75
FSG

ALSO BY TIMOTHY BRENNAN

Borrowed Light: Vico, Hegel, and the Colonies

Secular Devotion: Afro-Latin Music and Imperial Jazz

Empire in Different Colors (co-author)

Wars of Position: The Cultural Politics of Left and Right

Music in Cuba (editor)

At Home in the World: Cosmopolitanism Now

Salman Rushdie and the Third World: Myths of the Nation

PLACES OF MIND

PLACES OF MIND

A LIFE OF EDWARD SAID

TIMOTHY BRENNAN

FARRAR, STRAUS AND GIROUX

New York

Farrar, Straus and Giroux
120 Broadway, New York 10271

Grateful acknowledgment is made for permission to reprint lines from
"Goodbye Instructions," by David Lehman, from *Some Nerve* (New York:
Columbia Review Press, 1973). Reprinted by permission of the author.
All rights reserved.

Library of Congress Cataloging-in-Publication Data
Names: Brennan, Timothy, 1953– author.
Title: Places of mind : a life of Edward Said / Timothy Brennan.
Other titles: Life of Edward Said
Description: First edition. | New York : Farrar, Straus and Giroux,
    2021. | Includes bibliographical references and index.
Identifiers: LCCN 2020046890 | ISBN 9780374146535 (hardcover)
Subjects: LCSH: Said, Edward W. | Palestinian Americans—
    Biography. | Intellectuals—United States—Biography.
Classification: LCC E184.P33 B74 2021 | DDC 306.092 [B]—dc23
LC record available at https://lccn.loc.gov/2020046890

Our books may be purchased in bulk for promotional, educational,
or business use. Please contact your local bookseller or the Macmillan
Corporate and Premium Sales Department at 1-800-221-7945,
extension 5442, or by e-mail at MacmillanSpecialMarkets@macmillan.com.

www.fsgbooks.com
www.twitter.com/fsgbooks • www.facebook.com/fsgbooks

1   3   5   7   9   10   8   6   4   2

For the Palestinian people

. . . not as harmony and resolution but as intransigence, difficulty, and unresolved contradiction.

—EDWARD W. SAID, *On Late Style*

CONTENTS

Long after his death in 2003, Edward W. Said remains a partner in many imaginary conversations. For those who knew him, the exchanges when he was alive are missed almost as much as his person—the dark darting eyes, compassionate but fiery, of a man capacious and alert, a little daunting, and often very funny.

I found myself at the University of Madras, South India, in December of the year he died. Leukemia had had its way with him only a few months earlier, and now that he was gone, the memorials began to mount. Invited to speak about his work so far from his New York home, I expected to find myself in a small seminar room but was led instead to the chancellor's office for tea, a U.S. consular official beside him, both surprisingly well-informed about his writing, then to a lecture hall the size of a high school gym. The rows were vivid with the color of school uniforms, and the room alive with an excited bustle.

With all the seats taken, many stood along the walls and at the windows—students, community members, and some international visitors. They seemed to want to hold on to anything that had a brush with the man himself. The Egyptian novelist Ahdaf Soueif recalled that young people used to walk up to Said after lectures just wanting to touch him.[1] Moments before I took the lectern, two rows of students at the back abruptly stood up (their intervention had apparently been planned) and began to chant lines from Frantz Fanon's *Wretched of the Earth* as if at a political rally.

The tumultuousness of the event seemed at odds somehow with the more mixed reception Said had received over the years, and its third-world revolt a little distant from his own shifting positions and divided sympathies. In the previous decade, in fact, Said had threatened to disappear "into the front pages" (as Martin Amis once wrote about the novelist Salman Rushdie), having become an icon rather than the down-to-earth and rather insecure seeker he had always felt himself to be.

On the other hand, the energy of the event seemed just right for a man who had managed to turn street fighting into cultivated debates in foreign lecture halls. With Said, Palestinians had their urbane spokesman probing the manias of the metropolis; supporters of Israel found their malignant charlatan and terrorist; scholars of the Orient saw a well-armed foe in the rearview mirror; a nonwhite diaspora in the universities thanked him for blazing the trail of their own multicultural emergence; leftists within the university scratched their heads wondering how someone with his views managed to be so rewarded by the powerful. It had, in other words, become easy to turn Said into a series of placards without depth or nuance.

His overall effect, though, was hard to miss. A Palestinian American critic, intellectual, and activist, Edward Said is now considered one of the most transformative thinkers of the last half century. Poet and theorist, cajoler and strategist, he was equally at home in scholarly journals, popular magazines, and mass-circulation newspapers. His books and essays are still read in more than thirty languages and admired throughout the world. Said straddled an astonishing number of spheres of influence. He was an orchestra impresario in Weimar, a raconteur on national television, a native informant in Cairene newspapers, a negotiator for Palestinian rights at the State Department, and even on occasion an actor in films in which he played himself. His career was like a novel, right down to the fatal blood disease over the last decade of his life backlit by his own writing on personal and civilizational decline.

Born in 1935 in Jerusalem, the son of a businessman, he, along with his family, was dispossessed of home and homeland by the British mandate of 1948 and the military actions that followed. A brilliant if erratic student, and a gifted pianist from an early age, he grew up largely in Cairo, arriving in the United States in 1951. Later, he attended Princeton as an undergraduate and went on to Harvard for his doctoral studies before joining the faculty of English at Columbia University in 1963, where he remained for most of his professional life. By 1975, his career was already on its way to legend. Endowed lectures and honorary degrees poured in as he launched new fields of inquiry that changed the face of university life.

His politics belonged to more than books. Writing might have been their leading edge, but Said was also an original tactician, advocating political positions that were at first unpopular but later taken up by movements on the ground. He made unexpected alliances, carved out new institutional spaces, badgered diplomats, and counseled members of Congress—a harsh critic of the U.S. news establishment and, at the same time, a major media personality himself. As he confounded think-tank pundits again and again on the nightly news during the inhospitable Reagan and Bush years, he made the university seem to many a more exciting place and professors part of a vital conversation. More than anyone, he moved the humanities from the university to the center of the political map.

It was not just that along with Noam Chomsky and a few others he tore the "confidential" stamp off the official cover story, but he did it with a personality marked by impatience and vulnerability, by turns angry and romantic, that made the dense and difficult at the same time entertaining. By getting to the main stage with positions that only years before had been beyond the pale, he opened doors to others: "the mighty warrior, the Salah al-Din of our reasoning with mad adversaries, source of our sanity in despair," as the Iranian scholar Hamid Dabashi put it.[2] When he took his first university job, the defenders of Israel could ignore the Palestinian cause completely; a decade later, he had invented a new vocabulary and a new list of heroes. Almost single-handedly, he had made the Zionist stance no longer sacrosanct, and criticizing it had become respectable, even popular in some circles.

Although he put his imprint on them, the routines of university life did not always suit Said. A throwback to an earlier kind of intellectual—widely read on everything and interested in what he did not know—he was never much drawn to academic fashions like cyberpunk, affect theory, or posthumanism. He was much more the dragoman, cultivating the old-fashioned, the universal, and the "good," which he expressed in just those terms.

For all his writing on exile, he was a rooted man—imaginatively in Palestine and actually in New York, doting as always on its "restless, turbulent . . . energetic, unsettling, resistant, and absorptive" rhythms.[3] He lived there the longest and despite many opportunities to do so never left. Place and place of mind were to that degree at odds in him. If along with Chomsky, Hannah Arendt, and Susan Sontag he was the best-known U.S. public intellectual of the postwar period, he was the only one of them who taught literature for a living.

Said reveled in this fact. In his own mind literature was not just an avocation but the bedrock of his politics and the secret of his public appeal. Drawing on unusual sources ranging from musical scores to medieval Arabic transcriptions and finding inspiration in the likes of British media analysts and Pakistani socialist poets, he brought the humanities to the center of public life, deliberately reanimating the "great books" with the passions of war and anti-colonial revolution. As he saw the matter, this was his main contribution, much more than anything he managed to accomplish for the Palestinian cause. No one in the twentieth century, at any rate, made a better case that struggles over the meaning of secular texts, not just holy books, affect the destinies of rights and land.

THOSE WHO KNEW SAID only through his books did not see all of him. They missed his boyishness, certainly, as well as his fierce loyalties to friends, who in turn excused a fair amount of bad behavior—the vanity, the occasional petulance, the need for constant love and affirmation. Even admirers like the historian Tony Judt, for example, considered him an essentially angry man, although that looked completely past the gentleness many of us saw as he chatted with cabdrivers or sat rapt watching the hard-boiled, working-class cops of *Law & Order*. A childhood friend while visiting his apartment late in life remarked that if only his enemies could see the solicitousness and grace with which he served his wife tea, he could never be dismissed as a polemical or dogmatic man.[4]

I entered graduate school at Columbia in 1980 only vaguely aware of Said's growing reputation. Showing up at his office door expecting to be admitted to his seminar on postwar British Marxism, I was not chastised for cheekiness. He seemed to relish dealing with someone who had not learned the usual deference. "My dear boy," he said somewhat later after I submitted a proposal on cultural revolution for an in-house fellowship, "this is the age of Reagan. You cannot put things this way." Having come to graduate study after three years of political organizing in New York's black and Latino communities, I was amused, and a little surprised, to see him constantly prodding me for stories about life "on the street." Oddly, even though he came from a world of prep schools and was far too at home in it for my tastes, he became my mental refuge from Columbia's East Coast snobbery. A few years later, by then well into the program, I caught him marching up College Walk just after I had written an op-ed in the student newspaper on Ronald Reagan titled "The Making of a Criminal." Catching my eye, he smiled conspiratorially and, without saying a word, passed by me with his hand raised in a fist.

One day shortly after *The World, the Text, and the Critic* appeared in 1983, we found ourselves ambling across campus toward Butler Library. I marveled at his rhetorical achievement in that brash book on the politics of the university and told him so; his response was to discount his accomplishment because, he insisted, our job was first of all to have something to say, but also to emphasize that it was crucial not to get caught up in the displaced aesthetic longing of the critic as artist, as so many of the theorists of discourse at the time were doing, chiseling out their gnomic utterances as though they were parables from on high. "I am not an artist," he emphatically stated. Writing to get the word out and to be understood, he implied, was art enough. But he was an artist, a musical performer, an author of fiction, and a craftsman of the essay form, although he fought the artistic impulse at every turn.

At times, Said was a strangely vulnerable man. Once when I was having lunch with him and the novelist Elias Khoury (the two Arab Christians loved to joke that they were "honorary Muslims"), he winced while recounting the way Susan Sontag had recently reneged on a plan to collaborate with him on a project in France after she was awarded a major literary prize in Israel (both he and Nadine Gordimer had separately pleaded with her to decline, but were unsuccessful).[5] Because he seemed to be wondering aloud about what to do, I rashly proposed he publicly wash his hands of her. He smiled slyly, looked me in the eye, and said, "Don't you get it? *She's* dissing *me*."

He was an unpredictable mixture. Said's close friends at times poked fun by calling him a cross between "Eduardo," a dashing Italian Renaissance intellectual, and "Abu-Wadie," after the typical noms de guerre of Palestinian revolutionaries.[6] Improbably, Said's FBI file actually refers to him as "Eduardo Said, aka Ed Said"—seeming to operate under the impression that in 1979, on the eve of the contra wars, a terrorist was more likely to have a Latin name.[7] The charge would evaporate under continued surveillance. In fact, the files reveal that the FBI actually plowed through his books and articles for *The New York Times*, its informants providing faithful summaries for their superiors in the Washington office. Ultimately, their reports left the impression that they found his work rather interesting (a "skilled writer" with an "engaging smile and soft voice" whose works "have been translated into eight languages"), and they come off like the work of diffident students.[8]

Although prickly around criticism and quick to strike back, Said could also take a joke. In April 1999, only a month before his own death, his dear friend the Pakistani activist and scholar Eqbal Ahmad wrote to him in order to jab at his romantic aura. While thanking Said for a piece he had written on the war in Kosovo for the Pakistani newspaper *Dawn*, he teased him as only a close friend could, ending his letter in the tone of a supplicant: "Son of Palestine, Moon over Jerusalem, Light of the Semites, Refuge of the World, Shadow of the Lord on Earth . . . A humble particle of dust offers salutations from down under your expensively-dressed and glorious feet, and welcomes you back to the land of bombs and missiles, cold milk and canned honey."[9] The jest delighted him, making him, as another friend, the journalist and political commentator Alexander Cockburn, once put it, "clamber down from the pedestal of martyrdom and laugh at himself."[10]

Ahmad's playful excess recalled the worshipful ways in which Said had been treated over the years, the over-the-top reception that was simply a reality of his life. The Egyptian president Nasser's right-hand man and later a prominent journalist, Mohamed Hassanein Heikal, once looked at a now-famous photograph of Said and exclaimed, "He looks with his face full of noble suffering similar to the great paintings that embody the suffering of Christ."[11] No less extravagantly, the revered Sudanese novelist Tayeb Salih nodded as a friend declared, "Edward is a great and beautiful novel," and Salih replied, "It shall grow with days and grow more beautiful."[12]

But how long can an aura last? For an author who wrote with a fountain pen, he has been treated surprisingly well by the digital age. The internet is awash with websites, blogs, and short videos chronicling the life of this modern emissary of New York belles lettres, who despite such inauspicious credentials still manages to speak to youth after death. The old served the new even in his sartorial excesses, his Burberry suits and Rolex watches, never the latest from Milan and instead the duds of an English gentleman, and more Savile Row than Barneys in any case. Every friend had at least one story about his obsession with clothes ("Can you imagine a man too busy to go to his tailor?"), or his playful badgering of them in London to rush off with him to Jermyn Street to buy shoes because "I cannot be seen with you" otherwise.[13] Some found that being on the left and well dressed was a contradiction. But they missed the point, for his image, tweeds and all, did not prevent him from being routinely downloaded from the internet, photoshopped onto the T-shirt of an intifada militant, and placed on demonstration posters from London to Lagos.

Even adversaries like Joshua Muravchik conceded Said's staying power in the world of ideas, hanging on long after generational shifts. In *Making David into Goliath: How the World Turned Against Israel* (2014), Muravchik notes that more than forty books have been written about him and that universities all over the world teach courses entirely devoted to his writings. None of them, though, paints a full picture of his Arab and American selves as they come together, or accounts for the ways that Said's writings on Palestine, music, public intellectuals, literature, and the media intertwine. I take this to be the special challenge in writing an intellectual biography. All of his provinces matter, especially in combination, even though many of his readers know only some of them, ignoring the others.

On a different scale, Said made the humanities not only more visible but a great deal more unsettling to American, European, and Middle Eastern opinion makers. He did not just expose the outrages of the European and American empires, which some take to be his only agenda. He revived an older ethics of reading based on fidelity to what books say in their own place and time, part of his lifelong argument that what happened in the past is not hopelessly ambiguous but can be recovered through the work of interpretation. All along the line, in thought as in action, he created an attractive alternative to media authorities and State Department intellectuals, who (unlike him) were the "champions of the strong," as he liked to say.

Although a popular author (he once claimed to make more money from his books and lectures than from his salary), Said often wrote on technical questions of linguistics, philosophy, and social theory in three languages. We all know the sneer that comes over faces when the word "academic" is mentioned, but Said, as TV personality and bestselling author, was proud to be an academic and defended the university as a refuge from brute politics and a training ground for the freethinking that informs it. If the word "scholarly," similarly, means irrelevant or incomprehensible to those journalists who write about Silicon Valley dropouts as though they were geniuses and assume Vermont poets are sages, these attitudes are very far from the world Said tried to create. Theories of language, culture, and the image were not only meaningful to him but beautiful in themselves, and he consistently showed they had profound material effects.

By the force of his personality as much as anything, Said made literary and social criticism what every enterprising student in the next generation wanted to do and to have. We might even see today's "post-critical" age (including in academia) as the establishment's revenge on him and the world he so effectively brought about. But one doubts the vengeance will ever completely succeed. That may be because over three unpromising decades, Said kept the critical spirit alive against such difficult odds and gave it its warmest, kindest, angriest, and most honest shape.

PLACES OF MIND

CHAPTER 1

THE COCOON

Father and mother dear,
Brothers and sisters are in Christ not near
And he my peace my parting, sword and strife.
—GERARD MANLEY HOPKINS, "To seem the stranger . . ."

On November 1, 1935, a mild sunny afternoon in Jerusalem, Edward William Said was born to the soothing melodies of Mme Bear, a Jewish midwife. She had been asked to deliver the family's firstborn at the suggestion of the father Wadie's sister, Nabiha, in the family house at which they stayed when in that city. Said's initial world, then, was a home impressive for its grandeur and surroundings, situated in the still uncrowded neighborhood of West Jerusalem known as Talbiya, enclosed within gardens, and with open land beyond.

At his birth, the midwife chanted at times in Hebrew, at others in Arabic: "*Ya sayyidna Nouh / khalis rouh min rouh*" (Oh, our lord Noah, save one soul from the other)—a caution, perhaps, in that the baby was born unusually thin and had to be cared for by a child specialist, Dr. Grunfelder, a German Jew. Why "Edward"? His mother, Hilda Musa Said, would write in her journal, "Don't ask me why. We both liked the name. There was so much talk about Edward, Prince of Wales, and we chose that name, though the adult Edward hated it and would have preferred an Arabic name."[1]

Members of the extended clan crowded around the birthing room, his delivery in every way arranged to exorcise Hilda's traumatic experience in a maternity ward only a year and a half earlier in a Greek hospital in Cairo. On that earlier occasion, when Hilda was nineteen, a distinguished Austrian doctor, purportedly drunk at the time, had over-administered painkillers during labor with the result that the baby—also a boy—was born dead. That sadness would weigh on both parents in subsequent years and may explain some of the excessive affection his mother showered on the young Edward. His mother's evident joy in his presence, he would later recall, had to do with the fact that she had had "a child before me that did not survive," while his father "kept hoping he'd have one more son."[2] For the ill-fated delivery of the first child, Wadie had insisted on the latest medical technologies and practices, the most modern hospital, the doctor with the best Western education. When it ended disastrously, the parents were determined to rely next time on traditional ways, the reassurance of the homeland, choosing provincial Jerusalem over cosmopolitan Cairo—a pattern they followed for his sister Jean as well. They made the pilgrimage to Jerusalem in order to ensure that the new birth would take place in the capital of Palestine.

In family films from the 1940s, Said in Jerusalem—about age ten—appears rambunctious, somewhat chubby, stoop shouldered as in later life, and very aware of the camera. He is, in fact, at the center of the camera's focus in these home movies, jumping, climbing, a miniature version of the adult Said without the reserve. Throughout childhood, he has the appearance of a grown man in miniature, older than his years but immature at the same time. Today he might have been called hyperactive. In a few years, he would appear in college photographs more strapping than his classmates, a man among boys (though this would even out in high school). He was, along with everything else, simply big. Later, when added to the intimidating depths of his character and his sharp tongue, it was all in all an imposing presence. In family lore he claims he was considered a "delinquent" and a "fibber," but none of the family seems to have agreed with this harsh judgment. In their accounts, very little about him bore witness to that "solemn and repressed young man" that he described in an interview in the film *Selves and Others* while looking at a photograph of himself at age thirteen. He might have had bouts of brooding, but to those around him he was, as man and boy, "tempestuous, forceful, uncompromisingly outspoken to the point of rudeness, relentlessly restless, theatrical, and always very funny."[3]

In his generation, if not his social class, boys were forgiven everything. Tales of the mischievous young Edward fell, for that reason, short of disapproval. He loved playing on the armoire in his parents' bedroom during the day, and from atop a cupboard he would throw walnuts into the corridor at his sisters and their friends below, who squealed with pleasure as they dodged his missiles.[4] Inevitably, with all that climbing and jumping, the heavy piece of furniture once toppled over. The mirror on the front shattered, cutting his young sister Grace just above her eye. Beaten for the infraction, he became at the same time the subject of affectionate stories about this and other misdeeds told to visitors.

Said's family lived at 1 El-Aziz Osman Street in the Zamalek section of Cairo in a building that had a beautiful art deco lift, the signature architectural style of their neighborhood. Unlike other posh areas—the planned urban oasis of Garden City by the British embassy, or the suburb of Ma'adi farther to the south—Zamalek was both central and isolated, a picturesque island in the middle of the Nile that formed a stepping-stone by means of urban bridges from downtown to Giza and the Pyramids farther west. Unlike today, the island in the 1940s was filled with vast stretches of undeveloped parkland, woods, riding paths, golf courses, and exotic fishponds. The famous Gezira Sporting Club, the city's swankiest, can be found only blocks from their home.

This colonial dream of polo fields, bowling greens, and red-clay tennis courts "insulated from the *fellahin*," as Said later put it, was also a kind of nature park where he rode horses and bicycled in his family's "own private playground" free from the crush of humanity and surrounded by Europeans with whom they scarcely interacted.[5] When they tired of the Gezira club, there was always the Tewfikiyya Club for tennis and the Ma'adi club, where they would go for children's films featuring Tom Mix, the Lone Ranger, and Roy Rogers, but especially the Tarzan films that Said kept close throughout his life. In the 1860s, Egypt's khedive, Isma'il, remodeled Cairo along the lines of Haussmann's Paris. A socially engineered "greenbelt" separated the "dilapidated medieval city, with its winding corridors and over-populated slums," forming a buffer zone for Cairo's bourgeoisie.[6] Zamalek (from the Turkish for "vineyard") was called by Isma'il the Jardin des Plantes, and indeed the Grotto Garden across the street from the Said residence had a rare collection of African fish, its gardens the brainchild of a British captain.

The Gindy sisters, Hoda and Nadia, who lived in the same apartment building as the Saids, recalled that garden with fondness. There Said would compete with them to see who could climb to the top of the artificial grotto first. It was invariably Edward, who, once there, "danced and sang that most colonial of songs that we learned at school: 'I'm the king of the castle, and you are the dirty rascals.'"[7] Being the boy, he played the ringleader as the kids ran up and down the stairs of the apartment building making a racket and angering the parents. Yet his mother would tell of his transgressions to visitors with a sparkle in her eyes. It was all of a piece with the more constant refrain of "your brother"—an admonition to achieve as much as he, to match his triumphs, and be as good-looking. Not only their mother, but even the teachers at school, would flay the sisters with the refrain that their brother was the model of excellence. But then, in turn, springing from behind a doorway, letting loose the earsplitting Tarzan cry made famous by Johnny Weissmuller, he was a brother who tormented his sisters, learning how to burp on demand in order to annoy everyone.[8] The instigator of pranks, he was also simply the doer while others looked on, their job—according to the privileges of an only son, apparently—to assist, praise, and comfort him, or to attend his tennis matches, turn the pages of the Beethoven sonata scores, and carry the wild fowl he had slain during his rare hunting expeditions in the mountains around Dhour el Shweir. Once, while forced to pose with his sisters for family photographs in Cairo, he refused to put his left arm on the one beside him as all the others had down the line.[9]

Not that the sisters never held their own. They competed with him then as later, especially Rosy and Jean, who, although not as close to him in age as Rosy, would herself become an intellectual and author of a Middle East war memoir (*Beirut Fragments*, 1990) published before his own had appeared. The devotion to music of the two siblings was equal in intensity, and they talked about music often throughout their lives. As a middle child, Jean missed out on the alliances formed among her other sisters, gravitating to Edward, whom she "adored" and who affectionately called her "shrimp."[10] "We were from a culture of men," moaned Grace, who, being the youngest, took to calling her brother Uncle Edward whenever he reappeared during the summers from his studies abroad. Although Grace shared a room with Joyce, and Jean with Rosy, Edward had his own. That injustice felt keener whenever their mother stated plainly that Edward was her favorite.

There seemed to be two parallel streams in his life. The first— discipline, family order, schooling—dutifully performed but disavowed. The other, an "underground or subterranean" Edward who longed not only to read but to *be* a book.[11] Everything artistic belonged to this second version: his tastes in reading, his love of music, the creativity he unpersuasively palms off in the memoir as "fibbing." His childhood friends agreed: "Said was never really part of us . . . He lived a life separate from us, coddled, spoilt and adored in true Middle Eastern fashion by his parents and relatives."[12]

In revolt against his parents, he nevertheless complemented their traits. Hilda, his mother, was sociable and outgoing, whereas Wadie was "introverted and reticent." The same father whose shadow darkens Said's every phrase in his memoir, *Out of Place* (1999), had "a boyish sense of humour" that covered over his own "tendency towards morbid anxiety."[13] Indeed, there are hints of future self-criticism when Said casts his imperious paternal double as "an absolute monarch, a sort of Dickensian father figure, despotic when angered, benevolent when not."[14] The broad chest, the stooped shoulders, the athletic prowess, the fighting spirit, all repeat themselves in the relay from father to son, though tempered by Hilda's conviviality.

The Said sisters were appalled by his portrait of their parents in the memoir.[15] Quite unlike the stiff tyrant and emotional illiterate who had suffered nervous breakdowns and dealt out "harsh whippings," Wadie struck his daughters as a tender, quiet man who spoiled them with love and kindness, once holding Jean through the night when she was ill, singing to her, and doing magic tricks. Nadia remembers Wadie as a sometimes taciturn "smiling Santa Claus figure" who played that role at Christmas, visiting the children of the building.[16]

Although Said—the misfit "Cairo wonder," as his camp mates in Maine called him—portrays his private imaginative life as an escape from the harsh demands of an upwardly mobile family of overachievers, the burdens of a childhood without relaxation or leisure seem more the outcome of a relentless inner drive than the work of meddling parents for whom every achievement was a flaw.[17] The chronic sleeplessness, the cultivated solitude, were used to clear a space for what he felt needed to be done.

Andre Sharon, a lifelong friend and schoolmate at Victoria College (VC) in Cairo, hinted at other demons. A brilliant student with a talent for entertaining, Said was always tightly on display, gritting his teeth through a show of nonchalance.[18] The need for constant external validation had its flip side in a feeling of emptiness. Nabil "Bill" Malik, who had known him from early youth, recalled that every time he would approach Edward to play, he would back out, using piano, tennis, or French as an excuse. Around the immensely popular George Kardouche, another VC classmate, Edward shyly hung back.[19] George and his pack of admirers could see dark rumblings beneath Said's careful demeanor, but he labored to be fun as though it were another task on the day's agenda and largely succeeded, for, although he was better read, no one thought him a bookworm.

FOREIGNERS WITH LARGE BANK accounts and professional skills like the Saids got by fine in mid-century Cairo, although there were barriers to their climb up the social ladder. In a city of famed cosmopolitan openness, the Saids were a tiny Anglican religious minority within a Christian minority of roughly 10 percent dominated by the Eastern Orthodox Church. However small their faction, because they were congregants in the Christian denomination favored by the British, they might have been expected to receive preferential treatment. In fact, this was not the case. In Egypt as in Palestine, "Arab Episcopalians began during the mandate to face accusations of collusion and collaboration with the British occupying powers and, by extension, with the Zionist movement."[20] Because his father's business was the major supplier of office equipment to the British occupying army in Egypt, the family worked overtime to demonstrate their authenticity as Palestinian Arabs. In Cairo, they were seen by the British primarily as Shawwam—expatriates from Greater Syria, or Bilad al-Sham, an area that covered today's Syria, Jordan, Lebanon, and Palestine and that had been divided between French and British protectorates after the collapse of the Ottoman empire.[21] To be Christian, or Jewish, was simply to be the member of another tribe, although the tribes interacted in relative harmony. "We used to say about ourselves," explained his childhood friend Sharon, "'*Je suis Syrien-chrétien*,' or '*Je suis Syrien-juif*'" (I am Syrian-Christian; I am Syrian-Jewish).[22]

Said was, however, harder still to assimilate because, like his sisters, he was issued an American passport at birth on the strength of his father's American citizenship. His Americanness was, moreover, a cultural, not only a legal, status given his father's various quirks, which included turkey dinners at Thanksgiving and a taste for the American songbook. At the age of fourteen, he struck his Cairene cohort as more imposing for being American, and they were awed by his "American gadgets."[23] This aura was still apparent on his visits home each summer while an undergraduate at Princeton. By then, Hoda recalls, "he had become, to the rest of us left behind drearily continuing our schooling, an object of romance and envy as he was being 'educated abroad,' a phrase oft repeated in hushed, awestruck voices."[24]

Made up of writers, intellectuals, businessmen, and industrialists, the Shawwam constituted a closely knit social circuit, and much of the Saids' life was shaped by it. If they mixed also with non-Syrian Egyptians, and to a lesser extent with Europeans, these two groups remained marginal to their social lives.[25] For all the appearance of the Saids' elite status, they never occupied the highest ranks of Cairene society.

But Cairo was Said's childhood anchor all the same. While Jerusalem might have been the center of historical Palestine, the site of his birth and baptism, of frequent family pilgrimages and early schooling, he spoke of it only as sleepy and unwelcoming alongside Cairo's edgy urban excitements. Behind the latter's citadels of power stood a demimonde of pimps, con men, and shady characters who had fled to Cairo from Europe and elsewhere. By the 1920s, a fifth of the population were foreigners—native Copts mixed with Sephardic Jews, Greeks, Italians, French, and "uncounted numbers of White Russians, Parsees, Montenegrins, and other exotica" that Said dubbed a "crowded but highly rarefied cultural maze."[26] Between 1930, shortly before Said's birth, and 1950, the year before he departed for the United States, Cairo's population doubled. In time, the Zamalek of his childhood had become little more than "a bazaar."[27] Jerusalem's Talbiya, by contrast, sported mainly elegant homes with architectural motifs drawn from Moorish and Arab styles, tastefully surrounded by trees and gardens.

Even if they brushed shoulders with one another, the various tribal faiths of Jerusalem stayed mostly to themselves. The city's humorless doctrinal air was matched by a tacky religious tourism of "frumpy, middle-aged" men and women poking about the "decrepit, ill-lit" environs of the Church of the Holy Sepulchre.[28] Said considered the less bourgeois towns of Safad and Nazareth, where his mother had her roots, preferable to his father's "mortuary Jerusalem." Even his warmest recollections of the place, although respectful, are de rigueur: the cricket team photograph of his father on the wall of St. George's School that Said proudly shows his son on a visit in later life, his chipper memories of Jewish classmates when he attended the school in 1947 at the age of thirteen, and a shot of the family in storybook fashion facing the King David Hotel, replete with its Assyrian lobby, Hittite lounge, and Phoenician dining room. Jerusalem might have been the homeland but was never home.

Egypt, for its part, stood at the forefront of the Arab world with a revered literary culture and established newspapers read avidly throughout the Middle East. "Of all the countries of the Near East," a later mentor observed, "Arab and non-Arab, the first to attain her modern form and structure was Egypt. The westernizing reforms of the great soldier-leader, Mohammed Ali, resulting in some modest industrialization and in the emergent middle class, antedate the reforms of Ataturk and Reza Shah by well over a century."[29] More than any other Arab capital, Cairo was where the Arab world sent its children to be educated. During Said's time, it was still an enchanting, relatively uncrowded, largely secular cosmopolis on the threshold of radical political change. Not for the last time, Said was blessed by fortunate timing.

The daunting mélange of religious minorities in Cairo, at any rate, was offset by a radical division of space about which Said became increasingly sensitive: the less well-off Muslim denizens described in Naguib Mahfouz's novels *Palace Walk* and *Midaq Alley*, on one side, and the designer suburbs inhabited by upwardly mobile immigrants, on the other. Whatever his weaknesses, the great Egyptian novelist had accurately chronicled a trajectory he himself embodied, moving in his fiction (as in life) from the crowded working-class Muslim section of the old city (Gamaliyya) to the European-style inner suburb of Abbasiyyah.

The transformations of Said's Cairo were no less brash and theatrical. Between his father Wadie's escape to the United States during World War I to avoid conscription into the Ottoman army until Said's graduation from college in 1957, the country had gone from Turkish rule to a sultanate backed by British military occupation to the Free Officers revolution of Nasser. Said's youth and early adulthood, therefore, spanned two epochs, the major historical transitions of the Levant matching the arc of his life perfectly, from the end of khedival Egypt in the person of King Farouk through the interwar heights of British power over the Suez Canal to the era of Arab nationalism. Because of the strategic interests of the Suez Canal, Egypt had been occupied to varying degrees by the British military from 1882 until 1954, and their presence affected the culture in every possible way, from the organization of its clubs to its educational institutions. Behind the facade of Farouk, a foreign business elite thrived.[30] This *khawagat* (roughly what "gringo" means in the American context) had come to own an astonishing 96 percent of the nation's capital by the turn of the century.

By way of missionary schools, the American presence in Cairene society was palpable, although it was ultimately as marginal as the Anglican *shamis* themselves. Neither provided access to the most influential networks. And yet there was a distinction to being from America in the years just after World War II, before the United States' expanding empire had come to rival the British for most rapacious foreign occupier. Wadie had immigrated to the United States, where he was granted U.S. citizenship, as part of a more general movement of Arabs west during the Nahda—the Arabic "awakening" of the late nineteenth and early twentieth centuries. Part of Manhattan became known as Little Syria in the early twentieth century, its inhabitants winning a court case that gave them the right to be considered Caucasian under U.S. law.[31] The victory predictably led them to identify with everything mainstream, right down to America's racial prejudices, and their patriotism seemed more natural for embracing a country that had thrown off British rule.

IN ZAMALEK, SAID COMPLAINED of being "cloistered away" from politics by his parents, but the domestic idyll paved the way for his first political awakening. Life in the tightly knit family provided an ideal vantage point for witnessing Aunt Nabiha's volunteer work on behalf of Palestinian refugees to Egypt after 1948, some of whom were members of his extended family. Knowing little of the history, he could nevertheless chart the Palestinian calamity in the visitors' careworn faces.[32] Later he would find symbolism in the fact that he shared a birth month with the anniversary of the Balfour Declaration—the statement by the British government on November 2, 1917, supporting the establishment of a Jewish national home in the region. But his destiny was stymied less by parental protection than by family chitchat and the banalities of comic books.[33]

He first broke out of this tedium during his long summer stays in Dhour el Shweir in the mountains of Lebanon above Beirut. By his mid-teens, he had encountered his first serious ideas at the hands of Munir Nassar, a slightly older neighbor, the son of a high-level official for a London-based assurance company. Munir and his older brothers, who were part of the intellectual life of the American University of Beirut (AUB), located below them at the foot of the mountains, shared books with him and discussed Kant, Hegel, and Plato, whose names he was hearing for the first time.[34] He was a boy on the fringes of a circle of young men talking animatedly about ideas he had never known before: "Muhammad Ali, Bonaparte, Ismail Pasha, the Orabi rebellion, and the Denshawi incident."

Apart from these encounters, his major break from the relentless protectiveness of his mother was the piano in the privacy of his quarters. There, with "lordly magnanimity," he would let the girls at times have "a glimpse of the room and even, on extremely rare occasions, the right to cross the threshold of the sacrosanct place and gasp at his books and, in pride of place, his piano," to which he would retreat, playing for hours at a time.[35] It would be tempting to see the piano as a way of setting himself off from the rest of his family, but in fact it was a way of belonging. All five children continued to play long after the required lessons of childhood. Music, at any rate, became along with reading the principal source of his mental discipline and imagination and the first "theory" he explored before philosophy entered his field of vision.

In addition to his constant practicing of the piano, the first books he studied were musical, like *Kobbé's Complete Opera Book*, with its plot summaries of operas from Monteverdi to Janáček, selectively illustrated by representative passages from musical scores. He started playing piano at the age of six but became serious at ten and a half. By age eleven he was attending the opera at Cairo's miniature replica of the Palais Garnier, the very Khedival Opera House (Royal Opera House) that had canonized *Aida* at its premier production and about which he would later write so controversially. He noted particularly his keen memories of the *saison lyrique italienne* that he attended in the late 1940s—interesting because he grew to despise Italian opera later in life. A spectator living within, and above, Cairene daily life, he found in opera a glimpse of "an erotic world whose comprehensible languages, savage plots, unrestrained emotions" were all thrilling.[36]

Although he took these musical inspirations to a much higher level than his siblings, everyone in the family enjoyed them. His parents had a policy of taking each of the children to the Cairo opera as soon as they were old enough to appreciate it.[37] What's more, Said's immersion in music and his love of books (like his later infatuation with expensive fountain pens and luxury stationery) were the direct inheritance of his father's office supply business. The bonded paper, high-end typewriters, and fine writing implements from Wadie's shops found their way into the family's home in abundance, contributing to the aesthetic ambience. Over the keyboard of the family piano—a Blüthner baby grand from Leipzig on which all of the children played—lay a deep burgundy velvet cover with embroidered flowers on either side of the name "Alfredo Bertero, Le Cairo." It was not Wadie's merchandise, but it fit the household's old-world opulence perfectly.

The educational mission of the extended Said and Musa clans with their teachers and volunteer community workers was itself linked to the family business. His father's stationery company supplied many Cairo schools, one of which was Miss Badr's (that is, his aunt Melia's) school for young women. It also filled the "considerable library" of the Said family home not only with books but also with classical records.[38] The literary and vinyl largesse of the Palestine Educational Company in Jerusalem included *A Family Songbook*, which Said on long Dhour nights would sing from in order to amuse himself while softly humming such English standards as "The Minstrel Boy" and "John Peel."

Hilda would at times team up with her brother, Uncle Emil, performing Arabic folk songs on the *derbake* (a percussion instrument) to his *oudh* (an Arabic lute), an instrument that Hilda's father had played as well.[39] To an amazing degree, none of this seems to have stuck. Said would be moved late in his career to write appreciatively about the cultural pride instilled by the great Egyptian popular vocalist and film star Umm Kulthum but had very little to say technically about her music, which he likened to wailing. He once asked a good friend, Fawwaz Traboulsi, what he liked about Arabic music, because he could find little endearing in it himself, admitting to incomprehension rather than hostility.

As in everything else, Said was the most accomplished of the family's musical talents. The most famous of his teachers was Ignace Tiegerman, a Polish Jew, who quite apart from his association with Said holds an important place in musical history as an elusive, legendary performer of Romantic music, above all Chopin and Brahms. Only the very gifted were allowed to study with Tiegerman at his *conservatoire* at 5 Champollion Road behind the Egyptian museum. Nevine Miller, daughter of King Farouk's prime minister, was one of his students, and French was the conservatory's lingua franca. Lessons with Tiegerman, who charged one pound a lesson (a large sum at the time), were fairly rigid. "There was no discussion . . . He was always right . . . He demonstrated to you how the piece you were preparing should sound, and if you dared argue, all he had to do is show you the score and the notations by the composer, and that was that."[40]

One student, Henri Barda, recalled Tiegerman's "tyrannical rages when a pupil was less than prepared at a lesson: Often his studio door would swing open, the music would fly out, soon followed by the student . . . His eyes would go right through you like knives."[41] Said nevertheless idolized his teacher and spoke of him often, never about his pedagogical severity. Rather, he focused on the mind-boggling precision, grace, and understatement of his playing, especially while demonstrating musical passages in the practice room, where he concentrated heavily on the pedal, counseling his student to "clean" the sound at the beginning of each new chord.[42] Said occasionally invited Tiegerman to dine with his family and later, as a recent college graduate on leave in Cairo, would drive with him around the city.

A former student, Maurice Eskinazi, recalled that his instruction room was imposingly arranged with two Steinway concert grands interlinked and facing each other on which he and his charge would simultaneously play. He indulged in sarcasm—*"vous n'avez pas besoin de composer, pendant que vous jouez ce morceau"* (you don't need to compose while playing that piece)—when the student played notes that were not in the score.[43] In his U.S. years, Said went on to study with half a dozen eminent teachers, including at the Juilliard School in New York and again in Boston, but "all rolled into one [they] didn't equal Tiegerman's pinkie."[44]

Intellectually speaking, Tiegerman was Said's first sustained influence. Theirs was an intimate mentorship and, eventually, a friendship, meeting as they did in the 1950s "to play music, talk memory, and put ourselves back in time when Cairo was more ours—cosmopolitan, free, full of wonderful privileges." In the 1960s, Said even paid a call on his old teacher in Kitzbühel, Austria, where he had built himself a cottage.[45] Tiegerman offered him a glimpse as well into the illicit French underground Cairo of salons, theaters, and ateliers—gay Cairo, if you will. Having come to the city in 1933 attracted by its "possibilities," as Said cryptically put it, he made Said aware at a distance of a world of "unknown pleasures" and different kinds of human relationships.[46]

Said was actually important for Tiegerman's legacy.[47] It was he who unearthed a lost recording in Cairo that was then released to the acclaim of specialists, and he became the major living source for music historians seeking to fill gaps in the pianist's life. Ironically, Tiegerman's recordings were all the rarer because Egyptian radio had erased the pianist's broadcast tapes to reuse them in copying the LPs of Said's future confidant and friend Daniel Barenboim.[48]

DAILY LIFE IN THE Middle East of Said's childhood years was for most of its inhabitants relentlessly itinerant. In a very brief period, he had moved from St. George's in Jerusalem to the Gezira Preparatory School in Cairo, then to the Cairo School for American Children (1948–49), and finally to Victoria College, which he attended between 1949 and 1951. His stint at VC ended abruptly following a row with a teacher who, enraged by his students' unwillingness to

read Shakespeare, singled out Said as the chief insubordinate, wrestling him to the ground while other students, aghast, shouted with
outrage.

VC billed itself as a training ground for Middle East Etonians,
although Said's English pronunciation was never reliably British.
It changed over time, of course, the long American sojourn making itself felt in a mixed idiom that retained until the end a foreign
touch. He could speak French as early as Gezira Preparatory School
(his mother spoke it socially with fluency) and picked up more at VC
and at the "club," where it lubricated more formal conversations.[49]
The Arabic lessons forced on the children by their parents felt "like
a punishment," although they were not intended to be, but Wadie
did not speak Arabic well, and although Hilda did, and would use
it at home, her children typically answered in English.[50] Only much
later, in solidarity with their own embattled culture, did the children learn Arabic more formally, most relocating to the Middle
East after spending time abroad.

After his World War I–era stay in the United States, Wadie came
back to Jerusalem in the early 1920s only to honor his mother's
deathbed wish. Wanting to give his son a freedom he himself was
denied, he refused to force Edward to stay in Egypt to take over the
family business.[51] Wadie brought back with him a taste for Amer-
icana, which Said claimed (unpersuasively) not to share. Though
Wadie often had the traditional *labneh* (salted yoghurt) or *zayt wa
zaatar* (pita dipped in oil and a thyme spice mix) for breakfast, he
relished scrambled eggs with ketchup and pancakes with maple
syrup.[52] Thanksgiving featured cranberry sauce and candied sweet
potatoes. He prided himself on the whiteness of his skin, declared
he was from Cleveland, and often listed his name as William. In
a neat reversal, Edward's middle name was actually William, even
though critics have often tried to Arabize it by rendering it "Wadie."

When, after a dispute with his business partners, Wadie sailed
with his family to the United States in the summer of 1948, he
toyed with the idea of remaining there for good. The trip was

mostly planned around a serious kidney operation, which required American specialists. During the family's stay, Edward was trundled off to Camp Maranacook in Maine in order to acclimatize him to the new U.S. environment that would be their home. Miserable at camp, he was relieved when his father recovered enough to take them back to live in Cairo.

Apart from visiting relatives on family occasions, or seeking milder weather in the summer, the Saids' constant travel around the Levant had partly to do with Wadie's livelihood. His original interest in Cairo had been to expand the Palestine Educational Company into the Standard Stationery Company with branches eventually in Alexandria and Cairo and subsidiaries in the Suez Canal Zone. This arrangement demanded much moving back and forth, often *en famille*. Shifting conceptions of place, so fluid in this instance, often lay behind the spurious charge that Palestinians are nomads with no rights to the land because they set up no walls and established no bureaucracies to govern their legal claims. Their conventional disregard for the formal territorial boundaries of the British and French empires contributed to the confusion.

Much later, only a few years before his death, malicious articles played on this cultural difference, claiming that Said never lived in Jerusalem, had no family base there, and had always been safely nestled in bourgeois Cairo.[53] If the major tribune of the Palestinians had lied about his roots, it was implied, then all Palestinian claims must be fraudulent.[54] It was easy enough to counter the attack by establishing that Said had, in fact, attended St. George's (the "old bishops school," as locals called it) and that the Jerusalem house of his birth was collectively owned and therefore, because the papers were in Wadie's sister's name, shared property according to the custom of Arab extended families. The accusers had not even bothered to interview Said himself, nor had they sought out his fellow St. George's students then living in New York.

It was Israel, after all, that had turned the Palestinians' regional nomadism into a global diaspora. The Said and Musa clans, like many others, had been scattered as a result, taking up residence in Beirut, Amman, and the occupied territories or abroad. Staying in touch meant moving around. Hilda's brothers—Munir, Alif, Rayik, and Emile—lived in Palestine and, Said recalled, "we would visit them there with some regularity; after 1948, they flowed in and out of Cairo . . . We used to go down to Tabgha from Safad, which is where my maternal uncle Munir lived and where as a unique treat we would spend time in the summer."[55] If, as his sister Jean remembered, "from 1948 until the early 1960s, we were entrenched in Cairo," that did not mean there were not "trips into the Egyptian desert and the Lebanese mountains, when as children we were taken for jolly family picnics," and to light bonfires for Eid al-Salib (the Feast of the Cross). Upset by the insinuation that Said was not really Palestinian, his friend Andre Sharon set out to clarify what "home" meant to their generation in an unpublished letter to *The New York Times*:

> There were no meaningful frontiers when we were growing up, particularly mental ones . . . This was a positive legacy of the Ottoman empire. An Egyptian Jew, my ancestors came from Syria. My grandfather arrived in Egypt from Iraq by caravan . . . It mattered much less to the inhabitants that they were from Iraq or . . . Saudi Arabia or Oman than it did to the Foreign Office on the Quai D'Orsay. In short, that Said moved seamlessly from Palestine to Egypt to Lebanon is remarkable only for being so unremarkable to him and to those he grew up with. He was a Palestinian Arab like I was an Egyptian Jew.[56]

What Said perhaps did downplay, however, was the degree to which home involved incessant religious routine. Each morning at assembly, a reading from scripture began the day.[57] Even late in life, he kept his Book of Common Prayer from the Cairo years and was still consulting it in 1998 "as a way of regretting the pedestrianism of the New Standard Revised Edition."[58] Rather than scoff at the central text of Anglicanism, he scorned the newfangled revisions, preferring its elegant seventeenth-century form, replete with calendars, litanies, prayers of Whitsunday, and its commination, psalms, and catechisms. He had little use, perhaps, for the book's apocryphal end materials—for example, the weird thanksgiving for the deliverance of James I from the treasonous gunpowder plot. But even late in his career he accepted an invitation to become a member of the advisory committee of the Anglican Observer at the United Nations and proudly told anyone who asked.[59]

These trappings of piety were a natural consequence of his social and geographic location. In the words of an important presence in his life, Charles Malik (the husband of his mother's cousin Eva), Western civilization was an offshoot of "what was revealed, apprehended, loved, suffered, and enacted in . . . ten cities or their hinterlands": "Athens, Istanbul, Antioch, Beirut, Damascus, Baghdad, Jerusalem, Alexandria, Cairo and Mecca."[60] The rituals of religion, therefore, if not religious faith itself, were surprisingly central in his life, and he came from a region not only where East meets West in a territorial sense but where (as Said put it in 1969) one "carries the heaviest weight of competing monotheistic absolutisms . . . of any spot on earth."[61]

During his early schooling, those around him saw other effects of Anglicanism on his later thinking. As friendly rivals and antagonists at college, "the three of us would get together regularly for meals," Nazeeh Habachy recalled, "interesting because . . . the topic of discussion was frequently religion."[62] One friend, George Abi-Saab, was blunt about his atheism, Nazeeh confessing that he was a dedicated churchgoer, and Said combatively "somewhere between." Indeed, on a questionnaire Said responded to the query "Are you an unbeliever?" by answering "no." To the follow-up, "Then you must be a believer?" he left the answer blank.[63] Still later, Mohammad Shaheen, a frequent correspondent and accomplished critic of English Victorian literature, remembered Said responding to a question from the audience at a talk at the American University in Cairo (AUC). "What is your relationship to God?" he was asked by a clearly devout religious man trying to expose him as an infidel. He answered, "You are asking me about something which does not fall within the realm of my specialty. I am specialized in comparative and English literature. In any case God is in charge of the world we live in, and in charge of us all."[64]

Further ambiguities arose when Shaheen met Said for lunch in Amman after his talk at the Orthodox Club. Why had this, of all clubs, invited him? Said laughed and said, "Perhaps they thought I am a Christian."[65] Later in life, after he was seriously ill, he was having dinner at a local Lebanese restaurant with a former student. A Lebanese priest at the next table recognized him, came over to the table, and blessed Edward, with much waving about of his large crucifix. After the priest returned to his own table, Edward looked at the student, shrugged, and said, "It couldn't hurt!"[66] He seemed to put the matter to rest in a commencement speech shortly before his death in which he attempted to resolve the contradiction: "I am a resolute secularist, which doesn't mean that I am against religion, which, as far as I am concerned, is a matter of private choice and faith." But here as elsewhere Said was inconsistent. In a handwritten postscript to a letter sent to Tamar Jacoby of the *New York Times* op-ed page, after she interrogated him over his role in the Palestine National Council, he blurted, as if to assuage her, "I was baptized and confirmed in the Church of England—a not insignificant fact!!," as though belonging to the established faith kept his Palestinian advocacy from putting him beyond the pale.[67] Paradoxically, as Shaheen pointed out, because of the West's equation of Arabs and Islam, "Edward did more to promote Islam than all the sheikhs in the world," and had he actually been a Muslim, "he would be, like you and me, unable to defend Islam."[68]

A lack of clarity about his beliefs could certainly be traced to the care with which he resisted offending in matters of religion. A tactful dodge seemed appropriate when so many of his other positions were controversial and because people stop listening when they feel you have insulted God. Once, getting into a taxi, he struck up a conversation with the driver, an Arab, who asked him point-blank if he was Muslim. *"Alhamdulillah"* (Praise be to God), he replied—one of those filler words that can mean almost anything—leaving it to the man to draw his own conclusions. The evasion was typical. As a grown man around his family, he referred to himself as an atheist "about every other day" and told his children that the Bible was little more than "an interesting piece of literature." In all his years living in New York, he never once went to church, and while strolling the city streets, and coming upon a religious service where Protestant hymns could be heard from within, he never showed the least interest in stopping to hear them.[69]

But the paraphernalia of religion, which perhaps left a more lasting mark on his sisters than on him, was everywhere in his world. Hilda's father had been an evangelical minister, and her mother was never without her black leather-bound Arabic Bible, a habit she formed as the daughter of the first Arab pastor of the nascent Protestant community of historic Syria. It is hardly surprising that in the unguarded setting of the home Hilda herself would call out Christian maxims from time to time: *Khreisti sineisti* (Christ is risen) or *ya sater, ya rab* (O Protector, O Lord), accenting a reprimand or giving a homiletic gloss to a passing emotion. Wadie, though not usually devout, still punctuated moments with passages from the Sermon on the Mount: "The last shall be first, and the first last." With their mother, all of the children recited the Lord's Prayer every night before bed.[70]

When Christianity finds its way into Said's own accounts of his life, it is usually played down lightheartedly. And yet the national cathedral of Cairo (All Saints' Cathedral) was both the headquarters of the British in the city and the place the family and their circle of friends went to Mass each Sunday, attended Sunday school, and were confirmed. Every school day began with a Protestant hymn, a practice that did not stop even after Said left Egypt at the age of

fifteen. At Mount Hermon, "we were all required to go to chapel services four times a week (including Sundays)."⁷¹ At lunch too, again
every day, before sitting down to eat, students would stand behind
their chairs reciting, "For what we are about to receive," in unison.
"A Mighty Fortress Is Our God," "O God, Our Help in Ages Past,"
"Now Thank We All Our God," "Ye Watchers and Ye Holy Ones," set
the rhythms of his ear and drilled into him a peculiar English dic-
tion.⁷² Not all the influences were formal. The injunctions to treat
the poor with justice and charity meshed well with the basic political decency of a family that, despite its wealth, had good reason to
dwell on the fate of the dispossessed.

SAID MIGHT HAVE BEEN first among equals in the male-centered
Arab family of his youth, but he patterned his thinking on a Christian egalitarian ethos that he learned from the remarkable women in
his life, beginning with his mother. He could not have been blunter
about the family member with whom he shared secrets: "My mother
was certainly my closest and most intimate companion for the first
twenty-five years of my life . . . [whereas] my relationships with my
younger sisters . . . were attenuated and to me at least not very satisfactory."⁷³ The maternal intimacy, and the corresponding sibling tensions, would last until the end. Said bitterly claimed that his father
never wrote him "a truly personal letter," rather dictating them to his
secretary and signing them "Yours truly, W. A. Said." But such personal
letters from his father, filled with hurt and insecurity, are readily found
among his papers. A particularly abject Wadie at one point begs Edward to be more welcoming to visiting relatives and to contact a business associate on his behalf. The son replied that he was "rather tired of
being told what a bad person I am, and how I am always falling short of
the standards of . . . a good brother, son, etc."⁷⁴ He added, "I think the
time has come to start lecturing my sisters about how they should treat
me in a way more properly befitting an older brother."

His sister Grace, who looked after Hilda when she was in treatment for cancer in Washington toward the end of her life, had a close-up view of Said's behavior around his mother, marveling that the two of them could gossip on the phone for hours at a time every day. Nothing here of the sort found in *Out of Place*: the bittersweet force of his mother's emotional embrace, her role as "taskmaster," or the "weapon in her arsenal for manipulating us, keeping us off balance, and putting me at odds with my sisters and the world."[75] Nor anything of her fearful judgment that all of her children were "a great disappointment." Nadia Gindy, who found Hilda "indeed beautiful . . . high cheekbones, lovely skin," and always wearing "striking pieces of jewelry," remembers her as the opposite of how Said describes her, "always enumerating their accomplishments."[76] "I really think that we all got our political education from our mother," said Grace. "She was an Arab nationalist . . . [and was always] into social causes."[77] Nasser had, after all, abolished religious tribunals governing family law, sent engineers and doctors into the countryside, provided government subsidies to artists, promoted land reforms, and given women the vote. Hilda was no activist, a member of no party, but she was an enthusiastic supporter of Nasser and felt keenly the social injustices in Egypt.[78]

The mother's intellectual style rubbed off on her only son. As Jean puts it, "Mother had always been a maker and teller of stories. Even if she were recounting the smallest incident, she would embellish it with detail and colour, turning it into a matter of social and historic interest."[79] Like the magical realists of the Latin American novel, she found reality so strange only fiction could capture it. Hilda's mother, Teta Munira—the other woman guiding the Said household—set an equally forceful, if somewhat different, example that could not have gone unnoticed. She kept a "vast database on the subject of who left Palestine during and after the war of 1948 that displaced her and her children. She knew where each acquaintance in her large circle had lived, and where they ended up as refugees."[80] Theirs was "a family of storytellers and record-keepers."

Uncanny parallels bound the extended family more closely together. Hilda, as we know, suffered the loss of a male firstborn, but her mother lost a female child as well. This meant that just as Said had no brothers, his mother had no sisters. Surrounded by girls and women, Said had his opportunities for male bonding with his older cousins (Aunt Nabiha's children), Robert and Albert, about seven years his senior. But he established a more durable and formative relationship with a future friend who was also older: Ibrahim Abu-Lughod, "the father of three talented daughters and the husband of a greatly gifted scholar" and therefore "more tolerant of women than is normal for an Arab."[81]

His in-laws kept faith with the pattern. Mariam Cortas, whom he met in 1967 and, after divorcing his first wife, married in 1970, was the only daughter of a prosperous family known throughout Lebanon for canned foods and jams. With this marriage, he joined in-laws who were not only, like his own family, well-off because of recently established businesses, not only members of a small Christian minority (in the Cortases' case, Quakers), but also filled with socially committed women educators. The Cortas family's food preservation business grew directly out of their charitable work during the World War I–era famine created by the Turks' wartime rechanneling of supplies for troops. The food crisis was particularly acute in the Mount Lebanon area, where the family set up emergency food collection and distribution services. Noticed by visiting British Quakers, members of the family were invited to England to learn the techniques of canning. Like Wadie, Mariam's father built his business entirely from scratch and, also like him, was athletic and handsome, eventually the tennis champion of Lebanon.

Just twelve kilometers from the Said family's summer retreat in Dhour el Shweir, the tiny Quaker community of no more than five families established itself in Brummana, the site of the Cortas family home. Quakers, who reproachfully called Anglicans at the time "the congregation of the shilling," were as secular as a Christian denomination could be: communitarian, absent of preachers, and driven by good works alone.[82] Quite unlike Hilda's born-again Baptist father in Nazareth, Mariam's mother, Wadad Makdisi Cortas, having shown a penchant for the reading of scriptures as a child, was explicitly forbidden by her father to attend the local American evangelical school for fear she would become too devout.[83] In the end, she did become a missionary of sorts, a dedicated teacher of the humanities at the Beirut College for Women. In a community for whom the education of women was deemed an important step toward social reform, those who did not become teachers became writers or advocates for women's equality.

Even though Wadad, like Said's parents, loved to pass along little homilies about not wasting time, not littering, being nice to neighbors, and so on, she was in many ways "a nineteenth-century socialist."[84] Along with Mariam herself, she introduced anticlericalism into Said's life. One summer, Mariam recalled, Wadad "decided to change all the hymns that were sung at school, because they were in English, and their content was religious. Over the years, she lost her love for the Bible and deplored the role religion had played in the Middle East. She spent her days reading Arabic poetry and choosing poems to adapt to the music." Along with managing the Said home, and thereby keeping Said from any of the dreary financial and organizational tasks involved in bringing up two children, Mariam and her family introduced him to Beirut society and the intellectual life swirling around AUB.

The poles of his later life in Palestinian activism and university teaching, however, were symbolized in his youth by two dominant personalities above all: Aunt Melia (really a great-aunt, his maternal grandmother's sister) and Aunt Nabiha, his father's sister. The former—"Miss Badr" to her students, unmarried, small in stature with stern and piercing blue eyes—was, as Habachy recalled, "a very famous lady" in Cairo, acknowledged widely as a brilliant teacher and harsh mentor to young women molded to her sense of independence and propriety: "a bit of a tough guy."[85] Before this steely taskmistress of the American College for Girls in Cairo "generations of students stood in mortal dread."[86] It is not clear how Said broke through the shell of her forbidding manners to become her "particular favorite," as he put it. The semiformal teas over which she presided with the Said girls did not include him, and his sisters were as surprised as anyone to discover in later life his affection for her.[87] None of it was apparent when they were growing up. Yet he confided in her, and she, seeing something special in him, took the opening. It is tempting to think that at least some of her found its way into Said's poem "A Celebration in Three Movements":

> And those who knew her loved her: disciples
> Wafted forward pitilessly on the waves of her fulfillment . . .
> She was, I cried, a lovely thorn . . .
> We were told of perspiration, garrets, and dedication
> Sit you down and create, that is all
> Buy all you need at the corner store—light, glue, and a
> ruler.[88]

Melia's teaching was much more than the guidance of youth; it was a call for the discipline upon which national development depends. His affection, in that sense, was inseparable from the strictness that others feared in her.

Along with Melia, the short and stocky Aunt Nabiha, Edward's godmother, impressed him greatly with her "plaintive and scandalized" narratives of the hardships forced on Palestinians after 1948 during her regular Friday luncheons in the Said home.[89] Her heartrending litanies of malnutrition, dysentery, and homelessness, and her constant badgering of government authorities and charities to provide relief for the defenseless Palestinian refugees pouring into Cairo, had the effect of forcing Said to recognize his identity for the first time. Nabiha and Melia could not have been more unlike—one austere, the other patient and empathetic. They were also of different generations and from different sides of the family. Yet they embodied the poles at either end of Said's vast emotional range.

If the women offered steely models of political education, other guides were found among radical men in his midst. Even before his teens, Said showed a moral deference to left, at times far-left, political activists, without becoming one himself. When he remarked in *Out of Place* that the life and death of Farid Haddad, "an activist, committed Communist Party man . . . a partisan for a social and national cause," have been "an underground motif in my life for four decades now," he was not just confessing to a youthful predilection but announcing that Farid's example lay behind everything he later became, as well as that those who knew his career well in other respects overlooked the fact.[90]

As a boy in Cairo, Said already knew Farid but later spent time with him in the mid-1950s on annual summer trips home from college, finding him "aggravatingly parsimonious in speaking about either his politics or his extramedical activities," even as Said plied him with questions about both.[91] Shock followed when in December 1959 he learned that Farid had been beaten to death in prison as part of a sweeping "brutal repression in Egypt of all of the opposition—liberal Wafdists, communists and the Muslim Brotherhood."[92] At one with his political vision, Said was attracted most by what separated them—Farid's working without publicity or pay, his quiet modesty and indifference to advancement, the self-sacrifice of submitting to party discipline while dedicating himself to the poor. What he did, Said remarked, "he did as a human being and as a political militant, not necessarily as a Palestinian."[93]

With unmistakably Christian overtones, Said described Farid's work, like that of Farid's father, Wadie (the Said family's doctor and also an activist), as a "charitable mission," just as he had called Nabiha "saintly."[94] Much the same could be said of Said's second role model, Kamal Nasser, a Palestinian Christian, militant Ba'athist (Arab secular socialist), journalist, lawyer, and political scientist who worked for the Palestine Liberation Organization (PLO). Said had had dinner with him the night before he was killed in April 1973 by an assassination team sent into Lebanon by the

Israeli army.[95] With calculated understatement, he could find no better word to describe both men than "good."

Said was never really the detached, apolitical man that many supposed him to be until the 1967 war forced him into activism.[96] In a typed fragment on a half sheet of torn paper, one of many such notes buried in Said's undergraduate papers, he struggled to define himself: "To be a Levantine is to live in two or more worlds at once without belonging to either . . . [It is] not to be able to create but only to imitate . . . It reveals itself in lostness, pretentiousness, cynicism and despair."[97] Whatever self-reproach was evident when he described his childhood as a "cocoon" of privilege and pampering, cocoons nurture and enfold, preparing the vulnerable for independence. If anything, though, his was a premature adulthood.

In his youth, he had often listened to his cousins Yousif and George bemoaning the Balfour Declaration; although he did not yet know the declaration's significance, he appreciated their anger well enough. He remembered the checkpoints in mandate Jerusalem and the vague frictions between new and old settlers in their neighborhood of Talbiya and could still hear the radio broadcasts in Cairo belligerently denouncing the Zionist enemy.[98] Nadia remembers a less clueless, more militant Edward: "From an early age, Said was chafing against the trappings of British colonialism, rebelling against geographical centres of empire—but in those days he was a lone voice, an alien voice."[99] Just as strikingly, he described himself when visiting Tiegerman in Cairo in the 1950s and 1960s as a "Nasserite and a fierce anti-imperialist."[100] Only a boy less sensitive to his mother's political passions or less won over by his beloved aunt Nabiha's "one-woman aid centre for her compatriots" could have been anything else.[101] Just as Said was organizing his convictions into a program, he wrestled with the puzzling irrationality and dispiriting factionalism of Middle Eastern revolutionaries. Although he found their posturing a disincentive to joining organizations, his political character had, for all that, found its shape already as a teenager.

CHAPTER 2

UNSETTLING

. . . a troubling, disabling, destabilizing secular wound.[1]

Accompanied by his parents, Said arrived in the United States in 1951 at the age of fifteen to attend Mount Hermon, a New England boarding school in rural Massachusetts founded in 1881 by the evangelical preacher Dwight L. Moody. Although there was brief talk of moving the family to the United States (his parents looked seriously at houses in Madison, Wisconsin), they abandoned the idea, and soon returned to the family home in Cairo. Apart from being a fresh start, the school, his parents hoped, would provide much-needed religious discipline to the boy after his run-ins with the VC authorities. But he detested the place, calling it "extremely repressive," although there is little evidence of that.

To be sure, the narrow-mindedness of his new surroundings when compared with Cairo's urban attractions seemed stifling, but he was never subjected to excessive shows of authority. He resented the school's brand of moral education in which students were asked to show humility by performing menial tasks like peeling potatoes.

But this was far from the only manual labor in Said's youth. While still in his student years, he worked as a lifeguard and recreation director for the Pocono Plateau Christian Association, as a student cafeteria worker earning a dollar an hour, as a cashier at a football agency, and as a babysitter.[2]

Even the imposed moral uplift was less severe than the setting implied. Although central to the Mount Hermon curriculum, religious instruction was not of the dogmatic, born-again variety one associates with the term "evangelical." The psychological assault of New England winters on a boy from the Levant, along with the intellectual dead zone of McCarthy's America, contributed more to his harsh judgment than any indoctrination or corporal punishment. The truth is, his time there marked a creative flourishing, the discovery of a trusted mentor, and his first forms of public recognition.

Already an American citizen, he had not yet in any firm sense become American in his cultural disposition. But the fluidity of Levantine culture contributed to the ease with which he navigated the codes of his adopted land—particularly, as we will see, in his growing love for American popular film. From the start, though, Said found living in the United States radicalizing in a negative sense.[3] The country's intellectuals appeared to him repellently provincial, and he especially bristled at how many on the left had internalized their own government's imperial ambitions. The Zionist project, meanwhile, seemed only to recycle the country's proud self-portrait as a settler state displacing natives on its divinely ordained "errand into the wilderness," to use a phrase from a Massachusetts sermon of 1670.[4]

In the image of Puritans fleeing religious persecution in England, exile had always been a part of America's rhetorical repertoire, and this made him want to disavow the status. "To call me a refugee is probably overstating it a bit," he confessed.[5] However awkwardly, he did fit in a nation of exiles building a new world while anchored in the old, representing what his graduate mentor, Harry Levin, later recognized as the classic themes of American fiction, the

"Wandering Jew" and the "Flying Dutchman"—nomads who keep looking homeward in a state "between wanderlust and nostalgia."[6]

Eventually, Said would come to admit his Americanness in what might seem to many readers, given his political criticisms, an oddly patriotic sentiment: "Our country, we must never forget, is an immigrants' republic: that is what makes it so unique and so extraordinarily open, changing, and exciting . . . [America is] always in the process of revealing and transforming itself."[7] But he was far from consistent on this point. In acclimatizing himself first to New England, and developing there a contempt for what he found to be a cretinous popular culture ("my life was barren of soda fountains and soda jerks," he snidely remarked), he discovered in American film a vicarious glimpse into the sexuality he had been introduced to, but ultimately denied, in the forbidden nightlife of Cairo.[8]

To be both American and from the Old World was perhaps possible only in New York, a "chameleon city," as he put it, offering itself up, on the one hand, and unpleasantly from his point of view, as the hub of a "globalized late capitalist economy" and, on the other hand, as a cauldron of creatively dissident "urban expatriate[s]."[9] He was a New Yorker before ever moving to America. In 1948, 1950, and 1951, he spent significant stretches of time there sitting in its movie houses or wandering through its department stores and restaurants. His entry and exit from the country invariably passed through the high-rise metropolis.[10]

By his third visit, before being unceremoniously deposited at Mount Hermon by his parents, his addiction to the movie houses on Forty-Second Street was already well established—the site of mainstream cinema fare long before the area had become disreputable. Three years earlier on the way to the unloved Camp Maranacook, he had discovered in Manhattan the "lush Technicolor world . . . he had expected of America."[11] After graduating from Mount Hermon, he took a joyless tour of New England with his cousin Abie Said and family (who bored him), only partly salvaged by spending the last two weeks at the fashionable Stanhope Hotel across from the

Metropolitan Museum of Art in a New York that was by now no longer foreign territory.

Despite his abiding sense of isolation, Said was never completely alone in the New World. His relatives in the U.S. Arab community included the "polarizing, charismatic" Charles Malik, the future Lebanese ambassador to the United States, who lived in Washington, D.C., and whose wife, Eva, was Hilda's cousin. And there was Abie, who lived in Woodside, Queens. Both acted as Said's local guardians when funds were needed or emergencies arose, although both relationships became strained over time.[12] In the case of Abie, the son of his late uncle Al (Asaad)—his father's older brother—Said's only escape from the routines of Mount Hermon were the twice yearly school breaks when he would visit the family. He "loathed" them, skipping off to Manhattan at every opportunity so that he could watch "one movie after another."[13]

The little boy of *Out of Place*, pathetic in some ways, heroic in others, always ironized, never speaks. And so his feelings and thoughts remain prisoners to a sensibility that is partly his, but also more than his, because the older self knows the youthful one though not the other way around. By contrast, in his poetry and letters home from school at the start of this second exile (after Jerusalem), a character unrecognizable from the aimless and harried protagonist of his memoir comes into focus for the first time.

The move, after all, had at least brought to a halt the manic transfers to five separate schools in six years. He had left Victoria College under a cloud; that much is certain. Whether his suspension was because of insolence or bravery in standing up to in-class tyranny is difficult to say, but he was a hard child to cross—not "equable enough," as his Mount Hermon tennis coach later put it. The great unsaid seems to be that Said was surly around authority if not openly confrontational. The earlier altercation with the Shakespeare teacher was soon followed by a fistfight with a school bully. Unintimidated, he punched the upperclassman in the nose, sending him to the infirmary.

Said refers to his being "expelled" from VC, but technically this was not the case. It was more like a two-week time-out following the altercation with the teacher who had been frustrated by his students' insubordination, lost his cool, and then singled out Said as the chief troublemaker. His father judged it wise to remove his son from the school, recognizing that Said was languishing under the British-style education that had become a corporal as well as ethical affront and that had begun to take a toll on his studies. Other motives came into play. VC's acting headmaster, the dreaded S. Howell-Griffith, made it clear that Said had no future in the British system and that he had no confidence in Said's long-term abilities and warned that his letter of recommendation would be lukewarm. It turned out to be exactly two and a half lines long, followed by a report stating that he could think of "no notable achievements" in Said's school or religious life.[14] On a prepared form, Howell-Griffith ranked his intellectual curiosity and his courteousness at the second rank, presenting only "average promise" for college work.

The returning headmaster, J. R. G. Price, was less damning, assuring Mount Hermon that had Edward stayed another year at VC, he "should expect him to succeed" in admission to Oxford or Cambridge.[15] In any case, with these mixed reviews, it is not surprising that Wadie hedged his bets by petitioning a letter from a Mount Hermon alumnus and family friend, John S. Badeau, president of the American University in Cairo. It was he who introduced the Said family to Mount Hermon, with his recommendation shoring up the shaky application. He assured the school (and there is no reason not to take this at face value) that the father was "anxious to place Said in a school with good Christian influence."[16] In an effort to seal the deal, Said, no doubt in response to his parents' advice, bent the truth on his application by claiming, "I can safely say I had no disciplinary difficulties in Victoria College or any other school."[17]

There were other reasons for packing Said off to America. Wadie had come to feel that Edward's obsessive intimacies with his mother had become unhealthy and were stunting his emotional development.

Then there was the matter of retaining his U.S. citizenship, as Edward explained in his rather clumsy, handwritten application letter: "As I have lived in Egypt all my life, I have, according to the rule, got to live in the United States for five years until I am twenty-one years old. My age is fifteen and a half, so towards the end of this year, I shall be obliged to go to America in order to keep my citizenship."[18] If Wadie had returned home unwillingly from the United States as a young man in order to honor a promise to his mother, he was determined that Edward would have the opportunity to stay. The VC debacle only forced the issue.

At first, the signs were unpromising. His letter to Mount Hermon was primitive, even ungrammatical, and had the air of aristocratic caricature. His extracurricular interests, he carefully explained, included tennis, soccer, swimming, and riding; he was a member of the debating and scientific societies. He had reached "no final decision as to my purpose in life," although he was "inclined to study medicine." Only his studies followed the familiar pattern of premed students who discover they belong in the liberal arts after flaming out in calculus. In his final year at VC his marks were mediocre: A minus in English, C in biology, C plus in physics, C plus in chemistry, and a surprising C minus in French.

Whatever his demerits, he made a memorable first impression. He was, after all, a transfer student, arriving as a junior with two years at VC behind him. Not yet sixteen, in his application photograph he looks twenty-one, which may explain why so many demands were made of him during his stay there. His physical size, athleticism, and adult mien all contributed to the habit he retained in his life to seek the company of older friends. This was the case first, as we saw, with his Dhour neighbors Munir Nassar and his brothers but continued in his first romantic relationship (with Eva Emad, seven years his senior), with his cousins Robert and Albert, with his confidants while still an undergraduate at Princeton, and then among the members of the tightly knit circle of colleagues he assembled as a young professor at Columbia—all of them (again) roughly seven years older.

The evident weakness of his thinking registered in the school's psychological profile (a standardized multiple-choice test given to all applicants) was another mark of the fraught transition. Simple math problems on the test stumped him; he flubbed the questions on visual and spatial recognition. Overall his score was not terrible, but the mistakes exposed emotional vulnerabilities. In the last section, he was given a series of questions modeled on the sample "What is the opposite of hope?" where the answer is, of course, "despair." He was then asked, "Which would make the truest sentence: Fathers are ___ wiser than their sons: 1) always 2) usually 3) much 4) rarely 5) never." He answers "always" and gets it wrong. Similarly, to the question "A mother is always ___ than her daughter: 1) wiser 2) taller 3) stouter 4) older 5) more wrinkled," he answers "wiser" and is once more revealingly off the mark.

After this halting start, however, he came into his own in a burst of self-possession. Stored-up potential released itself quickly, with the before and after offering vivid contrasts. Within only a year, he had become a "pianist of distinction" and had learned to express himself confidently in a style that bordered on obsequiousness. His yearbook picture shows him to be handsome, not obviously exotic—one of three "non-white" students along with two African Americans from the glee club and choir. He would later quip that the place was so monocultural that a boy from Honolulu was recruited for the international club. Although no one was rude enough to say so to his face, his schoolmates considered him a "wog," according to his friends at the time.[19] William Spanos, the founder of the journal *boundary 2* and a frequent correspondent with Said later in life, happened to be a young instructor at Mount Hermon at the time. He later recalled to colleagues that the racial environment was tense. People called him "spic" behind his back because of his Greek heritage.[20]

As Said's confidence grew, he ventured for the first time into literature. His poem "The Castle" won the school's Hugh Findlay poetry prize in his junior year. He set the stage with predictable props. "High on a craggy mountain top . . . crusaders brave survey the motley Saracen host." To the castle walls, harsh screams rise up "from the dungeons foul," creating a "true symphony of discord."[21] In a weird blending of Franz Kafka and Alfred, Lord Tennyson, Said hints at his later political themes. Destruction comes to those who regard Arabs with "arrogant and contemptuous glance." The depressing scene is relieved only by a force greater than human cruelty—nature's grinding power, which slowly eats away at the stone walls until they crumble like a "clay idol into dust."

As an older man, Said would probably have treated his poem as mercilessly as he did the "simpering poetaster" Keith Bullen, a reviled former teacher at Gezira Preparatory School who caned him for delinquency. In *Out of Place*, he mocks the "mannered, even precious" verses of his former tormentor, "with its fancy words and word order ('peach incarnadine')."[22] But if so, he would have been unfair, because unlike Bullen's "perfumes violent," from a poem written for a pretentious wartime literary journal for British émigrés, Said wrote in rage against an obscene order. And he was, after all, only sixteen.

Even sustaining the castle conceit over thirty-five lines was in its own way impressive, developed in two distinct movements of potency and decay. These were not just random impressions but a worked-out narrative with an aggressive moral thrust. With an obvious ear for literary voices, he also had a weakness for Victorian formulas where "power" cannot be mentioned without "might," and "ivy" is inevitably likened to a serpent. Although marred by mimicry in this way, the poem tried to turn the loftiness of antique poetic language into a political weapon, blasting the castle not only because it is unjust but because it is against nature. It is hard not to see the crumbling edifice of its closing lines as anything but revenge on VC.

Happy about all he had escaped, Said was more tentative about what the present offered. Banished from a well-appointed home in a world city, he had now to contend with Northfield, Massachusetts, its opposite extreme. Phone service was erratic, and the opportunities for using it rare. The mail was as frustratingly slow as paperwork at a Calcutta bank. His "monastic" existence, as he put it, referred to much more than regular religious instruction or communal bathrooms with open toilet stalls. Mimicking the usual Ivy League arrangement, the sexes were housed on separate campuses, Mount Hermon's counterpart being the Northfield Seminary for Young Ladies (the two schools merged in 1971). He kept his mind from impure thoughts by nonstop activity in the international club (vice president), French club (vice president), stamp club (president), debating club, and choir, although now in a vastly less comfortable, snowbound setting. But none of it prevented him from having to endure insincere smiles and subtle put-downs or being denied a coveted honorary post on the yearbook or as a librarian—both usually reserved for students with his distinguished academic record. To say, as he did, that he never felt "fully a part of the school's corporate life" seems like a confession, but there is reason to take it as a boast. He was playing by the school's rules while disdaining them, manifestly there but not there at the same time.

The actual record shows him to be a rather eager participant in that "corporate life." In the administrative summary issued just before graduation, school officials found him "an agreeable personality" who "cooperates at all times." His headmaster, Howard L. Rubendall, wrote that he was hugely well liked and that his coaches held him to be "an outstanding member of the community." But his fellow students saw him as aloof. He was an intense, ambitious young man and far more worldly than they were. Unlike at VC, he got into trouble at Mount Hermon for coming off as a disgruntled know-it-all, later giving such trouble a different spin by declaring that he was disliked because "I was not a leader, nor a good citizen, nor pious."[23] He was inexplicably passed over for various distinctions, above all crushed that he was denied the library assignment. As the privilege usually given the year's best student, it was the prize he coveted most.

There was also the matter of imperial culture, which lurked in his observation that "just when the politics of the Arab world began to play a greater and greater role in American life," he was socially ostracized within his new academic home. Even at Mount Hermon, at least among his closest friends, Said was already known as a passionate partisan of the Palestinian cause. If not yet a campaigner, he spoke often of his people's plight as a teenager, and it was clear to anyone who listened that the issue was constantly on his mind. One of the witnesses to his views on the subject was Gottfried Brieger, a German fellow student. The two soon found solidarity in being othered by the natives and on occasion gave presentations to the local Rotary Club about their respective countries. After Brieger was asked, "Do they have cows in Germany?" he joked with Said that he should have spoken about Palestine and Said Germany, because no one would have known the difference.[24]

Toward the end of his first year, the composite talents he came to reflect at the height of his powers began to emerge. He vigorously studied Plato and Aristotle, the Enlightenment and Kierkegaard, which, to give a sense of Mount Hermon's relative openness, was assigned reading in the Reverend James Rae Whyte's Bible class. His amateur interest in classical music blossomed into a systematic study of the history of classical performance, opera librettos, lives of the composers, and the technical history of counterpoint. As he pored over the weighty *Grove's Dictionary of Music and Musicians* and worked his way through the entire 33 rpm disc collection in the school library, he joined the choir and the glee club, throwing himself once more into piano, practicing longer and more intensely than at any other period of his life. By the end of the second term, he had moved dramatically up the class rankings and won his second prize, this time for his talents at reviewing novels. These early liberal arts triumphs aside, he was still in his own mind a premed student, and his report cards list a bracing regimen of classes in algebra, biology, Math IV, and chemistry. In fact, the Florence Flagg award he won as a senior was for "excellence in the Biological Sciences."[25]

Inch by inch, though, he was drifting toward the humanities, although the transition was not a smooth one. His teachers acknowledged his intellectual promise but were more equivocal when it came to the very qualities the humanities require: creativity, imagination, and "expressing ideas orally." Following his parents' suggestion, the school authorities considered these defects likely fallout from the boy's shaky emotional state, which expressed itself as extreme lethargy even after a full night's sleep. Dr. W. F. Dodd of Mount Hermon went so far as to speculate in his health report that this waking up tired is "possibly an inherited condition" because it ran in the family.[26] He regarded the problem as physical, not psychological, and prescribed a "basal test" (to check blood sugar levels) and advised he be given a tonic to "pep him up."[27]

Exactly midway through his time at the school, chronic fatigue gave way to panic. He returned as planned for the summer break to Cairo and the usual Lebanese retreat of Dhour el Shweir in 1952, but as the time arrived for his return to Mount Hermon, he begged to be allowed to stay with his family. Even during the first year, the letters his parents sent to the Mount Hermon administrators were vigilant and beckoning, treading the line between doting parents unfamiliar with American cultural codes and overbearing watchdogs acting as their son's advocates. Hilda wrote to the school from New York just after his matriculation on September 21, 1951, urging that it deploy all of its expertise in dealing with their son's special challenges.[28] Five months later, she wrote again to say that Edward was suffering from more than garden-variety homesickness.[29]

By the summer of 1952, the "terrible events" in Cairo would push matters beyond endurance. As his sister Jean recalled, "We were in Dhour al-Schweir as usual when the Egyptian revolution took place on 23 July."[30] Everyone "listened to the radio endlessly" for what would come next. There had been forebodings earlier, in January 1952, only a month before Hilda's second letter to Rubendall begging for an intervention on behalf of her distraught son. In what is conventionally known as Black Saturday, in response to revolts in the Suez Canal Zone by Egyptian nationalists, the British clamped down hard, and angry crowds in turn marched en masse, attacking hotels, schools, businesses, and restaurants: anything that smacked of foreign privilege. Among the businesses burned to the ground was Wadie Said's Standard Stationery Company along with all the other establishments on Sharia al-Malika Farida (Queen Farida Street), which had been named after King Farouk's first wife.

A vivid contemporary account of the events, from the point of view of the colonial elite, was provided by Esmond Warner to the W. H. Smith & Co. Ltd. in Cairo, as well as to his father, Sir Pelham Warner, on January 28, 1952, and conveys the fear that prevailed in the foreign business community: "I regret to inform you that at approximately 5:30 p.m. on Saturday, 26th January, our premises at the above address were set afire by a mob and have been completely destroyed . . . [T]he mob numbering several hundred, were able to carry out their dirty work without the police making an attempt to restrain them; in fact, it seems the police assisted the mob."[31] Esmond continued in a separate letter on January 31:

> The town really is in *ruins*. All confidence gone. The Turf Club story is the most ghastly . . . [T]he last time I went on to town in the dusk at a quarter to 6, like Dante's Inferno. So many cars had been pulled on to the streets to burn as well as the burning buildings—if there had been a wind, Cairo would have been destroyed . . . [E]veryone very apprehensive of another flare-up of what is really a revolutionary movement with the excuse of the British occupation to set it off . . . Is he [the king] sufficient man to crush really their Serag el Din and other swinish "Democrats"? . . . Loot was forgotten everywhere in the passion for destruction . . . Shepheard's, the three great department stores in Fuad al Awad, all 4

Groppis, *every* cinema in Cairo, Barclays Bank, every restaurant and bar, most jewelers, the British Institute and its fine library, the fine Standard Stationery Co. (a 200,000 pound claim, I gather), which has just been done up with all up to date office machinery, all burnt, every motor car agent, every gunsmith in town has been clean looted.

Warner reasoned that the pattern of the arson was symbolic: British landmarks and places that signified "rich" (high-end stores, jewelers, car agents) were targeted by the "peace movement" (communists) and Ahmed Hussein's Socialist Party; and the "pleasure" sites (movie houses, bars, wherever there was "alcohol" and "vice") were targeted by the Muslim Brotherhood. He summed up: "The Christians here of all races are terrified."

Said's own later take on the events deviated crucially on points of fact: the Egyptian branches of the family business, he would later write, "were not nationalised, but sold to the Nasser government; nor were they burned by revolutionary mobs but rather by the Muslim Brothers."[32] At any rate, more than religion was at stake. Groppi's, for instance, was a cultural monument for anyone familiar with Cairene daily life—an ornately decorated Mediterranean tearoom with tall glass windows and curved facades, founded by Giacomo Groppi, an immigrant from Lugano, Switzerland. A popular meeting place, and not obviously restricted to the upper classes, it was famous for its chocolates, which were coveted by monarchs and pashas throughout the Middle East.

In the wake of the Cairo eruption, Hilda wrote to Mount Hermon, concerned that Edward would be traumatized because he was "rather too sensitive for a boy." Six months later, Said wrote an alarming letter home saying that his parents "should not at all feel proud of him, because he was far inferior to other boys at Mount Hermon." This "terrible inferiority complex," Hilda speculated, might have to do with the "many disadvantages" she felt crippled him, among them "too many changes in his schooling."[33] But the

Mount Hermon administrators were perplexed. They saw no evidence of any of this at their end. By January 1953, Hilda concurred, for he had dropped the dark broodings of his earlier letters, and he was finally given the job at the library after all and wrote home overjoyed. He was "our Eddie once more."[34]

Still, his time at Mount Hermon ended on a sour note. The worst slight was reserved for his departure when he was not named salutatorian, even though his grades were strong enough for the honor. He actually wrote to the registrar in June 1953 to confirm that he was indeed number two in his class (his lowest grades, curiously, being in English, his highest in Bible studies and music appreciation).[35] Years later, after his memoir was published, the actual salutatorian, Fred Fischer, wrote to him both to acknowledge that their grade averages had indeed been identical and to express his puzzlement at the slight.[36] Said took the affront as final proof that being in some mysterious way offensive to his superiors, he would remain a permanent outsider no matter what he did.

Before the uprising in Cairo, Said's feelings about the city had been curiously distant despite his formative years there. In his writing it appears less like a utopian ideal than a placeholder city around whose edges he was allowed to drift. Now consigned to an outpost abroad, he faced the added insult of having impotently to witness the violence abroad to his home and family. His helplessness foreshadowed the time only a few years later at Princeton when Israel invaded Egypt and the British shelled Cairo in response to the nationalization of the Suez Canal, "an event I experienced at a distance with great emotional stress since my family was there."[37] And then again, for the third time fully three decades later in 1982, when he was forced to watch from New York during the bombardment of Beirut, where his mother, sister, wife's family, and closest friends were then living. As he probed the back channels for hints of the realities on the ground, tapping inside sources for updates, the capital was pummeled for days from sea, air, and land before the Israeli army drove its tanks, in the face of great resistance, into the heart of the city.

The Egyptian turmoil did not prompt in him anything like that contempt for angry "mobs" found in Warner's letters to the company. If anything, like the rest of his family, Said applauded the insurrections that had driven Farouk from power and nationalized the Suez Canal Zone, agreeing with Jean that the events signaled how much "the distance between the fabulously wealthy Egyptian upper class[es] and the desperately poor peasants was dramatically reduced."[38] His friend Habachy, a Copt (Egypt's oldest Christian denomination), recalled that the Saids greeted the uprising, even the first that had swept away their store, as a favorable sign. As Hilda wrote, "The whole Middle East is still in turmoil, but Egypt seems to have found the answer to some of her problems, at least. We personally have done a beautiful job of reconstruction to our badly mutilated store, which made it look even better than before."[39]

Only in the early 1960s, after the volatile transformations had put their security at risk, did the Saids leave Egypt for Beirut, never to return. The relocation was prompted in part by the threatening political climate and the imposition of a series of socialist laws impeding the operation of the rebuilt business. Wadie's firm, it turns out, was never actually nationalized (many others were), but by 1962 he had closed its doors preemptively, reopening a branch of the business in Beirut and remaining there until his death in 1971.

Not all the political drama was taking place abroad. Entering the United States at the height of the Cold War would color Said's feelings about the country for the rest of his life. Although ambitious, eager to impress, and by his own account apolitical, Said deeply distrusted the Cold War mentality all around him, the anti-Soviet paranoia, the disregard for third-world realities, and of course the demand that thinking people toe the line. Mount Hermon's cheery conformism scandalized him—the Americans' "surface jokiness and anecdotal high spirits of teammates" hiding something more sinister. No straying from the "team" was allowed. But just as he would later carefully set the debate over social systems in Egypt, so Said understood the Cold War in national and ethnic terms. He found it impossible not to see McCarthyism as a nimbus surrounding the Arab predicament: "From the start of my arriving in the U.S. in the mid-1950s one is made as an Arab to feel in some way criminalized or delinquent . . . outside the pale."[40] Arabic "doesn't speak English."[41]

His aversion to 1950s America, then, was not hard to understand. Several of his childhood idols, as we saw—above all, the family doctor's son in Cairo, Farid Haddad—were communists. On top of that, the Maronite Christian communities of Lebanon, which he had had a chance to see up close on his many visits over the years, led him to associate anticommunism with blind pro-Western bias and hatred of the Islamic influences on Arab culture. When he arrived at Princeton only two years after coming to the country, he was exasperated by American indifference to the Cold War's cultivated ignorance. "Marx was barely read or assigned" at the university, he grumbled, and it "treated McCarthyism as a bagatelle."[42]

Even before the civil rights and antiwar movements made it safer to hold such views, Said faced down the logic of the Red Scare. He rather recklessly opened his Harvard grad school application in 1958 with an anecdote about meeting an "intelligent Cairene" bookseller who was "sponsoring a series of translations into Arabic of all the most significant Socialist thought." For hours they talked about socialism and "the so-called democratic systems." Frank exchanges like these were possible abroad, he implied, whereas in Europe and the United States exalted authors like George Orwell and André Gide were busy echoing the consensus by declaring their "disillusionment" with socialism. He agreed with the bookseller that they could "afford" to be disillusioned, because "unlike their brothers" in Egypt they wrote for an audience that no longer cared about ideas. He preferred the historian Richard Hofstadter, who explained this insouciance as well as this showdown between social systems by pointing out that U.S. education had become "acquis-itive" rather than "spiritual." Hints of Mount Hermon's mantras about moral citizenship, which he had earlier mocked, were evident as he drove this point home. The entire educational process, he as-serted, should find its energies in "a type of evangelical spirit which ideally should never wane." An educator "should be his own as well as others' gadfly."[43]

Far from the outcast lacking moral uprightness or the "right at-titude," as he tells the story in *Out of Place*, he was positively jaunty in his letters to his superiors after graduation. Looking back on his Mount Hermon years while visiting his family in Egypt, he wrote to Rubendall to share the happy news of his Woodrow Wilson Fel-lowship at Princeton, adding that "it is too bad that I am not a bit younger to be back in Mount Hermon to enjoy not only the gymna-sium but all the wonderful facilities the school offers. Don't worry Mr. Rubendall, Mount Hermon has a very good propaganda office in Cairo."[44]

And yet here he was, building his life in America, and like Tocqueville, Viscount Bryce, and Simone de Beauvoir he would di-agnose the United States with the peculiar authority that Ameri-cans have always granted foreigners when portraying their national character. This critical triumph relied a great deal on his ability to pass as an American himself. For it was always difficult for many of his critics to think of Said as authentically Palestinian. His detrac-tors never missed a chance to paint him as a New Yorker playing an ethnicity game. So at home did he seem in his adopted culture that his Arabness remained invisible for at least half his audience. While taking a walk in the early 1980s with David Yerushalmi, an Iranian Jew who tutored his wife, Mariam, in Hebrew, he was asked, "Professor Said, you don't feel any sense of alienation in America?" He said, "I do, but I overcome it."[45]

But it remained an effort. Judging from his essays, he had al-ways despised the U.S. entertainment industry, railing against the homogenizing power of American film, newspapers, and comics.

He built an emotional fortress to protect himself against the desolation of Middle America, pitying those "marooned in Brooklyn, their daughters overdressed gum-chewing, squeaky-voiced bobby-soxers."[46] He came to master American informalities over time but was never able to use slang without a certain self-irony in a vaguely Anglicized English (as when his daughter, Najla, many years later, turned him on to the phrase "lipstick lesbian," and he in turn found a way to work it into every conversation).[47] American leveling encroached even on his name. He hated being called Ed and would respond with hostility whenever anyone referred to him that way, although there were exceptions.[48] Or at least forgiveness. Noam Chomsky called him nothing else, and Said never corrected him. So did his school friends at Mount Hermon and Princeton as well as his father. He himself signed his letters "Ed Said" for the first five years of his American life.

As at other times when he tried to negotiate his mixed feelings as an American, he was inconsistent. He had internalized his father's upbeat take on American culture and certainly found success in the New World, like his father, as an improviser, experimenter, and self-inventor.[49] He even found bright spots in the otherwise bleak landscape of the McCarthy decade. Did not President Eisenhower force Israel to leave the Sinai Peninsula, ceding the territory to Egypt? Was not Dorothy Thompson, the doyenne of women's journalism, describing Zionism in these years as a prescription for perpetual war while portraying Arabs sensitively in her column for *Ladies' Home Journal*? The traditional high-mindedness of commencement speeches aside, he wrote from the heart in his Mount Hermon address only a year before he died when he spoke of "our republic . . . so unique and so extraordinarily open, changing, and exciting."[50] For America was also its dissidents—chronicled (as Said pointed out) by Howard Zinn in *A People's History of the United States*—the civil rights movement, the citizens movement of the Harvard law student of Lebanese descent Ralph Nader, and "the women's revolution, which took women out from the shroud of secrecy . . . and into the light of day."

His earlier nomadic existence helped explain his shifting cultural allegiances. "Popular culture means absolutely nothing to me," he declared, "except as it surrounds me," and yet he was clearly mesmerized by popular cinema as a boy and drawn to its guilty pleasures in later life.[51] As for sports culture, he called it an "anesthetization of the critical sense," musing that the mental world that surrounded him in childhood had "so little to do with the mind in any serious or academic sense" that it was a wonder he became an intellectual at all.[52] And yet throughout his most productive years, he was clearly watching a lot more television than he let on while devouring the novels of Robert Ludlum.

In an unpublished interview in 1993, he was more candid than ever about the impact of American film on his thinking in Cairo and the United States in the first two decades of his life. Before his escapades in the New York film houses, there was the Diana cinema on unfashionable Emad el Din Street, where he was allowed to see movies once a week, on Saturday afternoons, "the only escape I had from the unending regimen of boxing lessons and tutorials." Because he was prohibited by his mother from seeing any film twice, every scene was precious to him. When he was finally on his own in New York, he acquired the habit of seeing the same film repeatedly on Forty-Second Street, where the showings were continuous. But for him, even fun could become a regimen. In New York he saw Rita Hayworth's *Salome* five times in a row—for "that's what I was trained to do . . . everything with a tremendous intensity."[53]

His American tastes in film were already established in Cairo, where he had "developed a whole complex system of what [Hollywood] movies must have been about." Actually, his assessment was not all that complex. They amounted, he explained, to girls who "wore tempting dresses and looked like Debbie Reynolds and Cyd

Charisse." In 1946, when he was eleven, he longed to see *Gilda*, starring Rita Hayworth, and made a scene in front of his mother trying to force her to consent. She was adamant, though, and he remained, as he put it, "on a very tight leash."[54]

Unable to cross her, he found ways around her restrictions. Whatever he was prevented from seeing, he later tracked in *Photoplay*, filling out with Hollywood gossip what he missed on-screen and satisfying his adolescent curiosity by paging through the glossy photographs of, among others, Rita Hayworth. Trading screen lore was a constant pastime. With an older friend in Lebanon, he would argue about Robert Taylor, who seemed always to be coming home to Barbara Stanwyck so that she could fetch his robe and pipe ("he had this thing about a pipe"), but Said did not care for him and thought him "kind of a prick."

He also played on his mother's assumptions. As she and Wadie steered him toward the likes of *Lassie*, *Rin-Tin-Tin*, and *My Friend Flicka*, he fell instead for the sultry Jennifer Jones in *Duel in the Sun*, which was okay to see because it was a Western. *The Song of Bernadette* too seemed safe because it was about nuns, so there were no objections. Unwittingly, his mother was feeding his fantasies.

> Meant to be very devout . . . *The Song of Bernadette* . . . I thought . . . sexually very, very, very troubling. So I had this whole thing about Bernadette . . . She was the woman who founded Lourdes . . . I still think that Lourdes may be, if I ever get very sick . . . the place . . . I would want to go . . . Why Bernadette? . . . I think [her] purity as a person . . . coupled with her . . . sensuality . . . Our house was very puritanical . . . To have a . . . thing with Jennifer Jones, who was a nun and a saint in the film . . . That . . . turned me on.[55]

By high school, he became even more defiant. Just before leaving for America, at fourteen—the year his report card was filled with Cs and C minuses—he skipped school to see the "forbidden films" at last. Almost anything appealed to him more than the safe Middle East historical romances his parents were pushing—*Arabian Nights* and *Ali Baba and the Forty Thieves*, which, given his British education, were his only glimpse of that "part of the world I was living in, the Arab world."

Stereotypes were not limited to the Orient. It is true that the Arabian fantasies featured stock celebrities of color like Maria Montez, Sabu, and Turhan Bey (an Austrian of Turkish descent), but the Los Angeles of film was no less fake, filled as it was by types from "MGM musicals . . . taxi drivers, telegraph boys [who] all wore uniforms with little bow ties."[56] When he finally saw California for the first time in 1968 at the age of thirty-three, he could not stop himself from trying to discover these types in real life walking the city's streets.

Hollywood could not give him the louche Cairo demimonde of his old piano teacher Tiegerman, but it offered some of the same titillations. Up to a point, the two were fused in his mind. Mainstream popular culture, at any rate, had a surprising hold on him from early on and continued to vie with the highbrow tastes of his class and family station. Although he was a fan of *Masterpiece Theatre* in the 1970s and 1980s (especially *Upstairs, Downstairs, Brideshead Revisited,* and *Mystery* with Diana Rigg), and looked down his nose at what his children were watching, art house cinema bored him. Uplifting movies with a political message he especially avoided. "I don't want to see one of those anthropological movies," he cautioned.[57] For most of his professional life, action films were all he wanted to see—*Die Hard, Total Recall, Lethal Weapon.*[58] Still playing with improprieties, and finding in film a sensual escape, he wrote to a colleague from abroad with tongue in cheek, "I did see [the "porno chic" sensation] *Deep Throat,* ritually, just before leaving NYC . . . It does have social value."[59]

Long after receiving his Mount Hermon diploma on June 7, 1953, he kept in touch with his old mentor Rubendall. Said felt he could approach the gentle administrator who had so often managed

Hilda's fretful letters from home and like a second father helped him settle in. Apparently, the overwrought first years of Said's life in America were enough to create a firm impression in the man about what Said would later become. In his grad school recommendation letter, Rubendall observed that "Mr. Said's Middle Eastern background equips him in an unusual and pertinent way for effectiveness in stimulating the thinking of others."[60] Said's own sense of himself, and others' of him, was finally falling into place.

CHAPTER 3

AN IVIED APPRENTICESHIP

Poetry is the darling child of speech, of lips and spoken
utterance: it must be spoken, *till it is spoken it is not performed,*
it does not perform, it is not itself.

—GERARD MANLEY HOPKINS[1]

When Said entered Princeton in 1953, he was sure its familiarity would
allow him to forget Mount Hermon's New England severities. He chose
the school without much thought (he was also accepted at Harvard)
in part because he had already visited the campus with his parents in
the summer of 1951. Unlike Harvard, Princeton had the reputation of
being a safe haven for the children of foreign elites, and although the
Saids were far from royalty, they were certainly well-heeled. In the end,
he was disappointed, finding it a ramped-up finishing school "in the
wilds of New Jersey," offering more of the same upper-crust antics and
jejune conversation he had endured at Mount Hermon, although now
coupled with his classmates' incessant drinking.[2]

His only fondness for the place had to do with Princeton's experimental music department, which had recruited some of the most
daring composers in the United States, including Milton Babbitt
and Roger Sessions, as well as the jazz pianist and composer John
Eaton, and important musicologists like Arthur Mendel and Oliver

Strunk. Although few of his later readers might expect it, Said was quite uncertain about whether to pursue music full-time. His move to Princeton came on the heels of the most concentrated practicing of piano in his life, and now he had access to some of the country's leading figures in composition and music theory. New York was within striking distance, and when he performed well enough to win the Friends of Music Prize, he was allowed to study with the distinguished concert pianist Frank Sheridan in the city, later studying at Juilliard.

It was not so much literature itself as the way it was studied at Princeton that lured Said away from music. Unlike at the other Ivies, the most intrepid literary types at Princeton steered clear of the English department, opting instead for a degree in what was called the special humanities, which only Princeton offered. Open only to the most gifted students, this innovative honors program combined philosophy, literature, music, and French. It could not have suited Said better, and he eagerly signed up, inspiring a passion for broad, nonspecialized study that he never lost. In contrast, say, to Harvard's brilliant poet and Librarian of Congress, Archibald MacLeish, Princeton was more offbeat, sporting the eminent but eccentric critic R. P. Blackmur.

Said's most important activity was to gather around him a group of confidants and future interlocutors. The dearest to him were his classmates Arthur Gold and Tom Farer, who moved on with Said from Princeton to Harvard after college, forming a circle unbroken for nine of his most formative years. Nazeeh Habachy was just as close, although he joined the group only in grad school. Others in Said's Princeton cohort were important more indirectly: Hodding Carter III, through whom he later received an invitation to President Carter's State Department; and at Harvard, Ralph Nader, who helped him resist the draft, as well as his English grad student contemporary Erich Segal, whose *Love Story* Said admired for the cleverness of the young classicist in pulling off a bestseller with a brilliant piece of "self-promotion."[3]

At Princeton, Said seemed much happier than at Mount Hermon. An "attractive young man . . . admired by his fellows who accept him as one of their own," wrote the assistant dean in a recommendation letter.[4] In other words, he managed to be accepted even though he was *not* one of their own. Dr. Gerald Sandler (class of 1957) recalled that his classmate "Ed Said . . . probably felt as isolated as a Palestinian as we did as Jews."[5] Those around him during his college years heard him frequently take up the Palestinian issue with great passion.[6] A sense of the ethnic risks in doing so were suggested by some official notes scribbled in pencil on a Princeton Placement Bureau form that contained the anonymous observation, clearly meant for other officials to read, that Said was "very dark, big," and "of Arab descent."[7] Another professor, while praising his earnestness, singled out his appearance as "not a very refined type."[8]

He might not have cowered before such bigotry, but he did not confront it either, at least not then. Instead, his tactic was to outmaneuver it with a cosmopolitan flair that many found disarming. Not the only intellectual standout in his circles, for it was an impressive group, Said alone cultivated the image of "man of the world."[9] Money helped. He could afford every adventure proposed by his co-conspirators, and his political connections, which involved visits to prominent family members in Washington, D.C., or overnight stays at the Lebanese mission in New York, fed the aura. His closest companions at Princeton were mostly Jewish and urban, the children of store owners or professionals, whereas his roommates tended to be from obscure towns in the Midwest and working class. He helped one of them during the torture of Bicker (a frat initiation) by getting him accepted into the right social clubs. One friend, Alex McLeod, was surprised on one of their concert trips to New York by Said's odd behavior: "If an Orthodox Jew was walking towards us, he would cross to the other side of the street rather than face them." McLeod read this as a symbolic protest, the indignation he felt toward those in Palestine hurting his people, and agreed with those in

Said's cohort that he was "absolutely free of antisemitism."[10] But he was startled by the fury of the gesture.

Throughout college, "being Christian was very important to him," McLeod observed. To the admissions committee Said even declared that he planned to study medicine in order to become a "medical missionary" and later volunteered to sing formally at chapel, which exceeded the school requirement that students attend a religious service of their choice.[11] For all its anchoring, this return to ritual did not fool his schoolmates into thinking him well-adjusted. The anxiety of performing piano, the indecision about his career path, and his habit of seeing in his own dissatisfaction with himself his father's aloofness and tyranny eventually came to a head. Easygoing and fun he might have seemed, but it raised no eyebrows when he confided to his friends that he was seeing a psychiatrist. He would continue to do so throughout his life.

ALTHOUGH POPULAR, HE HAD, as his grad school classmate Michael Fried later observed, "a slight *méchant* [wicked] side."[12] He negotiated Princeton's customs perfectly, enjoying the rituals of the eating clubs in particular, but could be very ironical about them, mocking their excessive shows of ceremony. Each club had its own personality, and his own, the Campus Club, was for intellectuals. But his involvement in the various social activities at Princeton came at the cost of frantic late-night study, and he could not always bear the pressure. On the eve of the comprehensive examinations—similar to the French *baccalauréat* in that it determined one's academic future—friends found him in the middle of the night in a darkened common room, striking his head against the wall.[13]

Even as he fit in, he was at the same time odd—tortured, affable, and capable of surprising depths. A roommate discovered that when he spoke in his sleep, it was in Arabic. When awake, he adjusted his language to the visitor—Arabic when given the chance, a "beautiful

French" for those who knew the language, and two forms of English: one American, the other Oxonian, shifting abruptly between the two at a moment's notice either to make a point or to match the accent of his interlocutor.[14] An extraordinarily fast reader, Said reinforced this skill with a speed-reading course that he also recommended to his sister Grace.[15] Somehow getting his hands on an advance copy of *Doctor Zhivago*, he read the entire book in his dorm room between 7:00 p.m. and midnight, his hands constantly flipping the pages. "There, done," he declared as his roommate looked on in astonishment.[16]

It was Gold who made him question his dream of becoming a doctor, and soon literature and piano also competed for his attention.[17] No one at the time suspected that he would choose the former. For one thing, there was little happening in the field of literature—its biggest star was the Canadian literary taxonomist Northrop Frye—and it was certainly below the radar of anyone in his cohort except Gold. Said's choice, it turned out, was helped along by negative pressure. Despite its illustrious music faculty, Princeton was relatively weak in performance.[18] With a heavy theory component, and a focus on harmony, counterpoint, and composition, the music department had just been revamped by Roy Dickinson Welch, who had recruited eight or nine of the most eminent figures in the profession.[19]

These attractions could be found in the performance wing as well, if not as distinctively. By his senior year, he was studying under the legendary Erich Itor Kahn, yet another old-world Jewish émigré from Europe, who came down once a week from New York to teach him and a few others. Although he was dissatisfied with his other piano teachers in those years, two of the better-known instructors at Princeton, Edward T. Cone and Elliot Forbes, were hardly second tier.[20] The latter would eventually move to Harvard to become its éminence grise, and the former, Ralph Waldo Emerson's grandson, traveled in the Boston Brahmin circles that had the clout to launch professional careers.

Despite heavy doses of music theory, and exposure to the serial and atonal composers Babbitt and Sessions (as well as, through

Eaton, jazz), Said's tastes were quite conventional. The glee club's chief accompanist, he was particularly attracted to Bach, Chopin, and Schumann as a soloist, confessing that the deeper he immersed himself in piano, the more elusive he found the distance between his technique ("for all intents and purposes faultless," in one friend's view) and the mastery of the concert performer.[21] Everyone knew he was considering a professional career in music but that he "suffered from nerves" and at times would "push the tempo."[22] His skills were nevertheless impressive, and on May 11, 1957, he performed Bach's Concerto in C Major for two pianos with the Princeton orchestra under Nicholas Harsanyi, demonstrating superb modulation and lightning quickness as revealed in the extant recordings.[23] For piano he had the right physique: strong hands, a little stubby "like a boxer's," but with a body that fit the part, playing hunched over the keys as though mimicking Glenn Gould.[24]

As he softened his flirtation with medicine and business, and reluctantly vetoed a career in music, Gold became his "brother," as he put it in a phone call to Marie-Hélène, Gold's widow, right after his friend had died in late 1988.[25] Their special intimacy sprang in part from their respective family dramas, especially, as Marie-Hélène observed, a painful relationship with a domineering father.[26] The trials made other characteristics flourish: "Arthur's uncanny ability to imagine another person's point of view, his unusual gift for intellectual empathy."[27] It was Gold who introduced Said to the work of Giambattista Vico, the early eighteenth-century Neapolitan rhetorician and author of the masterpiece *The New Science* (1744), who would go on to frame so much of Said's thinking.[28] Although he had little to do with Said's innovative reading of Vico, Gold embodied the same impromptu erudition and impracticality that made intellectual life irresistible. Only his philosophy professor, Arthur Szathmary, another of Said's mentors at Princeton, could be considered equally influential in teaching him "the essentials of critical thinking."[29] Irreverent, skeptical, a partisan of his students' points of view, Szathmary gave him his first sense of the complexities and ambiguities of writing and speech.

Gold and Said had enrolled in the special humanities program in their freshman year and were inseparable over the next decade, even if there were tensions. It was Gold, for example, who finished first in the class; he was also the author of a brilliant one-act play and an ambitious thesis on Henry James and Flaubert that his professors, lamely punning on his name, called "pure gold." Politics were also at issue between them. The two young men quarreled bitterly over the Suez crisis, known in Arab circles as the Tripartite Aggression (the invasion of Egypt by Britain, France, and Israel), each seeing in his own side a beleaguered underdog.

With his European tailoring and wavy black hair, Said impressed women, whereas Gold was a classic "nerd." His thick glasses and baggy corduroys were of a piece with what Said described as "his lean wiriness, his nervous chain-smoking, his deeply furrowed brow, his gently gesturing hands, his tentative and groping voice, full of quizzical often funny and cackling self-interruption."[30]

A starker contrast lay in Gold's tragic unproductivity as his career progressed. His passing comments might have been more brilliant than those expressed in others' books, and his ideas for essays were limitless, but the magnum opus never materialized.[31] Unlike most of the Ivy League stars, Gold declined to move on to Oxford or Cambridge after graduation, instead accepting a Rotary fellowship to India because it was vast, world historical, and likely to change him. He was a defiant liberal in the age of Eisenhower. On his return from India, he rendezvoused with Said in the Cairo airport to discuss how productively small the experience had made him feel. Gold must have appreciated the texture of Said's "Near Eastern" identity (as Said described the region at the time), which was laid out clearly in Said's first published political essay—a piece on the Suez crisis that appeared in *The Daily Princetonian* in 1956.[32]

In this article, the cadences of Said's mature work are already visible, its assuaging tones accompanied by the high-minded reserve of one already at home in international relations. Nasser's nationalization of the canal, he wrote, was not the rash escapade of a radical but the logical expression of "a series of stalemates between the Arabs and the West." While agreeing to fund part of the Aswan Dam project, the World Bank set strict conditions, requiring that Egypt first make peace with Israel and that the West approve all loans at outrageous rates of interest. The Soviet counteroffer, he observed, was much more welcoming, a "pay when you can" scheme with no interest and without any stipulations regarding Israel. Granted that the Soviet offer undoubtedly concealed other agendas, the fact remained it was a better deal. Besides, Western intransigence had hurt the United States in terms of world esteem. It was Nasser's confidence *in the West* that had been shaken, not, as the U.S. secretary of state, John Foster Dulles, thought, the other way around. For the United States remained Israel's chief abettor, and all the other injustices in the region ultimately stem "from the Palestine question." None of the Western powers seemed to figure out that friendship with the Arab states was to the West's long-term advantage.

Whether for tactical reasons or out of genuine ambivalence, his defense gave little evidence of his family's ardent Nasserism. It is also striking that his essay ignored the Bandung Conference of 1955—the legendary meeting of twenty-nine third-world governments in Bandung, Indonesia, to express their independent support, free from the world's superpowers, for political self-determination. Talk of the watershed that was Bandung was very much in the air at the time, as his future mother-in-law Wadad Cortas explained when extolling Bandung's theoretical breakthroughs in shedding light on the crimes of colonialism, singling out Nasser, who by challenging Israel's legitimacy "won a symbolic victory for Palestine."[33] None of this found its way into Said's essay, which was puzzling because the crackdown on dissidents that would cost his friend Farid Haddad his life in an Egyptian jail was still in the future and because Nasser's inability to deliver a victory in his military showdown with

Israel had not yet happened.[34] The Egyptian leader, in any case, went loudly unmentioned in Said's roster of great Arab statesmen.

For all his accomplishments there, Princeton, unlike Mount Hermon, was not all about sublimation. Against school rules prohibiting students from owning cars (the infraction was grounds for suspension), he secretly kept his Alfa Romeo in a garage off campus, using it to escape to nearby campuses in the mostly fruitless search for the company of women.[35] By accident, his sisters helped the quest along. Rosy, the oldest daughter of the family, was studying at Bryn Mawr during his sophomore year, and it was through her that he met one of her friends, Nancy Dire, who became a romantic interest, although not at first. The year before, Said had become amorously involved with the francophone daughter of a wealthy soap manufacturer, Eva Emad, whom he had met during the summers in Dhour el Shweir. In these first awkward sexual encounters, he discovered the joys of an intimacy free from his mother's intrusive gaze.

Intense in his junior year, the courtship carried on long-distance for nine months of the year, resuming each summer in Lebanon; it lingered on even into grad school, although given their different lives and locations, only intermittently. In the end, without career ambitions and of the Greek Orthodox faith, Eva was not considered suitable.[36] Said's memoir implies that their love was the casualty of his mother's unmoving censure because of Eva's age, religion, and francophony, but other factors were more powerful. Eva was kind, proper, and devoted, but with only a secondary school education, and from a conservative family. She could only listen patiently as he talked about his ideas, not engage with them. Limping along until the late 1950s, already weakened and past repair, the relationship definitively ended when he announced his engagement to another woman in 1961.

As his ties with Eva grew distant, he found himself growing closer to Nancy Dire, and their bond was serious enough that he invited her to Cairo to meet his family. But this too came to an end in 1959 with a remarkable letter breaking off their relationship that alludes to some LPs he shared with her:

> Forgive my elegiac tone as I write this, but it is the melancholy trapped within me voicing itself for once—and I hope fervently—for all. The beauty of this music is the beauty of much recollected in sorrow and exultation. To you was revealed the bottomless bitterness of an Arab soul seeking its resolution in a sort of abiding harmony . . . For the brief moments of oneness we have much to be thankful for . . . I blame myself. Never, never be guilty of the sin of enthusiasm . . . Listen to this and be yourself in it, in the ineffable tones of perpetual, undiminished beauty—and maybe this is to be ours, only ours.[37]

A few years later, in 1962, by then in graduate school at Harvard, he married Maire Jaanus instead, a woman he met in 1959, once more through a sister, although this time it was Jean, who was then studying at Vassar and Maire's classmate. Much more than a lover and companion, she was a genuine collaborator, a woman whose intellectual intensity and linguistic talents equaled his own. Also working on her doctorate in literature, she was Said's partner in reading Continental theory. Their early years together were euphoric, the two of them multilingual exiles entering a profession just then opening itself up to their particular worldliness and philosophical tastes.

Just before graduating from Princeton in 1957, during some of the fiercest fighting of the Battle of Algiers, he met Ibrahim Abu-Lughod, a Palestinian graduate student at Princeton who hailed from Jaffa. Said had been working as a volunteer at a music club ticket booth on campus when Abu-Lughod approached him to make conversation. At first only a casual acquaintance, he became the man who later recruited Said to Arab American activism and collaborated with him on essays, books, and films, Said calling him his "guru" in a 2001 obituary. At the time of their meeting,

Abu-Lughod was on his way to work for UNESCO in Cairo, and Said for different reasons was headed there as well. This proximity allowed their relationship to deepen as the older Abu-Lughod tutored the French-identified Said in third-world political insurgency, especially the events then unfolding in Algeria.[38]

The meeting was all the more fateful in that Said had only recently acquiesced in his father's plea that he spend the 1957–58 academic year in Cairo, apprenticing in his father's business before entering graduate school at Harvard. The plan was more than a pretense to appease his father. Upon graduation from Princeton, despite the obvious release he felt in the life of the mind, he kept to his original scheme, stating that his aim was to settle in "the Near East" and that his top two choices for profession were teaching and "business (in a specialized branch of government)."[39]

So when he deferred the "fat fellowship," as he put it, to Harvard for a year, apart from his attempt to take pressure off his father, who for health reasons needed rest, he did so to put distance between himself and Eva, as well as to give Aunt Melia's advice to consider a life in business a genuine chance.[40] There was another reason as well. He meant also to reacquaint himself with Tiegerman: "I then went back to the Middle East for a year basically to play piano."[41] Even as he was learning about insurrectionary third worldism from Abu-Lughod, his state of mind remained conventional. As he left for Egypt, in a move that recalled his fawning letters to Rubendall at Mount Hermon, he made sure to have the *Princeton Alumni Weekly* forwarded to his Cairo PO box.[42]

Even with its many excitements, the year abroad produced a string of negative decisions. He decided he would not carry on the family business. Nor would he become a concert pianist or a doctor, even though he continued the premed coursework in chemistry and biology throughout his time at Princeton. In a letter accompanying the renewal of his grad school application following the deferral, he explained that "this one year in Egypt working in my father's firm has had its good points . . . I am more sure than ever what in the long run I would like to do: teach . . . [T]he troubled politics of the Near East have added a new dimension to my thoughts."[43] In fact, his recoil from a life in business was not entirely high-minded; it was clearly also personal. The sense of being a subordinate—the indulged young "Mr. Said" to Wadie's "sir" among the employees of the Standard Stationery Company—was a disincentive to follow his father's path.

What's more, his surroundings were simply too mundane. He was basically on a sinecure, and with time on his hands he began reading Kierkegaard, Nietzsche, and Freud intensively for the first time, puzzling over them while writing music criticism and poetry, some of which he published in small Beirut magazines.[44] It is anyone's guess whether he fled the life of sales contracts and import ledgers because of a higher calling, because of the unstable business environment of Nasser's Egypt, or because he did not have his father's head for numbers or iron command of trivial details. In any case, he had become almost without knowing it his own person for the first time in his life.

From the start of this year in Cairo, however, Said was plagued by concerns about the draft back in the United States. He wrote to Harvard in the summer of 1957 to say that he would indeed be in Cambridge in September "draft willing."[45] By 1958, he was classified 1-A, and so eligible for immediate conscription. He managed to hold the draft board at bay for a time, but in August 1960 he was required to appear in Long Island City for a physical, the final step before conscription into the army. He pointed out that his father was ailing and relied on him to help in the family business during the summers. It was Ralph Nader's counsel that proved the most effective, and with his help Said secured a student deferment.

OVER A PERIOD OF a little more than eight years, Said's intellectual life had been shaped by the imposing presence of four role models: Blackmur and Szathmary at Princeton, Harry Levin at Harvard, and throughout that time Charles Malik, the Lebanese statesman and philosophy professor at the American University of Beirut. All of them provided templates for his rhetorical style and research agendas, despite his antipathy to Malik's political vision. His contempt for Malik's right-wing Christianism was so strong that he later called him "the great negative intellectual lesson of my life."[46] But for all that, Said's work was a blend especially of Blackmur's diagnosis of America's doomed cultural panorama and Malik's missionary drive on behalf of a distinctively Arab humanism.

Blackmur was fond of saying that Europe's "force of mind," its ability to work at complex levels of conceptualization, was far superior to that of the Americans, and there can be no doubt that Said's pioneering promotion of various Continental philosophies in the 1960s and 1970s derived from just such a perspective. Said frequently complained of the "thinness" of American intellectual life and the "extraordinary absence" there of the kind of "philosophical reflection . . . one finds in French, German and Italian writing."[47] On the other hand, Americans, Blackmur continued, had superior "momentum." The irony is that this typically American drive and these European sensibilities could be found so strongly in a man whom readers of *Orientalism* later misinterpreted as anti-European.

Blackmur was never formally Said's adviser, although he did serve as the official reader of his senior thesis, titled "The Moral Vision: André Gide and Graham Greene." It was Blackmur who wrote his recommendation for the Woodrow Wilson Fellowship, which Said won. In a short handwritten note of December 13, 1957, he explained that his "personal knowledge of Said is negligible and amounts only to a general impression of vivid vigor and general attractiveness," and yet he read the thesis "with genuine interest because of its continuous intelligence, broad scope, and occasional surprising intuitions into the nature of moral vision."[48]

As for Szathmary, his special interest in the young man fell just short of devotion, finding Said's French "flawless" and campaigning among his colleagues to recognize him as "serious without being heavy, urbane but not blasé, cultivated but not jaded."[49] The two teachers were in different fields and had divergent styles but were genuine renegades, like Said himself, though, unlike him, not born to this milieu but sponsored by an establishment that protected and rewarded them for being acceptably edgy. Szathmary's influence, although crucial, was more general: he taught him "the essentials of critical thinking."[50] As an undergrad, the more lasting influence came from Blackmur.

What made his mentors unorthodox may seem obscure today, but it energized Said immensely. After World War II a showdown developed in the way literature was studied in the university. The uncritical history-mongering and dusty archival work of the old-school philologists was locked in battle against the radical challenges of the New Critics. Seen now as conservatives, the New Critics were in their own time insurgents. They insisted that reading literature was a matter of aesthetic appreciation and literary form, not just the tracing of etymological shifts or word derivations. Their emphasis on the unique figurative dimension of texts—more or less like the "revolution in language" in 1960s Continental theory—eventually became their movement's idée fixe.

Recoiling from the sterile specialized knowledge of old-school philology, they eventually bent the stick too far, erasing all history and politics from criticism and imagining an ideal reader to be one with no knowledge other than the poem or story before him or her. In this, the artwork became a self-enclosed meaning machine with its own codes. No need to unearth details about the author or track down information about how and why the work was written. Said, then, right from the start was drawn to teachers who, while still relishing aesthetic form, resisted these trends by unfashionably focusing on political and social institutions.

As an outlier of this sort, Blackmur launched trends that Said later helped promote. Although on the political left, both he and Said's grad school adviser Levin were skittish around Marx, treating him respectfully but keeping him at arm's length even with much borrowing. They spoke of capitalism wearily and with contempt, seeing in the art of language a revenge against a society that valued nothing that was not immediately useful.[51] In a handwritten note found among his papers for a novel in progress, Said seized upon an enigmatic line from Blackmur: "Knowledge itself is a fall from the paradise of undifferentiated sensation."[52] There is tragedy in knowing, he was implying, a foreclosure of the beauty of the original impulse to know, which, when satisfied, settles into an unsatisfying certainty. A life worth living was open to aesthetic mystery.

Not everyone, perhaps, would have agreed with Said's judgment that Blackmur was the greatest American critic of the first half of the twentieth century, but to most contemporaries he was one of a kind. He was not the sort of man to be "replicated, reproduced, reused as a lesson learned and then applied."[53] To his students, he was more than a teacher, something more like "a sort of high priest of modernism" who knew and was close with the poets (among them, W. H. Auden, Louise Bogan, and Wallace Stevens) whose work he was busy teaching. He would read poetry aloud to students for hours in class with cigarette in hand. Sitting in on his lectures, Said studied how physicality and character affect criticism, penetrating that part of persuasion that lies beyond words. If he later extolled the figure of the autodidact, it was Blackmur he had in mind, a professor who lacked not only a PhD but even a high school diploma.[54] Blackmur's appeal was, among other things, to have combined critical insight with a "sporty quirkiness."[55]

Far from apolitical and not only a formalist, Blackmur nevertheless was a New Critic as far as English departments were concerned. It is only that to return to the work itself, the signature New Critical move, did not preclude for him writing essays on the fate of reason, or protesting the idea that rationality was the private property of mathematics and technology, a theme Said later deliberately developed. Blackmur helped pioneer the skeptical study of news and entertainment media, nudging the study of fiction and poetry away from issues of talent or authorial voice to "the operative force of the whole social institutions which they willy-nilly represent."[56] He tackled the economy of literature, the "profit motive," the threat to art under "finance capitalism," and did so in many ways more plainly than Said did himself.

Said has always been considered a critic of narrative fiction and the novel above all, but it was poetry that lay at the heart of his intellectual formation. Blackmur had a direct hand in this, particularly through his love for Gerard Manley Hopkins, who believed that great writing possesses the qualities of direct speech. The phrase Said frequently quoted from Blackmur—"bringing literature to performance"—was, among other things, a way for Said to put his now abandoned career as a pianist to use, by imagining the ideal critic as a musician before an audience, but also a rhetor making a case in a court of law.[57] "Words are made of motion," Blackmur had written in *Language as Gesture* (1952), "the words in [the writer's] pen are not as viable as the words in his mouth."[58]

It is not just that Blackmur, following Hopkins, put his finger on that peculiar strength both he and Said mastered as critics, this ability to write with the disarming spontaneity, physical inflection, and personality of a conversationalist, but that both derived strength from Hopkins's religious vision to make criticism a secular vocation. It mattered that Hopkins was an ardent Anglican who converted to Roman Catholicism and became a Jesuit priest, and that his poems throb with a transcendent energy just beneath the surface of natural objects. Said's fascination with Hopkins was limitless for all these reasons, but also psychological ones. Setting out in grad school to write a monograph on the English poet, Said toyed with the thesis that "in the poetry of Hopkins . . . we find a very pure performance of polysexuality (sex transferred to text), of an omni-sexuality transferred from natural to literary life, underpinning the entire career and text."[59] If one wished to secularize religion without losing its transcendent force, sexuality would be the natural bridge.

It is hard to underestimate the mark Blackmur left on Said in other respects as well. Although a modernist, which then for most critics evoked a penchant for symbolism without referents or an enigmatic, self-canceling irony, Blackmur held that all creative writing is ultimately hortatory—that it has an ulterior purpose and argument—and he wanted to revive the didactic literature of Horace, Milton, and Swift. These views could not have been more heretical to the modernism then in vogue, and Said took notice. But Blackmur was not overtly political. He thought it best to remain "playful" and not to get bogged down in organizations or parties, which he memorably described as a "struggle in the marmalade."[60] Said later sneered at Blackmur's "bourgeois humanism in a church-yard," but this obscures the fact that Blackmur's political liberalism was essentially angry and middle-of-the-road—that is, anticommunist and anti-McCarthyite at the same time. He compared the "inventions of Moscow" to the "inventions of Madison Avenue."

Like Said later, he was both inside and outside literary modernism, which in the 1950s was consolidating itself as the central political and aesthetic outlook of the humanities and metropolitan art world. Although an iconoclast, Blackmur shared some of its central outlooks. Apart from meaning simply a period of art (roughly 1880 to 1940), "modernism" referred to a loose ensemble of aesthetic positions and artistic attitudes including avant-garde formal experimentalism, hatred of democracy, and revolt against mass culture. Unsettled by this antidemocratic thrust, Blackmur (and later Said) could nonetheless sign on to modernism's resistance to commercialism, patriotism, and repressive optimism. They willingly extolled the uncanny talents of deliberately unpopular, difficult, and dark authors (in Blackmur's words) to "have within themselves the capacity to generate by absorbing disorder into order."[61]

But Blackmur saw danger signs, finding in modernism some of the epistemological nihilism of physics and mathematics, where both the arts and the sciences seemed to claim that humans cannot really know and that the "person" is a fiction, an ensemble of mechanical stimuli. Said shared these fears but drew the line when it came to Blackmur's vision of criticism as a kind of heroic doom, waging its war in the hopeless space between the numen ("the power within us" that moves us "towards an ideal that overwhelms us") and the *moha*, a Sanskrit term, borrowed from his friend Robert Oppenheimer, alluding to the atomic bomb ("the contemptuous stupidity of man" who yields to "blind, necessary action").[62] Heedless of his mentor's advice, Said headed for the marmalade.

THE MOTIFS OF WORLDLINESS and authenticity that fill Said's first published writings will be misread without knowing about Charles Malik—a man who was much more than a distant relative by marriage. In the face of Malik's "harsh and unpleasant" religious views in which he "frequently denounced Islam and the Prophet Mohammed . . . using such words as 'lechery,' 'hypocrisy,' 'corruption,' and 'degeneration,'" Said became in spite of himself Malik's intellectual apprentice.[63]

By all accounts a giant of Middle East politics, international relations, UN history, and Lebanese public life, Malik was one of the great Arab intellectuals of the twentieth century. Among the original signatories of the charter that founded the United Nations, he was also a pivotal member along with Eleanor Roosevelt of the committee that drafted the Universal Declaration of Human Rights, serving continuously in the UN for fourteen years and eventually becoming president of its General Assembly. Although a man who made hard decisions as a working politician, he had a metaphysical cast of mind. He was minister of foreign affairs during the first Lebanese civil war in 1956–58, inviting U.S. troops into the country under the authority of President Camille Chamoun, who like all presidents of Lebanon after independence was a Maronite. He also revamped the philosophy department at AUB, working as a distinguished professor there from 1962 to 1976, with a list of honorary doctorates from prestigious universities.

Said had never met anyone who came close to Malik's intellectual distinction.[64] Malik had studied under Alfred North Whitehead at Harvard in 1934 and 1937 and was a student of the philosopher Martin Heidegger at Freiberg University in 1935–36.[65] On Said's visits to Malik in Washington when he was studying at Mount Hermon and Princeton, he deepened his relationship in a friendly atmosphere similar to the one he enjoyed at his parents' house in Cairo.[66] Malik might not have been a close relative, but Said, it turned out, was a favorite of Malik's wife, Eva, and Malik himself had a deep affection for Said's father, and so would visit the household in wartime Cairo. An imposing, some would say pompous, man with a "booming voice," he marshaled gravity and girth to empower his versatile roles as teacher, diplomat, and politician.

Malik's roles at political turning points, however, became increasingly problematic as they revealed themselves. He moved from spokesman for the Palestinians in the 1940s to the intellectual architect of the Lebanese Christian Right's alliance with Israel after 1949. Said took small revenge by gently mocking Malik in his memoir, painting a portrait of him as a know-it-all blustering about how ancient astronomers calculated the distance to the stars using terrestrial angles. Despite their different ages and status (Malik was already prominent when Said was only a sophomore at Princeton) and political views, the relationship grew, particularly in Dhour el Shweir, where the Maliks were regulars. Said found those summers increasingly dull, but his discussions with Malik allowed him to escape the familial torpor.

Their paths kept crossing. Malik was a guest professor at Harvard summer school in 1960 when Said was a grad student, and later, when Said was already tenured at Columbia and on sabbatical in Beirut, Malik was on the faculty there and very much in contact. By his own account, Said continued to seek Malik's guidance at least until 1967 and was dazzled by his linguistic mastery of Arabic, English, and German and his knowledge on subjects ranging from Fichte to Plotinus. Family accounts suggest that he was also reading his work closely, and the remarkable parallels between Said's interests and Malik's themes correspond to Malik's writing at just the time Said was visiting Washington as an impressionable teenager.[67]

In a major 1952 article by Malik published in *Foreign Affairs*—the advisory sounding board of Washington power circles—the Lebanese statesman lays out a research agenda for future East-West relations that could only have left a deep mark on Said's mind. In "The Near East: The Search for Truth," Malik not only highlighted themes that Said would later elaborate, but adopted a beckoning, tutelary style that he might well have learned from.[68] To deal with the rising fervor of Arab nationalism, Malik pleaded, one must understand its point of view. The nationalist movement has come to see the West not as a liberator but as a schemer intent to divide, dominate, and settle the region against the will of the population with "countless Jews on Syrian soil."[69]

Malik patiently reviews every Arabic and non-Arabic Islamic state in the region, noting its quirks of development to give a sense of both the illusory unity of the Near East and what does, in fact, negatively unite it: the Western powers' creation of the state of Israel. Geopolitics, he insists, has a cultural and spiritual dimension and cannot be reduced to a struggle over natural resources. Put figuratively, the conflict as its major actors conceived and lived it was never over land alone but over the children of Isaac and of Ishmael: "There is a profound intellectual and spiritual chasm between Israel and the rest of the Near East . . . History has not known an instance of a nation at permanent enmity with its immediate world."[70] The West must learn that Islam, even for Christians in the region, is one's fate. It is not just a religion but a total outlook, an understanding of which has been frustratingly rare, although initial advances have been made in the pioneering scholarship, he noted, of Albert Hourani, Louis Massignon, Philip Hitti, and Constantine Zurayk. These were names Said was reading for the first time and would remember.

At the end of this tour de force, Malik outlines key areas of knowledge to explore if cultural understanding is to be achieved: "the phenomenon in recent decades of 'the Orientalist.'" Malik wrote, "How much good and how much harm has Orientalism done? Why a corresponding phenomenon of 'the Occidentalist' did not arise?" Other suggestive notes are struck: "Is there an absolute beginning? If not, where do we start?" He then emphasized, as Said later would, the central problem of geography, the "geographical determinism" of Arab culture. He implored the aggrieved Arabs to engage in fundamental self-criticism and to stop blaming everything on the West, along the way raising the problem of originality versus mimicry in the colonial encounter. Offering a blueprint for what was to be done, he stressed the building of institutes of Islamic and Near Eastern studies in the United States and contended, in turn, that the most important thing for the Arab world was to publish each year in Arabic "one or two hundred volumes of the world's finest classics." He did not neglect the humanities, concluding that in the absence of a middle class the court poet in Arab countries rises in importance: "To rule you must employ a rhetorician or poet or be one yourself."[71]

Sharply aware of the national liberation movements sweeping across Africa and Asia, he built his counsel upon this shifting terrain. This struggle over the future of the third world provided an opening for Arab intellectuals to recognize the desperate warning it was giving to Christians everywhere, above all in the West. We must take notice that "Karl Marx and Marxism-Leninism do not belong to the dead past . . . They are a most living reality indeed, one which is raking us [over] all the time."[72] Through Marxism, he warned, "the non-West is gradually overpowering the West!"[73]

Said was much more begrudging with the Heideggerian influences on Malik's work, rejecting them in the same spirit that he had Malik's anti-Islamic prejudices.[74] But some of them lingered on. The term "fate," for example, intrigued Said as Heidegger had fashioned it, because there it represented the opposite of predestination. For the German philosopher, the human condition was one of radical freedom, which meant also responsibility, a view that fit well with Said's secular Christian ethos. The monstrous form Christianity took in Malik's anticommunist crusade cured him of any open attraction to his inherited faith and hastened his secularization. Despite Malik's acknowledging the cultural centrality of Islam to Arab identity, his sectarian arrogance as well as his endless paeans to the unique spiritual achievements of Europe drove Said toward non-Europe and gave him a lifelong distaste for anticommunism in all its forms.[75]

ONLY A FEW MONTHS before entering Harvard, on his first visit to the Bayreuth music festival at the age of twenty-three, Said had "a horrendously bloody, head-on collision" with a motorcyclist in Switzerland, suffering head injuries that required him to be hospitalized.[76] Just outside the town of Fribourg, where he was headed to visit his cousin George (a convert to Roman Catholicism who had set up life there in a religious commune), his Alfa Romeo rounded a curve on a steep mountain road and crashed into the motorcyclist, who was about his age and who died later that day in the hospital. Unconscious for twenty-four hours, Said awoke in intensive care to find his mother leaning over him and remained in Fribourg for the rest of the summer recuperating. The oddly detached account Said gives of this accident in his memoir matched his resistance to speak to his family about the incident, even when pressed. It was apparently too agonizing to discuss, and he never came to terms with it.

Except for his marriage to Maire Jaanus in 1962, Said's personal growth at Harvard was not nearly so colorful or so marked as it had been at Princeton. He lived with his new wife in relative solitude at a time that saw Mao's Great Leap Forward, the overthrow of the Batista regime in Cuba, the Sharpeville massacre, and the Bay of Pigs invasion. As he put it in a later interview, even his immersion in the piano was sacrificed as he plunged into his books: "I did really nothing else but study for five years."[77] Meanwhile, building on the deep companionship he had formed with Abu-Lughod during his yearlong hiatus in Cairo, Said was inching his way toward a new political awareness. It was still several years before Abu-Lughod helped launch his younger friend's political career by commissioning him to write "The Arab Portrayed" (1970), the essay that made Said's name in the Arab world. But there are traces of the defiant third worldism that Abu-Lughod inspired scattered throughout Said's student notes.

Life at Harvard moved along within the pleasant routines of concerts, standing lunches, an ongoing conspiracy of intellect with Gold and Farer. Between 1959 and 1962, he took advantage of his adopted city by attending every Boston recital of Glenn Gould, the most impressive of which took place in 1961 with the French conductor Paul Paray and the Detroit Symphony Orchestra. He continued visiting his sisters regularly and, as before, meeting new women. Michael Rosenthal, who later became one of Said's closest friends on the Columbia faculty, was part of the same dating circles and once walked in on him and his girlfriend in the dorms, clothes strewn about the room. Said already had something of a reputation, he recalled, for being dashing, confident, and fearfully smart. Without showing the slightest embarrassment, Said ignored the compromising situation and, having just taken his orals, started grilling Rosenthal on the novels of Wyndham Lewis as though nothing had happened.[78] Taken aback, but admiring the prowess, Rosenthal began a lifelong friendship with Said.

With Maire on the scene, Said settled down. The young couple was soon known for their fashionable garden parties at their colonial redbrick lodgings on Francis Avenue in Cambridge, the place to be seen at the time and a local legend. Like his father, he developed a taste for cigars and pipes and, when neither was available, for cigarettes as well, which he shamelessly bummed from friends. He remained a dedicated smoker all his life, but a particular one, who wrote letters to Alfred Dunhill Limited ordering tins of tobacco, "Mixture 34596."[79]

The "country of the blue"—Blackmur's image of the artist disappearing into his work—caught the mood of the Harvard years.[80] Apart from marriage, nothing much happened in his life, although his mind was exploding. He sought consolation in psychoanalysis and papered over emotional difficulties with productivity. Now in his mid-twenties, he dedicated significant time to mastering the books he would mine for the rest of his life—Vico's *New Science*, Georg Lukács's *History and Class Consciousness*, Jean-Paul Sartre's *Being and Nothingness*, and Maurice Merleau-Ponty's studies of phenomenology and perception. In comparison to that at Princeton, his writing suddenly had more originality and personality. Said's undergraduate essays on Henry James and on "the relation between greatness and perfection in art" are serviceable exegeses. The graduate essays soar.[81]

What they reveal should matter to anyone interested in the latent and manifest content of Said's signature ideas. Most striking, perhaps, is his deep investment in the classics of Western philosophy. Noteworthy, again, is his unexpected preference for poetry over fiction, but also his sustained study of the history of science. None of these is a focus in his published books, but they prevailed at his beginnings. There are extensive notes, for example, on Karl Pearson's *Grammar of Science*, which dealt with problems of "probability," "contingency," "fact," and "causation," and he compiled a lengthy bibliography on the philosophy of science. His essay on Hume's *Inquiry Concerning the Principles of Morals* prompted his professor Walter Jackson Bate to comment that his essay, although gracefully written, was not "belletristic" enough and too severely philosophical.[82] Other essays moved from the mystical poems of Crashaw to "Campion's prosody and text setting" to the political philosophies of Hobbes and Hume. Although part of his educational grounding was conventional for the time, other aspects were more adventurous. Under "philosophy and the arts" he was deep into his investigations of turn-of-the-century theorists (Benedetto Croce, Henri Bergson, John Dewey), artists and authors (Leonardo da Vinci, Piet Mondrian, André Malraux), psychologists (Carl Jung, Sigmund Freud, Otto Rank), and sociologists of culture (Georgi Plekhanov, Arnold Hauser, Siegfried Kracauer).

Buried in a note to himself for the essay "A Study of William Faulkner's 'The Bear'" (1960), a handwritten phrase in red ink leaps out, underlined on yellow lined paper: "Form as a Moral Complement to Theme." We find here another gesture toward Blackmur's efforts to reconcile opposites and deploy New Critical form in the service of right action.[83] Presaging his writing practices at the height of his career, this early effort, based on the surviving manuscript, was apparently written in one outpouring without serious revision, in mellifluous, lucid paragraphs. Many of the impulses at work in his extended readings of Hobbes's *De Cive*, Milton's political writings, and Ernst Cassirer are forerunners of his later principles of argument: the reclaiming of religious ideals for secularity and the idea that to be ethical, one must be political.

In "The Still Music of Meditative Poetry" (1959), he adopted a confessional mode, beginning with an anecdote: "An Egyptian medical student asked me what on earth I was doing studying literature. Egypt is a poor country, its people ill and under-nourished, her arable land scarce and thirsty." Said was embarrassed and had to admit that poetry cannot feed a poor man. But wasn't there some wisdom in the ancients who saw poets as practical philosophers, as "legislative seer[s]"? He felt chastened but not entirely persuaded and chose to fight back. The politics of poetry may be neither immediate nor direct, but it offered a unique social force: "the politics of the heart."[84]

The internal debates he was having in the early 1960s about the suitability of literary study to social action are revealing:

> [Because] all writing is political . . . one need not, I think,
> fear the implication of "politicianism"—bad taste and

mudslinging. Politics is a science of relation . . . I cannot concede it to be even remotely possible that either man [Plato or Milton] wrote simply to pass the time, because I am convinced that each man felt it a duty to speak and then to influence and reform . . . I am a Near Easterner . . . So when I look at the effect of books, newspapers, and magazines on the Egyptian scene . . . each idea in print, either isolated from its own context or lumped together with a mass of others' idea[s] can be interpreted (and indeed is) in the light of a really crucial political battle: Egypt *versus* the rest of the world.

It appeared to him that whatever was written in the third world would be greeted as rough and inelegant opposition. At this juncture, he was more interested in savoring the point of contact between a piece of writing's "original intention" and "what inordinate enthusiasm did to it."[85]

Such was Said's state of mind as he set off to pursue a PhD in English literature, gravitating toward advisers who only in retrospect seem likely choices. Monroe Engel, a novelist who had won awards for his writing on Gerard Manley Hopkins and an editor at Viking Press, was one of them and by far the more affectionate counselor of the two. Harry Levin, his other mentor, born in Minneapolis but an expatriate in Paris, was among other things a devotee of Thorstein Veblen, the iconic midwestern renegade, a sociologist and economist who scandalized academia at the turn of the century with his *Theory of the Leisure Class* (1899), an ethnographic evisceration of America's corporate warrior ethos.

Although not originally part of the Ivy League elect, Levin came to learn the manners of the establishment too well, playing the Harvard don almost to the point of caricature.[86] Still, like Blackmur, he managed to be odd and original. What Said took to be the rather pallid cast of literary study at Princeton ("conventional history and wan formalism") lived on at Harvard in the sanctimonies of Irving

Babbitt, a towering presence in East Coast academia between the wars and, with his protégé Paul Elmer More, one of the fathers of neoconservatism.[87] It was exactly this culture that defined Levin negatively, and upon accepting the Irving Babbitt Chair later in his career, he took the opportunity of skewering the man in his acceptance speech as an American nativist and a "religionist."[88] Babbitt's interwar crusade on behalf of a "New Humanism," which he understood as Puritan virtue drummed into students via the Greek classics, almost exactly paralleled the campaigns of Allan Bloom and Roger Kimball in the culture wars of the 1980s and 1990s.

Said downplayed his relationship with both of his mentors, noting casually that his dissertation was written "under the benign supervision of Monroe Engel and Harry Levin," as though the relationship were not deep or sustained.[89] In fact, it was both. Levin in particular opened the doors to key journals and played the part of a professional inside man, and Said continued to seek his advice even as a young professor. He might have been less dazzled by Levin's intellectual style than he had been by Blackmur's at Princeton, where he was part of a group his friend Michael Fried called "Blackmur barnacles," but the influence, if less theatrical, had for that reason a weighty, penetrating force.[90] Said would write to a friend from Beirut while rereading Levin's *Grounds for Comparison* years later to say that his adviser's stamp on his thinking was at last beginning to dawn on him.[91]

With a few others, Levin stood out at the time as a towering comparatist in a tidy environment of period specialists. Although technically in an English department, his essays were as likely to be on Cervantes, Goethe, and Balzac as Edgar Allan Poe or George Eliot. While the field was busy exploring the indecipherable symbolism of avant-garde language, he made his mark as a theorist of realism, which he defined as a literary movement dedicated to diagnosing "the greatness and decline of the bourgeoisie." His magnum opus on realism, *The Gates of Horn* (1963), impressed Said so much that he considered Levin an equal of the great German émigré

philologist and comparatist Erich Auerbach and the Marxist philosopher and celebrated theorist of realism Georg Lukács.[92] In a letter to Levin in 1965, he confessed, "The more I read it, the more it
strikes me as a great and deep book that will be fully absorbed only
by a later generation."[93]

To a remarkable degree, Levin anticipated many of Said's critical preferences, defending, for example, critical eclecticism, "a sense
of universal interrelatedness," and cautioning against the tyranny
of grand "systems" of thought that lose touch with contradictions
and chance discoveries.[94] Levin introduced Said to the great biblical
scholar and historian of religion Ernest Renan, who in L'avenir de
la science (1890; The Future of Science) had compared literary study
to the "old-fashioned botany of the amateurs," a major theme of
Orientalism.[95] With a reading knowledge of Arabic, French, Italian,
Latin, German, and Spanish, Said possessed the skills to become a
comparatist in Levin's mold and like him was eager to steer English
studies more in the direction of world literature.[96]

In Levin's hands as later in Said's, literary exile was no longer
automatically equated with American expatriates in Paris as it had
been for the generation before him. It now encompassed victims
of political flight, as well as the clash of idioms in Eastern Europe
and the Near East. Levin was especially harsh on Cold War writers
for hire like Arthur Koestler, complaining that he and others had
almost made deracination their profession, supplying American
public opinion with the ideological lessons it demanded by claiming the special authority of native informant. Said's investments in
Joseph Conrad were helped along by Levin's observation that as a
metropolitan émigré Conrad represented the larger "polyglot mis-
understanding of our time."[97] It is not just that his mentor wrote
about many of Said's intellectual touchstones before him—among
them Raymond Williams, Auerbach, Leo Spitzer, Swift, and Lucien Goldmann—but in essays like "Literature as an Institution"
he showed himself to be the American critic most like Williams

methodologically, tracing with the same sociological verve the impact of information technologies on literary studies.[98] In "Toward a Sociology of the Novel" (1965), Levin looked forward to Said's later applause for Goldmann's mixing of "an Existentialist stance with a Marxist ideology" to create a compelling *"paramarxiste"* amalgam.[99]

There is no question that Levin impressed on Said the importance of the work of Erich Auerbach, who taught at Yale until 1957. The Harvard don had been corresponding with Auerbach and the great stylistician Spitzer for years, having met Auerbach in 1947 by chance at a conference on Cervantes.[100] Their relations were cordial, and the meeting prompted a correspondence that rivaled his frequent letters to Spitzer, who was then teaching at Johns Hopkins. Levin recounts the relationship at some length in his essay "Two *Romanisten* in America," which Said read when it came out in 1972, calling it "marvelous," and then remarking "I hope you won't think it untoward of me to say that in your own way you represent the tradition of those two great scholars, and you do it with greater depth of effectiveness than any scholar in the U.S."[101] In contrast to the ponderous I. A. Richards, one of the most famous critics at the time (who in Levin's view had become a sort of second-rate messenger from the behavioral sciences), Spitzer maintained the vastly preferable "'chameleonic' approach of the philologist" in the sense that his free-floating erudition allowed him to experiment with new disciplinary approaches rather than be stifled by Richards's rigid formalism.[102] Levin had discerned a pattern for the coming decades, a new postwar type of "adaptable émigrés . . . trained in their homelands and by earlier travels to be experts on cultures other than their own. The Slavicist from Italy, Renato Poggioli, and the Anglicist from Czechoslovakia, Réné Wellek, arrived almost simultaneously at Harvard and Yale."[103] And then there was Said, a Palestinian from Jerusalem and Cairo writing about British modernists and America, who would soon arrive at Columbia.

CHAPTER 4

THE SECRET AGENT

To be, to remain what I will
A roguish elegist, the Arabic Till.

—SAID, "Song of an Eastern Humanist"[1]

Honeymooning in Greece in 1962, Said and Maire had every reason to see the future brightly. Their professional trajectories moved steadily upward, and within a year he would win the Bowdoin Prize at Harvard for his dissertation on Joseph Conrad, joining the likes of Emerson, Henry Adams, and John Updike in that honor.

Early in their relationship, Maire scribbled a note on the pages of Said's manuscript for a novel: "Double Dative: *Est auxilio mihi*—he is a help to me." Then immediately below: "Dearest husband, there is nothing on earth like the full heart."[2] Before it became a liability, their shared status as foreigners helped each to prop up the other. In Maire, he had also met his match: a modern woman who claimed the freedom to be everything she aspired to and with the steely will to bring it about. The prospect of a life mate who, unlike his former girlfriend Eva, knew all the nuances of what he was reading and thinking excited him deeply. The attraction was also physical, of

course. Some in the department found her "ravishing, a cross between Garbo and Bergman."[3]

Said's family, on the other hand, found Maire austere and off-
putting. An acquaintance called her "a real snow maiden from the
North," and she was, as Jean put it, "a strict intellectual, very German."[4] In fact, she was Estonian, though like many Eastern European intellectuals fluent in German. She had known sadness in her
life. Her father disappeared in the war, and no one ever discovered
what had happened to him. Edward and she, intoxicated by their
joint discoveries of German and French philosophy in graduate
school, possessed complementary talents. Said's convivial and vernacular powers of persuasion were balanced by Maire's expertise
in the eighteenth century (upon which he drew for his developing
.project on Swift). But as their varying prospects came into focus,
they became increasingly rivalrous, and there were differences
of style. Though Said and she were equally critical of Israel, his
friends, many of them Jewish, were troubled by her claims that
Yiddish was not really a language and, rightly or wrongly, detected
in the view a residual anti-Semitism from her Eastern European
childhood.[5]

There is no direct evidence that Said had Maire in mind when he
wrote a poem in light pencil on a Harvard blue book exam in 1962,
but it caught the rawness of their romantic entanglement:

> Force away, cajoling
> She writes of a kind song,
> Tuned in the halcyon scale
> And branded thus: affection
>
> Smarting with salt,
> Wrapped in a shredded leaf,
> A shoeless holiday in fantasy
> Scarred but ever—bright.

Careful alloy of ups-and-ins
Dropped through molasses and cotton,
Palatable, sticky, clinging
And now enter: chicanery.[6]

The volatility of love, where joy turns suddenly to suspicion, and the one to whom you have bared your soul suddenly appears an enemy: this is the sense Said captured in this poem in the blue book, which in later revisions he gave the title "Little Transformation." In the space of just a few words, the poem passes from longing to rejection, from the poet's hungering for attention to being put off by her clinging, and so even the ups and ins of the act of love are "alloyed."

From their wedding in Dhour el Shweir onward, it was clear that the issue of family would be their danger zone. Although she had escaped the violence of the war by fleeing to Germany with her mother, Maire could not understand Said's family obligations, where uncles and aunts were almost as close as parents and no one kept secrets from anyone.[7] It might have mattered too that Maire was a resolute atheist who lacked any of Said's fondness for religious ritual.[8] With hints of Maire's perspective, Said wrote a volatile letter to his father on June 2, 1965, detaching himself from the family's exhortations while making his mark as a critic and teacher in New York. With barely disguised petulance, he begged off from the "honor" of putting up a relative who does not appreciate the "sacrifice" he and Maire are making and the trial of living in the United States, where "in my profession I work a seven-day week, evenings and all."[9] His father's letters to him are surprisingly timid. Hilda's letters, however, filled with hurt and artful guilt-tripping, implore her son to get back on track as she senses him slipping away into the exhilarating challenges of his professional ascent.

At first, he wrote home bursting with excitement over all the important people he was meeting while summering on Long Island. In time, Hilda felt compelled to ask, "Why aren't you writing [us]? If you're busy, couldn't Maire write a card at least?" Throughout that summer and into the fall of 1965, a sorrowful exchange unfolded, with Said angrily charging his parents with being indifferent to his career and his father disappointed at his son's ungraciousness toward his sisters. This seemed especially an affront because first at Harvard, then later in New York, he saw a lot of his sister Jean in these years, when they spent a great deal of time at each other's houses. Nor can Wadie grasp why his son would flatly ignore his urgent request to act as a liaison with a business partner in New York. Said's response was harsh. "My whole attitude to my past is in ruin," he exclaimed, "money for money . . . it's the only thing that counts." His mother, with some justice, countered, "Where would you be without the SS co.?" By November 9, Hilda was barely able to handle her son's estrangement until, eventually, the target was hit:

> Edward, it was only normal for us to be wary of a foreign girl marrying our only son. But honest to God we tried hard to love her. Do you remember *all* that happened before your wedding—your reaction? Edward, we didn't know Maire then, we still don't know her, or know her even less. All we know and are sure of now is that she has no use *for any of us six*, in any way.[10]

Having met at Vassar, Edward and Maire commuted frequently between Cambridge and Poughkeepsie in the early stages of their romance, calling each other on the phone almost every other night. That set a pattern that would in time become a problem. Said was slightly more advanced in his studies. She had relocated to Cambridge to be with him and to pursue her PhD (Levin was one of the readers of her dissertation: "Thomas Mann: Biography and Form," 1968), only to face distance again when Said got the job at Columbia.[11] Another tiring commute, now between Cambridge and New York, added to the self-doubt and intellectual exhaustion that most everyone feels writing a dissertation.

The last straw came when Said accepted a fellowship at the

Center for Advanced Study at the University of Illinois at Urbana-Champaign. The venue was not as flashy, the distances were much greater, and there were too many distractions as Maire struggled to write her thesis. Visitors during their time in Urbana found the household mood dark, complicated by Said's old feelings of isolation.[12] Maire captured this inner turmoil in a remarkable note to him quoting from Mann's novella *Tonio Kröger*, whose protagonist is described at story's end as living in two worlds, at home in neither. She observed that "Saidus," as she playfully called him here, lived in three, at home in none. He "could have been a philosopher, a poet, or a critic—He *is* all 3 in one, a vexing trinity."

But he remained inaccessible, a "tripodic genius" who could not be understood through any one of his aspects because he was a "knotted fusion." "Poor me," she added, he "aestheticizes philosophy" and "criticizes literature and aestheticism."[13] Especially apt was the situation of Mann's tale, in which Tonio, born into a bourgeois family and expected to conform to its material values, is instead drawn to poetry. Rather than choose transgression over the mundane world of affairs, he splits the difference, trying to bring romantic rapture to ordinary life.

Between his year off in Cairo and the end of grad school, Said tried his hand at fiction. His most ambitious effort took place in Beirut in the summer of 1962 with a novel he gave the working title *Elegy*—about seventy pages of polished text and another thirteen of notes.[14] Happily, he left a record of his daily battles and his second thoughts:

> March 19: Why can't I fight this lethargy? It has taken me days to go to this book. What a terribly self-negating thing . . . March 25: Little or no work today . . . Am I sincere now as I write? I'm going as the man who "writes his thoughts" . . . I want a chance (which can never exist) to be myself to myself. If I could put that in either a very short short story or a long novel, I would be happy.[15]

In time, though, there was a breakthrough, which he recounted with some self-mockery. "Finally, I have mapped out" the novel, he exclaimed in a note to himself: "A triptych—3 stories as a whole . . . Experiences of non-un-failure!" It is clear from his notes that one of his inspirations was an author he did not especially like (along with Greene, the subject of his undergraduate thesis): André Gide. He fixated on one of the lines from Gide's *La porte étroite* (*Strait Is the Gate*): "*J'ai mis toute ma force à la vivre, et ma vertu s'y est usée*" (I have put all my energy into living, and my virtue is used up).

Like that of many first novelists, his story was a thinly veiled rendering of elements from his childhood, and an effort to bring 1940s Cairo vividly to life. Its large cast of characters, woven from the threads of every one of the city's classes, nationalities, and religions, blankets an ambitious cross section of Cairene society. A distorted version of his father is found among the players—Halim Khoury, a Lebanese Christian born in the city, a proprietor of a "failing printing company and a grubby stationery shop" who is mired in shady business deals. He wants to invest dubiously in fertilizers. With his paralytic wife "stuff[ed] away in a shabby apartment in Shubra," he spends every minute vindicating himself after having lost a lot of people's money in bad investments. Dr. Edwina "Miss" Thomas, president of the American College for Girls, around which much of the action revolves, possesses a "round, even dowdy figure [that] showed no trace of ascetic discipline," even though she punished herself trying, rising early like her Arab counterparts and wearing the same "rimless spectacles" as Miss Nasr, the frightening martinet who was the head of the school and one of its founders.

A native of Ohio, Miss Thomas "belonged to that Anglo-Saxon life-line of Americanism which gave the country moral tone and elevation . . . an industrialized Jane Austen." One of the minor roles goes to the rotund Totino, an imprisoned homosexual who "sports a jewel" given to him by his parents and is married to the elegant Antoinette Rahim, one of Miss Nasr's students. Miss Harfush teaches Arabic and music to support her career as a concert pianist. Judson, a seven-foot-tall American, is "skinny, unmarried and desperate."

In one of the two finished narrative segments, the plot centers on Miss Nasr. With his real-life aunt Melia clearly in mind ("Miss Nasr" for "Miss Badr"), Said recounts her battles with a colleague, Miss Forbes, who wants to recruit students for a school play. Miss Nasr, on the other hand, considers theater an affront to ladyhood and an obstacle to her pedagogical mission, which is to instill a steeliness with none of the presumed sentimentality of the female sex:

> She never made her opposition totally explicit, as if to pretend that the idea of a show was too unthinkable, too indigestible a bolus for her ascetically refined mind to absorb . . . At her death twenty years later, she was to be lauded by three generations of Egyptian women who effusively praised her as a whole chapter in the history of the Near East . . . Her personal habits, which made up her way of life in the College, were like a vast, fine, and yet immensely eccentric net . . . It was probably the work of an early morning hour when, quite alone, in the overcrowded solemnity of her room, its bed still hung with an old-fashioned mosquito net and overlaid with at least five blankets, she slowly sipped her Turkish coffee.

For those who dared, like her, the world held more than the insufferable posing of the good life preferred by the silly imitators whose minds were turned "like weathercocks to the West."

The phrase held a hint of self-reproach as though he had put it in Aunt Melia's mouth to expose his own weaknesses. Only occasionally in interviews, at any rate, does Said's gift for impersonation find the free rein he gives it in his fiction, where noticing odd details and capturing varied intonations are important elements of an author's ability to create the illusion of reality. There he let out fully for the first time what his friends often described as a talent for mimicry when, in the mood, he performed skits from *Beyond the Fringe* and *Monty Python*, put on a comical Indian accent, and did "a very vivid George Steiner."[16]

His prose was especially attentive to mise-en-scène. Michel and Elene Elias's petit bourgeois household is described with chilly disapproval: its black servants, high windows, cucumbers, arrack, scotch, and pipes. Kitschy Mahmoud Said Bey paintings decorate its walls—nostalgic vistas of the Nile valley, "overbearing enough to conceal a lack of finish and lopsided structure; mood dominates, washes, obliterates." The house is cluttered with various "hangers-on, poker players, wealthy friends." Even "the flies settled onto their resting places like demure students reclaiming their seats after having risen for an elder." Miss Cawley, who cheats her roomers, "died in an ecstasy of delight fourteen months later, clutching her *Pilgrim's Progress* to her bosom with a kind of fervid joy."

The second surviving fragment of the novel gives the impression that with more time and nothing else to do, he could have seen the project through to publication. The writing is fluid, assured, and quite complete. Partly in Cairo, partly in Heliopolis, the characters march forward in a dazzling array—Hamid, George, Samuel Abram (based on David Ezra from Said's days at St. George's in Jerusalem), and Maître Cortonsky, who is clearly drawn from Tiegerman. Two other characters, Mufid and Ahmed, are warped self-portraits. The latter goes off to work, scolding shabby policemen, studying Ovid's *Metamorphosis* "with dreary concentration," and barking instructions to his driver via walkie-talkie. In Mufid, Said's coy self-mockery takes its material from memories of his year off working at the Standard Stationery Company:

> For much of the time in his dusty and hot little office room, Mufid, today as always, would push his chair back from the desk, lean forward, elbows on his knees, hands under his chin, cigarette dangling from his lips, and stare down at the ink-spotted floor. The enormous ledger on the desk

was a companion he could not take seriously, for there was something comical, he mused, about the tiny unprotected figures—his own—which marched confidently across its endless pages. To him they were real only insofar as they were neat. And this neatness was *his* fastidious accomplishment: whatever sales, profits, losses they might represent to his superiors were utterly lost on Mufid. He was engaged on other things, which in turn were utterly lost on everyone else.

So Said saw himself on the eve of becoming a professor, still thinking that fiction might be a platform for expressing all those inner conflicts that his scholarly work largely skimmed over. *Elegy* would remain forever unfinished, but he did complete a fine short story, which he sent off to *The New Yorker* on February 26, 1965, a skillful confabulation whose material was clearly taken from Said's memories of his aimless summer nights in Dhour el Shweir.

"An Ark for the Listener" is the story of the Andraos family, a mother and her two corpulent daughters, who have come to a friend's summer home in Lebanon for a visit after being forced out of Palestine.[17] They drift from house to house among former neighbors and distant relatives like sleepwalkers. Although the story takes place in one site, its concerns are with another. In the Palestinian homeland many miles away, Jewish paramilitaries roam the countryside attacking the British. Here in the Lebanese hills, the impressionable narrator, tired of being tired, goes about his boring routines largely oblivious to the events with whose fallout he is now forced to reckon.

Taken from Hopkins's poem "The Wreck of the Deutschland," the story's title refers to the divine vessel ("ark") that protects the wretched in stormy waters, for the poet had meant to commemorate the death of five Franciscan nuns at sea. At the point where the line of the title appears, Hopkins has been drawing a contrast between those who hear God's call and those who do not. Mercy "outrides the all of water" providing an "ark for the listener," whereas the "lingerer" (who does not listen) "glides lower than death and the dark." The bounty of God's mercy, Hopkins implies, is to transform mere meanderers into the resolute, beckoning them to "burn, new born to the world." His narrator undergoes just such a transformation in the course of the story.

The most finished piece of Said's creative prose, "An Ark for the Listener" unfolds as a conversation. The setting is a lazy Sunday afternoon spent "high on the slowly eroding mountains of middle Lebanon." The young man, whose parents are away, grimly goes about his duty of entertaining the guests who have arrived unannounced. He already feels guilty for having whiled away his summer months and has no taste for wasting still more time with visitors he barely knows. The well-heeled surroundings of his parents' Dhour retreat and the bourgeois habits of the overfed Andraos family put him in a foul mood, and instead of empathy he has only contempt, thinking of "scapegoat Arabs taken from images spun by Western dreamers . . . dirty silent acquisitiveness exuding a brutal laziness that frightened me with its unrestrained moneyed power." His fear is that there is some truth buried in the caricature and that he himself is proof.

As middle-class Christians of means, the Andraos family, he reckons, is "too self-seeking for the relief camps . . . [T]hey had chosen their own way which had begun with them staring blankly out of a filthy car window as they drove into Beirut, their tired venal eyes sadly assessing the city's bustling and disorienting activity." Such rendezvous in his view had led too often to "afternoons spent in forums of gossipy self-laceration," where the fugitives punished themselves by probing open wounds. The narrator indulges in the same masochism, complaining that if in the West time is only money, for us Arabs it is like peanuts to "devour mindlessly" or "flick away." And yet, as he mechanically passes out bonbons as an unwilling host, he begins slowly to be assuaged on aesthetic grounds. For all his impatience with his own culture, he is forced to concede the beauty of the zajal—"the skill that lifted decorous chatter into high art."

On the screened veranda as night falls, hoping at first that his parents would come home to rescue him, he is gradually seduced by the woman's stories, she "hang[ing] the comically cut tatters of an unlovely tragedy on a slim stick of wailing prose." There is nothing dramatic, just the mundane details of a life now shattered and cut off—vignettes of a neighbor's experience with domestic abuse, anecdotes about Jews, Arabs, and Christians, rich and poor, living side by side. What strikes him is the dignity of the recounting and the Arab art of storytelling: "Our language was, when properly managed, a feast of every dish . . . the clothes of the Arabic soul." Only at the end as the last hint of daylight recedes has the palpable hurt of their collective fate sunk in. Pity and annoyance give way to resolve. Although Said sent off poems, worked and reworked in various drafts, to literary journals from the late 1950s until the mid-1960s (publishing two in *Al-Kulliyah* in 1958), when *The New Yorker* rejected the story, he withdrew. After 1965, he would not write fiction again for the next twenty-five years.[18]

IN 1963, SAID JOINED the faculty of Columbia University as an instructor in the English department, happily restoring him to the city he had never quite left. Upon arrival, he gratefully accepted the guiding hand of an older colleague, a former Trotskyist and labor organizer named Fred Dupee, who ushered him into the New York writing world. One of the founding editors of *Partisan Review* and a frequent contributor to *The New York Review of Books*, Dupee introduced him to various editors while helping him navigate the departmental hierarchies at Columbia.

In her funny memorial essay of 1983 (Dupee had died four years earlier), the cantankerous antiwar journalist and *Partisan Review* writer Mary McCarthy inadvertently laid out the evidence for what made Said and Dupee a marriage of minds.[19] The author of a brilliant short study on Henry James (1951) and a sparkling, irreverent, jargon-free book of essays on writers and writing, *The King of the Cats* (1965), Dupee was conscious about working within a genre he called simply "remarks." His critical oeuvre as a whole tended to be about "letters of authors, biographies of authors . . . autobiographies of non-authors . . . late works of authors . . . rather than about the primary work of authors"—exactly the pattern of Said's career. His models were the word painters of literary portraiture—Sainte-Beuve, Macaulay, and McCarthy's former husband Edmund Wilson. When one thinks of Said's constant return to a small stable of writers and thinkers whom he presents to readers almost as though they were friends or family, whose personalities are as important as their ideas, this model seemed to live on. A "continental sophistication ran in the Dupee blood," McCarthy added, "making him suaver than his fellow *Partisan Review* editors—Rahv and Phillips and Dwight Mac-donald." His art was to be brilliant in an effortless way, amusing, observant, nonchalant, whose "tone is that of conversation."

What's more, Dupee was clearly sympathetic to the achievements of American communism. He edited the *New Masses* in the 1930s and Trotsky's *Russian Revolution* in 1959, comparing that book to Thucydides's *Peloponnesian War* and Caesar's *Commentaries*. For like them, the historian had been (as Said would later write about Swift) a participant in the events he described, a "man of letters and the man of action."[20] Said admired Dupee's example of standing out-side grocery stores collecting signatures on petitions against the Vietnam War, although never doing so himself.

By the waning years of the 1960s, his breakout book, *Begin-nings*, still half a decade or so in the future, Said had settled into Columbia life as an upstart member of the New York intellectuals. His writing debuted in the same magazines as that group of mostly Jewish writers and critics, and he knew many of them personally, seeking counsel from the school's resident ironist and Freudian, Li-onel Trilling. But he continued to take his leads from Dupee, who introduced Said to McCarthy, whom Dupee had brought to Bard College to teach in 1946 before Trilling in turn brought him to

Columbia a few years later. It was a tight circle. Meanwhile, Said worked at refining a style that mixed belletrism with phenomenology and for which there was no real analogue in the "quality lit crit biz," as James Wolcott put it.[21]

Columbia, fortunately, rewarded such crossover tastes, and along with Said several of its faculty were liberally featured in New York's major magazines and newspapers, forming a professional guild. In this milieu, Said thought it wise to hedge his bets, scoping out familiar intellectual territory in a novel way. It was not difficult to do, because, coming from the Middle East, he was like a photonegative of his Jewish counterparts. The two themes they developed in book after book—exile and the immigrant experience—were his story too, but from a very different angle.

The polarities of the group stood out vividly in the contrast between Trilling and Dupee, the one "steeped in ambiguity, dialectical subtleties and flickering equivocations . . . a mandarin of almost excruciating courtesy and subtle indirection," the other "sounding a note of defiance, of boyish stubbornness . . . taking his stand as . . . an idle saunterer in an age of academic criticism, of 'field' specialists on the one hand and fanatic 'close readers' on the other."[22] At Columbia, Trilling enjoyed a special status among the New York intellectuals. His books were awaited, then exalted, arriving as if from on high with a weightless classical reserve. Noting both the pros and the cons, Said thought him a kind of American Matthew Arnold, a conservative with an ethereal taste for the liberal arts, diagnosing social mores and psychology from a distant literary perch.

He seemed to Said too above it all to get very close to new talent, although the intimacy of his letters to Trilling (as well as the latter's equally affectionate responses) suggests more amity, undermined only by their mutual studied cleverness. In the end, Said shared the sarcasm of a friend who, looking back, quipped that more than anything "Lionel lived the role of Lionel."[23] Said kept his judgments to himself but let his feelings spill out in a diary entry soon after arriving at Columbia:

Trilling is an impenetrable egoist. Unruffled; attempt at being godlike and elegant without realizing that the two can't
mix. He becomes funny; and yet, he is so remarkably intelligent that he has become shrewd, for, pushed to its logical
extreme, intelligence is the shrewdness with which one han-
dles the world . . . By comparison, I feel awkward, and want
to be silent.[24]

Years later when he wrote to Monroe Engel, his views had not
changed: "I'm slowly finding him too backward-looking . . . hemmed
in by . . . disillusionment . . . He associates 'mind' with 'gentlemen
and universities.'"[25] As might be discerned from remarks such as this,
Said did not particularly like Columbia at first. When the department turned down a colleague, Mason Cooley, for tenure after keeping him on the faculty for nine years, Said angrily told a colleague
that he had now "discovered . . . its arrogance and snobbery."[26]

Dupee, on the other hand, was considerably more likable, a
tweedy iconoclast, and so just right for Said's similar desire to be
an antinomian fit for the Ivy League. He owned an expensive house
upstate, was genteel in a subdued way, and enjoyed close friend-
ships with the likes of the subversive patrician Gore Vidal. Having
taken Said under his wing, Dupee thought him brilliant but not
always the best of writers.[27] The word on the street, in fact, among
Columbia's faculty was that Said's essays lacked the grace of Trilling's chiseled Freudian prose or Dupee's joyful erudition. Dupee
nevertheless detected in Said's somewhat credulous homages to
French theory the makings of a public stylist and, to keep critics
at bay, loudly announced himself a "member of the Edward Said
prose club."[28]

Said might have been most like Dupee in ignoring the academic
niceties of pleasing the old guard. He kept his nose clean as an un-
tenured and vulnerable newcomer, but it turns out that he was not,
as one might suppose, all that politic and did not go out of his way
to appease the departmental establishment.[29] All the same, in his

own mind he was too cagey by far. In a fit of self-reproach in a diary entry in January 1966, he wrote, "Necessity for me—and perhaps all—to speak only into a cushion of solid support . . . To win recognition and approval . . . is why I talk most—or perhaps all the time—how I look at the nuances of the math: watching it turn in agreement, appreciation, or disarray. Words—mouth—gesture."[30]

More than simply running interference or giving him access to publishing, Dupee was a dear friend. He was one of the few colleagues to visit him in Urbana with Maire and then, a few years later, in Beirut, where Said lived for a year with his new wife, Mariam. After Dupee and his wife visited for ten days, Said wrote to his old adviser Engel, "It's difficult for both of us to figure out our extraordinary attachment to and our really profound pleasure in them."[31] Like Dupee, Said the apprentice gave off the air of a man whose life was well lived, the indelible image being of him and his colleague Michael Rosenthal, his old acquaintance from grad school days, walking up Broadway smoking cigars in long winter coats.[32]

Clever enough to realize he would be more likely to succeed professionally by writing a conventional study of a canonical English author, Said was still torn by his discoveries in French and German philosophies of language. In time, they pried him away from the somewhat predictable project he had chosen, which was to explore Conrad as an invented authorial persona. He ended up injecting ideas from these philosophies between the lines of his otherwise safe dissertation, pleasing the old guard who missed the allusions while hinting at things to come for those with the eyes to see. The left-Heideggerian, existentialist, and Marxist theorists of France and Germany seemed to him richer and more unpredictable than did the prospects of spending his life as a "Conrad scholar."

In effect, he set out to decode French theory for readers of *The New York Times* and bring it loudly into an academy dominated by New Critics. For this task, he enlisted Wilson's demotic style, which he revered for its defiance of scholarly conventions, its lack of footnotes above all.[33] At the very moment Said was laboring through studies of ontology and semiotics, it was Wilson, of all people, he was extolling as "effortlessly well-informed, always interested in the human side of books and histories," and for that reason the most readable critic in English "anywhere and at any time."[34] These tastes probably explain his close ties to the Rutgers-based literary critic Richard Poirier, a co-founder of the Library of America and a lifelong friend, who just as actively sought to write about theoretical matters in a nontheoretical way and who after 1981 as editor of the journal *Raritan* highlighted serious but approachable essays while leaning on Said as one of its chief contributors.[35] Said considered Poirier one of the greatest American critics of the postwar period.

Writing as an informed journalist, Said insisted that modern Continental theories of language and being, however daunting, took insurgent positions on the politics of culture that were vital to contemporary life and art. The structural patterns of human behavior revealed by linguistic anthropologists and cognitive systems theorists like Claude Lévi-Strauss and Noam Chomsky constructively challenged, among other things, the uniqueness of Western achievement while questioning some of the benefits of industrial civilization. Everyone, he considered, should be able to understand those stakes.

Always an eager correspondent with established professors he admired or wished to know, he had begun to be noticed only a year or two out of grad school by leading-edge theorists. Figures like Richard Macksey, Eugenio Donato, and J. Hillis Miller made sure that he received a formal invitation in 1966 to attend the conference that made French structuralism a household word in American and British universities: "The Languages of Criticism and the Sciences of Man," held at Johns Hopkins University in October of that year.

It did not hurt that in the months before the conference he had published a gushing review of Miller's *Poets of Reality* (1965) in *The Nation*, followed by a highly laudatory treatment of Lucien Goldmann's neglected masterpiece, *The Hidden God* (1955), in *Partisan Review*. The Conrad study, meanwhile, after two years of revisions had just come out as a book with the help of Levin's intervention at Harvard University Press. We can appreciate, then, that the major figures in French structuralism, among them Roland Barthes, Goldmann, Jacques Derrida, and Georges Poulet, were not just names known to him from the covers of books. All of them were at the conference. He met them, watched them in action, and followed their arguments in French.

Not surprisingly, he was swept up in theory fever for a while and found himself corresponding with Michel Foucault, Barthes, Hélène Cixous, and others. A year after the conference, in a letter to Jean Starobinski, the Swiss phenomenologist then teaching at Hopkins, he remarked that Barthes was "over here for a short visit," and Said found him "fascinating, and yet hermetic."[36] Barthes himself sent Said a card thanking him for sending an essay: "so powerful, so subtle, so caring. A joy for me. Thank you from the bottom of my heart . . . Will you be coming to Paris? You must not forget to let me know."[37]

Said's new obsessions had become part of his makeup, pouring out of him even when at leisure. In 1966, he embarked on an elaborate trip to Spain with Maire and his colleague and dear friend Allen Bergson, staying exclusively in *paradores* ("because they're the best"), then buying a car that he had shipped by rail to France for the latter part of their journey, rendezvousing with it by sleeper train.[38] It was on this trip that Said developed an unlikely fascination with bullfighting, later impressing his second wife, Mariam, during their courtship only a few years later with stories of the experience and giving her a copy of Hemingway's *Death in the Afternoon* to underscore his devotion.[39] By his own account he had seen "a fair number of *corridas* in the sixties," including an event that featured the great Antonio Ordóñez, whom he saw "at a minor *feria* in Badajoz, a dusty and mercilessly sun-beaten town in Estremadura."[40] All these enchanting distractions aside, he could not contain himself during their journey, talking giddily in the various reception rooms of their lodgings about how criticism had exactly the same validity as literature and that each was in its own way primary.

He did not always sound like a theorist, though, roving back and forth between the vernacular and the technical. His friend the Palestinian historian Tarif Khalidi said he was at heart "a philosopher who had migrated into literature," and yet caught up in the intricacies of Gallic debates, he still considered his brief to be broader than picking fights with common sense on behalf of a newly assertive postwar linguistics.[41] Despite the beckoning style of Said's early essays and reviews in carefully chosen crossover venues for general audiences (*The Kenyon Review, The Centennial Review, The New York Review of Books*), literary theory changed Said forever. As he fell increasingly under its sway, he was returning in a way to the tastes he had shown throughout his schooling for the classics of philosophy.

Levin tried to discourage him. Clearly seeking his mentor's approval, Said had sent him the Miller review from *The Nation*, which, although accessible enough, dwelled on heady issues like "immanence" as well as Poulet's work on authorial consciousness.[42] Levin snapped him back:

> Dear Ed . . . I am touched that you should still be interested in my opinion, despite your publicly expressed enthusiasm for a work which so manifestly controverts those analytical and empirical principles which I try to impart; and since this cleavage seems so wide, I am not hopeful of bridging it in a brief letter . . . In a brusque word, this approach does not truly aim at the understanding of literature, but at deriving metaphysical paradigms from authors by superimposing certain abstractions supported by quotations taken out of context.[43]

Uncharacteristically, Said put up no fight, and by the time he wrote his farewell to theory in *The World, the Text, and the Critic* (1983), it was to Levin he wrote to say that his mentor had been right all along. Until then, though, his next two books would quietly disregard Levin's advice, reveling in those "metaphysical paradigms" while trying in his own way to recuperate them for everyday concerns by giving them a historical footing.

ON NOVEMBER 24, 1965, Said sent off to Levin an essay on Conrad's *Nostromo*, commenting that it will be "I think . . . the last of my work on Conrad."[44] The statement would turn out to be so extravagantly wrong that it called for speculation. He later observed more accurately and in a characteristically musical image that Conrad had always been "a steady groundbass to much that I have experienced," and there were at least several passages, sometimes major sections, on Conrad in every book of his thereafter, along with one seminal essay ("Conrad and Nietzsche," 1976).[45]

Conrad remained his secret sharer for powerful reasons. Both wrote in a borrowed language, witnessed colonial outrages, and had an almost morbid curiosity about political extremes. Like Conrad, Said was trilingual, loved French, and had a lifelong passion for Wagner.[46] Said was also endlessly fascinated by Conrad's harried awareness of being a prisoner of writing, chained to his desk like a slave, having to sculpt words to create a simulacrum of experiences that his native audience could never be expected fully to understand. At least it seemed this way in Said's tortured early career; later his writing—a little like Mozart—was more of a transcription, so easily did the words come to him.[47]

The devotion to Conrad seems straightforward, though, only if we ignore the antipathies. In Said's view, Conrad was an imperialist, a pessimist, and a misanthrope.[48] "Conrad," he later pointed out, "was a kind of high modernist, and he was about the aesthetics—or rather the aestheticization—of experience . . . I think he's really the opposite of me in many ways."[49] He was surprisingly explicit on this point in a heated roundtable exchange at Skidmore College with Conor Cruise O'Brien and others at an event he later described as an intellectual mugging: "*Heart of Darkness* is not only a book about imperialism, it is a book of imperialism itself . . . [T]he work is constructed with, with a kind of emptiness [about] . . . the backwardness of the natives, and the Blacks."[50]

Said was often drawn to writers he should have disliked. He championed the royalist Swift rather than the anticolonial visionary William Blake, although he adored Blake's poetry and quoted it to friends.[51] He dwelled on the politically dubious Conrad instead of his anti-imperial alter ego and friend, R. Cunninghame Graham, himself an accomplished author and socialist, to whom Said compared himself as the counterbalancing force to Conrad's dark view of the human soul.[52] The Polish novelist stood for everything he detested: a moral darkness without responsibility; the sense of Europe as the world's only beacon; and the idea of peripheral Poland as an outpost of the West against Pan-Slavism. All of these views, Said could see, were roughly analogous to Malik's ideology of Lebanese Christians saving the world from Islamic hordes.[53]

But, Said observed, even writers of the political Right can be astounding "verbal technicians . . . untimely, anxious witnesses to the dominant currents of their time," and this view enabled a taste for perverse allegiances.[54] His heart was with Sartre, but he devoted his creative early years to the anti-Sartre, Michel Foucault. He cherished Vico's lessons but conceded that Vico the man was vain, irascible, and nasty.[55] He later hinted that his delight in the great Polish modernist, despite his demurs, derived from Conrad's sharing with Nietzsche an interest in the radical paradoxes of human character, even though he gave no evidence of having read Nietzsche's complete works or (flirtations in graduate school aside) to having approached any of them with close textual attention.[56]

At any rate, by impulse and perhaps strategy, Said was becoming a partisan of ambiguity. He seemed to understand this move as a version of Blackmur's idea of "performance" in literature, a criticism "uncertain of its conclusions, prepared always to be solitary and self-limiting, without influence or disciples," although Blackmur's constant hedging, his "hidden ball play," as Said put it, irritated him. He demanded that one have conviction.[57] He was trying to capture, in any case, the flavor of the occasional, ad hoc quality of Blackmur's criticism as a direct conversational encounter in which "indeterminacy, the principle of complementary variable relations," prevailed.

In the language of Said's earliest essays, the word "dialectic" became the banner under which these critical notions operated, and the term is found, in fact, throughout his youthful writing. In an early lecture on W. B. Yeats, he explained that the word "dialectic" for him meant moving not in a straight logical sequence but in a succession of images that provoke new images in turn.[58] But it was more than just a call for open-endedness. He was looking for an idiom that could contain incompatible philosophies without appearing to be about philosophy at all.

There were other reasons for wanting to stake out this space between. At Columbia, he kept his Palestinian identity to himself at first. Consequently, upon his arrival, a rumor spread that the English department, in hiring him, had just hired an Alexandrian Jew.[59] And so in Conrad, he found a man who, among other things, was good at hiding himself. As he turned his dissertation into a book (it would appear as *Joseph Conrad and the Fiction of Autobiography* in 1966), he hinted that his obsession with Conrad rested on the fact that both were exiles in the imperial world capitals of their times and that both were contrarians: "There were *two* Conrads: one . . . the waiting and willing polite transcriber who wished to please, the other an uncooperative demon."[60] In time he would make the comparison explicit: "When I was beginning to teach at Columbia . . . I was really considered two people . . . the teacher of literature and . . . this other person, like Dorian Gray, who did these quite unspeakable, unmentionable things."[61]

It was not surprising, then, that in a poem written in the early 1960s, he referred to himself as a "roguish elegist, the Arabic Till," alluding to Till Eulenspiegel, an itinerant trickster figure in medieval German folklore who plays pranks on his fellows while acting the fool and exposing their vices, greed, and hypocrisy. He felt it necessary, then, in the Conrad book to devise a prose style that was accessible at the level of diction and syntax but deceptively layered and allusive. As he later described his motives, "I've always tried to develop my ideas further in ways that paradoxically make them ungraspable and unparaphrasable."[62]

The basic case of the Conrad book seemed to lie in his exposé of the mechanisms of authorship, the emphatic *thereness* of a person in the world who sets out to invent himself. This and his familiar mining of the themes of exile and foreignness (typical modernist tropes) lulled readers into feeling at home in convention. In fact, Said was subtly taking up the claim by French structuralists that authorship did not really exist, because all apparent creativity and choice was at the mercy of language as a finished system of grammatical rules and semantic functions—what in French is referred to by the word *langue*. By contrast, the structuralists used the term *parole* to refer to specific acts of speech, particularly of ordinary speakers, which as we have seen was where Said made his home. If authors are conventionally thought to engender their own work and therefore to have mastery over it, the structuralists thought the author dead. For meaning is predetermined by inherited linguistic structures.

Sensing how much novelty might be too much, he gave the impression that the originality of his thesis was to focus on Conrad's letters rather than his novels. This minor twist seemed acceptable. Few appreciated that he was choosing a genre of writing (the personal letter) where *parole* is much more in evidence than *langue*. A psychoanalytic impulse lay behind the move as well, for the book was also a vehicle for exploring a painfully familiar "personal dialectic," as he was himself.[63] Conrad's letters, he hinted, contained an "embarrassingly rich" testimony to an intellectual life based on a biological fiction.[64] Using slightly different means, Conrad too had used "the sea as a mirror to throw misleading reflections of himself out to the public," exploiting what he was often "cynically to call his 'foreignness.'"[65] Somewhat unfairly, because he had worked so hard to produce this outcome, he later complained that the book's reviewers, although mostly positive, had no clue what he was really trying to do.[66]

The "structuralists" were varied, and none was quite like another. Said particularly stressed their differences in his seminal reflections on structuralism in *"Abecedarium Culturae*: Structuralism, Absence, Writing" (1971), an essay he originally proposed to *The New York Times* and that more than any other essay made his name in academic circles. They did, however, have common motives, as Gilles Deleuze pointed out when describing what Foucault shared with his contemporaries:

> A cold and concerted destruction of the subject, a lively distaste for notions of origin, of lost origin, of recovered origin, a dismantling of unifying pseudo-syntheses of consciousness, a denunciation of all the mystifications of history performed in the name of progress, of consciousness and the future of reason.[67]

It is a small register of Said's contrariness that he recommended Deleuze to his friends, letting them know that he had been reading "a lot of [him]," even as every one of these objectives, which Deleuze was applauding, controverted his own views.[68]

After the 1966 event at Hopkins, structuralism became almost overnight an immense subterranean force, and the feeling among avant-garde critics and writers was that a new paradigm was forming, a Copernican shift of thinking about the centrality of language to all political and social meaning. Said found this emergent sensibility intoxicating, not only (following Blackmur) because European philosophy seemed so much more grown-up than American down-home pieties, but because "theory" could not be written off as the pastime of bookish elites. On the contrary, it spoke confidently and rebelliously to matters of power, communication, and historical meaning and with a withering intelligence that no one could look down upon.

Attracted to its insurgency, but not wanting to jettison history and progress, Said tried to square the circle. When looking at Conrad's fiction, he did not find there, as others did, the nice Romantic formula whereby an author invents an imaginative world. His point was rather that authors make *themselves* in the act of writing.[69] One's being-in-the-world was to this degree dependent on writing, and to that extent, he was following a familiar structuralist lead. But other influences were at work as well. Lurking also in this way of putting things was Malik's older interest in the "ground" of everyday experience—the worldliness of one's existential being-there (*Dasein*)—an idea impressed upon him by his former teacher, the philosopher Martin Heidegger. In Conrad's case, though (according to Said), this self-invention was essentially devious; he changed his character by wearing "eccentric masks," which Said took to be Conrad's main objective.[70]

In that latter spirit, there were plenty of jabs at structuralism in the Conrad book. To say, for instance, that in Conrad "style . . . and grammar" should be understood "in purely physical terms" is to deprive language of the autonomy that structuralism wanted to give it.[71] Elsewhere, he even dismissively referred to structuralism as "a minor intellectual industry in France" and complained that while it may be fascinating, it was also infuriating.[72] He lavished with compliments Lévi-Strauss himself, the towering instigator along with Roman Jakobson of the structuralist turn, while subtly undermining him.

As always, Said was especially interested in language in the form of speech. He had no interest in drawing dire conclusions about the inability of individuals to act or to mean on the basis of the tyranny of written language. He found an ally in the fascinating linguistic studies by Émile Benveniste in *Problèmes de linguistique générale* (1966; *Problems in General Linguistics*), which in contrast to the prevailing French intellectual environment—then, as now, dominated by the posthumanism of Nietzsche and Heidegger—conceived of people as historical actors and as fully integrated persons.

The structuralists made much of the term "subject," which they relished as a pun. For the word reflected what Freud called the antithetical meaning of primal words, referring both to the doer of an action (as in the phrase "subject of a sentence") and the vassal of a ruler (as in "the queen's subject"). As such, it was useful to structuralism for suggesting a supposed but really imaginary freedom. We imagine ourselves conscious citizens, historical agents, and individuals when in fact the inherited rules of language force us into predictable patterns of behavior and make certain thoughts and topics of discussion impossible in advance.

Like Said, an immigrant from the Middle East, Benveniste (a Sephardic Jew born in French mandate Syria before moving to Marseille for graduate study) made a celebrated distinction between the *énoncé* (statement) and the *énonciation* (utterance)—the difference between what is said and how it is said. Using a notion of language swept up not so much by universal structures and codes as by the contingencies of an active verbal exchange, Benveniste argued that literature itself was a mode of writing dependent on "reported speech."[73] Said seized on the idea and used it as a way of mitigating structuralism's unwelcome attacks on history making and agency.

By far, though, his most influential ally along these lines was a thinker largely overlooked by readers of Said's work, although his importance cannot be overestimated. Lucien Goldmann's *Le dieu caché* (*The Hidden God*) was not only a finely textured study of two contrarian figures of the Enlightenment (the mathematician and philosopher Blaise Pascal and the neoclassical tragedian Jean Racine) but an ambitious, if deliberately veiled, effort to forge alternatives to the structuralism then dominating the French intellectual scene.[74] A Romanian Marxist writing in French who considered himself a disciple of Georg Lukács (he translated two of his books into French), Goldmann had, by the mid-1960s, come to mean a great deal to Said, in part because he helped introduce Lukács to American universities. As such, he was a unique emissary on behalf of Lukács's key argument in *History and Class Consciousness* that only those intellectuals who identified with early twentieth-century revolutions on the global periphery could find their way out of the tired dichotomy between "subject" and "object" inherited from Kant. Goldmann gave Said the tools to pacify Malik's borrowings from Heidegger and to bring that philosopher's existentialist preoccupations over to the clash of current events from a distinctively left perspective.

Said's aside in *Out of Place* that in graduate school he was "deep in the study of Conrad, Vico, and Heidegger" and that they have "since remained a strong presence in my intellectual work" is initially puzzling.[75] The first two are everywhere in his writing, whereas Heidegger is glancingly mentioned, often negatively and, as time wore on, dismissively.[76] We find Said, though, in early career chiding critics for taking from Heidegger without acknowledgment, which suggests an intimacy with his work, and in 1969 he was invited by the Society for Phenomenology and Existential Philosophy to its annual conference at Northwestern, which implies a reputation in the field.[77] And he does, it is true, reserve one of the last pages of his dissertation on Conrad for one of the few substantive allusions of any kind to the philosopher in his work.[78]

His debt, or lack of debt, to Heidegger is nevertheless significant for many reasons. The pervasive presence of Heidegger's ideas in French theory of the 1960s and 1970s—the turn, for instance, to questions of being (ontology) rather than knowledge (epistemology), the view that humanism is a form of "inauthentic" existence, or the doctrine of the untranslatability of language (which implied that we are imprisoned in our native cultures and cannot get out)—seems, point for point, to be in conflict with his own interventions. Said for that reason complained of Heidegger's "patient but agonized doom within language," which causes his acolytes to accept culture rather than "rebel[] against it."[79] More familiar would be his remark when narrating a memorable evening spent with Jean Genet about being surprised that the activist Genet called Derrida *un copain* (a pal) because Said had assumed Derrida was just "a quietist Heideggerian type at the time."[80] But Heideggerian undercurrents in Said are nevertheless real, if likely to be misread.

For one thing, while Said enlisted Goldmann as Heidegger's antagonist, the Heidegger he *did* deploy was that of Jean-Paul Sartre, who had outmaneuvered the great German philosopher in *Being and Nothingness* (1943). There Sartre turned Heidegger's antihumanism into humanism and did so precisely on the grounds of the individual's radical freedom and responsibility—just the opposite of Heidegger's intention. The word "being," similarly, as a quality or state of things now became (again with the deliberate aim of subverting Heidegger's original sense) the conditions of historical experience. Hence, in the Conrad study Said calls for a "psychographic" rather than psychoanalytic method of criticism, because the latter tended to bury the self in a maze of helpless symptoms.[81]

This delving into the phenomenological philosophies of Edmund Husserl and Sartre was necessary, from Said's point of view, in order to expose the fundamental weakness of literary studies at the time, which was that it took for granted what literature was.[82] He wanted to problematize the term "literature," which meant, among other things, vastly extending its scope. That range was reflected in handwritten notes for an early course on language that he taught repeatedly in the late 1960s, where he was assembling not only different theories but thinkers from entirely different disciplines and habits of mind: the Latin polymath Varro (one of Vico's mentors); the biolinguist Chomsky; the Danish grammarian Otto Jespersen; the structural linguist Ferdinand de Saussure; and several Arab lexicographers.[83]

Said's reading in phenomenology, existentialism, and psychoanalysis was extensive, but his allegiances were skin-deep. He learned an immense amount from these approaches but kept his distance. For what mostly interested him was the way artworks were created "in a whole environment." Just as these theoretical movements were acquiring prestige, he was looking for the authority to throw off the straitjacket of a criticism based on a mere reading of novels and poems. For that reason, as he later confessed, he used their vocabulary "shamelessly."[84] His devotion to the work of Sartre, however, went further and deeper, for his attachments, and finally his withdrawal, were political as well as intellectual.

Although he wrote very little about Sartre's work, apart from transient allusions in the Conrad book, Said was completely immersed in his writing, especially from the beginning of grad school to the early 1980s. The attraction was in some ways natural. Sartre was already a celebrity among Arab intellectuals, his concept of *littérature engagée* having been rendered as *adab multazim* (committed literature) and as *iltizām* (commitment) in the poetics of the Palestinian writer Ghassan Kanafani.[85] Sartre's consistent anticolonial positions, his open-mindedness toward the actually existing socialisms, and his famous preface to Fanon's *Wretched of the Earth* moved Said at one point to proclaim him "one of the great intellectual heroes of the 20th century, a man whose insight and intellectual gifts were at the service of nearly every progressive cause of our time."[86] Said had met Sartre briefly at the Russell War Crimes Tribunal in 1966 and expressed to friends his eagerness to get to know the man personally. This could have been easily arranged through the London-based journal *New Left Review*, which by the 1970s was close to both men, but despite his perennial eagerness to make new connections, Said never took the initiative.[87]

Said's admiration had at any rate noticeably diminished following his early praise for Sartre's June 1967 special issue of *Les Temps Modernes* dedicated to the Arab-Israeli conflict. Even then, Sartre's intervention was not the anticolonial gesture Said had expected of the great man, for the philosopher, with specious balance, had lamented that two protagonists of living history sat next to each other in the Near East, "each inert to the other except as pure antagonist."[88] In the end, Said was never able to forgive Sartre for his support of Israel. Ultimately, in a late piece for the *London Review of Books* in 2000, he delivered a bittersweet portrait of the old man filled with regrets for lost possibilities, telling the story of a second meeting with Sartre in the all-white underfurnished apartment of the celebrated philosopher Michel Foucault in 1979, where a gathering of invited luminaries (including Said) held a *Les Temps Modernes* roundtable on Palestine.[89] Already enfeebled by age and surrounded by pro-Israeli protégés, Sartre remained mostly silent at the event until shamed into speaking by Said, at which point he could manage only platitudes.

If not Sartre himself, Said did seize upon another figure from the same French milieu: Maurice Merleau-Ponty, who with Sartre and Simone de Beauvoir edited the influential journal *Les Temps Modernes* and who became in effect a Sartre substitute. As the author of the *Phenomenology of Perception* (1945), Merleau-Ponty offered an inviting middle ground between the frank engagements of Sartre with race, class, anti-Semitism, and anticolonialism, on the one hand, and the apolitical withdrawal from such questions in structuralism's archaeological approach to language, on the other: that is, its atemporal obsession with linguistic patterns divorced from all intentional meaning. For his part, Merleau-Ponty offered what Said called "a third genre of being between the pure subject and the object," thereby seeing human encounters as forms of embodiment.[90]

While not afraid to take political stands, Merleau-Ponty was much more critical of the communist movements than Sartre, and therefore a more acceptable leftist with whom to associate. His mark on Said's thinking is undeniable. Merleau-Ponty's hostile takeover of the term "intentionality" from Husserl, the father of phenomenology, is turned by Said in his later book *Beginnings* into "will and intention." Similarly, the key term "worldliness" in Said's work, although undoubtedly derived from Erich Auerbach's *Dante: Poet of the Secular World* (1929), where the German term *irdische* (earthly, grounded) can be translated either as "secular" or "worldly," finds its way to him also through this idiosyncratic translation by Merleau-Ponty of Husserl's notion of the "life-world" (*Lebenswelt*). Merleau-Ponty stressed the worldly nature of the subject, which was in the end, above all, a physical body. And Said joined Merleau-Ponty's battle against *la pensée de l'Absolu* (the theory of the Absolute) by stressing the ambiguity and contingency of truth.

All of these sources struggled to speak between the lines of his rather unassuming book on Conrad, but there was one other as well. Said was at the same time taking on the giant of structuralist thought, the movement's very founder in most people's minds: the anthropologist Claude Lévi-Strauss. In one of Said's most important (and certainly most influential) early essays, "The Totalitarianism of Mind" (1967), he compared Lévi-Strauss's theory of the "law of mind . . . to the laws of modern scientific thought."[91] It was not a compliment. Too one-sided in his faith in scientific logic, more misanthropic even than Conrad in believing humans a species that poisons the environment with the toxins of modernity, Lévi-Strauss was the paradigm for Said of the dogmatic intellect.

With his usual perversity, though, Said could only admire his "wittily engaging, even lyrical descriptions of native practices all over the world."[92] For all their arrogance, Lévi-Strauss's studies of ancient myth were, among other things, an antidote to "the snare of personal identity," although in his attempt to account for massive cultural differences by means of a universal system of patterns, he felt that Lévi-Strauss's imperious method in the end "swallowed his work."[93]

With these forays into existentialism and phenomenology, Said was quickly becoming known as the apostle of "theory," although the thought horrified him.[94] In a little more than a year, he had gone from being an invited observer at Hopkins to sharing the podium with Poulet, Derrida, and Hans-Georg Gadamer at a symposium in Zurich titled "The Theory and Practice of Literary Interpretation" (1968). He was now in many people's minds the academic face of Continental theory itself.

AS HE MOVED TO the academic center between 1963 and 1968, two events shattered his relative security. The first was the disastrous

June, or Six-Day, War of 1967 (called in the Arab press an-Naksah, the "setback"), which signaled the beginning of Israel's occupation of all Palestinian territory with the apparent intention never to leave. The second was the collapse of his first marriage the following year, although he would not divorce until 1970. The rightward turn of the New York intellectuals following the 1967 war amplified his distance from some of the groups he was busy courting. A journal such as *Dissent*, which had little to say about Israel before 1967 except to refer sarcastically to its nationalist zealots, suddenly turned passionately Zionist. "Irving Howe was so extreme," Chomsky wryly noted, "that he was actually satirized in the Israeli press."[95] People who had never done so before began to support Israel even as they turned against the Vietnam War.

On a brighter note, the Battle of Karameh (Jordan) took place in 1968 when Palestinian refugees backed by the Jordanian military stood their ground against an invading Israeli force and acquitted themselves well. In the same year, on his way to the conference in Zurich, where Paul de Man had helped him with his lodging, he stopped in Lebanon to visit his ailing father, remaining in Beirut for a week.[96] Somewhat later, Said recalled, he had been "in Amman during the summer of 1969 and then again in 1970 . . . a visitor but also an exhilarated participant in the national revival that I saw taking place."[97] He witnessed some of "the bitterness and appalling violence of Black September 1970, when tensions between the PLO in exile in Jordan and the Jordanian military led to considerable loss of life on both sides" but also generated remarkable institutional achievements, "the greatest of which was the rise in regional and international visibility of the PLO itself."[98]

Even before 1967, Said was far less apolitical than many have come to think. The myth of his abdication from politics, as we have seen, was partly his own doing, remorse for not having been more active earlier, as he put it mercilessly in his first published analysis of the Palestinian situation, which appeared in a Columbia alumni magazine in 1969:

[After 1948] I said I was from Lebanon, which was as cowardly as saying nothing since it meant saying something
deliberately intended to be not provocative. As time went
on, I earned my degrees, I became a professor . . . That did
me no good during that awful week in June [1967]. I was an
Arab and we—"you" to most of my embarrassed friends—
were getting whipped. I wrote one or two eloquent letters
to the *Times* (they were not published) and with a few other
Arabs had sessions of group-think that were really group
therapy . . . [W]ith a dose of self-pity, I wrote "The Arab
Portrayed."[99]

Despite his flogging himself about it, his students remember
this period of his life very differently. After the first five years or so
of his teaching at Columbia, no one had doubts about his origins.
Many of those who cared were Jewish—either observant or connected to the Jewish renewal movement, among them Alan Mintz,
David and Michael Stern, and David Lehman, who wrote to him in
1973 to say that he had dedicated "a sequence of 17 neo-sonnets
(5-7-5 like haikus)" to him.[100] The group considered this Palestinian
who "didn't hide" it fascinating and attractive, sought him out, and
found it oddly easy to talk to him about almost anything.[101] The essay
that brought his name for the first time before an Arab public—
"The Arab Portrayed"—was, then, actually not his first public declaration of political engagement, even if it was written before. His
announcement, at any rate, signaled that just as he was affiliating
himself with the linguistic revolutionaries of theory, he was joining
a second revolutionary camp.

He would try to bring the two into harmony in, of all places, Urbana, Illinois, where he had been awarded a yearlong fellowship for
the 1967–68 academic year. When he left New York for the Center
for Advanced Study there, he had a clear project in mind. Originally
called "Swift in History," this study, which had already been com-
missioned by Harvard University Press, would explore how the great

eighteenth-century Irish novelist, poet, and satirist Jonathan Swift offered unexpected insights into "the sociology of knowledge."[102] He wrote half of the Swift project as a fellow but was also torn in the direction of another project entirely, one that would later take the form of his second book, *Beginnings*. While at the center, he published a version of this second book in microcosm—"A Meditation on Beginnings" (1968)—quickly followed by two other dry runs: "Narrative: Quest for Origins and Discovery of the Mausoleum" (1970) and "Witholding, Avoidance, and Recognition" (1971).[103]

Once again, the influence of Goldmann was evident. As he explained in his original proposal for the book (which went by other titles—"The Coherence of Swift," "Swift as Intellectual"), if he had taken some of his "guiding principles" in the Conrad book from contemporary critics like Jean Starobinski and Roland Barthes, here because of the "distinctive political importance of Swift's life" his interest was "similar to Goldmann's who in his study of Pascal and Racine shows the structural similarities between the political realm and the aesthetic form of the author's works."[104]

The creative intensity of the year outstripped any earlier period of productivity. This is not to say he always repaid the center's largesse with gratitude. At first, he was cautiously praising: "Urbana is not a beautiful place—as you must know—but it is surprisingly pleasant and easy to live in. The library is absolutely splendid (certainly it is better than Columbia's)."[105] Less than a month later, his first impressions gave way to scorn:

> Up until a week ago it was a curious . . . place—sociologically, that is. It's hideously ugly, but then so are most American towns, except, possibly, a few New England ones . . . A sculptor, Jonathan Shahn, and I have made a fairly extensive catalogue of the linguistic clichés that abound as well as the *idées bien reçues* that govern life: an amusing and never-ending occupation . . . Excuse the ghastly stationery.[106]

It is on this stationery, however, that readers of his collected papers can see some of the most penetrating notes of his career. On the same futuristic letterhead—a yellow blotting in the shape of the sun—he sketched the outlines of what would become *Beginnings*, side by side with the Swift book that would never be realized.[107]

Feeling exiled to the provinces, he kept up with news from home, writing to his New York neighbor, the classical pianist Jerome Lowenthal, to complain that the music in Urbana was "heavy on the unlistenable avant-guard. John Cage, himself, is a member of the Center for Advanced Study, though he's away most of the time, or collecting mushrooms" (although Said later boasted of performing Cage on the piano).[108] In a letter soon after, to keep Said entertained, Lowenthal supplied tidbits of gossip about his dinner at Claudio Arrau's, Jacqueline du Pré's marriage to Daniel Barenboim, and above all mocking anecdotes about Leonard Bernstein.[109] Said did not much care for Bernstein, mentioning him only once or twice in his many essays on music and then only when the topic was bloated egos. He never forgave the conductor for once insisting on equal billing with Beethoven in a program at the Philharmonic.[110] He delighted, then, in Lowenthal's account about "the familiar Bernstein style, vulgar without being funny," comparing it to the slapstick antics of the comedian Danny Kaye.[111]

Despite hard feelings between them during their time in Urbana, Said and Maire meanwhile were at work on an important collaboration. Their joint venture, a translation of Auerbach's essay "Philology and *Weltliteratur*," which they had done in 1965, was now approaching publication four years later, finally coming out in 1969. It was in every way seminal—both ahead of its time and boldly against the structuralist stream.[112] In their short, heavily reworked introduction to the translation, they broke away from narrow national literatures in the name of "a concert among all the literatures by man about man," extolled historicism, embraced a universalism poised against the standardizations of the market, and took the then scandalous view that criticism had to be more than evaluating novels or poems and instead a political and social decoding of "all, or most of, human verbal activity." In these gestures, they could not have been more out of tune with critical trends at the time, but they marked the crucial first step in the rise of "world literature," which four decades later became one of the most influential fields in the humanities.

With mounting tensions in his marriage, his longing for New York, and the wild shuffling between projects, he unsurprisingly described his sabbatical year as "hectic."[113] It was also frustrating. For all his frenetic creativity, he could not quite bring home the projects most on his mind. Over the course of his career, there were two huge undertakings that he worked on for decades and never completed. One was a study of intellectuals, the other, this book on Swift that he had had good reason to believe he would complete in Urbana. It was not so much that they never appeared, for scraps of the arguments, random paragraphs of the texts, are artfully strewn throughout the oeuvre and, in the case of the Swift project, it eventually appeared as a book under a different guise. The latter project, at any rate, could not have been more central to Said's long-term intellectual aims.

Swift had been on his mind from the first, among those writers he discovered as a boy in Cairo alongside Enid Blyton, Lewis Carroll, and Edgar Rice Burroughs. More than anything, though, Swift offered a way, just as Conrad had, to wage war on contemporary theoretical trends obliquely. In this way, following Goldmann's strategy, he was able to deflect his contemporaries' resentments by dramatizing twentieth-century debates dressed up as eighteenth-century ones.[114] Like Levin, Said appreciated Swift's brilliance in using (in Levin's words) "the spider as a prototype of the latest moderns, with their ingenious mechanisms, their cobwebs spun from entrails, and their renunciation of sweetness and light in favor of dirt and poison." In English letters, no one more than Swift lent himself, Levin added, to exposing the "antihumanistic thrust of so much recent writing."[115]

In fact, in Said's own words, the project's major focus was "the manner in which literary criticism constitutes and/or transforms the object of its practice."[116] Literary criticism was to be understood as the primary place where knowledge is produced and agendas formed. It was completely expected, then, that one of the first seminars Said taught after arriving at Columbia was devoted to Swift, and he had completed his book proposal for the project in the same year that the Conrad book appeared. It was again to Swift that he turned in his course offering at Harvard in the summer of 1968—a declaration of sorts, because a favorable impression was paramount in that setting, that Swift was at the heart of his professional identity.

His proposal for the book was warmly greeted. It prompted Daniel Bell, then at Columbia, to recommend him for the Illinois fellowship he eventually received. Writing to him as a familiar, Bell expressed unreserved enthusiasm. He loved Said's turn to Goldmann and was happy that, unlike Karl Mannheim's, his approach did not make ideas mere functions of social forces but set out to show how "the artistic imagination parallels the structure of overt political and social thought."[117] After Bell advised that he look up a 1934 study by Franz Borkenau, then a member of the Frankfurt Institute for Social Research (popularly known as the Frankfurt School), on the *bürgerliche Weltbild* (bourgeois worldview), Said followed his suggestion, later scolding Goldmann in his review of *The Hidden God* for not consulting Borkenau, whose work he took on in some detail in the longest of his Swift essays.

Though the study on Swift always seemed on the verge of appearing, he kept it back in part because he no longer felt it could be effective in this Augustan form. The academy's stern protocols of expertise would ultimately put him, as a specialist in modern British literature, at the mercy of the judgments of those he preemptively labeled "the professional guild of eighteenth-century scholarship." He realized it was likely to frown on his restless rescue of Swift from the official portrait of him as "a rather dry and abrasive Anglican divine."[118] Still, in a letter of 1969, he referred to his "forthcoming book" with Harvard, now under the title "Swift's Tory Anarchy."

In a later letter to Lionel Trilling, he mentioned his Swift book as being bloated and said he was busy rewriting it.[119] In fact, the Swift book was perennially reinvented: a collection of glittering fragments that never quite fit together. He intended to publish both books (on Swift and on intellectuals), one with Harvard, the other with Basic Books, and although his modes of presentation shifted radically between the 1960s and the 1980s, making the idioms of each version of the Swift project starkly dissimilar, it was in *The World, the Text, and the Critic*, its avatar, where he laid out what he wished to accomplish there.[120]

Within English letters, Swift embodied the active politician for whom language was a theoretical problem. In Said's essay "Swift's Tory Anarchy," he articulates this problem concisely: "highly dramatic encounter between the anarchy of resistance (agraphia) to the written page, and the abiding tory order of the page."[121] Certainly, a suspicion toward writing is discernible here, but also an allusion to Blackmur's observation that anarchism has a tory flavor, which might be said to mean that authoritarian rigidity is the paradoxical outcome of a freedom from all rules.[122] Against this, Said seemed to propose a kind of discipline ("order"). Without explicitly naming the deconstructive and hermeneutical theories of the 1960s, which were then spinning refined interpretive webs to problematize all textual meaning, he complained that this intricate machinery for working *on* texts oddly failed to ask what a text is in the first place.[123] And that, with his bid to extend criticism beyond imaginative literature, is what he proposed to do.

Swift, of course, was literally a Tory, but despite being a monarchist, he had learned from hard political experience the need for verbal order in a style that was "unyielding, hard, tight."[124] And he achieved this, Said suggested, by complicating the definition of "text" in two ways: first, by nimbly switching from one genre to another depending on the needs of the occasion in which a direct address of the reader was required. *Gulliver's Travels*, for instance, seemed troubled by the way that writing becomes a substitute for events. Swift's writing, therefore, was for Said "a far less integral activity than speaking."[125]

The speaking/writing dichotomy, again, had political ramifications. One was the way that the literary establishment and publishing world ignored the oral cultures of the non-Western world, where speech and physical presence obviously loomed above the private scholarly volumes of a library. Writing as opposed to speaking, moreover, naturally recalled the doctrinal fixities of monotheism itself, the religions of the Book (Judaism, Islam, Christianity), which had plagued so much of the history of the Middle East. Against such fixity stood his own earlier rescue of the "subject" from the structuralist version of it as a mere phantom effect of texts. Speaking, by contrast, meant a person physically before one, tactile, worldly, and concrete. If the Conrad book surreptitiously brought the English literary canon face-to-face with Continental philosophy, the Swift study was to have quietly exposed the political disaster lurking in theories of the autonomy of language. Swift stood as a cautionary tale, an engaged auteur, an Irish outsider in the English metropolis, a man of revolutionary temperament with conservative leanings, but above all a political activist who saw firsthand the sordid realism of a power that eventually beat him down.

When the Tories fall, so falls language, and is given over to verbal masturbation, of which there were depressing signs in Swift's late career. Poring over Swift's manuscripts, Said found "dazzling" evidence of the Irish author's "queer pastimes." His incessant word games made it hard to read anything by the man without suspecting there "*might* be a trick, or a meaning or a coded message concealed therein."[126] This led to the second, countermanding stand: Swift stood for the idea that "the writer's integrity derives exactly from the strength of his position vis-à-vis the actual state of things," even if Swift's impressive mastery of realistic detail took shape as scatology, sadistic asides, and a hatred of the rabble. He was a man, Said added, "very hard to like."

While forging his own path, Said clearly meant to heed the lessons of Swift's political career. For at first Swift's pamphlets meshed seamlessly with the political reality they were affecting, although later the man impotently opposed language to political actuality, assuming the role of a mere commentator.[127] Swift's shifting attitudes toward writing registered momentous changes in the political climate. The gradual delimiting of the power of the monarchy brought with it a move from gifted amateurs to professional politicians, and from a period of radical debate to one where politics was bureaucratically predictable. Said's important equation seemed to be this: the more powerless and hopeless the political situation, the greater the move toward a theory of autonomous language.[128]

It was therefore the opposite that Said set out to applaud—Swift's "highly polished fury of language," putting "proper words in proper places." Interestingly given Said's later writing on the political fiction of the Middle East, he raised the intriguing possibility that Swift's texts resisted irony itself: "What it says is what it means . . . the irony completes itself in the reading." Again, direct speech and the art of conversation are given the highest regard, and by Swift as well, whose choice of genres brought both to the fore: the modest proposal, tale, letter, argument, and sermon.[129] In short, the trajectory of Swift as a writer chronicled the tragedy of over-literariness in a political world.[130] Ultimately, Said confided in a friend about why he decided to let the Swift project drop: "In the end I found . . . [an] inability to sympathize with the anger and pride of the man, along with the comparative lack of interest one must perforce take in his personal life, which was always subordinate to a cause, and service for aristocrats."[131]

Meanwhile, he fended off pressures from Illinois to stay on as a full professor with a salary he took relish in describing as "astronomical."[132] By 1972, the first of several offers to move permanently to Harvard had arrived, along with other offers from Buffalo and the University of California, Santa Cruz. Following Illinois's lucrative proposal, which included a position for Maire, Columbia gave him an associate professorship with early tenure, and Maire a position at Barnard as part of the retention. As he triumphed, so did she, defending her dissertation in the very months of their estrangement in 1968. Their intellectual camaraderie was such that she continued to sit in on his lectures even after their divorce in 1970.[133] They were together at last, only now it no longer mattered.

CHAPTER 5

BEFORE OSLO

brighter
than the sun's image on a scimitar
stands the past's waste . . .
impassioned prison
of our humane dreams.

—SAID, "Desert Flowers"[1]

Although a very respectable place to land, Columbia was still gritty in the late 1960s and early 1970s. Perched on Morningside Heights on Manhattan's Upper West Side, the campus abutted some of the poorest parts of the island and had a reputation for being perilous. One of Said's Lebanese friends then studying at Teachers College wrote in exasperation about "endless stabbings, muggings, rapes and just malicious violence of every description. One young professor was left bleeding from the head . . . in the middle of Broadway . . . [I] avoid Amsterdam Avenue at all costs."[2]

With buildings that showed signs of shabbiness, Columbia was not as sought after as its peers in the Ivy League and was easier to get into than now. Its students were not all products of East Coast prep schools but native New Yorkers from public schools, many of them Jews.[3] If it was not yet as racially diverse as it would become in the 1990s (helped along by Said's deliberate efforts to make it so), it was edgy, urban, and intellectually alive.

Columbia did, however, have its own mystique. The school was divided between "the college," as it was known—the wing passionately devoted to undergraduates—and graduate studies. The two faculties, although side by side, rarely mixed.[4] From the start, Said knew where he stood. His office was in Hamilton Hall, the seat of the college, not Philosophy Hall, where the English department was housed.[5] For the first decade and a half of his teaching career, he fit in well with the gentlemanly ease of the college, which had no interest in turning students into hyper-professionals in pursuit of the academic game. Students were encouraged rather to wrestle one-on-one with the great books, without a scholarly apparatus, until they could live and breathe them.

The antiwar protests of 1968 and 1969 not only shattered this outpost of high-mindedness but added to the perception that the school was a war zone. The Columbia student actions against the Vietnam War were among the most emblematic of the 1960s. When Levin wrote proudly to his colleague Henry Hatfield (they had been corresponding about Maire's dissertation) that Said had just accepted Columbia's offer to stay, he wryly added, "I'm not so sure who wants to be at Columbia these days; the morning radio has just announced that the administration has called in the police."[6] Still on sabbatical as the demonstrations broke out, Said was desperate for news, and Herb Leibowitz, a friend, supplied him with eyewitness testimony:

> The violence of revolutionary rhetoric was . . . surpassed by the actual violence of the police action . . . The shock of seeing students you've taught bloodied in the head, or bumped and banged along the ground as they were thrown out of the buildings and into paddy wagons; tactical police dressed like storm troopers, their faces contorted in sadistic rage.[7]

Just as at Mount Hermon during the Cairo uprising, Said was again in the wrong place at the right time. While his students faced police batons or published protest letters in *The New York Review of Books*—Dupee did both, ending up with a black eye—Said was still sequestered in Urbana, but eager to discover how the events might unfold. Some of his colleagues were on the front lines—Homer Brown, a junior faculty member who looked and sounded like Raymond Williams, and Leo Braudy—but Said was far away.[8]

When he returned to Columbia in the fall of 1968, the aftershocks were still evident. He recalled that he got "quite involved in the anti-Vietnam campus activities" because many of his students "had been part of the revolution."[9] He was one of only a handful of professors, for example, to support the national student strike, sponsored by Students for a Democratic Society (SDS), against the elections that year, agreeing not to hold classes on campus in solidarity.[10] His take on the college Left, however, was complicated, as Robert Friedman, a journalist, activist, and one of his students, knew well. In their many conversations at the time, Said could not get enough of Friedman's stories about his political activities and wanted all the details.[11]

As the character of their complaint sank in, he recoiled. He found the protesters' blanket anti-authoritarianism misguided. To reject all social constraints is to fail to recognize that the university is partly there to produce authoritative judgments; its role is not to abolish law but to evaluate laws fit for a government worthy of the name. At the time, he was on the other side of his future comrade in arms Eqbal Ahmad, who had a role in starting the antiwar movement and could even be considered one of its figureheads after the Department of Justice under the Nixon administration absurdly charged him and Daniel Berrigan in the 1970 plot to kidnap Henry Kissinger.[12]

As Abu-Lughod had done, Ahmad brought to life the humane and militant Marxism of the global periphery and knew many third-world revolutionaries personally. Born in Bihar, India, in 1934, the son of a zamindar (landlord) who moved to Pakistan after India's partition, he witnessed his father's murder during a peasant uprising as he slept beside him. Like Said a student at Princeton in the 1950s, he left to fight with the insurgents against the French in Algeria, working alongside Frantz Fanon on the party's newspaper. Said would later lean heavily on Ahmad's counsel when dealing with the PLO, and his views on student protest evolved through his friendship with Ahmad, whom he met for the first time in 1970 as a result of Ahmad's reading Said's "Arab Portrayed" essay and asking Abu-Lughod to introduce them.

Said had other gripes with the student protesters. If U.S. antiwar dissidence was far from cost-free—the students risked jail, fines, and expulsion—the protesters had less on the line than the Vietnamese cadres of the National Liberation Front to whom they at times pretentiously compared themselves. He would have none of such comparisons and mercilessly criticized students who adopted the unearned pose of guerrilla fighters.[13] Thinking of the Israeli occupation, and the assassination of PLO representatives (some of them his personal friends), he thought the students had little idea of true political danger. Soon after he returned to teaching in February 1969, SDS disrupted about forty classes in six university buildings by forcing their way into classes uninvited and handing out leaflets for a sit-in against the U.S. Navy Reserve Officers' Training Corps.

According to the *Columbia Daily Spectator*, three SDS students entered his class while Said was still lecturing. He demanded they go, threatening to leave if they stayed. Most of the seventy-five students clamored for the disrupters to yield, but before a vote could be taken, Said stalked out, calling campus security from his office to have the disrupters removed.[14] The classroom was the last place to wage war against the state, he argued, later pressing the point with one of his activist students on the steps of Low Library: "What's this all about? I don't understand."[15] He took the position of many other faculty that despite the obvious justice of the students' demands, intellectual life should not be disrupted. On the other hand, when Mike Stern, one of his students, once jumped out the first-floor window of his class in Hamilton Hall in order to cover a demonstration, Said was won over, laughing at the student's audacity while admiring the ingenuity of the gesture.[16]

In a long handwritten note to Said from All Souls College, Oxford, where he was then on leave, Trilling would later complain of the "declining intellectual life" at Columbia, pointing especially to the "distressing effect on our morale" that the 1968 protests had produced and the need for "curricular reform to counteract the prevailing permissive tendency in the college."[17] In replying, Said tactfully held his tongue, because Trilling had clearly misunderstood Said's letter of three months earlier where he had complained to Trilling that the "love of mind and learning [is] threatened." For he had not meant to indicate the protests but rather "a fate of silence, or the fate of thinness, modishness, ephemerality."[18] It was not, then, that militancy threatened the serenity of learning but that fashionable withdrawal was an abdication of the intellectual's duties.

Even if he carried no picket signs for the Vietcong, Said was not above the sweat and noise of campus organizing. In 1970, he co-organized with his friend Sami Al-Banna—a computer graphics professor at Columbia—an impressive sit-in on the question of Palestine at Columbia, in which Said spoke to the crowd.[19] That same year, a long feature on the Palestinian resistance by Ahmad Besharah appeared in the campus daily, expressing support for the cause after the June War.[20] At a time when Palestinians were stripped of their identity (by convention they were referred to exclusively as Jordanians), Besharah's language must have been shocking to many students as he defended the "rebirth of a nation that has taken up armed struggle to secure the basic rights of its homeland."[21] Said too spoke animatedly with friends at the time, arguing that symbolic acts of violence in support of the victims of Israeli bombing, torture, and collective punishment were justified in a military confrontation they had no part in starting.[22]

.   .   .

THE COLLAPSE OF HIS marriage had made the late 1960s gloomy for Said, and he later admitted that his writing at the time came "out of a very dark period in my life."[23] For a time, he was lost.[24] In 1967, a year before his relationship with Maire collapsed, he met Mariam Cortas in a New York hospital room where he was visiting his sister Joyce, who had broken her leg. As she entered the room, he was "sitting in a chair, eating popcorn," apparently aloof.[25] Quakers from Brummana, Lebanon, her well-known family was loosely part of the Saids' social circle. Later, as they were falling in love, Hilda was ecstatic but given the Maire debacle cautioned him against committing himself to the relationship until he was sure. As it turned out, Mariam—a business and economics major working in real estate—had taken a job temporarily as a librarian at AUB during a downturn in the market, and the familiar university setting no doubt helped the romance along during Said's frequent visits to the country during the summer and holidays.

By 1970, he and Mariam were married. Everything seemed now to fall into place as he was warmly welcomed into Mariam's progressive Christian family, one very much like his own. On a Guggenheim fellowship two years later in Lebanon, newly married and with an infant son, Wadie (named after Said's father), he took on the role of family man. Meanwhile, after a decade of battling metastatic skin cancer, Said's father died in February 1971. The emotional wall that separated them in life was finally gone, but so much had been left unsaid, and would now remain so. In a tearful session with his psychotherapist, Said poured out his feelings about the long-sought-for connection with his father that had always eluded him. For the moment, all he could do was to bear up stoically. Recalling his last meeting as his father slipped in and out of a coma, Said hugged him and found in the impending death a symbol of the "eerie finality" of Palestine, a closed house with drawn blinds that he was no longer allowed to enter.[26]

Said spent the 1972–73 academic year in Beirut, traveling briefly to give invited lectures in Krakow and in Linz, Austria, at the Bertrand Russell Centenary Symposium ("Spheres of Influence in the Age of Imperialism"), and vacationing in Iran at Mariam's prompting ("silly not to see Persepolis," because it is "in the vicinity" of Lebanon, and Isfahan, a "thoroughly magical place").[27] That year, he plunged into the study of literary Arabic, made new contacts with the PLO after its relocation to Beirut from Jordan following the tense and bloody events of Black September (1970), and thoroughly revised *Beginnings*, the book he had begun in Urbana, with Mariam typing its various versions. As always, he complained bitterly of the taxing family obligations but found the city a fascinating, maddening mix, part "Shangri-la" and part "fanatically un-intellectual" outpost.[28]

The years leading up to the publication of this second book represented a sea change in Said's life and work. Not only did he rewrite the *Beginnings* manuscript, half of which he had composed in 1967–68, but the period marked another, more unfortunate beginning. The grueling Lebanese civil war—"the events" (*al-ahdath*)—erupted the year the book appeared and would drag on with bouts of carnage and brief lulls for another decade and a half. Writing to his friend Morris Dickstein (a Columbia alum then teaching in New York) from the Lebanese capital in January 1973, Said reassured him that they were "all well here despite the occasional raid or border skirmish . . . The heavy hand of the U.S. is so clearly implicated."[29]

Wanting release from the work of revision and unable to ignore the violence around him, he yearned to become more politically involved, seeking out Hanna Mikhaïl, a contemporary of his at Harvard now living in Beirut, who opened up another world to him. After grad school, Mikhaïl had moved to the University of Washington to teach, before abandoning his safe academic life to become a full-time cadre for the PLO in Amman. Now relocated to the Lebanese capital, he became Said's first political contact, introducing him to local notables, among them the celebrated playwright

Jean Genet, who made Mikhaïl a character in his *Prisoner of Love* (1986) under his nom de guerre Abu Omar. By 1976, Mikhaïl was dead, the victim of an assassination under obscure circumstances.

Said's awkward first meeting with Genet gave a taste of the time's unscripted encounters. Living with Mariam at the Cortas lodgings in Ras Beirut on the edge of the palm-tree-lined adobe-colored splendor of the AUB campus, he was visited one night by Genet, who dropped by unannounced. "He's a very strange bird given to long scary silences," Said reported. "He wouldn't leave until both of us yawned long and impressively at around 1:30 a.m. I've seen him since skulking about the streets. He talks a lot about his childhood and about religion."[30] Other characters he encountered—the fiery intellectual Sadik Al-Azm, for instance—were every bit as odd and unforgettable, drawn as they were to Beirut's peculiar attractions.

For the city's grandeur had not yet been ravaged by a war only a few years over the horizon. An incomparable mix of antiquity and modernity, with traces of Phoenicia, Rome, the Ottomans, and the French on every side, the city's steep tumbling streets and charming side lanes, Armenian restaurants, and greenery were legendary. The campus of AUB itself with its bell towers, public sculptures, archaeological museums, and iron gates recalled UCLA or USC but was more topographically varied. As ancient as Athens and Alexandria, and along with Istanbul and Aleppo the region's major crossroads, Beirut was then still the most enchanting coastal city of the eastern Mediterranean and by far the most politically welcoming. As a refuge for the region's political and intellectual exiles, the city played much the role in the Arab world that Mexico City plays in Latin America.

Said boasted of its *discordia concors*, a city "able to accommodate everything" by choice and by fate, once a splinter of Greater Syria, now a choice destination for its location and beauty:

> To live in Beirut means, among other things, having the choice of doing, feeling, thinking, speaking and even being

the following, in a huge assortment of possible combinations:
Christian (Protestant, Maronite, Greek Orthodox, Melchite,
Roman Catholic, etc.), Muslim (Sunnite or Shiite), Druze, Armenian, Jewish, French, American, British, Arab, Kurdish,
Phoenician, part of pan-Islamism, part of Arab nationalism,
tribal, cosmopolitan, Nasserite, communist, socialist, capitalist, hedonist, puritan, rich, poor, or neither, involved in the
Arab struggle against Israel . . . disengaged from the Arab
struggle against Israel, and so on. The poverty of labels like
left-wing and right-wing is immediately apparent.[31]

Said's own affinities fell between registers. If he shared the sympathies of Mariam's mother, and his own, toward Arab nationalism
and Lebanese autonomy, he was now surrounded by more militant
influences.[32]

The terms "left" and "right" might not have captured every subtlety, but for Palestinian partisans they did their job rather well. The
Lebanese Phalange, for instance, was an explicitly fascist party whose
aim was to break the labor unions, as Said remarked when pointing out that the Phalangist leader, Amin Gemayel, fancied himself a
"Lebanese Shah."[33] When the civil war erupted in 1975, the country's
class character revealed itself in a resentment toward the Palestinians who were perceived by right-wing Lebanese nationalist militias,
mostly Christians, as a military threat to the country's political order.[34] In much earlier times, AUB was the birthplace of Arab nationalism, the first gathering of Iraqis, Jordanians, Palestinians,
and Syrians debating a common future.[35] After 1948, the crisis in
Palestine, which hovered over every argument, drove that nationalism left.

Said sensed Lebanon's fragility, observing that the country's very
openness and virtuosity deprived it of a solid foundation. Its neighbor Israel had never specified its own boundaries and had obvious designs on the Lebanese South. The country's multicultural tolerance
unsettled the favorite narratives of sultans, strongmen, and religious

extremists, making it a greater threat to its enemies. This also made it ripe for fracturing within and the logical site for organizing Arab political demands. The arrival of PLO *fedayin* (militants, guerrillas) fleeing Jordan following its clash with the Jordanian military during the events of Black September exacerbated both.

Said's entrée into Lebanese society through Mariam's family during his Guggenheim fellowship year, then, took place just as Beirut was undergoing a dramatic radicalization. As scholar, spouse, and father of an infant son, and increasingly as a local activist, he was no longer just passing through the Middle East. Since he had left the region in 1951, as he once explained to Chomsky, this was the first real time he had spent there since adolescence.[36] Day-to-day life was beyond full, though often frustrating, because he found conversations at home and university for the most part unchallenging, even anti-intellectual.

The great exception to these routines was Constantine Zurayk, the most distinguished professor at AUB and the author of *Ma'na al nakba* (1948; *The Meaning of the Disaster*)—the book whose popularity had made the term *nakba* (disaster) synonymous for most Arabs with the founding of Israel. Married to Mariam's aunt on her father's side, Zurayk was a familiar presence in Said's life. An even greater confidant that year, however, was Sadik Al-Azm, his Syrian-born ally in dissidence. The two met several times a week for long discussions, fortified by Al-Azm's explosive *Critique of Religious Thought* (1969), which by 1972 had already been banned in every Arab country except Lebanon and condemned by the grand mufti for blasphemy.[37]

Despite the allure of these street-fighting influences, he was cautious about wandering very far from his study. His first lectures at AUB during the fellowship year were not on the Palestinian resistance but on Foucault, and it was in Beirut that he published his first extended essay on the French philosopher's work.[38] He would not meet high-level PLO operatives until 1974, a year after he had left Beirut for home. One of his closest friends and collaborators was Shafiq Al-Hout, a poised and remarkably brave operative in the PLO leadership whom Said affectionately described as "swashbuckling."[39] Alongside him were Salah Khalaf, Khalil Wazir, and Yasser Arafat himself (a.k.a. Abu Ammar), whom Said got to know only in 1974, when Arafat arrived in New York to deliver his inaugural speech to the United Nations, the first time the PLO was publicly recognized in an international arena. By that time Said had already developed a close friendship with Kamal Nasser, a member of the secular, socialist, and anti-imperialist Ba'ath (renaissance) Party and a Nasserite whom he had seen frequently when growing up in Cairo during the 1950s. Another militant close to his heart, Kamal was assassinated by the Israelis in 1973 on the very night he had spent chatting for hours with Said and Mariam while attending the wake of Aunt Nabiha.[40]

Al-Hout later recounted the event: On April 10, 1973, Israeli commandos carried out an operation aimed at the core of the PLO's Beirut leadership. "A group of Israeli commandos led by the future prime minister, Ehud Barak, entered two buildings in Verdun Street near Al-Snoubra and assassinated Kamal Nasser" as well as two others, failing to kill Arafat by mere chance.[41] Earlier that year, Said had been busy interviewing members of Arafat's Fatah wing of the PLO. He and Al-Azm had been trying to figure out the inner workings of the organization, not liking what they saw. They concluded that it was less a matter of clear factions than of ad hoc "non-action." The level of bureaucratization was already alarming—compensation, Said ventured, for diminished guerrilla activities. When Said approached the avant-garde poet Adonis (Ali Ahmad Said Esber) to draft a letter protesting the rough treatment of student protesters in Egypt, the poet sat on it for six weeks because he was "not inspired." Similarly, Said had tried to set up a research group, but no one showed up after the second meeting.[42] Despite his disillusionment at seeing these weaknesses, their sobering effects only further politicized him.

This new resolution formed the backdrop of his labors on

Beginnings. In his lectures on Foucault in Beirut, one of his chief tasks was to decipher Foucault's use of the term "discourse," a word Said provisionally, if somewhat idiosyncratically, defined as "the possibility of, as well as the rule of formation for, subsequent texts." He was referring to the fact that any statement, apart from its literal meaning, announces the scope of an inquiry, a particular lexicon, and an appeal to one rather than another authority. Any declarative statement, Foucault suggested, is much more than the claim it contains, for it dictates every statement to follow by foreclosing other options that can no longer survive outside its verbal universe. As a result, Said was especially concerned (in writing as in politics) to make the right first move.[43]

A tidy exegesis, as in the Conrad book, seemed unequal to this particular task, so he searched for a different principle of organization, something that would remain true to what he was then calling the "molestations" of language—his term for the dissimulation that authors use as they create their fictional realities.[44] This coinage, which he first used at the Zurich symposium in 1968 and then again in an essay in 1971, caught the attention of the profession's movers and shakers and helped launch his career in the circles of an emergent French theory.[45] For it seemed to them to embrace the experimental modernism on which theory was premised and to champion the willful subversion of direct intention and meaning. In fact, he had not intended the term to be taken this way, but that only became apparent later.

The formal innovations of literary modernists like Paul Valéry and Ezra Pound, their theatrical ruptures with the past, and their injunction to "make it new" governed the book's ostensible field of vision, so that its central question seemed to be, Can authors be original or are they condemned to repeat? This drift toward writerly origins and away from the existential self-making of authors marked a subtle departure from the Conrad book, although he would come back to the earlier concern by decade's end.

As the drafts neared their final form, he could tell he had

formulated something unique. Among other things, he was inviting the profession of American letters to open its doors not only
to Continental theory but to Arabic lexicography. A skilled media-
tor who nudged his enemies and friends alike away from the intellectual parochialism of Anglo-American academia, Said arranged
with National Public Radio to give radio broadcasts on Foucault
and Lévi-Strauss.[46] For all its challenges, *Beginnings* operated in a
similar spirit, intending to make this rigorous thought coming out
of France and the Arab Middle East accessible to larger audiences.

In a letter to Basic Books, his publisher, he seemed to want to
reassure his editors that his "fat advance" had been justified.[47] "Let
me put modesty aside—the book will be a major one . . . The . . .
methods are, I think, completely original, and the scope very wide.
Since I am well-grounded in a major non-Western tradition, I can
do comparisons in history and literature between the whole range
of Western stuff and the Arabic."[48] He wrote in the same vein to
others, confiding to his old Harvard adviser Monroe Engel that the
process of crafting the book, although agonizing, had been worth
it.[49] He had been holed up, working incessantly on the manuscript
for months, not taking on the usual side projects or moving rest-
lessly from one deadline to the next as he had always done before.
Now, finally past the labors of research and at the point of fine revisions, he found himself capable of no reading whatsoever except
some short stories by Graham Greene.

The process of composing the book had been fitful. He would get
up in the morning, pace around, fiddle with things.[50] His daughter,
Najla, recognized the pattern later in life, her father always anxious, restless and energetically moving, tortured. His work, then as
later, took place in spurts.[51] "I felt the freedom of virtually creating
the subject as I went along . . . Thus, I discussed what I wanted to,
no prescribed material, no ritualistic attempts to 'cover' scholarly
studies, etc."[52] A few years on, he would confide to a younger colleague that he had had doubts about ever being able to write a book
conceived whole from beginning to end: "I think I'm good at essays,

like Barthes' *fiches* [index cards], assembled into a book."[53] Because he managed in this case a unified whole, however much the seams showed, the book always remained a project close to his heart.

Unlike the Conrad study's silence on culture in the Middle East, this one reflected, and in some ways subtly narrated, Said's own return to Arab life. In the course of the year, he seriously thought about leaving Columbia for Beirut and even took the initial steps of doing so before Mariam dissuaded him. Jettisoning the plan was easier as his compromised status in Beirut came into focus. Apparently out of envy, the faculty at AUB gave Said the cold shoulder, ignoring his offer to teach a course for free and even putting meaningless obstacles in his path of obtaining something so simple as a library card. The resentment derived, no doubt, from Said's growing fame and Ivy League connections. In a letter to a colleague in Egypt in 1972, he vented his frustrations: "I think it's an absolutely hopeless and even pernicious place, and for my own relative strength of mind, I won't have anything to do with it . . . [T]here is no one—no one at all, literally—doing anything of interest . . . Anybody good—although poor old Halim B[arakat] [the Syrian novelist] is a mild enough man compared to Sadik Al-Azm—is just shelved, castrated, or thrown out, whatever can be done most cheaply."[54] In this humiliating milieu, where respected writers like Barakat were treated with the same disrespect as firebrands like Al-Azm, only Malik invited him to lecture at the university and to address his seminars.[55]

His intensive study of Arabic, nevertheless, colored every line of *Beginnings*. For one thing, he shared Abdallah Laroui's bold argument in *The Crisis of the Arab Intellectual* (1974) that no civilization more than the Arab had invested its sense of "truth in the structures of its language."[56] Laroui had also suggestively argued, in a move Said later adapted, that French theory's assault on the study of history—its undermining of the quest to recover the truth of the past by reading texts—had strangely aligned it with Sunni Islam's "fundamental givens."[57] From the progressive Arab's point of view, which had always been attentive to French intellectual leads, it was dismaying to watch the European avant-garde come to resemble the conservative Arab cultural tendencies they would be assumed to denounce. Only historical knowledge, Laroui continued, could bring out what was "genuinely attractive but perhaps also misleading about them."[58]

Said's tutoring in formal, written Arabic (he was already fluent in its Palestinian and Cairene spoken forms) affected his understanding of the word "origin" itself, which was obviously central in a book with the title *Beginnings*. Arab philological expertise, after all, had predated Europe's by many centuries and became particularly refined in the years immediately before and after Al-Ma'mun's ninth-century preservation of the classics of Greek antiquity in Arabic translation. This attention to language and its structures, though, derived ultimately from the "dogmatic fixity" (in Said's words) of classical Arabic itself, which was thought to have attained perfection in the Qur'an, and therefore was seen by Arab scholars as an absolute textual beginning. Said's letters home attest to his excitement as he labored over Arabic grammar, which he conceded after twenty-two years in the United States had fallen into "disrepair."[59]

He had, as he put it, first "learned to speak Arabic and English at my mother's knee."[60] Now in Beirut he found himself involved in "fact-gathering of a queer sort" stemming from his ongoing fascination with the problem of language as he had explored it in graduate seminars in the mid- and late 1960s.[61] He found Al-Khalil (Ibn Ahmad Al-Farahidi, the eighth-century author of the first Arabic dictionary) "damn interesting," adding that he wished he had time to study all of the Semitic languages, with a special interest in Ugaritic, a language from the fifteenth century B.C.E., written in cuneiform, from Ugarit in present-day Syria.[62] During the fellowship year in Beirut, the role of Arabic philology and of Vico became fused in his mind, although he politely said nothing about the disparagement of Arab learning in Vico's autobiography or his reference to the "impious Averroes":

To a modern educated Arab anywhere . . . eloquence . . . is much closer to what Vico experienced and talked about than it is for English-speakers . . . Rhetoric and eloquence in the Arab literary tradition go back a millennium, to Abbasid writers like Al-Jahiz and Al-Jurjani, who devised . . . complex schemes for understanding rhetoric . . . that seem startlingly modern.[63]

While doing the research for *Beginnings*, and working on its drafts, he found time for regular lessons with a retired professor of Semitic, Anis Frayha, a friend of the family who gave him short courses in "remote corners of the language."[64] Depending on his mood, he shrugged off the effort as practically useless even if culturally valuable. At other times, he declared the opposite, announcing that the philology and grammar of Arabic made "'*les mots sous les mots*' [the words beneath the words], and all that"—a phrase taken from the father of structuralism, the Swiss linguist Ferdinand de Saussure—appear amateurish. For two months he waded through ninth- to thirteenth-century Arab learning, finding it dazzling: "Barthes et al. could learn a lot from the analyses done in the middle ages."[65] In the future, he promised, he would consider it the essential preparation for all his work.[66]

Against Beirut's increasingly militarized backdrop, Said moved on to a neglected if not forgotten Arab literary tradition from the medieval past. The great fourteenth-century historian and sociologist Abd Al-Rahman Ibn Khaldun, born in Tunis in 1332 but descended from a family of Sevillean patricians, brought him face-to-face with a major influence on his work thereafter. It was through Ibn Khaldun that he began to consider the possibilities of an indigenous Arab aesthetics, which was all the more attractive because of its obvious parallels with Vico, who was almost certainly influenced by his Maghrebian precursor.[67] Said would recall two decades later that "for at least thirty years I've been planning a seminar on Vico and Ibn Khaldun," and actually spent significant time in some of the essays collected in *The End of the Peace Process* (2000) charting Vico's many resemblances to this Arab forebear, calling Vico's *New Science* and Ibn Khaldun's *Muqaddimah* (1377) "books of the millennium," "the most extraordinary achievements of secular thought."[68]

Ibn Khaldun anticipated Said's literary sensibilities very closely. In the Arab historiographer's masterpiece, the *Muqaddimah*, the watchword was *asabiyyah* (group feeling)—the principle upon which all communities depend for their cohesion. If originally such fealties were based exclusively on blood ties, Ibn Khaldun sought to expand them to include solidarities based on ideas or shared goals, in that way moving beyond tribalism. The *Muqaddimah* indirectly gave support to Said's contemporary case that the politics of literature should not be understood so literally as to be equated with the radical views expressed by authors, on the one hand, or the formal experiments that supposedly explode older modalities of thinking, on the other. Literary politics was rather to be understood in terms of the role of human eloquence in the formation of polities as well as the textual record of their rise and decline.

Said was not unique among Arab intellectuals of his generation in finding Ibn Khaldun a valuable resource, although he was the only one to build a specifically Arab aesthetic strategy on the basis of its source. On more than one count, the *Muqaddimah* seemed to anticipate Said's intentions in *Beginnings*. In a twelve-hundred-page manuscript, the book—whose title suggests both an introduction to history and a judgment of it (as in a court trial)—Ibn Khaldun was every bit as obsessed as Said with the "how" of intellectual work, laying out lessons, patterns of argument, rhetorical strategies, and methods of investigation to be employed by any intellectual who wishes actually to affect policy. Along the way, the boundary lines between imaginative literature and sociological or historical analysis were effaced. Ibn Khaldun brought the science of history to bear on the study of rhetorical figures, literary genres, and the character of language, the topics of the *Muqaddimah*'s entire final movement. Keenly aware of this fact, Said drove home the literary consequences of Middle Eastern politics as they had been shaped by the linguistic prehistory of Ibn Khaldun's thought:

> During the eleventh century in Andalusia there existed a remarkably sophisticated and unexpectedly prophetic school of Islamic philosophic grammarians, whose polemics anticipate twentieth-century debates between structuralists and generative grammarians . . . One small group of these Andalusian linguists . . . turn[ed] the question of meaning in language into esoteric and allegorical exercises . . . [This] Zahirite school [was the] antagonist[] of the Batinist school. Batinists held that meaning in language is concealed within the words . . . The Zahirites['] name derives from the Arabic word for clear, apparent, and phenomenal; *Batin* connotes internal [suggesting that] . . . words had only a surface meaning.[69]

The Swift study's nod to "clear and apparent" writing seemed to resurface here in a new guise. At stake was Said's rejection of a number of ideas prominent in 1970s and 1980s academia, which included the doctrine of creative misinterpretation, the idea that the meaning of books is determined by their readers rather than by authorial intention or the inherent properties of the text. At the same time, he was resisting the epistemological pessimism of Hans-Georg Gadamer's hermeneutics as well as the French structuralist Marxist Louis Althusser's notion of "symptomatic reading" with its invitation to use texts as raw material, in effect permitting texts to say whatever one considered it politically expedient for them to say. Interpretation, he was saying, is complex, fraught, and often ambiguous, but not mystical and never merely willful.

He was also seizing upon the term *bayan* (eloquence), a theme running through the *Muqaddimah*, where it meant being (in Ibn Khaldun's words) "able to combine individual words so as to express the ideas [one] wants to express, and . . . able to observe the form of composition that makes . . . speech conform to the requirements of the situation."[70] *Bayan* was a key rhetorical category in Arab humanism, referring to the kind of eloquence that clarifies or elucidates and declaring—as Ibn Khaldun does following the Qur'an—that the dignity of human beings derives from God's having created them with the capacity for eloquence.[71] Two other connotations were equally important: first, that in its clarifying function, the term could also mean "manifesto" or "communiqué," and indeed Said later in the wake of the first intifada issued a call for an international conference under the title *Bayan*.[72] But also, that in Arab rhetorical theory, one speaks of Elm al-bayan, where "Elm" refers to the "science" of the humanities and of literature, much as one refers to the science of chemistry or mathematics.[73]

This meditation on the collision of politics and language was Said's constant theme just before and during the Guggenheim in Beirut. The groundwork for it had been laid by his disarming candor in a testy exchange with the great linguist Noam Chomsky over "Speaking and Language," his review of Paul Goodman's *Defence of Poetry* in *The New York Times* in 1972.[74] Like many others of his generation, Said had been transfixed by Chomsky's magisterial broadside "The Responsibility of Intellectuals," which appeared in *The New York Review of Books* in 1967. Inspired by this call for professors to speak out against the state, he soon became an avid correspondent and met Chomsky frequently at gatherings around the Israel/ Palestine issue. Emboldened by Chomsky's example, and already on his own political quest, he kept a clipping of this celebrated *J'accuse* in his files along with a massive dossier of Chomsky's articles, later writing the foreword to Chomsky's *Fateful Triangle: The United States, Israel, and the Palestinians* (1983), where he exalted him as an epochal groundbreaker.[75]

Despite their many solidarities, the two public intellectuals— already close friends by the early 1970s—held opposing views on key aspects of language. The setting for the conflict arose a year earlier in Said's elaborate treatment of Chomsky's linguistic revolution in an essay Said titled "Linguistics and the Archeology of Mind" (1971), in which he provocatively pitted him against a thinker Chomsky considered a charlatan, the post-Freudian analyst and quintessential French theorist Jacques Lacan.[76] For his part, Chomsky recalled being "utterly astonished that Ed could even begin to take this stuff seriously"—"this stuff" referring to language as pure creative expression or, in Lacan's case, as the mirror of the unconscious and the structure of social and libidinal desire.[77] Said respectfully held his ground.

In the archaeology of mind essay, Said seemed intentionally to place two incompatible positions side by side: the social scientistic and cognitive approach of academic linguistics proper, over which Chomsky then reigned supreme, and the speculative aestheticism of a motley group of French critics, poetic enthusiasts, and philosophers. He did this, moreover, with faux naiveté, each foot in the other's foreign camp, as though the pairing were altogether natural.[78] The maneuver puzzled and irked both sides with its jarring eclecticism, and neither group recognized itself in his accounting.

What Said liked most about Lacan was his "concrete situational analyses," which, he implied, were unlike Chomsky's overarching paradigm of universal grammar. In the sometimes angry and defensive correspondence between them after the Goodman review appeared, he pressed Chomsky to read Barthes, advising him that studying Benveniste would also be worth his while.[79] Chomsky would have none of it, considering them dabblers who did no real research, read little, and bungled the sources they did read. He was especially put out by Said's enthusiasm for Goodman's irreverent non-specialism (the subtitle of the review was "A Good Man Against Theories"), along with Said's romantic fixation on acts of speech, rather than his own approach, which was to study the linguistic grounds for any possible speech or, indeed, thought.

In answer to Chomsky's position, Said declared that "the complexity of everyday speech can [not] be reduced to variations on simple declarative sentences."[80] Goodman, he averred, was right to suspect that grammatical structures are not semantically neutral, and was correct to wonder whether the whole Chomskian hard-wiring approach to language was not too cut off from the roundedness of life, which it replaced "by the impersonal 'format' of 'communication' or of message 'transmission.'" According to Goodman (and Said agreed), Chomsky could not really account for "inflection, tone, gesture, silence [which] all play a significant part in verbal behavior."[81] Further, Chomsky was too bullheaded not to grant that universal grammar, whatever its insights, was irrelevant to the actual scenes and events of language, where individuals manipulate words by inexhaustibly expressive, often very personal, means.

Said detected in Chomsky's implicit indifference to human agency a flawed political vision. Chomsky's masterful compilation of facts laying out the lies of empire in his political books was, he thought, ambiguous. "You end by depressing yourself," he complained, "making it hard for your reader to know what to do about the whole business."[82] These exposés, however bold and upright he implied, did not give his readers any idea about how to fight these injustices, or why or how to act against them. Goodman, on the other hand, was no panacea, and Said assuaged his friend by slamming Goodman's self-flattering portrait as an anti-intellectual maverick. Endlessly invoking the "individual" and "freedom" like some Romantic poet, Goodman lacked an astute analysis of the constraints imposed on freedom by the media, corporations, and the state. "He leaves his reader at the level of language," marveling at its beauty or expressiveness, Said explained, but "unable to see the way back to the actual world, there to change it." This "classically liberal ethic," he protested, was a dead end.[83]

Even more on his mind was another essay he published a month later on the eve of his arrival in Beirut. This other facet of *Beginnings*'s background story can be traced to an essay of his that never appeared in English: "Witholding, Avoidance, and Recognition" (1972), published in Arabic in the literary journal *Mawaqif*—a Beirut quarterly run by Adonis.[84] After three years of being badgered by Adonis to write for the journal, he finally gave in.[85] It would prove to be a painfully direct address to his people, the first of his Palestinian essays intended exclusively for an Arab audience. A more caustic and radical version of his dry run for the book—the essay "Beginnings" (1968)—"Witholding, Avoidance, and Recognition" covered related ground from a different angle.[86]

Guarded and unguarded by turns, he moved along nervously in the essay, aware that he might be seen as a New York interloper testing uncertain waters.[87] He wisely let the essay be vetted by Adonis himself, a literary modernist of some importance in twentieth-century letters and a friend of Said's Lebanese confidant the novelist Elias Khoury. As not only a poet but a literary theorist and translator, Adonis found the piece intriguing and "quite original" but gently disagreed with its methodology, finding parts of it untranslatable and faulting the essay for raising provocative issues it left unresolved—above all, the relevance of English literature to the Arab dilemma. Too much on the likes of Nietzsche, he counseled, and too little on "national sources."[88]

The essay's reception was also complicated by the crowded field it was joining. A number of Arab intellectuals at the time had written postmortems on the "setback" (an-Naksah) of 1967, with hard talk about where to go from there. The important Palestinian novelist Ghassan Kanafani frowned on the wave of self-criticism as "a masochistic festival of self-disparagement."[89] Essentially, Said's essay, though, belonged in that company, and he was well aware of it. Many Arab intellectuals at the time would have considered the pinnacle of the genre to be his newfound Syrian Marxist friend Al-Azm's *Self-Criticism After the Defeat* (1968), which was a bombshell. Along with Al-Azm's book of the same period critiquing the foundations of religious thought, it made him the Arab world's enfant terrible. Said seemed to emulate Al-Azm's provocations by closing his essay with a reading of *Othello* in which he summoned Shakespeare's wronged hero as a paradigm of the contemporary Arab leader, conspired

against on all sides. Dwelling on the line "When you shall these un-
lucky deeds relate, speak of me *as I am*, nothing extenuate," Said insisted that the real tragedy was not Othello's jealousy or gullibility
or the vile plots against him, but his assuming he knew who he was.

With "self" on the agenda, psychoanalysis was on full display
in the "Witholding" essay, which Said described as "a critical psy-
chohistory of contemporary Arab reality."[90] "Why," he asked, have
Arabs no sense of "efficiency, of progress . . . of science or cultural
vivacity"? We are clearly "an amalgam of Western and traditional
influences," but for that very reason "no one can or should say flatly
what an Arab should be." Our progress need not pattern itself necessarily on the West's mastery of the technologies of writing, which
have turned us into second-rate Europeans. Under the power of "Bible, blackboard and printing press," the West has managed globally
to disseminate its version of reality. Now that the world has become
a "complex of interconnected systems" in which digital information trumps print, the species itself seems of slight consequence in
the face of "trans-human phenomena like cybernetics or planetary
space." In this web of specious modernity, the Arab is "produced to
be consumed by an aggressive, acquisitive culture."

In a torrid letter to his friend Sami Al-Banna in July 1972 just
after arriving in Beirut for the fellowship, Said explained why he had
had to write the essay, which had appeared a few months before.
The letter's guileless fury and sheer length were testimonies to his
complicated debut in Middle East politics and letters, and it gave
perhaps the best single portrait of his thinking in one of the most
revealing exchanges of his career. Everyone here in Beirut behaves,
he complained, as if nothing had changed (dress, greetings, and so
on), although it had terribly. "In the past two weeks . . . Egypt, Iraq,
Lebanon, Morocco, and the Sudan have lost several generals, and
several thousand Palestinians have been decimated, have surren-
dered to Israel, or just disappeared," and yet everything goes on "as
if all that happened was a coffee break."[91] Infuriated, he diagnosed
the reasons: "The society . . . has no memory, no sense of dimension

(no projection into the future, no capability to plan), no stability except that of mere equilibrium."

In a striking foreshadowing of his worries about third-world originality in *Beginnings*, he bitterly concluded that "the characteristic movement of the Arab is circular . . . Repetition is therefore mistaken for novelty, especially since there is no sense of recognition." Despite all the "Marx mongering" among the radical poseurs, he grumbled, they have no idea how to make a revolution. "Reality is—to us [Arabs]—a function of language. Although this is in a way true in the West, there is in the West a consciousness of this; here there isn't." He had defined the problem well in the "Witholding" essay when he complained that Arabs have had their language stolen from them by making it the language of God. It must in that form be immutable and cannot change with history. They speak either the language of the West or the language of God and are caught between the two.[92] The potential offered by the demotic is foreclosed by the "highly ornate" language of classical Arabic, "unchanging and perfect," leaving one only with "zero-sum repetition."[93]

Like Malik, he thought it justified to speak of an "Arab Mind" across the national borders of the Middle East; there was, he felt, a common template, despite myriad differences. What a pity then, he says, that in response to the 1967 war intellectuals like Taha Hussein in Egypt used the unexamined thought structures of the West. Even Fanon, to whom he appealed, used Freud and Marx as agitational devices against European colonialism and in that way postponed the task of creating a distinctly native culture.[94] As unlikely as it seemed, given the book's long passages on Verlaine, Eliot, and Freud, this task of mapping out an indigenous Arab culture, politics, and aesthetics is what he sought to complete as he worked on *Beginnings*.

AS HE LEFT BEIRUT for home, the book remained unfinished. With the eventful year in the Lebanese capital finally over, Said returned to New York by way of Europe in the summer of 1973, only a few months before Egypt and Syria launched the October War to reclaim Sinai and the Golan Heights lost to Israel in 1967.[95] Cheered by news of the Watergate hearings as he stopped with Mariam in France in June, he wrote letters to friends from the Columbia residence, Reid Hall, at 4 rue de Chevreuse in Paris, revealing his mixed response to what he had experienced in Lebanon: "The censorship is very heavy."[96] Clashes between the Lebanese and the Palestinians were common, as were Israeli raids.[97] "But my feeling is that the movement has done very well militarily and politically during the last confrontation."[98]

Not long after his return and still in this mood of optimism, he threw himself headlong into the Palestinian resistance. His Beirut contacts paved the way, but the trajectory was inevitable given the success of his "Arab Portrayed" essay, which had by then circulated widely throughout the Middle East and in the Arab diaspora. Already a known entity, he was asked to help with the English translation of Arafat's address to the UN General Assembly in November 1974. One of Arafat's closest advisers, Al-Hout, was a very close childhood friend of Abu-Lughod, both refugees from Jaffa, "the Bride of Palestine." During the PLO delegation to the UN, Said and Al-Hout hit it off immediately, which gave Said ready access thereafter to the upper echelons of the organization. Said would eventually dedicate *The Politics of Dispossession* (1994) to Al-Hout and his wife, Bayan, and they remained lifelong friends.[99]

The original draft of Arafat's speech had been composed in Arabic by Nabil Shaath and then sent to Al-Hout for review.[100] The text was reworked with input from Walid Khalidi, Salah Dabbagh, and Mahmoud Darwish, who, despite his towering stature in Arabic letters and his role as the Palestinians' poet laureate, knew very little English. In this form it was given to Huda Osseiran to work on the translation with the Arafat team, but the results were wanting. Al-Hout then approached Said, who agreed to give it shape. With

Randa Khalidi Fattal, a professional editor, he turned the speech into the form in which it was finally delivered by Arafat at the UN on November 13, 1974. Said added elements he knew would resonate with American audiences and enthusiastically passed along the document's famous closing line: "Don't let the olive branch fall from my hands." Because Mariam was the only person in the group who could type, she finished the final version on the rickety Smith Corona at home before Al-Hout delivered it by hand at 4:00 a.m. on the day of the speech.[101]

On this occasion, Said's advice was heeded. It rarely was thereafter, although he made his impact felt in other ways. When PLO delegations came to New York in the late 1970s to deliver speeches at the UN, Said arranged meetings with small groups sympathetic to their cause but critical of PLO positions. These forums were designed to let the leadership hear from trustworthy partisans of their cause (such as Chomsky, Ahmad, and the Russian historian Alexander Erlich) how they might present a fresher public face. Chomsky found the PLO unique among third-world liberation groups in its inability to think strategically.[102] The fancy New York hotels, the lavish dinners—all were morbid symptoms of a proud and previously ignored PLO cadre suddenly thrust into the limelight by international recognition in the 1970s. At one point, Ahmad sardonically dubbed such events "banqueting as the latest form of struggle."[103]

Now with a firm base in Beirut, Said returned often to the city in coming years, routinely visiting Arafat. In *My Life in the PLO* (2011), Al-Hout recounted with all the drama of a thriller the dangers of being a public spokesman for the Palestinians. Al-Hout himself improbably survived six assassination attempts, which ranged from the bombing of his office to Israeli snipers wounding him by shooting from a parked car as he left his home.[104] In Arafat's case, apart from the Palestinian people's love and support for him, he was physically striking, with sharp eyes, a friendly smile, and an imposing presence. "He was not a movie star by any means," recalled Bayan, "but he was always very attentive, never without a pencil and small notebook."[105] In person, he was the reverse image of the one created for him by the Western media—sensitive, extremely polite, gentle, frequently laughing, and funny. His diasporic credentials also fit Palestinian realities, born as he was in Jerusalem, but with his family living in Egypt, speaking with an Egyptian accent, and based in Kuwait before returning to the Middle East to lead the PLO.

When Said and Arafat met, they spoke exclusively in Arabic, Said adopting a Levantine rather than an Egyptian accent, although he could "put on" the Egyptian accent of his childhood whenever necessary.[106] Until the Oslo Accords, Said remained doggedly loyal to the "old man," as he called Arafat, for which he was severely criticized, even by his allies. Despite Arafat's failings as a leader—his mercurial style, the top-heaviness of the leadership with its flipping back and forth between sectarian intransigence and needless concession, as well as his inability to understand, and therefore properly address, American culture—the Palestinian movement was, for well or ill, inextricable from Arafat's singular presence. But even in the rosier pre-Oslo days, Said put pressure on him indirectly, once getting Alexander Cockburn to chide Arafat in print for stubbornly holding on to his keffiyeh, stubbled beard, and military attire, which made him ripe for mockery in American magazines.[107]

Still, it was Arafat who, through Fatah, "built institutions, dispensed arms, and instilled a sense of hope and pride."[108] It made sense, then, in the years to come, that Said would mount a strategic defense of his leadership following a mutiny within the PLO backed by Syria and the crises caused by the Israeli invasion of Lebanon in 1982, which forced the PLO from Beirut.[109] Before their falling-out, Said never wavered. In the dubious venue of *Interview* magazine (an Andy Warhol vehicle and the last word in postmodern fashion), he warmly recounted a rendezvous with Arafat in the PLO's new headquarters in Tunis. There he provided a memorable sketch of Arafat's personal charm and dignity, revealing his affection for him despite disappointments at Arafat's failings.[110]

One of the effects of writing the "Witholding" essay had been to stake out a middle ground between philosophy and activism, and thereby sharpen his understanding of what a phrase like "the politics of literature" (which at the time was the rage in universities) might actually mean. His unwillingness to segregate his professional and political lives gave his antagonists an opening. Summoning popular misconceptions about expertise, they mocked his avocation. One of these, Amos Perlmutter, a media analyst with close ties to the Israeli government, dismissed him on *The MacNeil/Lehrer NewsHour* by quipping that as a professor of English, Said "like[d] fiction," as though his charges against Israel were simply invented.[111] It was not the first time that think-tank intellectuals lagged behind his arguments. Of all political conflicts, Said had often observed, the Israeli-Palestinian issue was to an unusual degree an image war: "In no modern conflict has rhetoric played so significant a part in legitimating one preposterous thing after another (also known as 'creating facts')."[112]

Said's writing had always been concerned with the power of the imagination to organize belief and action. His position, when compared with those of other literary critics of his day, was just the opposite of the one targeted by Perlmutter's jab. He believed that whereas reality may be independent of the stories told about it, the meaning of that reality never is. Facts are "created" to the extent that some facts are ignored, others selectively chosen, then arranged in the form of a narrative, which is the only way they make sense. More often than not, a naive insistence on "the facts" reveals a "contemptuous dismissal of opinion and interpretation," usually favoring what already passes for fact in conventional wisdom, and is therefore part of a larger "cult of 'objectivity' and expertise."[113] While working on *Beginnings*, he had still not fully worked out his position on the responsibilities of representing reality in this sense, but by the end of the 1970s he found his voice in a note scribbled on Cornell University hotel stationery:

> Recent critical theory has placed, I think, undue emphasis
> upon the limitlessness of interpretation . . . This is a view I
> oppose not simply because texts are in the world, but also
> because as texts they *place* themselves, they *are* themselves
> by acting in the world.[114]

This view clearly evolved as he struggled to reconcile philology with Foucault in *Beginnings*. He would remark late in life that although he "began with the notion that there is no such thing as the correct interpretation," he worked his way out of it. What he failed to add is that he did so for practical reasons as he toiled over position statements and UN resolutions where precise meanings were essential to legal and political sovereignty, not to mention the creation of a Palestinian state in which the factual basis of competing narratives was paramount.[115]

As several of his closest allies were being killed or threatened, Said's activities as he moved between New York and Beirut during the 1970s had dangers of their own. At one point, at the height of the civil war's passions, he failed to refer to a suicide car bombing as the act of "martyrs" (the preferred honorific) and, worse, suggested the tactic was ill-advised. He soon learned that a group had singled him out for assassination. He and his family lived under a pall, fearing the sentence might actually be carried out, because it had been for others who similarly transgressed. Making matters worse, in an interview in the journal *Middle East* a few years later, he was understood to say (though later denied it) that armed struggle was "a mere slogan or an outdated concept."[116] As he explained to the Middle East historian and political analyst Fred Halliday, "The furor that this has caused . . . is beyond belief. Most of the attacks . . . have accused me of being a traitor, a capitulationist, a quisling, an agent of American imperialism, a stooge, a lackey, and on and on . . . *Al-Hadaf* in its most recent issue in Beirut has launched a murderous campaign against me."[117] The danger soon subsided, but he came to feel exasperated by such encounters, which made his second life in literature seem all the more attractive.

His travels to the Middle East were not always to Lebanon. In Cairo in the summer of 1975, he found the city of his upbringing sprawling and dusty, with no social services, and claimed he had no desire ever to return (a pledge he would not keep). Still, there was both opportunity and time enough to see a satirical play featuring the great Egyptian belly dancer Tahia Carioca, whose politics, he sadly recounted, gave voice to an emergent and increasingly vocal Arab right wing, thereby adding another unforeseen roadblock to Palestinian statehood.[118] In 1977, Said stayed behind at Columbia as Mariam, his young son, Wadie, and new daughter, Najla, traveled to Lebanon in January during a lull in the fighting, later joining them on a separate trip in June. By the following year, the civil war had begun to make travel there too dangerous.[119]

But he managed trips to Lebanon when the fighting permitted, struggling, among other things, to enlist academics to the cause. In 1979, a key recruit, he thought, might be the American literary critic Fredric Jameson, who took classes with Auerbach and who had been on Said's radar after Jameson's breakout book, *Marxism and Form* (1971). He had already introduced Jameson to Al-Azm, and now with Jameson visiting the Middle East on a trip organized by him and Eqbal Ahmad and with David Dellinger, Ramsey Clark, and other peace activists taking part, he saw his chance.[120] Writing to Robert Alter from Beirut, he later talked about his motives:

A funny coincidence is that Fred Jameson, and a small group of others whose trip here was encouraged and to a certain extent arranged by me—I thought it was time for them (especially Fred, who I like and admire as you know) to get involved seriously in a political issue, involving people, movements, struggle, war even, and not just theory, if you see what I mean. The situation here is really desperate, and desperately tense: there is violence everywhere . . . I'm taking Fred and the others to the south tomorrow so they can see it with their own eyes.[121]

By 1982, in the wake of the Israeli invasion, the city's "once glamorous bay" gave way to bullet-riddled walls and former apartment complexes hollowed out by Israeli missiles. Previously a familial escape from sweltering Cairo summers, Beirut had by then become a second home, although one increasingly difficult to visit.

CHAPTER 6

THE GENTILE INTELLECT

Not begun at all till half done.

—JOHN KEATS[1]

As he witnessed them in 1970s Lebanon, the promises and failures of the Palestinian movement moved Said inexorably toward the role not simply of intellectual spokesperson but of active cadre. Already a skillful campaigner through his essays and speeches, he was considered by many of his friends unsuited for practical political work. From the mid-1970s onward, nevertheless, he found himself more or less constantly flying to meetings, debating colleagues, editing position statements, proposing policies, and building institutions behind the scenes. For what it was worth, the intensive FBI surveillance of Said revealed that, in the bureau's opinion at least, Said was the "unofficial liaison between the U.S. and the PLO" and that "his advice is sought [by Arafat] over that of other . . . representatives at the PLO Permanent Observer Mission at the United Nations."[2]

His political essays, beginning in the late 1960s but hitting their stride in the 1970s and 1980s, are not simply informational or emotive responses, or speculative reflections, but insistently pragmatic calls to action. Taken together, they became a blueprint for the movement, unpacking its otherwise unnoticed complexities, although a blueprint not always followed.[3] Several of his essays transcended their immediate use to become classics. For instance, no more penetrating a statement on the slippery character of violence can be found than in "Identity, Negation, and Violence" (1988). "The Essential Terrorist" (1986), similarly, is not just a complaint about how the term was used to blacken the PLO's name but the dissection of the obsessions of an entire era of British and American media. The historian Perry Anderson believed it the finest statement on the pernicious term "terrorist" to be found anywhere.[4]

For Said, being a professor complemented his political work. "You always got the feeling with Said," recalled JoAnn Wypijewski, a former editor at *The Nation*, "that he was containing quite a lot."[5] Having to prove his case again and again led to "a certain volcanic feeling" that was calmed somewhat by having an intellectual world into which he could retreat.

Said's political correspondence especially formed a prism through which to view the different facets of his life.[6] One was to be a mentor for those undertaking original research on Palestine, or uncovering media untruths about Iran, Iraq, or other parts of the Arab world.[7] Beginning in the early 1970s, most of his day was spent on the phone coaxing, cajoling, informing, planning, putting people in touch with one another to create a network of like thinkers. The archive bulges with letters from those not simply empowered by his example but seeking him out as a sounding board. Arab student organizations, dissident Jewish organizations, the American Friends Service Committee, the Arms Control Research Center, the ACLU, the Confederación Sindical de Comisiones Obreras, the Democratic Socialists of America, the European Coordinating Committee of NGOs (nongovernmental organizations), the Einstein Forum, Common Courage Press, the Abington Presbyterian Church—these are a fairly representative if random sampling of the organizations writing to him every day for three decades.

Another role was to outline research agendas by hectoring magazines, think tanks, foundations, and individuals to begin looking for x or y, expanding on this or that inchoate initiative. At the same time, after he had become famous, he was busy opening doors at elite institutions for scholars from the Middle East, or from the formerly colonized world, setting up publishing agendas for Arabic scholarship and literature (at Columbia University Press and elsewhere), helping found new departments, or expanding those already in existence. As he called in favors or applied pressure to get key allies hired, he created institutional support that did not exist before.

Recognizing the weakness of the Arab presence in the media because of its ignorance of American culture, he was an indefatigable proponent of setting up American studies programs at universities throughout the Middle East. At the same time, he agitated for developing Arab studies in the United States so that the media had a greater understanding of Arab culture. He repeatedly wrote to schools and universities in Lebanon and the occupied territories assuring them, "I am at your disposal if you would like me to lecture or teach or do anything."[8] In 1972, Mariam and he sponsored a book drive for the Birzeit school for girls in Ramallah and contributed subscriptions of *Ramparts* and *New Left Review*. A decade later, in the wake of the massacres of Palestinian refugees in Lebanon, the couple set up the Palestine Defense Fund. Along with counseling those in need, he welcomed others' advice in turn. For instance, in 1976, he wrote to Linda Foxworthy, the head of Our Health Center, a free community clinic, looking for a reading list and advice about how to set up community clinics in the occupied territories.[9]

Similarly, in addition to analyzing institutions, he also created them. For years he and Abu-Lughod worked to found a Palestine Open University in the West Bank. The first push came as the result of a UNESCO-sponsored feasibility study in 1979–80 under Abu-Lughod's direction. Modeled on its English counterpart, the distance-learning format of the Open University seemed to them perfectly suited to a dispersed and dispossessed population. Said was the main force in fashioning its largely humanistic curriculum, and he took on the task of fund-raising, writing letters to key Arabic officials in Qatar and elsewhere.[10] The Open University never materialized, but some of his important academic initiatives did. With Abu-Lughod and Fouad Moughrabi in 1978, he co-founded *Arab Studies Quarterly*, co-editing it with them for eight years. The journal became a key outlet for Arab and Muslim scholars and is a still-vital venue for hard research and dispassionate argument on the Middle East from an alternative perspective.[11] At the request of the former congressman James G. Abourezk, Said also served on the national board of directors of the American-Arab Anti-Discrimination Committee.[12]

Even outside the university, his political work involved documenting, ordering, and preserving a library of Palestinian existence. In a late interview, he announced that he had been compiling an archive of eight to nine thousand Palestinian photographs since 1948—a comment that recalled why, during the Israeli invasion of Beirut, he kept urging his family and friends to keep diaries, make drawings, write an account of what was happening.[13] Fact-finding was a key component of his organizational efforts. He pushed for years for a Palestinian census, compiled a lengthy profile of the Palestinian people for the Institute for Policy Studies, and (with Abu-Lughod) drew a succinct portrait of Palestinian history, land use, and demographics for a special subcommittee on international relations of the U.S. House of Representatives in 1975.[14] In September 1980, he wrote a detailed response to a request by the U.S. Department of State that he provide "observations and comments on that year's State Department report on Human Rights in Israel and the Occupied Territories."[15] The answers to this roughly thousand-page document were precise and frequently critical. They demonstrated not only a command of particulars but the energy and patience to savor the details and reproach the document's authors diplomatically.[16]

Never having joined political organizations before, Said made an exception with the Association of Arab-American University

Graduates (AAUG), founded in Chicago in October 1967. Set up primarily to combat anti-Arab racism, the AAUG (for well or ill) built its core around middle-class professionals rather than grassroots activists in the territories or temporary workers abroad in the Arab diaspora. The times were dire. The Nixon administration in 1972 launched Operation Boulder, which like the Patriot Act three decades later was intended to silence Arab Americans by threatening them with deportation, even as it turned a blind eye to anti-Arab discrimination on campus and institutional prejudice against critics of Israel. The risk, and it was keenly discussed, was that an organization of university graduates rather than everyday workers might seem elitist. But this fear was counterbalanced by its implied message: namely, that Arab Americans held advanced degrees, and that most of those who immigrated to the United States did so to study. Its primary purpose was to "provide knowledge."[17]

Not all of his comrades appreciated this conscious choice. Al-Banna, for example, begged him in the early 1970s to be less the cautious professor and more the intellectual *engagé*. Said responded defiantly: what the movement needed were more intellectuals and fewer activist types like Sami, whose "radical" meetings were essentially social gatherings. Much more could be accomplished by being "an influencer, a moral thinker in academia."[18]

In this spirit, some of Said's proposals for a more effective political activity took the form of lectures to the AAUG or articles for its working papers. At various times, Said acted as the organization's vice president and sat on the board of directors. And yet, to the AAUG's rule that "work—even the most banal—was to be evenly distributed," Said was the exception, which led to resentments. The organization's chronicler, Elaine Hagopian, admitted that she at first thought him a "dilettante." Her judgment changed as she began to notice the particular province he occupied in the formidable duo he formed with his right-hand man and co-conspirator, Abu-Lughod. If the latter was better at rallying support behind the scenes or pulling strings with Arab businesses and UN agencies, Said was the articulator of grievances, a walking "library exposing in full naked relief the vast colonial and Zionist institutional foundation."[19]

He did not come to the role naturally. Nubar Hovsepian, an activist from a younger generation who thought of Said like an older brother, remembered meeting him first at an AAUG event in Chicago in 1975. Said was already considered a luminary, but not yet the confident author of *The Question of Palestine* (1979). As the master of ceremonies at the banquet, he was clumsy and ill at ease, smart but not yet eloquent.[20] Invited the next year to present at the Council on Foreign Relations, Said arrived over-prepared. His thumbtack presentation, graceful and succinct, and clearly the result of enormous labor, stood out uncomfortably next to his Israeli counterpart's rote rehashing of all the old positions. A few questions, and the event was over. The emotional pressure and ridiculous disparity between his own care and his opponent's privileged ignorance overtook Said as he flagged down a cab. After bidding farewell to his friend, he threw up in the street.[21]

Despite his shaky debuts, the FBI sensed his importance. With the usual redactions, the 147 released pages of Said's 238-page FBI file make it clear that he was under scrutiny from the start, above all because of his activities with the AAUG. The FBI specifically targeted his chairing of the panel "Culture and the Critical Spirit" at the Boston convention of the AAUG in October 1971. Their surveillance was even more intense after the attacks at the 1972 Munich Olympics. His background and citizenship, his voting, banking, and credit records were all pored over with the shameful cooperation of informants at Princeton and Columbia as well as the Harvard Alumni Office. In May 1982, a special agent for the FBI in New York delivered a secret report to the director, William Webster, "saying that Said's name had 'come to the attention of the N.Y. [FBI office] in the context of a terrorist matter.'"[22]

The suspicions, based on guilt by association (Said had once corresponded with someone the bureau deemed subversive), proved groundless, and the case was dropped. Yet the file betrayed an obsession with Said's journalism and academic writing. The agents, for instance, in 1970 worked up a detailed analysis of a *Boston Globe* article by Said titled "Columbia Professor Blames Racist Attitude for Arab-Israeli Conflict." They later prepared forty-nine separate abstracts of his articles for *The New York Times*, arguing that his published opinions were dangerous, especially to Israel, and would become more so.[23] Their suspicions proved well-founded. Stanley Kurtz, an anthropologist at the conservative Hoover Institution, would testify before the House Subcommittee on Select Education in 2003 "that Said's post-colonial critique had left American Middle East Studies scholars impotent to contribute to Bush's 'war on terror.'"[24] That eventual triumph found its seeds in the 1970s, when the man who described himself as "not a joiner" had effectively joined, and largely led, the U.S. wing of the movement.

In 1977, he was elected an independent member of the Palestine National Council (PNC), the Palestinian parliament in exile, which usually entailed declaring a party affiliation. Although initially sympathetic to the Democratic Front (DF), a faction that broke from the Popular Front for the Liberation of Palestine (PFLP) in 1969, Said never joined the group, resolving to stay out of interparty fighting.[25] His flirtation with the faction, though, hinted at his political leanings at the time. The DF represented the far left of the Palestinian organizations and, although not explicitly communist, was Marxist in orientation. These two trends within the PFLP, related but organizationally separate, reflected Shafiq Al-Hout's observations on the deeply rooted character of communism in the history of Palestine, to which many Palestinians (although not Al-Hout himself) subscribed because it was the clearest way of expressing one's contempt for the imperial policies of the United States and Britain.[26] Similarly, the driving force within the Israeli Communist Party was almost entirely Palestinian. Fatah, the PLO's largest party, had always been for Said too nationalist and too prone to court political Islam.

Even at an early date, Said could see the threat of Islamic funda-
mentalism within the movement.[27]

These struggles with factionalism aside, he remained essential
to the Palestinian struggle. His tentative first efforts as the movement's main international spokesman were helped along by the
relative welcome of the Carter years. More openings for a Palestinian state existed then than before or since, and the AAUG, it turns
out, was exactly where the administration went to negotiate. Before
long, Said's Princeton classmate Hodding Carter III approached
him for a meeting with Cyrus Vance, then secretary of state. With
other AAUG colleagues, he met Vance and Undersecretary Philip
Habib on November 8, 1977. Just after the Egyptian president, Anwar Sadat, made his controversial trip to Jerusalem to address the
Israeli Knesset in November, Carter himself met with the group
on December 15, although Said was absent because of a speaking
conflict abroad. The following year, Said was urged by the State
Department to see if he could get the PLO to formally recognize Israel. In exchange, Carter promised to promote a two-state solution,
guaranteeing that the post-1967 Israeli-occupied territories would
become the national territory of the Palestinian state.

The entreaty was no doubt inspired by Said's sudden high profile in the wake of Sadat's unexpected, but also unmistakable, allusion to him three weeks earlier in a public speech as "an American
professor of Palestinian origin" who he felt would be the most
acceptable head of a Palestinian delegation at the Geneva peace
talks.[28] While Said took the offer from Carter to be a rare opening,
and transmitted it eagerly to Arafat, the chairman did not respond.
Vance had to go back to Said seeking reasons for Arafat's inexpli-
cable silence. Meanwhile, seeing the lay of the land, Said thought it
wise to downplay the Sadat overture. Without shutting the door on
it entirely, he explained in media interviews that he did not think
he was the best person for the job, not least because he lived in the
United States.[29] His better option was to remain in the background.

For almost four months, Arafat sat on the Vance proposal as

Said called up Al-Hout frantically to make sure it had been received. Finally, Said flew to Beirut personally to force the issue, but Arafat declined to accept the overture on the grounds that the Americans had always been unfair and that the PLO did not need their recognition.[30] Embarrassed and distraught, Said brought the unwelcome message back to the White House, later reflecting on the irony that Arafat would urge him in 1982 to intervene with George Shultz, then secretary of state under Reagan, to prevent the annihilation of the PLO leadership as Ariel Sharon's tanks rumbled toward Beirut.

IN HIS FIRST YEARS at Columbia, Said was known mainly as an innovative young Conrad scholar. His essays on such demanding French theorists as Poulet and Lévi-Strauss, or the formidable old-world polymath and philologist Auerbach, were noticed, but they remained on the sidelines until his foray into French theory with *Beginnings* (1975). He saw the book primarily as being about the role of the intellectual and the goal of criticism, and he reasoned that it would make or break his career. Initial impressions, then, were everything, which is why the coalition he fashioned there was so unusual, placing as it did Vico, the great early eighteenth-century Neapolitan rhetorician and student of Roman law, alongside Michel Foucault, the heir to Sartre and his nemesis.

To most readers, Vico and Foucault seemed a curious pairing. On all their preferred points of focus—language, history, agency—each was the other's antipodes. Vico considered the myths of antiquity forms of rational philosophy poetically expressed; Foucault, following Nietzsche, considered truth a mythological construct of language. Vico argued that *verum* (the true nature of a thing) can be known only by *factum* (making it), whereas for Foucault history had no agents and change came about through anonymous shifts of perspective.

Vico, an ardent humanist, called the "age of men" a stage of history when the lower classes finally come into their own and institute the first common law, breaking from the slavery that characterized the age of gods and heroes. By contrast, Foucault relegated "man" to a fantasy, famously comparing him to writing in the sand that the tides of time efface. Law itself for Foucault was suspect, for he tended to see the modern state as even more tyrannical than the absolute monarchies of the past, replacing the former's direct punitive violence with a "benevolent" discipline that penetrated every aspect of waking life, regulating our thoughts, sexual desires, and biological functions. Modernity had substituted surveillance and "education" for public hangings as it mercilessly subjected with the weapons of reason and moral guidance anyone living outside its norms.

Said's effort was somehow to weave these two disparate strands into a single fabric. He had described his thesis in earlier drafts of the book in just these terms: "finding a common language between warring or conflicting cultures and languages."[31] Every version of *Beginnings* except the one that was actually published, in fact, concluded with a long section dedicated to common language—an idea he took from Vico, who projected a "mental language common to all nations . . . the verbal community binding men together at the expense of their immediate existential presence to one another."[32]

His political education in Beirut, meanwhile, had altered his thinking about the possibilities of literature and left its marks all over *Beginnings*. He had already peered out from the protective cover of the European canon in 1972 by writing on the Egyptian novelist Naguib Mahfouz.[33] Now, two years later, he turned that knowledge to new use in an extraordinary essay that many of his readers overlooked, "Arabic Prose and Prose Fiction After 1948," which originally appeared as the introduction to Halim Barakat's novel *Days of Dust* (1974), set during the Six-Day War. Easily the defining literary essay of his early career, it brought rhetoric and policy together in a way that recalled the Swift book:

What concerned me [after 1969] was how . . . a language
could be formed—writing as a construction of realities that
served one or another purpose instrumentally . . . I also
wrote a longish study of Arabic prose fiction after 1948 in
which I reported on the fragmentary, embattled quality of
the narrative line.[34]

The view he developed here was severe and unromantic. Culling
ideas from Sartre's *What Is Literature?* (1948), he flirted with social, if
not socialist, realism. Such a view was scandalous in the academic
circles in which he traveled, and that might have contributed to its
being ignored. He would later return to Mahfouz in several prominent essays in the *London Review of Books* and elsewhere, trying gingerly to carry out the program initiated in the "Arabic Prose and
Prose Fiction" essay. Dwelling at length on Mahfouz's eminence as
the unparalleled chronicler of Cairene life, and an inspiration for
all the Egyptian novelists who came after him, he also considered
him too lofty and serene, an insufficiently critical fellow traveler of
Nasserism, and one of the first public intellectuals to support the
Egyptian-Israeli peace pact (for which he was in Said's view rightly
censured in the Arab press).[35] In private, Said referred to Mahfouz
in even less flattering terms as the Egyptian Bulwer Lytton—the author of ambitious but grandiose novels written in a stilted, pseudo-
Shakespearean language.[36] He was eager to move beyond Mahfouz's
"Flaubertian dedication to letters [which] . . . followed a more or
less Modernist trajectory," standing in stark contrast to other, more
neglected Arab novelists such as Jabra Ibrahim Jabra and Taha
Hussein.

The writing in the latest generation of Arab novelists, Said suggested, was more significant than that of the much-decorated Mahfouz both artistically and politically. The younger novelists were, for
one thing, more "mobile." Ghassan Kanafani's "disintegrating prose"
and multiple narrators, for example, captured the weightlessness of

life among the Gulf's Palestinian guest workers, forcing fate and character into a series of jarring collisions. Emile Habibi's "wildly experimental" humor in *The Secret Life of Saeed, the Pessoptimist* (1974) mixed Aesop, Dumas, and Walt Disney in a "free-wheeling" Palestinian take on the picaresque.[37] A deliberate formlessness, he pointed out, allowed these writers to escape the demands of inherited genres, staking out a territory indistinctly situated between essay, autobiography, and fiction. Each experimented with codes that shunned ironic distance to produce what Said intriguingly called a "well-articulated earth language." Said seemed to be looking for nothing less than a new shape for the art of the global periphery.

The novel arrived late to the Arab world, just as it did in Africa and Asia, but there were some advantages in that. In the West, writers easily distinguished between types of historical narrative—for example, Marx's *Class Struggles in France* (1850) and Flaubert's novel *Sentimental Education* (1869), both about the 1848 revolution in Paris, but the one a political critique and the other a novel. Western authors could therefore ignore the history of forms, because its distinction among genres was already assumed, which freed them up for more introspection and textual play, as in the West's foundational novel, *Don Quixote*, whose story is more or less about the reading and writing of novels.

The task of the Arab novelist, by contrast, was delightfully unconditioned by these prior determinations. Appearing to readers in Paris or London as primitive documentary realism, their fiction grew out of the special needs of Arab artists to articulate crisis as an urgent contemporary record. In this light, it was not just a flourish to call the writing of fiction a historical act and even, as the Egyptian literary critic Ghali Shukri argued after 1967, an act of resistance: "Writing was not and could not be free: it had to put itself at life's service."[38] Said in this essay fully assented to that view, drawing on popular Rihani stage comedies to describe scenes of verbal attack (*radh*), like human cockfights, and looked to the traditions of Hariri's classic medieval text, *Maqamat* (1237)—a compilation of stories in poetry and prose, basically a "swapping of yarns" that probed the everyday lives of the lower classes. Toward the end of the essay, Said brought together Arab and Marxist elements by turning to Al-Azm, whose writing illustrated best, he argued, the possibilities offered by these rich new currents. A "didactic, even pedantic, quality of Al-Azm's prose" should be seen, he urged, as working in the interests of precision, willing to take flak for not adopting a hypocritical self-deprecating posture or indulging in "absurdist pastiche."[39]

Beginnings was written with these conflicts in mind, itself a product of double strife in that it appeared in the year that the Lebanese civil war began and the Vietnam War officially ended. There it met head-on a public mood characterized best by the low comedy of Gerald Ford and a popular culture symbolized by the anti-establishment cynicism of *Saturday Night Live*. The political exhaustion following a decade of protest seemed unfriendly to his call to arms. Feeding off the unpropitious time, and along with his writing on Arabic poetry and fiction, he launched essays on Joyce as an anticolonial writer and on the shameful absence in U.S. fiction of novels about America's own empire, the country's defining theme.

Writing to the editor of the journal *Diacritics* two years earlier, he looked for camaraderie: "Do you feel, as I do, that there is an incredible wave of pseudo-writing sweeping the country, with every scholar and/or intellectual turning himself into a mini-Tom Wolfe, and everyone looking for glamor, and easy acceptance, and the latest ideas all thrown together?"[40] He sensed the "me decade" just over the horizon and in his own way looked to strike first. Although many missed the nuances, not everyone overlooked the book's Middle East subtexts. Hunting between the lines, Richard Klein, a professor at Cornell (where *Diacritics* was published), thought he detected "powerful intellectual tools . . . put in the service of Arab nationalist interests," as he put it in a bitter letter to the editors, later passing along the comment to Said himself.[41] The journal had paid tribute to *Beginnings* by dedicating an entire special issue to it, including a long interview with Said, and to that Klein objected because the book, rather deceptively from his point of view, was really offering people an attractive alternative to the received Judeo-Christian narrative.

As Said had predicted, the book was a huge success, reviewed everywhere by the who's who of the profession. The outcome, though, was in some ways unexpected. The book's vast and complicated armature made it tough going for most readers. His old PhD co-adviser Engel, for instance, threw up his hands, regretting that he lacked the philosophical training needed to understand the book.[42] A former student, now a well-known journalist, set out to read it but gave up, saying he just "didn't have the gene."[43] Tony Tanner, a distinguished professor at Cambridge and a dear friend, pleaded for sympathy: "There are parts of the book which my Anglo-Saxon mind simply can't bend to even when it tries with all its might (or mightlessness)."[44]

Said realized from the start that he would have to create an audience that did not yet exist if the book was to be fully understood. Most lit professors at the time, if they had a taste for theories of language at all, got it directly from the poets and novelists they were reading. The poems of Paul Valéry and T. S. Eliot, like the novels of Marcel Proust, were a great deal like theory in the sense that they were fictions about fiction, writing about writing and the snares of language. For their own part, the essays of Barthes, Foucault, and Derrida deployed the semantic feints and wordplay of poets and novelists, savoring the ambiguities and opacities of language—the sort of language that called attention to itself as though the words had created the authors rather than the other way around. In the *Diacritics* interview, Said even joked about this role reversal. The common prejudice, he quipped, is that the critic is to the artist as Howard Cosell is to Muhammad Ali, a straight man to the other's genius.[45] His point in *Beginnings* was to suggest that fiction and criticism were equally foundational and that criticism, not necessarily fiction, was where the deepest cultural recesses of society were laid bare.

In correspondence with his editors, he laid out his intentions

in plain English.[46] The book was to be a monument to comparative literature and a demonstration of what might emerge from the
study of English, French, Italian, German, and Arabic sources in
their original languages. Freud was also central, following on his
turn to Arab psychology in the "Witholding" essay. Its point of departure was to turn upside down the English literary critic Frank
Kermode's celebrated book *The Sense of an Ending* (1967), whose fascination with apocalypse and Bible criticism provided precisely the
wrong models for the present. "The issue of dependence and independence, or freedom and subjugation," was his primary concern,
and it would demand a new "framework for theory and method . . .
in the human sciences—that is, a framework based upon the real
world."

Originally written as twelve independent essays, the final version
of *Beginnings* took the form of six interlocking chapters in dissimilar
styles. In the first movement, he roved brilliantly among multiple
meanings of the word "beginnings" itself, arguing that the historical approaches to meaning in texts found in classical philology were
paradoxically more avant-garde than current fashions in theory
themselves. From there, he moved on to explore how various authors
had put the idea of beginnings to work, moving from nineteenth-
century realism (Charles Dickens's *Great Expectations* was his chief
example) to the modernist novel (Conrad's *Nostromo*), where realism
gave way to a mockery of history and social reform.[47] Throughout,
he pitted the current state of French structuralist and poststructuralist theory against Vico, to whom he dedicated the book's final
chapter, declaring it had been his destination all along.[48]

Beginnings's distinction between origins and beginnings was to
be understood as the difference between religion and secularity. The
opening words of Genesis, "in the beginning," mark an ontological
starting point. At one moment there was a void, in the next a world.
There cannot be a more precise and dramatic point of departure,
nor one more alien to human effort and understanding. An origin,
therefore, underscores the impotence of human endeavor anchored

by the divine Word. A beginning, by contrast, refers to what one does; it is not singular, for there are many beginnings, and one can always begin again. Said's intense interest in Vico—a contemporary, as Said liked to point out, of Swift and the Marquis de Sade—was rooted in this distinction. The point was to skirt, as Vico cleverly had, "religious notions of the creation," religion being "the most dangerous of threats to the humanistic enterprise."[49]

His often personal, even confessional, voice made the argument unpredictable as it seemed to alight on various volumes of the library, plucking phrases from far-flung books. The patterns of Said's curiosity were nondenominational but so historically varied as to be discordant with his supposed role as the cicerone of French theory if only because so many of his sources seemed chosen to destabilize its basis. In *Beginnings*, in fact, Said was clearly starting to move beyond the structuralism of Lévi-Strauss to the poststructuralism of Foucault, Derrida, and Deleuze, although without resting there either. He could not view language, as they did, as a medium of desire, of "meaning-effects" rather than knowledge properly speaking. He refused to follow them into that abyss, even while admiring the brio of their triumph in getting intellectuals to feel the dizziness of thought as its ground was cut from beneath their feet. His analysis was, to most ears, astoundingly novel and well ahead of its time. For it is easy to forget that most of these figures in French theory were still untranslated at the time. Just as he was introducing these theorists, all still living and at the height of their powers, to American readers, he was moving beyond them. Said instead brought their radical doubts about knowledge into harmony with philology—a critical school, as we saw, that represented just the opposite: confidence in the accuracy of texts and the possibilities of correct interpretation.

One of the key tasks of the etymologists, classical editors, and historical grammarians of philology, for example, was to establish the authenticity of texts from antiquity. For such scholars, the ur-text of a work was a kind of phantom whose proof could be found only indirectly by comparing the mistakes in later corrupted versions. In practice, a text was always patched together from surviving scraps, in other words, glued back together again with guesswork to form a whole. Over many centuries, paper rots, pages are misplaced, ink turns faint, redactors corrupt, censors destroy. The researcher never holds in his or her hand a physical object that can be called the original.

Said used this image to great effect, reminding contemporary theorists that, like them, older humanists had also questioned origins. What's more, both schools found origins "intransitive" on Said's terms (that is, inactive, effacing authorship). Unlike philology, though, theory overlooked that we are all driven by a desire to find those origins in any case, relying on the "intention and method" (Said's subtitle for *Beginnings*) of critics to reanimate these texts by force of will. For how can we know who we are if we do not know where we came from? In an unpublished note on Foucault from the period, he explored the stakes of this difference clearly:

> The more I . . . remove myself from my natural and habitual centers of gravity, the greater the chance of my grasping the foundations I am obliviously standing on . . . I am trying to find their origin . . . the constraint they impose on us; I am therefore trying to place myself at a distance from them and to show how one could escape.[50]

Reasserting in this way the active side of origins, he was brought back logically to beginnings, which the poststructuralists asserted were a myth and which the modernists believed absolute—an entirely new way of seeing without any debt whatsoever to the past. Said had no such confidence in absolute novelty. He did not wish to deny origins; he only wanted to escape their tyrannical effects.

This meditation on beginnings was also, obviously, a declaration of his own. Seizing on the term "philology" was perhaps his most unexpected move in this respect. For "philology" had always had the musty flavor of the study of Latin, Greek, and Hebrew as they were forced on students in nineteenth-century classrooms. In that sense, it recalled the pinched and plodding study of comparative grammar, etymology, and lexicography, and so seemed anything but apt for sorties into contemporary French experiments in speculative thought. Years later, Said joked that philology was the least "sexy" of any of the branches of learning associated with humanism.[51] All the same, he found it alluring. He saw in it what Vico had: the study of "all, or most of, human verbal activity," not just poems or novels, but law, sociology, economics, and history; a total art and a new science. His attractions date from his earliest teaching as a graduate student in Harvard's History and Literature program in the late 1950s, where philology was the theme of his courses even then. Late in his career, he flatly declared that his life project could be put very simply: to "renew[] the tradition of the great philologists."[52]

By saying this, Said was rejecting specialization. Moved by their hunger for all things verbal, philologists were not that far, he implied, from the spirit of literary modernism itself. For if philology's giant step was its generous taste for the expanse of knowledge, French theory's insurrection (as Said put it) might be summarized in a complementary, if different, way as "the irregularity and discontinuity of knowledge . . . its lack of a singular, central *Logos*."[53]

Rather than a complete rupture with the past, Said was looking for an originality based on *tradition*, paradoxically, and here Foucault stood in his way. Hence his ambivalence about the French thinker, who provided him with intellectual riches while raising doubts:

> The origin and the beginning are both hopelessly alien to, and absent from [what Foucault means by] the stream of discourse. (This is a structuralist position which, in the course of this book, I have implicitly been criticizing and modifying; here, however, I am presenting the position as they have argued it.)[54]

Such throat clearing hinted at why the book was such roundabout reading. In fact, significant dimensions of *Beginnings* echoed the "Witholding" essay very directly. Both dealt with problems of "representation" in the dual sense of depicting reality in words (mimesis, or imitation) and of speaking on behalf of a constituency, as in the phrase "political representative."

For writing to be faithful to reality, it must copy it. According to Said's logic, to "mime" reality gives too much authority to writing. It was to modernism's credit, then, that it exploded the pretensions of literary realism, not only because copying is never genuinely real but because the very effort places one forever in debt to the original, a condition that recalled the Arab dilemma vis-à-vis Europe. Drawing on Vico, Said imagined a past that was not in thrall to imitation, in part by rejecting the illusion that invention is ever wholly new and by adopting Vico's seminal observation that one can repeat in an original way. Every *ricorso* (return, retrial) is a new possibility in Vico's famous theory of historical recurrence.

He observed how in the Arab literary world, given the status of the Qur'an as a text orally recited by the angel Gabriel to Muhammad, there was "a dialectic between oral and written language near the surface of any text"—the oral (popular) struggles breaking through the tyrannical screens of the written (official). If in its own cultural myths, Arabic was immutable (the language of God), then the conflicts over meaning that animate the humanist enterprise in Western literature are impossible in Arabic, for in that language no one can be a genuine author. Authorship is always *elsewhere*.[55]

This impasse within Arab letters had haunted Said since graduate school, where in his student notes he wrote that because in Arabic there is no "mediating presence of formal verbal structures directly related to, and embodying the changing world," the result is "an unmediated ornamental" kind of writing. To this "there are," he lamented, "sad consequences."[56] Forced to "speak either like Westerners or like God," Arabs had found it impossible to create "a form [of language] that might reveal us to ourselves."[57] Foucault at the time seemed conveniently at hand to help him fashion the tools necessary for the enterprise of finding just such a form of language, but only one tempered by Vico.

BEGINNINGS'S BACKGROUND STORY MUST be seen, ultimately, as a collision of intellectual types vying for influence within Said. Vico was as foreign to Parisian fashions as it was possible to be. An irascible bookworm and Latinist, he occupied a humble position in Naples on the margins of Europe, then firmly in the grip of the Inquisition, looking with resentment northward at the center of intellectual life in the freethinking Netherlands—a refuge at the time for heterodox thinkers from throughout Europe, including Vico's alter ego, Descartes. He buried himself in a brand of scholarship that had hit its peak in the city about a century earlier, one whose philological techniques of literary interpretation were grounded in the study of Roman law.

What's more, his masterpiece, *The New Science*, was a hodgepodge of linguistic archaeology, iconographic readings of antique prints, and imaginative stories about the prehistory of primitive humans. The book appeared to follow no pattern, written as it was over a lifetime. Always arresting and often bold and boastful, it bound together axioms, apothegms, and heated marginal commentaries while oddly claiming for itself a "geometric" precision. All the same, Vico's story was far from drily archival. It was filled with tales of class conflict, insurrection, intertribal warfare, and accounts of the fall of empires. Its overarching moral could not have served Said's purposes better: that no one people, race, or region has priority in the story of human civilization. Nations (etymologically linked by Vico to the word "nativity") might have begun as clans, but they developed over time into states that were no longer based on racial privileges.[58] As against Foucault's idea of "discourse," which refers to an ideology imposed from above through the official language of institutions and the state, Vico was saying that what humans can know, and should spend more time trying to know, are the civic institutions that express our order and capacity to know.

In the mid-1970s, Said was far from a lonely renegade on Vico's behalf. The proceedings of an international symposium on Vico had been published in 1969, and in a meeting planned two years earlier, the Vico Institute sponsored a weeklong international conference called "Vico and Contemporary Thought" in January 1976 on the heels of *Beginnings*'s appearance.[59] Held at the Casa Italiana at Columbia and at the New School, the events of the conference were significant enough to be covered in *The New York Times*. Leading Vichians entreated Said and publishers begged him to produce a monograph, but he kept his distance, having no interest in making a name in Vico studies.[60] His fealty was more personal than that.

For just as the word "nation" has encoded within it the idea of nativity, so do the origins of civilization require a theory of "birth." For Vico, it was the word "gentile" that captured this sense of birth. Although the term colloquially refers to non-Jews, "gentile" for Vico conformed entirely to the Christian doctrines of his day regarding the primacy of the Jews in the story of God's plan. All the same, his argument throughout *The New Science* has secular implications. The word found its roots, Vico observed, in the Latin *gentes*—the extended families that grew logically out of the institution of marriage, one of the first acts of gentile religion. At the dawn of prehistory, bestial humans crept out of the forests to build the first cities, and those who led the way became rich and powerful, enslaving those who arrived later and who were forced to seek the others' protection. The gentiles, then, were forced to make *their own* history, inventing the institutions of marriage, religion, burial, and government because, unlike the Jews, their path was not foreordained by God.

Let the chosen have their pact with God, Vico seemed to say; for the rest of us, there is the largely untold story of mankind's struggle to recognize God on its own, and to use its fear of Him to build civilization by means of language, custom, and laws. It mattered a great deal that, like the *Muqaddimah,* Vico's book, although centrally about history, sociology, and comparative religion, was essentially a work of literary criticism. It offered a literary interpretation of the fragmented documents of the past in a very special sense. For it ventured an account of the birth of gentile history as one whose protagonists spoke only in poetic characters. Poetry, Vico discovered, was not at first the heightened or imagistic language of ritual or artistic performance but the everyday means of communication. Our ancestors thought and spoke in metaphors and images, and their first laws were poems. This historical pattern of movement from the age of gods to heroes and to men was cyclical in Vico's view, with much backsliding and returns to barbarism. In this sense, repetition could be more than mere mimicry. The intellectual discovers new relationships, "to use a favorite Vichian term, by refinding them (*ritrovare*)."

In tandem with Vico, Foucault's influence was overwhelming on many levels, stylistic, linguistic, and biographical. Apart from being the "central figure in the most noteworthy flowering of oppositional intellectual life in the twentieth century West," as Said put it, and part of a brilliant coterie that "we are not likely to see again for generations," Foucault was a nimble rhetorical tactician.[61] It would have been impossible for Said to have written *Beginnings* in the idiom he did without Foucault's ingenious manner of expressing himself, where writing seemed disembodied: an autonomous technical function in a field of political forces. For Foucault, Said explained, a "text does not simply record, is not the pure graphological consequence of an immediate desire to write." Rather, it "distributes various textual impulses."[62]

Foucault's bringing of linguistic notions into a critique of social institutions seemed similar to Vico's as far as it went.[63] But in the closing pages of *Beginnings,* Said complained that although Foucault had spoken persuasively about the rules of "transmission" in language—that is, its gathering of power by dispersal through institutions—in all this attention to the "systems of discourse" there was nothing regarding the world of corporate monopolies, advertising censorship boards, and the mass media. About these, Foucault had little directly to say.

Nevertheless, Said found it easy to identify with Foucault's early career writing on the sick and the insane, where he exposed how those on society's margins had been punished by the beneficence of a state that branded them as abnormal. He taught one of these studies, *Madness and Civilization*, in his courses in 1972.[64] He was equally drawn to Foucault's style, at once "ironic, skeptical, savage in its radicalism, comic and amoral in its overturning of orthodoxies, idols, and myths," and was generally in awe of the philosopher's inimitability.[65] Foucault did not just make points, but made them through form itself, piling up gerundives to make "doing" a form of "being," organizing ideas under sets of four examples rather than the usual two or three, proving a point by appealing to a past vacuumed of all causation and agency. Said reveled in Foucault's "anti-dynastic" thinking, that is, his insouciance toward established authorities while inventing his own unique patterns of order.[66]

As with Sartre, his attractions also had to do with the Middle East, and in particular with Foucault's pro-Palestinian bona fides. In a letter to Hélène Cixous in January 1973, Said exclaimed that he had just seen the *"appel pour les Palestiniens"* (Palestinian appeal) published that day in *Le Monde* on which she, Genet, and Foucault were signatories. He was "touched and grateful," complaining of the backwardness of the American Left on the issue: "For me the example of names like yours . . . all of whom I've read and none of whom, except yourself, I've met, is to invigorate and enliven our thought and determination."[67] After publishing his most penetrating essay on Foucault in the fall of 1972 ("Michel Foucault as an Intellectual Imagination"), he took the chance of sending it directly to the philosopher like a message in a bottle. In November, apparently surprised by the delicacy and thoroughness of Said's rendering of his project, Foucault sent him a handwritten note brimming with cordiality:

Upon my return from America, I found the article that you were willing to write about my work. I do not need to tell you how grateful I am for the effort you have made reading, understanding, and analyzing the stutterings I have managed to get out . . . I infinitely admire your intelligence, your mastery, and the rigor of your analyses to the point that on many points you have helped me clarify the nature of my own future work . . . I would like to find out about your work, and where it is heading.[68]

Flattered, Said returned the favor, dashing off a note about meeting Genet, who had told him to his surprise that Deleuze, Philippe Sollers, and Derrida, among others, were pro-Palestinian. He was delighted to learn that the "spirits" he had already admired held such progressive positions: "I add my Palestinian and political thanks . . . delighted to have grasped in your theoretical work a revolutionary trajectory that might contribute to the development of an Arab-Palestinian and revolutionary thought."[69] Foucault and Said did meet, although much later, but by then their solidarity over Palestine had frayed.[70]

As he worked to fit Foucault into the shape of Vico's thought, the alliance became more and more dubious. Still, he persevered. Yes, Said conceded, Foucault did stand with Heidegger's "bleak" view of human freedom, very unlike the resourceful *homo faber* (the human as maker) of *The New Science*. But, he pleaded, Foucault merely "absorbs" these bleak prospects; he is not a "partisan" of them.[71] Foucault may be a posthumanist, but he has a "humanizing" effect.[72] In time, the philosopher's oracular mode began to bother Said.[73] For a thinker who gave primacy to "impersonal rules, authorless statements, and disciplined enunciations" and who claimed authorship did not matter, Foucault seemed oblivious to the "'infamous' egos, including Foucault's own," of the French intellectual scene.[74] Unlike Vico, he ignored or effaced his precursors, making his ideas appear more original than they really were.[75] "What linguicity cannot do," he added, "is show us why structure structures." Eventually he was inclined to accept Levin's judgment that this body of thought was the "Alexandrianism of our time"—that is, an ornamental criticism like that of the scholars of ancient Alexandria, obsessed with form, bordering on mysticism, and reviling anything commonplace.[76]

As the years passed, building on what was already a mixed message, Said grew more openly disappointed in the French master. "I am off Foucault," he testily informed his correspondents.[77] Evaluating the work of a former advisee, he quipped that the student would have been better off reading "less Foucault and more Gramsci and C. Wright Mills."[78] He was particularly hostile to the argument of Foucault's "Truth and Power" (1977), where the philosopher denounced "universal" intellectuals who speak for political collectives like the proletariat, Algerian freedom fighters, or the French resistance, in favor of "specific" intellectuals who modestly keep to themselves.

In the closing pages of *Beginnings*, Said began to announce his solidarity with the kinds of intellectuals Foucault derided as "universal," among them the left historian Gabriel Kolko, who dedicated his *Main Currents in Modern American History* to the Vietnamese revolution "and the people who made it," and who dubbed the U.S. wars in Vietnam and Korea "holocausts."[79] His other endorsements at the time were equally notable—Harry Bracken, whose essay "Essence, Accident, and Race" was often on his mind throughout the 1970s and into the 1980s, and Jonah Raskin, whose *Mythology of Imperialism* (1971) touched Said deeply.[80] He later confided to the author that "no one, it seems to me, has come close to dealing with the issues you raised," an unexpected comment given the modulated voice of *Beginnings*, because Raskin had written in his book of "gangsters, conspirators and terrorists of the literary page," issuing "Wanted posters" for T. S. Eliot, F. R. Leavis, and Lionel Trilling and looking forward to the "burial of Amerikan [*sic*] imperialism."[81]

Ironically, a year after it appeared, *Beginnings* received the first Lionel Trilling Award at Columbia. Many years later, Said still felt that the book deserved elaboration and that its themes were richer than the treatment he had given them, especially when it came to Vico.[82] Among those whom *Beginnings* did not please was Levin, who, quoting Dante's *Inferno*, confessed that he had lost his way in Said's *selva oscura* (dark wood). Applauding Said's unique perceptions, he still wondered whether the figure of "beginnings" was a genuine idea or only what Roget's called an "abstract relation . . . a category of such generality that any context would give it another content." But he knew Said well enough to pick up on his double consciousness: "You are not so far from philology or historicality—or, thank God, so anti-humanistic—as on occasion you resonantly declare."[83]

Although Said often took criticism poorly, especially when his reputation was at stake, on this occasion he put up no fight. "Dear Harry," he wrote to him, "what in the book was perhaps a too polemic and dramatic 'open break' is now something I find myself embarrassed by. That is, I now find myself arguing against the kind of anti-historical and starkly theoretical position I seemed to be advancing in *Beginnings*." He was now at work, he proudly announced, on something that would please Levin more—something primarily historical, "even positivist," on "the fortunes of Oriental studies in the West."[84]

CHAPTER 7

FROM SAIGON TO PALESTINE

Phantom flyers of the sky,

Persian pukes prepare to die.

Rolling in with snake and nape,

Allah creates but we cremate.

—SONG OF THE SEVENTY-SEVENTH TACTICAL
FIGHT SQUADRON, U.S. Air Force[1]

Orientalism was an unlikely bestseller. Begun just as the Watergate hearings were nearing their end, it opens with a stark cameo of the gutted buildings of civil-war Beirut. Then, in a few paragraphs, readers are whisked off to the history of an obscure academic discipline from the Romantic era. Chapters jump from nineteenth-century fiction to the opera buffa of the American news cycle and the sordid doings of Henry Kissinger. Unless one had been reading Said over the previous decade or was already familiar with the writings of the historian William Appleman Williams on empire "as a way of life," or the poetry of Lamartine, his choice of source materials might seem confusing or overwhelming. And so it did to the linguists and historians who fumed over the book's success. For half of his readers the book was a triumph, for the other half a scandal, but no one could ignore it.

In much of the Middle East, its audience felt little other than rapture. "Here for the first time," explained Tarif Khalidi, "was a

book by one of 'us' telling the empire basically to go f— itself."
"We know your tricks," Said seemed to be saying, and he brought
to the table not just a critique of static, essentialized identities but
a whole theory of knowledge in the service of power. It "opened up
myriad doors, and a flood burst through."[2] As an indictment of English and French scholarship on the Arab and Islamic worlds, *Orientalism* made its overall case clearly enough. The field of Oriental
studies had managed to create a fantastical projection about Arabs
and Islam that fit the biases of its Western audience. At times, these
images were exuberant and intoxicating, at times infantilizing or
hateful, but at no time did they describe Arabs and Muslims as Europe's neighbors or contemporaries or as people facing the everyday
problems familiar in the West.

Over centuries, these images and attitudes formed a network of
mutually reinforcing clichés mirrored in the policies of the media,
church, and university. With the authority of seemingly objective
science, new prejudices joined those already in circulation. This
grand edifice of learning deprived Arabs of anything but a textual
reality, usually based on a handful of medieval religious documents. As such, the Arab world was arrested within the classics of
its own past. This much about *Orientalism*'s meaning, it seems, was
uncontroversial, although readers agreed on little else.

Most failed to notice Said's genuine ambivalence toward Orientalists. Clearly, they came across as the story's very culprits, the
scholars whose "known facts" gave scientific authority to a portrait
of the Arab and Islamic other. This was a story that revealed more
about the West's need for Arab villains than about the real peoples
living in the Levant, whose "brute reality," Said added, was "obviously
greater than anything that could be said about them in the West."[3]
On the other hand, were these scholars, not philologists, and was not
philology a way of reading and studying that he wanted to revive?

His assessments are, for these reasons, complicated. In essays
composed just after the book's publication (and originally intended for inclusion), he demonstrated his high regard for many of

the Orientalists he criticizes in the book, marveling at Louis Massignon, "a mind altogether of another sort of magnitude," admiring also Raymond Schwab's "ingenuously obvious motif[s]."[4] He was in part arguing that Arab scholars and dissident intellectuals had a lot to learn from the Orientalists' "images, rhythms, and motifs" and that he had every intention himself of taking notes on the evanescent stuff of style and presentation, quite apart from the awesome sweep of their knowledge.[5] In Said's mind, *Orientalism*'s success had everything to do with his having learned their lessons well.

Misunderstandings plagued the book's reception. It would be going too far, of course, to say the book was not really about the Middle East, or that Palestine did not lurk behind his accounts of nineteenth-century caricatures of Arab "backwardness" floated by the likes of Disraeli, Lord Cromer, and H. A. R. Gibb. On the other hand, the book was not only, or even mainly, about the Orient and its scholars. Those who had followed his writing before *Orientalism* were unlikely to miss that the book was a meditation on the degree to which *representation* is part of reality, not just its rendering in words. Rather than try to gauge the accuracy or inaccuracy of the Orientalists' accounts of Arab and Islamic life, he meant to dwell on the echoing inner chambers of representation itself.

Within that self-enclosed construct of gestures, terms, and statements, one would find signs of the mechanism by which ideas circulate, how they acquire authority, how they reinforce themselves untouched by the actual world. What many wrongly took to be a failed attempt to map the scholarly discipline of Orientalism as a whole (a project he had no desire at any point to realize) had an entirely different aim. So, if there was one thing *Orientalism* was about, it was that the humanities have political consequences, not only because of the weight and scope of influence wielded by Orientalist scholars but in the particular sense that literary critics (rather than politicians, journalists, or social scientists) study representation. Only they can explain how a mania like Orientalism takes shape and acquires, as he put it, "mass density and referential power."[6]

Even those left cold by his account of the coteries around Silvestre de Sacy or the antique verbiage of Flaubert's novel *Salammbo* sensed at least some of his underlying point: that the media, think tanks, and universities were witting or unwitting collaborators in the foreign policy adventures of their respective states. He had not invented the word "Orientalism" and was not even the first to explore the field's baleful effects, but he gave the term new resonance. The surest sign of its impact was the number of books (some of them longer than *Orientalism*'s 329 pages) written precisely to demolish it.[7]

JUST AFTER COMPLETING THE first draft on August 2, 1976, Said decided to give the book the title "Orientalizing the Orient."[8] The work that area studies experts later assaulted as the last word in nihilism was, in his own mind, nothing more than a fact-based correction of the record. His desire to be seen as a sober materialist was even clearer the year *Orientalism* appeared, when he invited Levin to be a panelist at the prestigious English Institute, which he headed up that year at Columbia. After the Welsh socialist and literary maven Raymond Williams and the former British Communist Party historian E. P. Thompson turned down his invitation because of scheduling conflicts, he turned to Levin, who, sensing the new affiliations, proposed to speak on the German Marxist media critics of the Frankfurt School.[9]

Knowing that *Orientalism* was likely to be thought iconoclastic, he found his friendship with Chomsky, another iconoclast, all the more valuable. The linguist's jeremiads had always made him controversial, and that gave him plenty of experience with bad press. Chomsky's *Intellectuals and the State* (1978), which appeared as a lecture the year before, was known to Said—a critique of the complicity of academic institutions with the Vietnam War. Said briefly considered co-authoring with Chomsky a book on spurious cultural portrayals of the Middle East, and *Orientalism*, it appears, began with just such a plan. Chomsky, though, was unable to see the project through because of other commitments, so Said forged ahead alone, with *Orientalism* the result.[10]

The MIT linguist lent a hand in other ways. He was the first to read Said's initial draft, reading the manuscript "virtually at a sitting."[11] He admired its penetrating analytical rigor but cautioned him to pay more attention to "the balance between analysis and direct quotation." His critics "will not be few," Chomsky added, and are likely to seize on the relative lack of documentation. "It might be useful to add something about the matter of racism, Orientalism and the Vietnam war—I think we've discussed it."

Begun in the aftermath of the Arab-Israeli War of 1973, the first version of the book was completed only a year after Nixon's last bombing campaigns in Indochina. It set out to portray the Middle East conflict as an anticolonial insurgency very much like the one in Vietnam.[12] Why, he wondered, were there no flag burnings or occupations of the Capitol in Washington on behalf of Palestine? Much like Goethe's *Weltliteratur* (world literature), which had been conceived in the wake of the Napoleonic invasions of central Europe, *Orientalism* was, among other things, a response to war.[13]

In early 1978, writing to Israel Shahak—a Holocaust survivor, chemistry professor, and chairman of the Israeli League for Human and Civil Rights—he described other motivations for the book. Cultural heroes in the West like John Stuart Mill and Matthew Arnold "not only did not oppose racism, imperialism . . . they actively supported it by lending their names and prestige to the dignity of the 'culture' and 'race' promoting evil." They knew exactly what was going on and said so, which made them prototypes "of the modern liberal intellectual," not only like the liberal apologetics of administration white papers and *New York Times* editorials, but their direct ancestors.[14]

Where Said wrote the book colored his outlook considerably. The brunt of the first draft was composed at a research center, oddly enough, dedicated to work in the natural and social sciences—the Center for Advanced Study in the Behavioral Sciences at Stanford in 1975–76.[15] Apart from an art critic or philosopher here and there, humanists were not typically welcomed among the scholars invited to the center. He was the lone literary critic in his cohort.[16] He happily reported to his friend, the British historian Roger Owen, in July 1976, "I have completed two long chapters (about 250 pages) already, and I am well on my way to completing the final section," which was, in fact, done by August of that year.[17]

The CASBS, moreover, is not a fellowship for which one applies. The selection committee's awareness of his crossover tastes did not come from an intriguing proposal in which he might have overcome initial impressions. Those selected are plucked out of the academic crowd by an anonymous list of venerables. One day a letter of invitation mysteriously arrives in the mail. What did the philosophers of science, sociologists, and psychologists in those rarefied circles see about Said that his later critics missed? We know that it was not his argument in *Beginnings* about Khaldun's and Vico's roles in the birth of historical sociology, because the initial invitation came in 1972–73 before that book appeared. Apart from his frequent appearances in *The New York Times*, his Manhattan connections among the literati, and his broad circles of friends among the academy's power brokers (Dick Macksey, Hazard Adams, Hayden White, David Riesman), there seemed to be two reasons. In his CASBS statement of purpose, after highlighting his plan to study "the rise of the discipline of Oriental philology" that "will result in a book," he added, "I am now interested in the contemporary Arabic novel, particularly the cultural and political role played by the novel."

The center apparently wanted to learn more about the Middle East. And, in the politically progressive interregnum of Carter's America—which, as we saw, led to the most promising White House openings for the PLO—Said's comparative radicalism was itself a draw for the open-minded researchers at Stanford. As he bluntly put it in his letter to Owen during his time there, he had no desire to transform himself into a Middle East expert; his message was rather more forthright: "I find the work on Orientalism to be a contribution to the struggle against imperialism."[18] It had simmered in his mind on lingering walks around Columbia's campus with Sami (a friend of Mariam whom she knew before ever meeting Said and his best man at their wedding). Why, he wondered aloud to Sami, were all the great works on the Middle East written by Western scholars?[19] Why are the Arab regimes so despotic?[20]

In 1975, after Anwar Sadat scrapped the blacklist that had been in effect throughout the 1960s, Said returned to Cairo with Mariam as a tourist in the summer, staying for a week in a hotel but disenchanted by the city's overpopulated lanes and filth. His home base outside the United States in Beirut was only slightly more comfortable in the months prior to his moving to Stanford, for the civil war had broken out that summer. The letters he received from friends while at the center all spoke of the "terrible carnage" in Lebanon, sympathizing with him, asking about his family.[21]

Despite writing to friends in England that he was "not enjoying the Center that much," the California weather reminded him of the eastern Mediterranean, and he soon discovered a Lebanese restaurant in Berkeley. His "high, tennis-playing spirits" made him sociable, particularly with women, in whom he found it easier to confide.[22] Jonathan Cole, later provost at Columbia, was a fellow that year as well and remembers Said being the center of attention, at ease with others in long and lively conversations over lunch.

With uncanny symmetry, one of Said's co-fellows that year was Yehoshafat Harkabi, the former head of Israeli military intelligence and a renowned Israeli Arabist. Deeply cultivated, a lover of Arabic poetry, "secret police like" in his quiet reserve, according to the art historian Svetlana Alpers, he described himself as a "Machiavellian dove."[23] Some feared the duo might prove combustible and start a Middle East proxy war at the center.[24] In fact, Said and Harkabi retained their decorum and if not warm were mostly polite to each other, often conversing about safe topics of mutual interest.

Recalling nonetheless their many "comedic, hurtful frictions," Alpers felt their relationship strained.[25] In the years before arriving at the center, Harkabi had evolved from a hard-liner (his "clever innovations," Chomsky drily observed, included "letter bombs in the Gaza strip in the 1950s") into an outspoken proponent for a Palestinian state.[26] Whether under Said's influence or not, shortly after leaving the center, he began to urge that Israel negotiate with the PLO and withdraw from the occupied territories to make way for an independent Palestine.

Fabulously literate, Harkabi arrived at Stanford having written a political dissection of the Arab psyche, *Arab Attitudes to Israel* (1972), based on the analysis of hundreds of Arabic books, newspapers, and radio programs. In *Orientalism*, he made an appearance briefly as "General Yehoshafat Harkabi," a man Said described as arguing that Arabs were "depraved, anti-Semitic to the core, violent, unbalanced."[27] Whatever its intentions, Harkabi's book belonged to a genre with which Said was already familiar and obviously meant to address in *Orientalism*.

Its clearest successor was Raphael Patai's *Arab Mind* (1973), an anthropological case study by a Hungarian-Jewish Orientalist who taught at Columbia and Princeton, in which Arabs were said to avoid all work that dirties their hands, to be preoccupied with sex, and to be indiscriminately hostile to outsiders. Probing the paranoia supposedly at the root of Arab perceptions, the book, which was very positively reviewed, eventually caught the eye of the Pentagon. In an essay for *The New Yorker* in 2004, Seymour Hersh revealed that it had become "the Bible of the neocons on Arab behavior," used by interrogators at Abu Ghraib to attack the weaknesses of Arab prisoners believed to be especially vulnerable to sexual humiliation.[28]

Even before spending time together at Stanford, Harkabi and Said had a tense history. Five years earlier, the Association of Arab-American University Graduates, of which Said was a member, held its annual convention in the Orrington hotel in Evanston, and by coincidence Israeli students based in the United States were holding their annual meeting only a few blocks away, with Harkabi their keynote speaker. Impulsively, the "good general" apparently led ninety of them without advance notice to the Orrington for a good-faith dialogue. The Popular Front subgroup to which Said was then sympathetic because of his friendship with Sami (who was a member) was the first to hear of the approaching delegation. Enraged by what he considered sheer "provocation," Said led the PFLP group to confront them. As they approached, Said shouted, "Provocateurs." After a tense standoff on the stairs, with Harkabi shouting over the noise that they had come in peace, the Israelis finally backed off and left.[29]

Harkabi and Said met once again in Paris in 1979 at Foucault's apartment for the *Les Temps Modernes* roundtable on Israel/Palestine. On that occasion, Said described him, with simmering reserve, as being in "the process of changing his position, to become Israel's leading establishment dove."[30] Ostensibly about nineteenth- and early twentieth-century Arabists, *Orientalism* also clearly had more immediate offenders in mind, and behind the philologist-scoundrels C. Snouck Hurgronje, Theodor Nöldeke, and Edward Palmer could be discerned the faces of Harkabi and Patai.

Orientalism's good forefathers, though, outnumbered the bad ones. In the years before arriving at Stanford, Said had diligently corresponded with the doyens of Middle East studies along with major critics of academic Arabism such as Anouar Abdel-Malek, who happened to be the cousin of Said's childhood friend Nabil "Bill" Malik. Abdel-Malek's "Orientalism in Crisis" (1963) had been seminal, for example, and the two men openly corresponded for years. He sent Said a list of his works after reading Said's précis for *Orientalism* ("Shattered Myths," in a collection of 1975), complaining that Said had not cited him.[31] This led to an amicable exchange in which Said wondered why Abdel-Malek had never referred to him either.[32]

Despite this initial touchiness, Said soon wrote to express admiration: "No one in our part of the world (i.e., the Third World, or the

Arab World) has the ideological intelligence and methodological grasp of civilizational and cultural issues that you have."[33] Some reviewers later charged Said with borrowing without attribution, but from his first essay on Palestinian issues of 1969 (in the Columbia alumni magazine) he listed his precursors very early and, more to the point, very plainly: Jacques Berque, Maxime Rodinson, Abdallah Laroui, Hussein Fawzi, Constantine Zurayk, George Antonius, and Albert Hourani.[34]

Said considered Berque especially to be one of the most gifted scholars of the century.[35] A French *pied noir* born in Algeria, Berque had been on Said's radar for several years, and they warmly corresponded from the early 1970s onward. Unlike his peers, Berque was fascinated by contemporary Arabic literature, departing from the conventional stance that anything of interest in the Orient was ancient and the East stagnant. Maxime Rodinson, whose *Islam and Capitalism* (1966) Said reviewed for *The New York Times Book Review* in November 1974 under the title "A French Marxist Explains the Mysterious Near East," was an intellectual of whom Said was "in awe."[36] Said relied heavily also on some Israeli sources, especially Shahak, whose "scouring of the Hebrew-language press" was invaluable to him, making public the Israeli policies, court decisions, or off-the-record utterances of political leaders intended only for domestic consumption.[37]

It was by way of *Orientalism* that Said most clearly emerged as a representative intellectual type produced by the Nahda, the nineteenth-century Arab awakening. Indeed, in his preparation for *Orientalism*, he consciously apprenticed in the work of Nahda intellectuals, joining, among others, Clovis Maksoud, the great Lebanese American pan-Arabist and ambassador to the Arab League (1961); Hourani, the man who created Middle East studies as a field in the English-speaking world; Mohamed Hassanein Heikal, a leading independent journalist in Cairo whom Said called "a veritable encyclopedia of information on Egypt and the Arab world"; Laroui's extraordinary *The Crisis of the Arab Intellectual* (1974); and Philip Hitti, whose *Islam and the West* (1962) positioned him, just as *Orientalism* would Said, to give informed testimony before government agencies.[38] In 1944, for example, Hitti argued before a U.S. House committee that there was no historical justification for a Jewish homeland in Palestine.[39]

Inasmuch as *Orientalism* exposed Western caricatures, it was joining a long and honorable tradition, including Mikhail Rustum's often forgotten *A Stranger in the West* (1895), whose author complained bitterly about the racist calumnies of Dr. Henry Jessup's *Syrian Home-Life* (1874) and even more slanderous *Women of the Arabs* (1873).[40] He systematically cataloged Jessup's techniques of selecting certain facts while ignoring others to pass judgment on an entire people.[41] If Maksoud's *Arab Image* (1963) dealt with similar problems of negative images as *Orientalism*, and Hourani's *History of the Arab Peoples* (1991) highlighted the Foucauldian watchwords "truth, power, and wealth," it was Laroui's Marxist sociology that provided the most points of contact. There Laroui dramatized the crisis felt by Arab intellectuals who had to settle for being mere "illustrators" of Western theory, on the one hand, or seeming aloof and cosmopolitan, on the other.[42]

The chief influence, though, had to be Zurayk, a man with whom Said spent long hours talking intimately at family gatherings. Zurayk was in many ways Charles Malik's alter ego. A secular Syrian Greek Orthodox Christian born in Damascus, a diplomat, and a revered educator at AUB, Zurayk wanted nothing to do with Malik's style of confessionalism. Mariam's parents and the Zurayks were so close that she grew up like one of his daughters, and the Zurayks and Saids lived only a few blocks from each other in Beirut. Spending long dinners in often combative conversation, they might not have had a marriage of minds. For one thing, they parted ways when it came to the greater influence of "Freud, Nietzsche, and Gramsci in my work," as Said later reflected.[43] But however much he chafed, he sought Zurayk's advice and depended on his patronage.

In February 1974, he wrote to Costi (as Zurayk was known in the family), prodded by Mariam's mother, Wadad, to see about the possibility of a permanent teaching position at AUB. Despite his disappointments two years earlier, Said reasoned that that university was "obviously the only place of any consequence for what I do" in the Middle East. But, then again, Johns Hopkins, Harvard, and Columbia were all recruiting him, and it was time to make a decision. He was at a turning point and tilting east: "Whatever knowledge of the Middle East I now possess is being pressured into the service of the American Empire, and why not put it to *our* service?"[44] The offer he eventually received was to become the head of research at the Institute for Palestine Studies, which was organizationally independent of AUB. At Mariam's urging, though, he dropped the plan. For apart from having no desire to live full-time in Lebanon, she feared his leaping into the quagmire of Middle East politics, giving up a tenured position he had worked for his entire life with no chance of return.

Zurayk's great study, *The Meaning of the Disaster*, argued for the basic unity of Arab culture, finding its cohesion in its spiritual vision, universal outlook, rejection of the relativity of truth, and openness to other cultures. Zurayk's impact on Said was perhaps most obvious in conveying the message that only the consummate scholar, free from personal vendetta, would prevail in the attempt to make these inherent qualities a conscious guide for action. Unlike Said, Zurayk scorned the literariness of Arabs as well as their absurd talent for expressing political fantasies in ornate language. Nevertheless, he too focused on *thaqafah* (culture) as the vehicle of social transformation.[45]

Ijtihad—personal witness, or simply the capacity to use one's own reason—was the principle Zurayk borrowed from his Muslim counterpart, the embodiment of the spirit of the Nahda, Abd al-Rahman al-Kawakibi (1854–1902). If Malik, like so much of the Christian Right of Lebanon, despised Islam and sought membership in Euro-America, Zurayk's question in *The Meaning of the Disaster* was how can we "transform Arab society from an affective, delusive, mythological and poetic society into a practical, realistic, rational and scientific one?"[46] Any project of national self-assertion, he argued, required understanding the West, not just insulting it, and above all learning from its science and technology. Said noted that Rodinson had observed that Zurayk understood and appreciated the importance of those Western Orientalists who had done so much to elucidate the great classics of Arab civilization, and "felt a certain twinge" hearing those words, since "I have often been accused in my book *Orientalism* of attacking every Orientalist [whereas] in fact, I was *not* as undiscriminating as people have imagined."[47]

Zurayk's natural reserve, though, fit ill with Said's more fully alive writing, in which emotion, humor, reminiscence, and anecdote all played a part. Guarded calm must have struck a sour note for a man on the fringes of the DF—Zurayk a reformer, yes, but still in the solid center of the Levantine liberal establishment. Now that he had become part of the family and was already an intellectual force in his own right, Said thought the possibilities for collaboration with Zurayk endless. But there were hurtful episodes and misunderstandings. As a fellow at the Institute for Palestine Studies (founded by Zurayk and Walid Khalidi), Said was in line for a position on its board of trustees when Wadad Cortas, Mariam's mother, died in 1979. He and others assumed he would take her place, but he was quietly passed over without explanation. Walid, he was later told, did not want him, and Zurayk had gone along.

After the snub, he kept his feelings under wraps, but when asked to contribute to a Festschrift for Zurayk in 1987, he promised an essay that never quite arrived. He later wrote two essays about Zurayk's legacy in which he gently criticized his mentor.[48] He wanted Costi to double down on the persona he had created: "one of the first and most brilliant Arab minds to know the West, not simply as a military and political power, but as a vast, complex, and deeply interesting culture."[49] The depth with which Costi had grasped this point about culture—roughly Said's advice to the PLO—made his avuncular presence vital to the peace process and to Palestinian aspirations, and yet at the age of eighty-one, when there was still so much he could do, he took himself out of the game.

In other letters written as he was at work on the book, he brought unexpected matters to the fore and, although not yet at the point of seeing the book's unity in the theoretical problem of representation, still confounded many later understandings about what *Orientalism* was trying to say:

> My thesis, although crude, is an effective way of studying the modern phase [of the East-West conflict]. I begin with a handful of coincidences, near the end of the 18th century: . . . the Napoleonic expedition in 1798, the consolidation of the East India Company, the birth of the *Société Asiatique* and the Royal Asiatic Society . . . the rise of comparative philology . . . and—not least—the distinction drawn first by Schlegel, but carried forward by Humboldt, between Indo-European and Semitic. For my subject is the history of British and French Orientalism in the near-Islamic world (including occupation of Algeria, 1830, of Egypt 1882 and so forth through the century) and its relations with political control . . . I argue [that] a certain view of Islam and the Arabs develops (this has a pre-18th century history, going back of course to the first anti-Islamic polemicists all of whom were Syrian Christians, ancestors of the Maronite zealots in Lebanon today) . . . It is the official culture itself, not just media distortions, which has complicity.[50]

It was a remarkable statement, for nowhere here can one find that substitution of the Middle East for the whole Orient for which he was later mercilessly attacked. North Africa and Indologists like Anquetil-Duperron are here clearly part of his original plan. Nor does he simply overlook Orientalism from the Middle Ages and Renaissance as critics later claimed. Instead, he deliberately excludes them to achieve a better focus.

For Said, the East-West divide was never etched in stone, some essential and unbridgeable gap, as authors like Rudyard Kipling and E. M. Forster had portrayed it. He wrote *Orientalism* precisely to contest that claim, in fact. The divide, as he saw it, was rather geo-strategic.[51] To have mastery over the Orient, Europe felt it had first to master the subject matter, and because knowledge is power, that mastery took the form of determining the essence of the Orient, its true inner character (as though there were only one). This was a project Europe undertook "because it could"; it had the resources, the global designs, and the geographic proximity to the Orient that for just that reason must be portrayed as the other.[52]

A good deal of this general case can be traced not to Arab sources at all but to works such as Raymond Williams's *The Country and the City* (1973) and the 1920s-era linguistic theories of the Italian communist intellectual Antonio Gramsci.[53] For years, Said kept perched on a bookshelf in his office a poster of his joint appearance with Williams at an event at the University of London in 1987. It obviously meant a great deal to him, for no other posters of the sort had this pride of place, memorializing one of their rare meetings toward the end of Williams's life when they took the stage to answer questions about screenings of recent films about their work. They had met the year before on the set of the British television program *Voices* along with Roger Scruton, the oddball conservative of the culture wars whose vituperative assault on the New Left had just appeared, singling out Said as one of its principal offenders.[54]

In later articles, Said described himself as Williams's acolyte, but at their meeting they were more like peers. Although wed to similar ideas, they displayed mutual reserve. At lunch with him and his wife before the taping of the *Voices* program, he described their apprehension, finding it hard to get beyond "friendly chit-chat."[55] Their different upbringings did nothing to allay the discomfort. Williams had been born into a mining community and was a lifelong socialist from the Welsh countryside, a novelist, and later a drama professor and media theorist. His experience teaching working-class students in adult education courses after World War II was no stopgap job but a political avocation. Despite the clash of pedigrees, they managed all the same to spend a long afternoon walking the streets of Bloomsbury lost in conversation after the event was over. Said had especially admired Williams's ability to remain "optimistic, hopeful, gentle and large" in the face of the *Voices* program's "inane babble."

Usually funny and charming in such encounters, Said held back, partly stopped short by the two men's clashing idioms, but also on account of his immense admiration. He was meeting for the first time a man whose work he had consistently taught in his seminars over the previous decade.[56] *The Country and the City* appeared in 1973 on the eve of Said's beginning work on *Orientalism,* and he later frankly admitted that the book had been one of his primary models when writing *Orientalism.*[57] Williams's convictions that culture was no mere aftereffect of the economy and that the government's techniques for social control still left a space "for alternative acts and alternative intentions" were exactly his own, although he credited Williams with having pioneered the effort.[58]

With demotic intelligence, Williams invented an approach to English letters that was sociological and personal at once. While involved in the large movement of ideas, he remained attentive to individual authors, seeing texts not as inert objects within the library but as elusive and transformative points of departure. In this, he departed from both the styles of Oxbridge and the parties of the Left then in the ascendant (on whose margins he hovered, while keeping his independence). Allergic to the technical vocabulary of the social sciences, he nevertheless pioneered a vernacular study of literature's sociological forms.

By the early 1970s, he had turned these traits into a masterpiece, and Said took notice at an impressionable moment of his own development. *The Country and the City,* Said observed, rivaled Erich Auerbach's *Mimesis* for its "majesty of structure and fineness of detail."[59] On at least two grounds, Williams gave aid and comfort not just to Said's assault on the English department old guard but to his Palestinian writing. For, unlike Foucault, Williams found systems of social control vulnerable: "by definition [they] cannot exhaust all social experience, which therefore always contains space for alternative acts and alternative intentions."[60] For Williams, it was the literary critic who had all the advantages for being conversant with the wiles of representation, alert, as they were, to the mischief that happens when reality is symbolically reproduced: "Representations are part of the history, contribute to the history, are active elements in the way that history continues . . . in the way people perceive situations."[61]

At first glance, *The Country and the City* had little to offer an exposé on Arab stereotypes, for it was about eighteenth- and early nineteenth-century English rural life as seen through the prism of country house poems—paeans, basically, to the estates of wealthy landowners. Behind this screen, though, Williams was interested in how the utopian idylls of the gentry had subverted the histories of terrain and landscape, superimposing on harsh rural conditions a distorting self-portrait.[62]

Nor was the anti-imperial thrust of *The Country and the City* buried.[63] Explicitly (and the gesture was unknown in English criticism at the time), Williams wrote of poems that bore witness to a transitional era of English social life in which a new kind of political control was being exerted over the colonies both within and outside the country. The war between rural and urban territories within England mirrored the antagonism between the periphery and the global metropolis, reproducing each other on a different scale. Williams captured the surprise, as Said would later, that the pervasive effects of empire on the English imagination had been so consistently ignored by critics and novelists alike, and indeed Williams's book was one of the first to right this wrong. For Williams, it is the critic rather than the poet who leads us out of euphemism to the crescendo of his argument: "one of the last models of 'city and country,' is the system we now know as imperialism."[64] Long before the rise of postcolonial studies—the field Said was said to have founded—Williams was already moving beyond his contemporaries in search of alternative traditions. Toward the end of the book, he looked to the colonies and former colonies themselves, addressing writers from

Turkey, Malaya, Kenya, and South Africa, who at the time were un-known to his colleagues—Yashar Kemal, Han Suyin, James Ngugi [Ngũgĩ wa Thiong'o], Ezekiel Mphahlele [Es'kia Mphalele], and others at the receiving end of a "brutal alien system" who managed to depict "unidealized" rural societies "from the other side." They are vital, he insisted, for giving us "a different and necessary perspective."[65]

By linking language and geography, Williams had helped give Said one of *Orientalism*'s central themes. But so too had Antonio Gramsci, a prisoner in Mussolini's fascist jails, one of the founders of the Italian Communist Party, and a culturally Catholic revolu-tionary in a twentieth-century milieu dominated by brilliant Jewish Marxists.[66] A geographic imperative shaped Gramsci's identity. As a Sardinian from Italy's rural South, he pursued his studies in Italy's industrial North, and so was seen there as racially and ethnically inferior. In "Some Aspects of the Southern Question" (1926)—an essay Said taught frequently in the late 1970s and early 1980s—Gramsci found in this clash between country and city an instance of what Said in *Orientalism* calls "imaginative geography," where land itself becomes a symbol of invidious cultural distinctions.

Even more important, for Gramsci it is language that defines territorial conflict. In Turin, Gramsci had studied under Matteo Bartoli, one of the era's most outspoken proponents of a school known as spatial linguistics. Bartoli and his circle had argued that language was the embodied record of migration and foreign con-quest, not only the "soul of a people," as the Romantics had it. In territorial conflicts, two idioms are violently thrust together and there forced to compete for prestige.[67]

With these sources in mind, *Orientalism* mobilized a series of spatial metaphors. One of these, "strategic location," referred to how an author is positioned in regard to his or her own writing; another, "strategic formation," to how works acquire more "refer-ential power" so long as they are positioned within a constellation of complementary works rather than standing on their own. Again, he was obsessed with learning about how certain texts gather force and influence whereas others do not. By "imaginative geography," then, Said was referring to the paradox that the proximity of the Middle East made the Oriental especially potent and dangerous in the Western mind. Precisely because of the region's adjacency to Europe, it could be more easily visited by travelers, colonial adventurers, and missionaries. Their experiences, then, had to be managed by a shared story that gave them their "true" meaning. Land may be the material stuff of geography, but ideas tend to dematerialize place, making neighbors appear distant. In the form of Sinology, Indology, and Islamic studies, Orientalism pretended to encompass more than half the world. How, he asked, can a discipline so proud of its attention to minute detail propose to cover so vast a cultural terrain except by filling in the blanks of an already imagined script?

AS SAID LABORED ON the first drafts of the book, the year was drawing to a close. Unlike other moments of his life (except when he was in graduate school), there were few dramatic encounters or political intrigues. He spent his days at Stanford mostly at work in his study. After he made a brief trip to Libya to give a lecture in the spring of 1976, the fellowship was at an end. His plan was, again, to return to Beirut, but with the airport bombed, he was forced to abandon the idea. He remained instead with his family in California, rendezvousing with his sister Jean and family before returning to New York in late August. Shortly thereafter, he took part as an invited guest in the Arab American symposium of the American Enterprise Institute in Washington.

Even before *Orientalism*, he was offered distinguished professorships from, among others, Berkeley and Johns Hopkins. In early March 1978, he planned a short trip to Beirut alone, but the Israelis invaded southern Lebanon as he was en route with Mariam in Paris, and so he decided to return to New York. He had arranged the stop in Paris in order to give a lecture on *Orientalism* at the Sorbonne, confessing to a former student in Cairo that after he had decided to give the talk in French, he was filled with "anxiety and dread."[68] His fears were unfounded, although his lecture's ecstatic reception gave no hint of the uproar to come.

At first, *Orientalism*'s reception was jubilant. On its way to being translated into thirty languages and destined to inspire a full-length documentary, the book was nominated for the National Book Critics Circle Award in 1978, losing out that year to the award's dual winners: Garry Wills's history of the Declaration of Independence and Maureen Howard's *Facts of Life*, a sassy autobiography of a writer's journey from love to art. Enviably reviewed, it took several years to become a scandal, even though Said had clearly laid out its controversial theses two years earlier in an article in *The New York Times Book Review*.[69]

In 1979, he met Dominique Eddé, a young Lebanese woman who would later become a novelist. At the time an employee at Seuil, *Orientalism*'s French publisher, she had read the book in French and wanted to promote it. They had a brief affair, but later resumed their rendezvous in 1995 after a long hiatus before falling out a few years later over her use of Said's name on a petition he had not endorsed. More international contacts and newfound friends gathered around him as the book's reputation steadily grew, and there was a constant stream of fan mail, exemplified by the philosopher and political activist Cornel West's letter of 1978, whose exultant tone caught the feeling among dissident intellectuals, especially intellectuals of color, all over the world: "You are on the frontier—a Gramscian frontier."[70] With Said already an academic sensation, his sudden global fame had the unfortunate effects that pride often bestows, and because everyone wanted a piece of him, he took advantage. His sister Grace complained of a new haughtiness, a "nastiness" in dealing with his sisters that was not evident growing up.[71]

Family relations were not helped along by his emotional distance from his brothers-in-law, for they had few interests in common and would not even look each other up on visiting the other's city. When there were shared commitments, as was the case with Rosy's husband, Antoine "Tony" Zahlan, over Palestine, other obstacles prevented real friendship. In this case, as a physicist at AUB with business interests in Iraq and Syria, Zahlan worked with governments Said could not abide. Jean felt also that his sharp tongue around them, although it could be written off as his "wicked sense of humor," revealed that he did not say much about his sisters because "not much was felt either."[72] From Said's point of view, his sisters never gave him his due. None congratulated him or complimented him on his accomplishments, and the resentment was exacerbated by his mother's having long played the children against one another. While they loved each other, they nonetheless found it difficult to be together.

Meanwhile, the book's detractors grew to be as invigorated as its champions. On November 10, 1980, Said replied to his old friend Sadik Al-Azm's roughly forty-page review of *Orientalism* just dispatched by him to *Arab Studies Quarterly* (which Said then coedited). Al-Azm took issue especially with Said's insinuation that Marx was just like the British colonialists in thinking the third world unfit for self-rule, a "travesty" of Marx's views, he thundered. Moreover, to trace, as Said had, the roots of Orientalist impulses back to Homer and Dante was to give credence to an unchanging Orient. What was *Orientalism* against if not this?

Entirely missing Said's theory of representation, Al-Azm exclaimed (like the social scientists who also missed the point) that it was not enough to claim that scholars got the Orient wrong. You had to show what an undistorted knowledge of Arabs and Muslims might look like. Said's epigraph from Marx, "They cannot represent themselves; they must be represented," from a book on the 1848 revolution in France, was dubious, he added. Marx, after all, was referring to *political* representation, the isolated, individualistic conditions of the peasantry that made it susceptible to charlatans like Napoleon III. Said, by contrast, used "represent" in the sense of mimetic representation in order to ride the book's motif about fantasies projected onto the Near East. It was, Al-Azm believed, a prefabricated charge and in the end a distortion.

Al-Azm thought *Orientalism* a little like the Islamic greeting "May you be protected from Shaitan [Satan]." In effect, Said had opened the door for his protégés to begin every argument with a ritual denunciation of Orientalists.[73] The book's timing was most unfortunate, he pointed out. At the very moment the Arab Left was trying to promote Western science in its struggle with religious obfuscation, Said "poured cold water" on that, supplying a gift to the mullahs who were just then railing against Westoxification. In a similar attack, Azmi Bishara, a Christian Arab then living in Israel and working at the Van Leer Jerusalem Institute, balked at *Orientalism*'s message because, like all ineffectual liberalism in the region, it fixated on art and culture just when the Left was prodding intellectuals into dealing with the hard material facts of political economy.

Thirty-six years later, then living in exile in Berlin and still stung by the exchange, Al-Azm moodily recalled the collapse of their friendship. As he remembered it, Said had written him a "nasty, virulent letter . . . really quite frightening in its unalloyed hostility and anger."[74] The letter itself, though, which still exists, was often more assuaging, a mixture of cajoling, even warmth as Said struggled to preserve their relationship while indulging in some savage digs. Sizing up Al-Azm's review, he conceded that it was "carefully worked out" and "makes a cogent and often impressive document," although it needed to be cut by half (not on the strength of his own demand, but that of his co-editors Abu-Lughod and Moughrabi). Said reserved his sarcasm for the letter's end: you have never really gotten past the Marxism of the Second International, whereas "I am a skeptic and in many ways an anarchist who doesn't believe, as you do, in laws, or systems, or any of the other claptrap that inhibits your thought and constricts your writing." In his bitterest moment, he charged Al-Azm with being a "Khomeini of the Left which is one thing my heroes, Gramsci and Lukács, could never have been."[75]

A month later, after receiving Al-Azm's refusal to make any cuts,

Said extended more than an olive branch, promising to argue at the journal's next editorial meeting to publish Al-Azm's review in full with his own response: "I am prepared to concede that *Orientalism* is not really a very good book, but I do insist that it contains, with a few exceptions, excellent readings and interpretations." He then proposed to meet him in Beirut in January, but the damage had been done and was later pushed beyond repair after Al-Azm, teaching in Syria and in the grip of the Assad regime, accused Said in a magazine article of working for U.S. intelligence. Despite the efforts of Khoury and Darwish, mutual friends who were hoping to patch the rift, the two men never reconciled.

Assaults on *Orientalism* came from four angles: first, from contemporary scholars of Arabic, Islam, or the Near East who believed that Said had recklessly ventured into a field whose demands on knowledge overwhelmed him; second, from Pakistani and Arab Marxists (like Aijaz Ahmad and Al-Azm) who felt that his East-West line in the sand, however militant, was undialectical and gave comfort to the Islamic Right, which was as paranoid as he about a ghostlike, undifferentiated "Europe"; and, most hurtful of all, from his mentors in Middle East studies, especially Berque and Rodinson but also Laroui, who thought his training in literature an obstacle to his grasping the sheer disciplinary variety of Oriental studies in practice. A fourth group was ensconced in right-wing think tanks or hostile media whose task was not only to undermine *Orientalism* but to erase Said's entire career. Their titles betrayed their contempt: Joshua Muravchik's "Enough Said" (2013), Martin Kramer's *Ivory Towers on Sand* (2001), and the pseudonymous Ibn Warraq's *Defending the West* (2007).

It did not help that the first Arabic translation of *Orientalism* was widely considered a disaster.[76] Never one to mince words, Al-Azm pronounced it "terrible" for trying to be too clever, like Edward FitzGerald's translation of Omar Khayyam, resorting to neologisms and bizarre syntax that made the text practically unintelligible.[77] The translator himself, Kamal Abu-Deeb, insisted that his rendering was well received in the Arab world, if a "bombshell" that broke all the rules, reinventing the very concept of translation.[78] Whatever the truth, it added layers of perplexity and resistance.

Confident about the logical supremacy of their case, few critics bothered to reckon with any of Said's philosophical points of departure. When, for example, Said claimed that critical positions first require a cultural space for their articulation, his detractors were puzzled, unused to dealing with such complexities. In their view, facts were simply facts, and the form of writing had no bearing on its meaning. Because they occupied a different cultural space, and were unwilling to enter his, their criticisms often missed their mark.

However incongruous their starting points, most of the critics of *Orientalism* kept coming back to the same kinds of points. Daniel Martin Varisco, an anthropological expert on thirteenth-century Yemeni agricultural texts, for example, claimed that Said's enthusiasm for the role of the amateur in intellectual inquiry only dressed up his own amateurism when entering his field half-cocked.[79] With such large gaps in his knowledge, it is no wonder that "there is no such thing as truth" for Said or that "his problem is with reality, not about it." Ibn Warraq complained, similarly, of Said's "endless postmodern jargon," the language of a man who, in the words of Robert Irwin, thinks "evidence . . . reactionary."[80]

Irwin particularly pushed the Saidian counterassault to the limits in *For Lust of Knowing: The Orientalists and Their Enemies* (2006). A student of Said's nemesis, Bernard Lewis, and a medieval specialist on the Mamluks, he mocked Said for suggesting that Orientalists could have lent their services to the empire when the truth was that no one cared what they had to say. Nor was there the coherence to the field that Said implied; it was little more than a baggy collection of devotees, bookworms, librarians, and eccentrics, ranging from "Nöldeke's Prussian jingoism, Hurgronje's colonialist approach to Islam, . . . and Margoliouth's crossword-solving approach to Arab texts."[81] He and Varisco together added that Said's constant recourse to literary examples from Flaubert, Dante, and Greek tragedy expanded the field of Orientalism to the point of meaninglessness.[82]

Even those who admired Said, like Rodinson, concurred with some of these accusations: "As a specialist of English and comparative literature, he is inadequately versed in the practical work of the Orientalists." The Lebanese Marxist Mahdi Amel—often called the Arab Gramsci—denounced Said's gratuitous jibes against Marx while again striking Al-Azm's note that *Orientalism* was guilty of attributing unchanging characters to entire cultures.[83] To make matters worse, some former students revolted. David Stern felt that a book with the title *Orientalism* should have dwelled on the Hungarian Jew Ignác Goldziher, the most important Orientalist of them all. Alan Mintz worried that Said missed an opportunity by not making the book about Jews and Muslims together, the joint Western fantasy objects of Orientalist discourse.[84] His old confidant Berque probably struck the most damaging blow when he implied that *Orientalism*'s thesis was not so much outrageous as commonsensical: "Obviously . . . every work, whether of science or art, reflects the conditions of its composition."[85] So it was not really news that scholars of the Victorian era reflected Victorian biases.

None of these critics, though, knew anything at all about Said's earlier work or how that related to *Orientalism*. And for some, there were personal scores to settle.[86] Irwin, for instance, left academia to write novels with titles like *The Mysteries of Algiers* and *The Arabian Nightmare*, and his profile was strangely similar, in fact, to that of Ernest Renan, who is unsparingly dealt with in *Orientalism* as a nineteenth-century popularizer and independent spirit with an unquenchable hunger for all things Oriental (Irwin briefly converted to Islam while studying in Algeria). Whether noticing these parallels between Renan and himself or not, Irwin pronounced *Orientalism* "malignant charlatanry." In 1982, Said had written to Westminster College, Oxford, complaining of Irwin's crudely ideological review of his book, his "scarcely veiled innuendoes about my racial origins."[87] Bernard Lewis, Irwin's teacher, whom Shahak contended was working more or less directly as an Israeli agent, was a renowned Orientalist at Oxford and Princeton, and the one with whom Said most prominently sparred over *Orientalism* in the pages of *The New York Times* and *The New York Review of Books*.[88]

More than a public drawing of swords, these encounters were often bitterly personal in part because *Orientalism* portrayed Lewis, along with State Department intellectuals like Fouad Ajami and, somewhat later, Daniel Pipes, as the modern descendants of the racialized scholarship his book set out to expose. They are, he was saying, the Renans and Carl Beckers of our day, no more no less. If Ajami was the native informant who interrogated the danger and fragility of the Arab psyche on television talk shows, Daniel Pipes—whom Said skewered in several of his post-*Orientalism* essays as a "scholar-combatant" in the service of the state—carved out his own media space by emphasizing the geostrategic threat of Arab wealth, and in 2002 (shortly before Said's death) he founded Campus Watch, a group that surveils and harasses progressive professors.[89]

It was inevitable that *Orientalism*'s fame would force a public confrontation between Said and his detractors. The definitive showdown took place between Said and Lewis on November 22, 1986, at a meeting of the Middle East Studies Association in Boston.[90] With the large assembly room packed, and six hundred more attendees outside, many had to sit on the floor. Said's animosity was clear from his mischievous humor before the event, conspiratorially whispering in Arabic to Assaad Khairallah and others at lunch, "I am going to f— his mother."[91] In fact, Lewis appeared to have lost the encounter, evading questions about his scholarly independence and jesting lamely about popular Middle East stereotypes. Because Western travelers to Arabia, he quipped, were obsessed by the unbridled sexuality of the sultans' harems and travelers from the East found Western women licentious, it is a mystery the two sides did not get along better. His debate second, the *New Republic* columnist Leon Wieseltier (one of Said's former students and an antagonist), proclaimed the evening "a nightmare for me." Bernard was his "brother from another Orientalist planet, saying outrageous things, I felt horrible, startled, because I am not like that. He gave the debate away."[92]

All seemed to misunderstand that *Orientalism* was about an interlocking system of images that made conquest easier by making the superiority of Europe seem natural. It was never about something so vulgar as this or that Orientalist being an agent of foreign occupation, although in the case of Hurgronje this too was literally the case (as Irwin conceded).[93] Massignon, for example (who is prominently and admiringly treated in *Orientalism*), worked directly for French military and espionage forces. That Said was supposed to have overvalued literature, another frequent line of attack, seemed equally ill-considered. Did readers forget his discomfort in *Orientalism* with what he called the "textual attitude"—that is, precisely the overvaluing of literature? His whole point about Orientalism's power and perfidy was based on others' misconception that the "problematic mess in which human beings live can be understood on the basis of what books—texts—say."[94] One cannot learn about sixteenth-century Spain by reading *Amadis of Gaul*, he bitingly remarked. On the other hand, Said turned the tables on his critics in another sense as well, foregrounding the very thing they took to be its weakness: "I am positive you will find literature to be the least represented of the Orientalist sub-specialities, for obvious reasons, since literature muddles the tidy categories invented for Oriental life by Orientalists. The plain fact is that Orientalists do not know how to read, and therefore happily ignore literature."[95]

As for the familiar charge that Said was a postmodernist who believed there was no reality, he went to great lengths in lectures on the eve of *Orientalism*'s publication to attack postmodernism.[96] He was equally unyielding toward poststructuralism, undermining the celebrated deconstructionist Jacques Derrida's claim that reality "is literally a textual element with no ground in actuality."[97] Said disliked Derrida's writing, in fact, and thought him a "decadent thinker, mannerish, a dandy fooling around," whose followers were involved in a kind of low-grade skepticism.[98] When he declared in an essay on Derrida that "there is no such thing as a 'real' Orient," he meant not that people do not exist in Jordan or Iraq, walk the land, feel pain, or die.[99] His point was simply that the reality "out there" is inaccessible without shared conceptions communicated by words. All reality for us, insofar as we are human and not gods, is necessarily mediated by language, even though that reality may be physically independent of our thoughts. This view would have been common sense to anyone schooled in literary theory in the 1970s. For physicists and sociologists every bit as much as for literary critics, reality acquires its sense and shape only by way of the concepts we form of it, and this acquires its social meaning only in language. In this sense alone, concepts are not secondary to reality but constitutive of it.

If Said had not believed that the Middle East existed independently of our ideas about it, he would not have spent the last chapter of *Orientalism* contesting the U.S. media's distortions of that reality in Palestine and Israel. The war that mattered, clearly, was over interpretation, and not every interpretation is equally valid. His strategy in this book, then, was not to paint a more accurate portrait of the Orient in its true essence, thereby repeating the misbegotten desire of his antagonists. What mattered was to demonstrate the indifference of the Orientalists to the Orientals' accounts of their own lives.

That said, not all of the book's supposed weaknesses could be explained away. Even Said's admirers found *Orientalism* at times unalert to contradiction, too willing to corral unlike thinkers into the same camp.[100] For instance, could any European on Said's terms ever work cross-culturally without an entirely dominating disposition? His sarcasm often overwhelmed those moments when he praised the Orientalists' sheer range of learning, and overstatements marred his argument, for example, when he claimed that "rarely were Orientalists interested in anything except proving the validity of these musty 'truths' by applying them, without great success, to uncomprehending, hence degenerate, natives."[101] Such a claim clashed with his own vignettes of the careers of Raymond Schwab, Edward Lane, and other scholars whose crime if anything was excessive rapture over the triumphs of the Arab and Islamic past. Wanting to stake out an indigenous Arab theory that owed nothing to Europe, Said downplayed the anti-imperial novelty of Western philosophers and campaigners like Michel de Montaigne, Denis Diderot, J. G. Herder, and Victor Schoelcher.

At times he sounded close to denying that any non-Oriental could ever write an account of the Orient without identifying with his or her own country's foreign policy. In one passage, for example, he declared that one is always a "European or American first . . . an individual second."[102] The risks of such a comment should have been obvious: there can no longer be an interpretation that is unswayed by one's identity. Nineteenth-century Europeans as a whole, he continued, were "almost totally ethnocentric."[103] Counterexamples to this bald charge were not hard to find, although he did not mention them: the ethnographer Leo Frobenius, for example, widely praised by black scholars for struggling to have Africa's dignity recognized; or the novelist Eduard Douwes Dekker, who passionately exposed the pillage of Java by the Netherlands in writing that explored many of the same problems of language and reality debated in *Orientalism*.

On the other hand, there was a method to the madness. Said's overstatements were designed to unleash a purifying indignation in his readers. Close friends observed that Said knew he ought to qualify his statements more, but he felt he had to be strong and definite for political reasons. Subtlety, generally, was his beat, but "he didn't want to get lost in it," as his colleague and friend Michael Wood put it.[104] Said raised this very point in *Orientalism* itself. The danger was that he might end up with "a coarse polemic" so unacceptably general "as not to be worth the effort"; on the other hand, he might lose track of the "general line of force informing the field."[105] While he warned against seeing Orientalism as "some nefarious 'Western' imperialist plot to hold down the 'Oriental' world," his presentation had to be just blunt enough to be heard. His politics of blame brought a number of scholars from the former colonies on board and had everything to do with the book's international success. As one hostile critic observed, "It became a manifesto of affirmative action for Arab and Muslim scholars and established a negative predisposition toward American (and imported European) scholars."[106]

Having single-handedly put an institution under a magnifying glass, *Orientalism* also gave safe haven to English department misfits, Latin American exchange students, and shipwrecked Arab activists in Middle East area studies. The U.S.-based Pakistani scholar Aijaz Ahmad, who like Amel, Al-Azm, and others was scathingly critical of the book from the left, put his finger on the book's immense demographic implications: it had opened the doors of academia by giving power to "the social self-consciousness and professional assertion of the middle-class immigrant and the ethnic intellectual."[107]

THE TWO BOOKS THAT quickly followed *Orientalism—The Question of Palestine* (1979) and *Covering Islam* (1981)—were essentially outtakes of the original project and with it formed a trilogy. In fact, his first design was for *Orientalism* to be a very short book that would appear side by side with a brief informational study on the Palestine question.[108] Not only would *Orientalism* grow into a tome, but *The Question of Palestine*, although primer-like in some respects, had much deeper theoretical ambitions. Its impact was more explosive than he could have predicted. Following its publication, his notoriety became obvious in a snide, if generally respectful, portrait in *The New York Times* just after the book's release: "Edward Said: Bright Star of English Lit and P.L.O."[109] With this billing, it was inevitable that some of its subtleties would be lost on its readership, although he did his best to lay out its premises simply:

> One of the enduring attributes of self-serving idealism . . .
> is the notion that ideas are just ideas. The tendency to view

ideas as pertaining only to a world of abstractions increases among people for whom an idea is essentially perfect, good, uncontaminated by human desire or will . . . When an idea has become effective—that is, when its value has been proved in reality by its widespread acceptance—some revision of it will of course seem to be necessary, since the idea must be viewed as having taken on some of the characteristics of brute reality.[110]

He went on to argue, though, that this adjustment to reality had never been undertaken by Zionism. On the contrary, it had always presented itself as an *"unchanging* idea" and had now acquired doctrinal solidity in the form of a state. As such, it was difficult to trace Zionism's "kinship and descent, [its] affiliation both with other ideas and with political institutions." The passions and partisanship of the Israel/Palestine question had partly to do with the creation of this tangled, portly, immovable myth of a biblical Zionism outside history.

Insistent, as we saw, on the material coordinates of struggle following his disappointments in Beirut, and having reassured Levin of his "positivism," he seemed to be saying here that ideas were more powerful than armies, guns, and land. In this crossover study, when the importance of making Palestine's case factually, as in a court of law, was paramount, he offered philosophy. For all the book's pedagogical gathering of data about Israel's prehistory, the genesis of Zionism as an ideology, British (and later American) imperial patronage, Jewish terrorist organizations, and Palestinian claims to the land, what held the book together was a point of theory. More than anything, the book was saying that ideas, images, and stories do not reflect reality in a secondary way but are its very ligaments. He repeated the claim often in different ways: "the massive architectural, demographic, and political metamorphosis" of Palestine by Israel took place first as a projection. Middle East reality followed upon, and was brought to realization by, images.[111] The implicit injunction was: and therefore we need our own.

The book's relentless clarity and patience—especially in its provocative central chapter, "Zionism from the Standpoint of Its Victims"—made it unlike anything the U.S. public had seen on this fiery issue, and as a result Said had a very difficult time publishing it.[112] The original house, Beacon Press, not only turned down the manuscript after long delays but refused at first even to give it back, asking for the advance to be repaid. Said had to rally his agent to apply pressure simply to have the manuscript returned. In a letter to Said, the editor let slip that the reasons for rejecting the manuscript were, in fact, political, just as Said had suspected: "What needs to be evoked is the Palestinians as a people rather than the crimes committed in the name of Zionism."[113]

By September 1978, after Simon & Schuster passed on commercial grounds, he decided to stop trying to publish it until the following year.[114] No Arabic press would touch it either, alarmed that his talk of the region's dismal model of the "top-heavy national security state" might offend Middle East leaders.[115] Zurayk called it a "breakthrough" but then added that some of its presuppositions were not acceptable "on our side" and feared it might even bring harm to Said in the Arab world.[116] In a packed lecture he gave at Teachers College at the time, Said was heckled from the floor. *The New York Times* feature of February 1980, prominently placed on the second page, insinuated that he was in the PLO camp, if unofficially. The attention made him notorious, and several of his colleagues tried to get him fired.[117] Meanwhile, "Auntie Wadad," Mariam's mother, wrote to her son-in-law after the book's appearance, saying, "I hope you will continue to write in realms that seem to be yours alone to explore. The Israeli[s] will bow their heads in admiration of the Arab mind only when such studies are available."[118]

Spun off from the Iranian hostage crisis of 1979–80, *Covering Islam*, which he dedicated to Mariam, put the idea (if not the actual word) "Islamophobia" into respectable circulation for the first time. More than in any other book, it was in this one that Said created a dignified standpoint from which an anti-Arab and anti-Islamic ideology of irrational fear could be recognized and diagnosed and seen as a pillar of American policy.[119] *Covering Islam* was not simply a reflexive response to hysterical media coverage during the Iran hostage crisis; the PBS film *Death of a Princess*, which aired on May 12, 1980, and which he analyzed at length in the book, was one of the most extreme examples. It saw itself very consciously as part of a new wave of critical work on the U.S. media, joining figures like Chomsky, Herbert Schiller, and Fritz Machlup.[120] He was also following the lead of Israel Shahak, to whom he had written two years earlier to thank him, saying that Shahak had inspired him to take up the problem of intellectuals and the state.[121] To that degree, the turn to media demanded not only a criticism of the information industry but a plan to use media more creatively. The plea to think beyond dead-end military strategies—"all the rage at the time" in Beirut, he lamented—went hand in hand with using film, television, and magazines to appeal to extra-governmental organizations such as churches, mosques, and universities.

He chided close friends in English lit circles for not knowing the media theories of anti-establishment radicals and policy-oriented sociologists like Edward Herman, Régis Debray, and Armand Mattelart.[122] In one of his most revealing essays, "The Limits of the Artistic Imagination" (1995), he took the media's "mind management" as a special case of the "distortion or effacement of the human (or inhuman) agency," a theme dear to him over the previous two decades.[123] His analysis was significantly strengthened by the fact that he himself was by then a media celebrity and would appear frequently over two decades on major television news and policy analysis programs: *Evans & Novak* (CNN), David Brinkley's *This Week* (ABC), *The MacNeil/Lehrer NewsHour* (PBS), *The Phil Donahue Show*, *The Charlie Rose Show*, and *Nightline*. His interlocutors over the years included Benjamin Netanyahu, Yasser Arafat, Jeane Kirkpatrick, Henry Kissinger, George Will, and Sam Donaldson. By the time *Covering Islam* appeared, that process was already well under way.

The book thrived in this milieu but also played with double meanings. His punning title—where "covering" referred both to addressing and to obfuscating—implied more at first glance to those in his field than outside it, skillfully combining the standard focus of the seminar room on problems of representation with a global critique of the information state. The two realms came together most clearly in his rendering of the typical literary term "narrative." Storytelling, as he explained in his most ambitious Palestinian essay, "Permission to Narrate" (1984), is not some luxury of the middle classes. All power relies on it. No one wins respect, or even exists in the eyes of others, unless they can tell their own story and be heard. The Zionists had Exodus, the heroic biographies of dashing generals with eye patches, or saintly existentialist philosophers like Martin Buber. The Palestinians had no story at all as far as the public was concerned.[124] Israel's imaginary congregation included anyone anywhere deemed Jewish, which gave it substantial leeway in the *non*-imaginary and depressingly real military occupation and invasion of its neighbors.

Far from simply decrying the lack of a Palestinian narrative, *The Question of Palestine* supplied one of its own, which he called "Palestinianism."[125] His people were itinerants, moving fluidly in, among, and between other peoples and long-established nations. These features were often used, in fact, to deny them a state of their own, because as nomads they lacked a clear national identity. Refusing to view Palestinians as victims huddled in squalid camps, Said fashioned a portrait of a people whose styles of movement and exchange evoked a loosely linked regional identity without strict borders. This was not their weakness, he implied, but their strength.

As a story, Palestinianism had certain advantages over Zionism. Even though it too was about a people's struggle for nationhood, it had come to stand for universal principles. First, it was the symbolic rallying cry for the entire Middle East. All non-Jews there felt the pain of the wound inflicted by Western occupiers in the form of Israeli settlers. Second, for anticolonial activists everywhere, it was proof that colonization was alive and well and the acid test of one's anticolonial convictions, because criticizing Israel usually meant sacrificing one's reputation or even losing one's livelihood. Third, Zionism's supposedly airtight divisions between Jews and non-Jews were not only impossible to establish in practice but an offense against the region's shared history, because they "inflated one, relatively immodest period of Israelite domination" in order to obscure "the teeming, diverse, multicultural history of Palestine."[126] Zionism's essence was exclusion, while Palestininism's was inclusion.

To arrive at this positive image, he first had to dwell on the negative power of institutions. The first step in social change, therefore, was critique, and this saying "no" to power was developed best and most thoughtfully, he argued, in the humanities. *Covering Islam*'s ambitions, then, were not limited to establishing that Islamaphobia was now the go-to myth used to justify America's imperial designs. The book was also a practical demonstration of the political force of literary theory (especially given its insights into narrative) to probe the logic of state and corporate truths. After completing the trilogy, he reasoned it was time to interrogate another institution with the capacity to manage minds—the university—and, by doing so, to bring the war back home.

CHAPTER 8

AGAINST FALSE GODS

Theory is a cold and lying tombstone of departed truth.

—JOSEPH CONRAD[1]

Working at the same time on three books and dozens of essays, Said felt tired by decade's end. Despite a number of victories, his friends had begun to notice his ill health and a creeping depression. Writing to a companion in July 1978, he complained of "a bad lingering case of viral pneumonia" and two cracked ribs because of coughing.[2] A string of invitations had fallen by the wayside over the previous five years because of illnesses he could not shake. Abdel-Malek was alarmed enough to address his poor health, begging him to exercise more and get some distance from the relentless pace of his life.[3]

Somewhat earlier, Said blurted out in a letter to Sami that he feared he had not long to live.[4] This gloomy self-diagnosis was, apparently, a tic of the Said family, who always feared the worst in health matters. No doubt this taste for melodrama was what Salman Rushdie had in mind when he affectionately described Said's hypochondria, remarking that "if Said had a cough he feared the onset of serious bronchitis, and if he felt a twinge he was certain his appendix was about to collapse."[5] No one then knew about the cancer looming (any more than Rushdie knew that Said's appendix had been removed in childhood), and as the novelist himself pointed out, when leukemia struck a little more than a decade later, he stopped complaining and simply bore it.

Orientalism's fame certainly added to the physical strain. With redoubled media exposure, he found the joys of lingering over texts for the sheer love of reading harder to come by. Distractions multiplied as he struggled to clarify and defend what *Orientalism* had managed to express, and for a stretch of twelve years (1981–93) he would not write another monograph, even though he tried. Apart from an informational anthology on spurious scholarship on the Palestine problem—*Blaming the Victims* (1988)—what he did manage were two of the most innovative outpourings of emotion and accusation in his oeuvre: a photo-text collage, *After the Last Sky* (1986), in many ways an impromptu book, and in 1983 a gathering of essays—most of them written in the 1970s—that would finally bring the Swift project to completion. The collection of essays, a study of the university's role in American society, would be the boldest, most radical, and most finely written book of his career.

With the coming to power of Margaret Thatcher in 1979 and Ronald Reagan two years later, the 1980s seemed most unwelcoming for a defense of dissident intellectuals, especially in the university, which both leaders were trying to defund. Gritty working-class films like *Alien* and *Blue Collar* gave way to Melanie Griffith and Michael J. Fox movies about twentysomething entrepreneurs. Shortly after a Palestinian settlement seemed possible under Carter, the new decade saw a wave of U.S. military invasions of upstart satellites in Nicaragua, the Philippines, Grenada, and Lebanon. Now well-known fund-raisers and media strategists like Richard Viguerie, Ralph Reed, and the Scaife and Olin Foundations took charge of America's rightward drift as the New Christian Right fought its way into the mainstream. With campus resistance no longer to be counted on in the new post-Vietnam mood, reactionary political attitudes began to look hip, symbolized by "me decade" pop music icons like Elvis Costello and the Police and a postmodern art scene that glorified corporate mass culture as a site of inventiveness and freedom.

These were the years, improbably, that *Orientalism* found its audience. As its message spread, it seemed less and less to fit the prevailing mood. The crusades against unions, government regulations, and social welfare launched by the Reagan White House, although resisted, were portrayed by much of the media as popular initiatives, and the effects of that story seeped into the university with every new incoming class. As the Right gained visibility while organizing election campaigns, taking over radio stations, and setting up think tanks, the cultural Left in the university seemed stalled, fighting a largely symbolic war with psychoanalytic or semiotic theories about sexuality, racial otherness, and the evils of any and all politics except the politics of representation. In August 1979 in a letter from Beirut, Said expressed guilt for his own part in complacency, plugging away at essays on Conrad and Swift as the Israeli military raided Palestinian refugee camps in the South, only forty or so miles away, abetted by Israel's fascist allies, the Lebanese Phalange.

Earlier that summer in June, he had managed a respite from the troubles by vacationing in Andalusia ("Arab Spain") with his family, a place that along with its tourist attractions was the medieval site of religious tolerance among Arabs, Christians, and Jews.[6] In 1981, given the ravages in Lebanon, he took his family holiday not in the customary hills above Beirut but in Tunisia, where, in the friendly company of the poet Mahmoud Darwish, he and the family stayed in "an enormous house that had a pool and a grand piano" that Said played every evening before dinner.[7] In early September, he was off to Paris for a five-day speaking tour.[8] With *Orientalism* as backdrop, the National Endowment for the Humanities informed him of his election to the New York Council for the Humanities.

Offsetting the welcome news, Israel had launched a full-scale invasion of Lebanon by the summer of 1982, sweeping through the South, eventually occupying Beirut, and putting many of his family members and friends in imminent danger. The Phalange threatened his sister Jean's family directly with the note "We know where you are," making it clear that they had to either move from their flat or be killed. His old friend and collaborator in the AAUG Abu-Lughod found shelter at Hilda's apartment after his own had been destroyed by an Israeli missile.

Lebanon had gone, Said wrote, "from bad to worse: the Israeli army lootings, and now the Lebanese army arrests of hundreds, perhaps thousands, of people on suspicion of something or other is terrifyingly similar to [the military coups in] Argentina, and yes, Chile. A new era has begun, and it doesn't bode well."[9] His role on the ad hoc committee to protest the Israeli invasion attracted some of his first real hate mail, and letters poured in calling him, among other things, a "commie sympathizer" and a "dirty, sneaky, Arab."[10] His and Mariam's Palestine Defense Fund received letters that included anything from five to twenty to fifty dollars, to used condoms in swastika-bedecked letters of extraordinary violence about "wanting to stick a fence post in your eye," as his grad assistant at the time recalled. Over the years, he routinely received such letters whenever an Israeli bombing campaign inspired his protest. For instance, someone wrote,

> You're a stupid son of a bitch. You are now under surveillance and two of your associates know it. They lie for us. You got that? Talk to him again about anything and you get microwaves. Microwaves to the head. It's a lot cleaner than bullets. Don't think you're too small for this. Look for cameras—you won't find them.[11]

In a few years, his office would be firebombed, a cigar left burning on his desk making a hole in the leather blotter, ink poured over his papers, and forty books stolen from his shelves.[12] "I was visited by the FBI and they told me it was one of the militant Jewish groups . . . They [the groups] then threatened me in the pages of the *Village Voice*."[13]

No one was ever arrested, although the FBI gave specific instructions to be on the lookout for suspicious packages after the massacres in Sabra and Shatila, two Palestinian refugee camps on the outskirts of Beirut in 1982.[14] The killings had been carried out by the Phalange with Israeli encouragement and protection. At about the same time, a stern woman dressed in army fatigues knocked at his office door on campus, then rushed menacingly past his assistants with the words "Where is he?" Apart from the president of Columbia, only Said's office had bulletproof windows and a buzzer that would send a signal directly to campus security.[15] His father's last words to him a few hours before his death were "I'm worried about what the Zionists will do to you. Be careful."[16]

Not all his enemies were Israeli. His sister Jean remembers him terribly agitated in Beirut after an interview in late 1979, genuinely fearing for his life. Rumors circulated that he was on a hit list.[17] Some militant pro-Palestinian factions interpreted him as denouncing armed struggle in place of diplomacy. To clear the air, in a letter to the journal *Middle East* shortly thereafter, he denied he had been fully understood.[18] A decade later, in a separate incident, while supporting the asylum petition of a Palestinian intellectual, he complained that he could not visit West Beirut for fear of the Shiite militias and the Syrians. For their own safety, his children were forbidden to visit their uncles, aunts, grandparents, and cousins in the wake of the incident.[19] Although Mariam visited Beirut with the children in 1983, and by herself the year after, it was out of the question for Said himself to travel to the city in the years just after the Israeli invasion of 1982. Adding to the pall was the news in 1983 that his mother had terminal cancer.

The baleful political turn both at home and abroad made

him yearn to get involved. By 1983, though, the movements on the ground in Lebanon were unpromising: "As to the Bekaa rebels . . . since I know the ringleaders there, I can't say I sympathize in the slightest either with their aims or their ways of attaining those aims. They're a bunch of stupid and brutal people."[20] At one margin, there was unthinking violence; at the other, indolence. After a trip to Tunis in July 1983 to visit the new headquarters of the PLO, which had been forced out of Beirut by the Israeli invasion, he was despondent at the inactivity of the organization, eager once more to do something concrete, "except I don't know what."[21] Making matters worse, he was prevented from participating in the historic PNC meeting in Algiers that year because his son, Wadie, then eleven, contracted osteomyelitis and fell gravely ill.[22] His son's death was a real possibility, forcing Said to stay behind.

It was logical, then, that when invited to the prestigious School of Criticism and Theory at Northwestern the previous summer, he chose to lecture on the "institutionalization and professionalization of literary studies," for it was the closest thing to policy he could actually affect. Obviously disappointed by his profession's clueless response to Reagan's assault on living standards, third-world liberation struggles (in Nicaragua, particularly), and the separation of powers, he grimly dubbed the era "the Age of Ronald Reagan" and saw in it a return of the Cold War.[23] Just as snidely, he referred to literary "theory" as "the new New Criticism," implying that the staid literary formalism of the 1950s had simply changed clothes in the 1980s, appearing now in the insurrectionary costume of deconstruction, Lacanian psychoanalysis, and postmodernism.

The same theories that a decade earlier seemed an intellectual adventure had given way to coded jargons of accreditation where the university was involved in little more than an assembly-line production of dubious professional "theorists." And he was also put off by its theatricality as gullible American professors courted their French counterparts—Jacques Lacan calling Foucault from a university office phone just to run up conference expenses or moving all the furniture around his five-star hotel room before demanding a whisky as he taught his seminar.[24]

He felt an equal, if somewhat different, dismay toward the academic field that welcomed these theories and solidified their hold on the U.S. and British university. This field, known as postcolonial studies, had entered the academic mainstream directly through the opening created by *Orientalism*'s runaway success. Seen by many as the field's founder, Said had no trouble applauding its efforts to bring more non-Western authors into college curricula and to challenge the subtle prejudices found in so much of the Western library. He also supported its attempts to diversify faculties in terms of ethnicity and national origin. But the sectarian conflicts of Lebanon, not to mention the lessons of Ibn Khaldun and Vico, had made him abhor fixations on personal "identity," which was rapidly becoming the field's reason for being as nonwhite students and professors fought their way into formerly closed positions of authority.[25] He had led the way, creating a movement larger than himself but one that was now outside his control and inspired by a body of thought he was busy rejecting.

By the end of the 1990s, postcolonial studies was no longer simply an academic field. Its watchwords—"the other," "hybridity," "difference," "Eurocentrism"—could now be found in theater programs and publishers' lists, museum catalogs, and even Hollywood film. It had become part of the general culture, partly due to his influence, which posed a problem because he denied that a *post*colonial condition even existed. "I'm not sure if in fact the break between the colonial and post-colonial period is that great," he said, and later confessed to a colleague, "I don't think the 'post' applies at all."[26] The duty of the critic was to show that colonialism was still thriving, yesterday in India and Egypt, today in South Africa, Nicaragua, and Palestine.

Ironically, despite his mocking phrase for the era, the Reagans sent him a Christmas card in 1987 wishing him "a joyous holiday season and a happy and healthy New Year."[27]

THE LONG STRETCHES OF time off from teaching while in Urbana, Beirut, and Stanford had given him space to write, but in December 1981 he declared with relief that he would be "resuming my teaching duties for the first time in about eighteen months." He welcomed the return to New York after the long absence spent making the film *The Shadow of the West*, which he wrote and narrated for the BBC's television series *The Arabs* and which aired in 1982.[28] Back to teaching full-time, and in a new mood of introspection, he managed to finish the book that had dragged on for so long and that highlighted in the boldest way possible the defining interests of the first half of his career.

The World, the Text, and the Critic was nothing less than a critique of criticism itself. But its portrait of the splendors and miseries of academic theories of language, psychoanalysis, and the body was no outburst. It did not erupt as a late response to the depressing turn in American political life. On the contrary, it took shape as a revenge on the disturbing undercurrents of that turn already visible in the more experimental 1970s.

In the view of his earliest grad students, *Beginnings*, for all its "ungainliness, . . . was a kind of teacher's book."[29] Even those who had never taken a class with him could witness in its pages his style of navigating the unscripted exchanges of a seminar room. For the second wave of his students, *The World, the Text, and the Critic* was a teacher's book in just this sense, but more sober and a good deal angrier. He put on hold the charms of *Beginnings*'s intellectual play, at least temporarily, in order to undertake the pragmatic task of describing the social role of the humanities. Audaciously, he sought help in this effort from Cardinal John Henry Newman, sharing with that Victorian divine a conviction that the university should free itself from implanting moral doctrines or preparing students for careers.[30] Nothing about education should involve "direct utility or immediate advantage."

He held firm to the principle that professors not agitate for causes. "In 30 years of teaching, I've never taught a course on the Middle East. I don't believe in politicizing the classroom," he wrote, and not even his detractors could deny it.[31] As during the antiwar demonstrations at Columbia, he took the view that the university should be a refuge from politics, even if one rife with political implications. *The World, the Text, and the Critic* set out to describe the most important of these, which had to do with the methods of the humanities, above all, as he presented a case for what they offered that the physical and social sciences did not.

As early as 1968, Said had already found his way to *The World, the Text, and the Critic*'s major point, that theoretical inquiries that appear to be about reality are frequently "an unconscious fantasy or cluster of fantasies of importance to our emotional welfare."[32] The Swift project, after all, had among other things targeted the mandarin style of letters in favor of direct speech; here, its avatar was to remain true to that intention, although the complexity of the modern university, and its shifting relationship to the state, were difficult to capture, and the sheer scope of the book's arguments was holding him up. A similar fate had befallen his long-planned study of intellectuals, which he hoped would rival master statements on the subject by Gramsci, Alvin Gouldner, and Debray, even announcing to his colleagues that his major study on intellectuals was under way.[33] In both cases, though, he felt that his original conception would demand more time than his other activities allowed him, and so reluctantly he let the intellectuals project drop.

In regard to *The World, the Text, and the Critic*, he pleaded in late 1979 with Maud Wilcox, his Harvard editor, for patience, saying he was working hard and felt he could get the manuscript to her by the end of the year. The delay, he explained, had to do with his work on a completely different book, which he had decided to write in lieu of the study on intellectuals. This project, which he related to friends was very close to being finished and already had a publisher, was dedicated entirely to Gramsci and Lukács. He was just then tying its loose ends together but did not want to leave "great swatches of the subject untouched," and so needed more time.[34] Between 1978 and 1982, his seminars oscillated between a course on British postwar Marxist thinkers (including Eric Hobsbawm, V. G. Kiernan, and J. D. Bernal, the celebrated interwar Irish molecular biologist, socialist, and historian of science) and a seminar dedicated to Gramsci and Lukács.[35] The first draft of that study had to be revamped, he explained, in order to acquaint himself with an immense amount of work on the two thinkers so as not to make "a complete fool of myself."[36] Of course, other forces stood in the way as well: lectures in Beirut and the National Endowment for the Humanities summer seminar on "modern critical theory" that he had organized at Columbia in 1978.

In every sense a prologue to what *The World, the Text, and the Critic* eventually became, the National Endowment for the Humanities seminar also demonstrated Said's shift to a more open embrace of left political lineages, one outcome of the partisan pressures he had faced crossing swords with the U.S. media. Said considered the gathering (which met sixteen times over an eight-week period) a united intellectual front against the state's and media's silencing of the critical faculty itself: "I was interested in trying to read a set of critics greatly influenced by Marxism, by linguistics, by formalism, and by historicism, [who] never turned methodologically what they got out of any of those schools of thought [into] dogmatic, mechanistic, cliché-ridden critical tools."[37] In this new attitude, he encountered thinkers—Theodor Adorno and Walter Benjamin particularly—who had played little role in his writing up to this point but would be central thereafter. Perry Anderson, the force behind the London-based international journal *New Left Review*, sent him the influential collection *Aesthetics and Politics* (1977) just after its appearance—a collection of debates among Marxist playwrights and philosophers (Bertolt Brecht, Ernst Bloch, and Benjamin)—along with Susan Buck-Morss's *Origin of Negative Dialectics* (1977), a study of Adorno's thought. The two books were important for moving Said's thinking more into the German philosopher's orbit.[38]

In 1983, Said at last made good on his promise to Wilcox to deliver his Swift book manqué. For years he had been trying to persuade her to allow him to jettison his original idea for the Swift study in favor of a more flexible and episodic book because he wanted "a different kind of audience."[39] As Swift had before, Gramsci now stood for him as the paradigm of a tension, in politics as in writing, between the immediate if evanescent now and the mediated if more formative *longue durée*. In letters, he had proudly announced that "two books of criticism" were about to appear, even though it was already clear that the projects were blurring into one.[40]

If he had set out in both books to critique sovereign systems (he specifically mentioned psychoanalysis and semiotics), then he was in the course of that endeavor "indebted to certain kinds of anti–Second International Marxism," as he put it, the ostensible subject of the second book. The Second International meant for him, as it conventionally did for others, a sort of clockwork, evolutionary Marxism of Europe in the late nineteenth and early twentieth centuries, positivist in its methods and eager to don the mantle of "science." The more supple and intelligent Marxist thinking that arose in the Third International inaugurated by the Russian Revolution was more to his liking. In other words, Lukács and Gramsci, to whom he was referring in the phrase "anti–Second International Marxism," were the logical precursors to *The World, the Text, and the Critic*'s rejection of "the new jargonism, hermeticism, and dogmatism proliferating everywhere" among the literary theorists he had himself inspired in an earlier phase of his career.[41]

Realizing by the early 1980s that he would never finish the Lukács and Gramsci book, he condensed the material into a single long essay that he intended to include in the book of essays, but in the end he withheld that too from the volume and never published it anywhere.[42] He might have felt that lauding communist intellectuals muddied the waters or that it would make his assault on the academy too rebarbative, because his criticisms were already so stringent. But he might simply have run out of time and felt he could not do the two thinkers justice. Despite differences between the harsher first and the more ameliorating final form of this explosive volume, its attack was clear, and the generals of the new New Criticism (as he had dubbed poststructuralist theory) fought back.

Diacritics, for example, which had so loved *Beginnings*, rejected a favorable review of *The World, the Text, and the Critic*, telling the review's author that they "wanted someone to come down hard on it."[43] Meanwhile, the editor of the French publisher of *Orientalism*, Seuil, while praising "the mélange of subtlety and violence that is for me the mark of your critical reflections," turned the book down for being too academic and too American.[44] The displeasure of both did not prevent him from snagging the prestigious René Wellek Prize that year, given by the American Comparative Literature Association to the best work in comparative literature, in part because of the elegance of its organizational principle. Said had not arrived at it easily.

He gave a hint of that principle by originally calling the book simply "Method," the title, he explained, that he had had "in my mind all along."[45] Rather than explore, as he had in *Orientalism*, how to compose a book that acquires gravitas and travels globally, he inquired why certain texts and ideas acquire authority based not on originality or even accessibility but on the basis of toeing a mainstream ideological line. More crudely, the question nagging at him was this: How, when it comes to the circulation of prestige, does it happen that a Derrida or a Richard Rorty commands so much attention when there are Ali Mazruis and Lucien Goldmanns around? All students are expected to read Descartes but are free to ignore Vico and Herder. Why is that? Dominant culture, he responded, owed its hegemony to "the sovereignty of systematic method."[46]

Clearly, one of the main casualties of the West's must-read list was Arabic literature, which he was busily promoting as he wrote *The World, the Text, and the Critic*.[47] Rather than bring deconstruction to the Middle East, his agenda was to introduce M. M. Badawi's study of modern Arabic poetry to *The Times Literary Supplement*. Having already discovered Naguib Mahfouz in 1972, he spent the 1980s getting him translated and published in the United States, a project made infinitely easier after Mahfouz won the Nobel Prize in 1988.[48] In response to his gentle badgering, Jacqueline Kennedy Onassis, then a senior editor at Doubleday, wrote to him appreciatively, finding it a "privilege to discover" the great novelist through his prodding and sending Said the bound galleys of Mahfouz's *Palace Walk* (1956), to which he had earlier introduced her, signing her letter in exquisite penmanship "with admiration for your work."[49]

In pursuing this question of method, *The World, the Text, and the Critic* was like an archaeological dig portraying all the earlier phases of his career. None of his books had been exactly tidy. All bulged at the seams, each with at least one runaway section. But here the imbalance was of a different order. The various phases of his mental life stood in the harsh light of a judgment on his earlier role as an apostle of the critical avant-garde. He had already started interrogating this very idea, wondering aloud to friends "whether such a thing as a critical avant-garde is a legitimate one, the kinds of problems associated with being a so-called advanced critic, and so forth."[50]

He included essays (on Raymond Schwab and Louis Massignon) that clearly belonged to *Orientalism*, then also two essays, one on originality and the other on repetition, that obviously belonged to *Beginnings*. The essays on Conrad and on Swift were afterimages, in turn, of the dissertation and the never-realized book. But the collection was held together by the weighty essay toward the end, "Criticism Between Culture and System," which not only was the longest and most uncompromising of the volume but originally bore the title given to the book as a whole. There he demolished the "new orthodoxy" established by the American reception of Foucault and

Derrida.[51] The other essays he had at first proposed for the volume—
"Bitter Dispatches from the Third World," a review of V. S. Naipaul
for *The Nation*, and "The Forms of Arab Writing Since 1948"—were
left out, because they did not contribute to the study of "method."

His correspondence with Wilcox gives the false impression that
he delivered the book, drastically revamped, as something of a grab
bag at the eleventh hour. In fact, it was the pinnacle of his life as an
essayist, as several of his friends and colleagues eagerly asserted.[52]
Assured of tone and boldly antinomian, the book showcased the
full range of his talents, seizing the moment of Reagan's counter-
offensive to appeal to his university colleagues to take responsibility for reversing the disaster. In a stormy meditation on the point
where teaching, political understanding, and speculative theorizing meet, he risked the censure of colleagues by putting bluntly into
print what until then he had kept to private conversation. Although
he had not been in regular touch with Arthur Gold for years, his
old friend wrote to applaud him for his "masterful" response to an
American scene that sees "French criticism as [an] invitation to but
another hypostasis of the Romantic imagination."[53]

The first idea for the volume, at least in the form in which it
finally appeared, arose at a conference in St. Louis in 1974, where
he gave a lecture titled "The *Word*, the Text, and the Critic." As he
moved over the next decade from "word" to "world," his task was
not simply to present authors to students, or to appreciate with
them their formal artistry, but to ask how texts circulate, how etymology and philology themselves inspire novels rather than simply make sense of them after the fact. The great eighteenth-century
experimental novel *Tristram Shandy* by Laurence Sterne, he pointed
out, owed its style and outlooks to the scientific inquiries of John
Locke, just as Balzac's imagination thrived because of his borrowings from the naturalist Georges Cuvier. Tugging at a thread from
Beginnings, he unraveled the status of literary works as independent
creations and, to a degree, as the by-products of scholarship itself.
In the specific case of English literature, one of his main points was

to remind readers what Schwab had already shown: namely, that much of literary Romanticism was the direct offspring of Orientalist scholarship, not the other way around.

In part, *The World, the Text, and the Critic* was taking aim at the public's uncritical esteem for anything scientific. He joked that the fixations of university administrators on technological gadgets were like "car repairing."[54] When still in Urbana, he wrote of the "horrid affair" sponsored by the center there, "Science and the Human Condition," which convinced him after sitting through the interminable bluster "that the human condition is hemorrhoids."[55] Now, sobered by the task at hand, he allied himself with the great sociologist Pierre Bourdieu, a friend of his, to find relief from the sciences' "symbolic tyranny."[56]

Instead of limiting himself to describing the different methods of the sciences and humanities, he delved to the roots of the false antagonism between them. The sad fate of critical thinking, he suggested, mirrored a larger problem in the culture. His diagnosis of that problem was clearest in the essay he did not include in the volume but that expressed the book's intentions perfectly, "Opponents, Audiences, Constituencies, and Community" (1982), one of the most important essays of his career. ,

In "Opponents," he argued that the mystification of science lay at the center of the Reagan era's culture of military Keynesianism. Its organic intellectuals worked hard to make citizens think that their side's progress, as against their inferiors' backwardness, derived from a self-regulating market. Rationality was palmed off as manageability, and democracy as productivity and competence.[57] In the university, this onslaught was met with unseemly awe. Factions of the old guard mimicked the sciences by worshipping the elaborate "febrile machine" of Northrop Frye's summa, *Anatomy of Criticism.* For a time, this book reigned supreme in English departments, considered the last word in literary science for having mapped every possible component, in every combination, of the grand machinery of the literary imagination.[58]

Meanwhile, in a distinction without a difference, youth in their French reverie stormed Frye's barricade but offered little better, serving up a new scientism based on delusions of precision in the clocklike workings of linguistic structures. As Said described it, the obsession of literary theory with structuralism was in the end a version of the social scientific world of "'value-free' functionalism" with its "cult of behaviorism and quantification."[59] The living world of contestation, debate, and ideological conflict was thereby erased in favor of the illusion of an objective certainty achieved at the expense of human choice. For all its achievements in upping the intellectual ante, literary theory had sunk into a discourse of "occultation and legitimation" by adopting the appearance of scientific methods in a pseudo-artistic wrapping in order to win legitimation for itself in a culture that valued nothing else.

This line of thinking, he complained, relied on ignorance of actual scientific procedures. Historians of science, he pointed out, like J. D. Bernal, Thomas Kuhn, Georges Canguilhem, and Gerald Holton had struggled to make the public understand that the circumstances of scientific work are "notoriously imprecise determinants of that work in ways that humanists (and even scientists) haven't adequately dealt with."[60] Scientists relied on the speculative leaps often considered the humanists' weakness. There were interesting thematic similarities, in fact, between aspects of *Orientalism* and Thomas Kuhn's *The Structure of Scientific Revolutions*, a book that Said frequently touted, including in the "Opponents" essay. Both zeroed in on the role of convention in knowledge, where scientists and critics are carried away by already known habits of inquiry, leaving whole areas of their practices unexamined.[61] In just this spirit did the question of "method" enter his narrative.

Said had written a great deal by this point, and very irritably, about the way Renan, *Orientalism*'s scholar as villain, annexed himself metaphorically to the work of Cuvier, where Semites and Semitic were fictions "invented . . . in the philological laboratory."[62] For Renan, the sciences were revelatory in an almost religious sense, "*telling* (speaking or articulating) definitively to man the word [logos?] of things," as though things had a language only science could read. These classificatory motifs borrowed from the natural sciences produced what Said disparagingly called a "philosophical anatomy."[63] Inasmuch as theory demoted human beings, he considered it, along with the general scientism of the media and government, "an assault on thought itself."[64]

If he playfully taunted his friend Sami, a computer graphics technologist, to read more novels, he regarded Chomsky's judgment that the humanities "lack the intellectual content of the natural sciences" to be naive.[65] His essay on Schwab in the book especially explored this methodological showdown between the humanities and the sciences. The former had an intellectual voracity that freed them from the pretentious austerities of science's supposed rigor. Schwab embodied the talents of the scientist for digging up endless detail with "vertiginous minuteness" even as he offered what the scientist could only dream of—a "romance of ideas" within a "tremendous cultural drama."

Schwab wonderfully represented the humanist's generous awareness, combining vast erudition with a free-associative movement to which Vico had given the name *ingenium*—the principle of "joining together into one things which are scattered [and] diverse."[66] This deliberately general, cross-disciplinary mode of attacking questions was held up in *The World, the Text, and the Critic* as offering certain advantages over the sciences' tendency to zero in on discrete parts of nature without regard to the social whole or the tainted perspectives of individuals, believing it could in this way unravel nature's mysteries. The roving intelligence, often dismissed as dilettantism, nevertheless allowed the critic to see broad connections that experts always miss.

AS A TEACHER'S BOOK, *The World, the Text, and the Critic* built itself out of the assembled data of massive lecture notes. It was not only Said's strange couplings of unlike figures but his obsessive discipline in accumulating biographical details and quotations that leap out in these notes, where he would often copy out extended passages longhand, pasting them onto pages filled with line diagrams, interlarded commentary, and insertions of marginalia. At times, they appear as drafts of an essay, the paper plain white, then ruled yellow, then ruled white torn out of a spiral binder combined with scribblings on hotel stationery. Friends doubted him when he claimed that his best ideas came from teaching, but anyone who has read his class notes between 1964 and 1984 would find it persuasive.[67]

He wrote a piece titled "History of Critical Theories" in 1971, for instance, that never saw publication. Dozens of pages typed or scribbled on Shelley, Plato, and medieval laws of interpretation give way to an extended study of Plato's *Phaedrus*, where he is excited by the philosopher's model of philosophical virtue. Rather than writing "by way of pastime," it is better, Said thought, to be involved in "the art of dialectic. [For] the dialectician selects a soul of the right type." A few pages after these quotations, he pens a note to himself: *Phaedrus* is about a language that, "because rational, invites the play of the intellect, takes time, is *polysemous*. Not directly one."[68]

This was no random quotation. In the early 1970s, he explained the rationale for his seminar reading list to students as being made up of writers who are "anti-dialectical in the sense that dialectics as Hegel used it provided for a final transcendence and/or resolution."[69] Hegel, it turns out, did not actually believe that thought could be stopped in its tracks this way, or that it arrived dutifully at its destination, at which point the world suddenly ends, being freed from all antagonisms between self and other, consciousness and things. But it is certainly true that France's Nietzschean philosophers ascribed this view to Hegel and that Said, who read very little Hegel, subscribed to the view as well.[70] Once in conversation with the novelist and political activist Tariq Ali, he jokingly asked, "Have you actually read any Hegel, and don't lie," as though no one but a masochist would bother.[71]

This conflict between resolution and the "play of the intellect" lay behind his original plan to make the chapter on Gramsci and Lukács the centerpiece of *The World, the Text, and the Critic*. He pitted the emphasis on history and time in Lukács against Gramsci's interest in geography, although, as he posed it, the difference was hardly an either-or.[72] He asked a friend, "Have you ever read Perry Anderson's 'Components of the National Culture'? I was trying to develop some themes out of that." Anderson, a British Marxist historian, had charted there the deadening effects on British culture of the wave of conservative intellectual immigrants to the U.K. after World War II (among them, Karl Popper, Lewis Namier, and Ludwig Wittgenstein). Said seemed to be saying that the pair of interwar thinkers offered a corrective to the apolitical thrust of American intellectual life, emboldened, moreover, by its own wave of right-wing or pro-establishment immigrants (among them, Edward Luttwak, Henry Kissinger, and Ayn Rand).

He had been frustrated for some time that Lukács was not widely known in the Arab world and that there had never been an Arabic translation of his masterpiece, *History and Class Consciousness* (1923), one of the twentieth century's most influential works of philosophy. Generally, even those third-world intellectuals who knew Frankfurt School authors like Herbert Marcuse or the anticolonial theorist Frantz Fanon knew next to nothing about the debt both owed to Lukács, the main figure in what Merleau-Ponty had called "Western Marxism."[73]

When the *New Statesman* asked Said to participate in its "Influences" column, he was emphatic about the centrality of Lukács and Gramsci to his thinking.[74] In the very short list of books he identified as his major influences, he cited *History and Class Consciousness*, Gramsci's *Prison Notebooks*, George Antonius's *Arab Awakening*, and Marx and Engels's *German Ideology*. When it came to films, he chose Gillo Pontecorvo's *Battle of Algiers* and Bob Rafelson's *Five Easy Pieces*; in music, Wagner's *Siegfried* act 3, Bach's *Goldberg Variations*, Berg's *Lulu*, and Beethoven's *An die ferne Geliebte*. Curiously, one found no mention of Swift, Auerbach, or Vico, and no Conrad either except in the form of one novel, *Nostromo*. This did not mean that they had ceased mattering to him, only that the trauma of the previous decade had given him a preference for those with more unyielding credentials when it came to combating system philosophies.

Essentially, "On Critical Consciousness: Gramsci and Lukács" brought to life what he later called the "Italian materialist tradition that runs from Lucretius through to Gramsci and Lampedusa," identifying it as an important corrective to the German idealist tradition of Hegel.[75] Grand philosophical systems, he suggested—and this included French theory—acted very much like religions in their "canons of order" and their effort to "compel subservience or to gain adherents."[76] He titled the final chapter of *The World, the Text, and the Critic* "Religious Criticism," counterbalancing the introduction, "Secular Criticism." Why, he wondered, when American politics were being dismantled by Reagan had a trend of academic criticism arisen that could speak only of unthinkability, undecidability, and paradox?[77]

Signs of the crypto-religious impulse were everywhere, from the kabbalistic readings of deconstruction to Frank Kermode's eschatological investments in Bible studies as a model for literary criticism.[78] Bookstalls at academic conferences were filled with titles like *The Genesis of Secrecy*, *Kabbalah and Criticism*, and *Violence and the Sacred*. Surely there were better models from the past such as Francis Bacon's *New Organon* (1620), which waged war on the "social idols of the cave, the tribe, and marketplace"—that is, the warping prejudices of one's circles of like-minded thinkers, inherited cultural norms, and the profit motive.[79] His writing in the volume was more than usually passionate in part because its two central thinkers mirrored opposite sides of his personality. For Lukács, it was combativeness, *Sehnsucht* (yearning), and a feeling of lost transcendence; for Gramsci, a geographic imagination and a refusal to allow anything morbid into self-awareness. Lukács roved in deep philosophical waters; Gramsci, the sacrificial soldier and organizer, found his inspiration in a revised and more humane Machiavelli.[80]

He might have been at odds with academic theory, but he continued (literally) to share a stage with its leading lights, including Julia Kristeva, Louis Althusser, Lacan, Barthes, and Foucault.[81] Despite his polemical edge at times, he usually softened the ferocity he actually felt. When Jean Stein, the editor of *Grand Street*, for example, asked him to review a book by the celebrated postmodern firebrand Jean Baudrillard, he revealed his contempt. "Listen, I read this piece finally by Baudrillard . . . It's hard to say he's got too many ideas. None of them is quite an idea. They're all sort of like little burps." Publishing this essay would be a disservice "unless you want to put it there as an example of the satiety to which French thought has sunk or risen depending on your outlook."[82]

He was equally unyielding about Kristeva, a Bulgarian émigré to France and an icon of the cultural Left. In his obituary for Raymond Williams in *The Nation* in 1988, he recalled the taping in London of the BBC's television program where he had first met Williams. The organizers had wanted balance, he explained, so he and Williams were there apparently to represent the Left, David Caute the middle, and Kristeva (along with "the rather odd reactionary philosopher" Roger Scruton) "constituted the Right."[83] *The Nation* eventually cut the passages on Kristeva, ostensibly to improve the column's focus, where he had complained that she constantly interrupted the discussion with "an insistent affectation that was intended to dignify her threadbare clichés."[84]

The World, the Text, and the Critic unleashed the full force of his sarcasm. Phrases like "the last word of high Theory still hot from the press," a "priestly caste of acolytes and dogmatic metaphysicians," and "the jaw-shattering jargonistic postmodernisms that now dot the landscape" flowed from its pages.[85] Although as a writer he reserved his greatest wrath for Middle East pundits, even the language of those attacks borrowed suggestively from his scolding of the academy. In interviews, he could find no better way to respond to the *New York Times* correspondent Judith Miller (later of Fox News), except to say that "she has a disdain for facts worthy of the airiest deconstructionist."[86] One of his great nemeses of the 1980s, Joan Peters, a freelance journalist, rehashed the long-standing Zionist thesis that the Palestinian people were an invention and therefore had no claim to the land. Her bestselling book *From Time Immemorial* (1984) was lauded by U.S. newspapers but ridiculed almost everywhere else (including within Israel) for research so shoddy as to be called "ludicrous" and a "forgery." Said's acidic refutation, aptly titled "Conspiracy of Praise," hammered away at the necessity of "facts," how they are arrived at, why they matter, and how she abused them.[87]

Academic Marxists were not spared either. Said found the blithe deployments of postmodernism in Fredric Jameson's book on Wyndham Lewis a "positive nuisance."[88] The pet notions of theory, he complained, were passed along by Jameson as uncontroversial truths. A year earlier he had sent Jameson a letter expressing his impatience with his purely textual Marxism: "I wish you were more active politically, but perhaps you are and I don't know about it. There's a lot to be done."[89] He thought that Jameson's view of the world was essentially nostalgic, and that his work resembled Thomas Aquinas's scholastic theology. Jameson, he said, consequently acts as though he had lost something and keeps trying to find it in "history with a capital H."[90]

He knew he was disappointing old mentors like J. Hillis Miller, who had opened so many doors for him earlier and who found *The World, the Text, and the Critic* wrongheaded when it established ties between academic theory and the culture of Reaganism.[91] Said, however, doubled down, writing to a publisher that while still admiring Foucault's "agile mind," he had now passed from "becoming a champion of the oppressed to a great Establishment figure . . . taking general anti-Left positions on such matters as Soviet dissident figures like Solzhenitsyn and Cuban dissenters."[92]

As for the postcolonial studies he was supposed to have founded, he neither engaged in their debates nor had much truck with them, except when he indirectly chided one of the field's leaders, Homi Bhabha, for "trashing" Fanon or when he lamented the tragedy of identity politics in his essay "The Politics of Knowledge."[93] Pressured from two sides, he pushed back in both directions. Soundly critical of the so-called vanguard, he at the same time advised publishers to reject manuscripts by old New Critics like W. K. Wimsatt for being filled with "the musings of forty and fifty-year-olds."[94] As theory journals pushed back, he was getting it from more traditional humanists as well. For instance, Said assembled a volume of Erich Auerbach's selected essays and planned to write the introduction, but Auerbach's family vetoed the idea, adamant that someone so "politically committed" not be associated with the estate.[95]

After the Last Sky, Said's only other single-authored book of the 1980s, opted out of these conflicts and sidestepped an unwinnable war by changing the subject.[96] He had always marveled at phototext collage as a genre and wrote glowingly about John Berger's collaboration with the Swiss photographer Jean Mohr in *Another Way of Telling* (1982), which Said reviewed with great enthusiasm for *The Nation* in December 1982. Berger, an unconventional art historian and Booker Prize–winning novelist living in rural France, had with Mohr perfected the genre in *A Fortunate Man: The Story of a Country Doctor* (1967) and in *A Seventh Man* (1975), about European migrant workers, creating new ways of seeing the offbeat, nonconformist, or dispossessed of society.

Accompanying Mohr's unsentimental black-and-white portraits of farmers and Eastern European émigré artists, Berger's evocative and often enigmatic texts resisted all poetry, irony, or double meaning. Often about laborers, Berger's prose deliberately worked its subjects over in a language made to appear as ordinary as possible. Admiring these traits, Said defended him against the charge of being too earnest, too showily proletarian, but chided Berger as well. As a great observer, Berger settled for brilliant storytelling. What he lacked, and what Said sought to add, was "aesthetics with action."[97]

It was, at any rate, primarily Berger and Mohr who inspired the project, and Said's own experiment with the photo-text form was to train his eyes on the everyday lives of Palestinians in the occupied territories.[98] He kept his models' sensibility, refusing to use elegiac images of poverty to ramp up emotions. In fact, when making his final cut of the photographs, he rejected some of Mohr's favorites on the grounds that they were "too aesthetic."[99]

The least planned of his books, *After the Last Sky* was written quickly, an impromptu response to an international UN conference Said attended in 1983 at the Palais des Nations in Geneva, where Mohr was then living. It was on this trip that Berger, a friend of Eqbal Ahmad, introduced Said to Mohr, the two then traveling to visit Berger at his home in Quincy in the mountainous eastern region of France not far from Geneva, where they spent a long afternoon and evening eating and talking. Because the UN conference was held to discuss the aftermath of the Israeli invasion of Lebanon, the organizers agreed to permit a display in the Palais lobby of photographs of Palestinians that Mohr had taken while working for the World Health Organization and the Red Cross, provided that the captions identifying them as Palestinian be removed.

At a restaurant on Lake Geneva afterward, Shafiq Al-Hout, Said, Mohr, and Nubar Hovsepian conspired to counter this outrage, and the idea for the book was born. After many months of plotting it out, Said and Mohr rendezvoused in the summer of 1985 in New York, Mohr carrying several hundred photographs to the Saids' flat for a working ten-day stay during which the final selections were made. Before leaving them early on other business, Mohr's wife, Simone, sat down to play with Said a piece for four hands on the piano.[100]

However accidental, the book opened new emotional registers, and as he conceded, the effort had no intention of being "objective."[101] After Said sent him a copy with a personal inscription, Derrida wrote back expressing his admiration for this "magnificent book" and shrewdly recognizing its anti-aesthetic thrust. "In every line the political and poetic gestures are tied together in the same analysis . . . Your text and these extraordinary photographs," he added, "work at once as an allegory of a people in its destiny which, given its unending suffering, it no longer allows to be allegorized."[102] Just the opposite of documentary, it was meant to express the imagination of diasporic yearning. A photograph of a mother scribbling a note as her bored daughter looks on begged for interpretation. This picture offered what the book does throughout—not dispassionate testimony, but a snapshot of Said's own psychology. The point was less to educate the public about unknown aspects of the territories than to chronicle the helplessness of one who must project his own personal meanings upon them because he has been physically cut off from it all.

In his rendering, then, the mother's pen is transformed into a symbol of resistance to the tangle of Israeli legal regulations in the territories, as though her writing were directly answering theirs. For all its desire not to aestheticize the Palestinian tragedy, Said relied on a voice of reverie and romance that rivaled his unpublished fiction. In phrases like "the swirl of noisy chiliastic visions" and "how much trivial malice can we bear?" he for the first time in print let himself play with the novelist's art. Inspired by the experiment, in late 1986 and early 1987 he began work on a draft of a novel about Beirut, stealing moments from his work on the film *Exiles*, which aired on BBC Television on June 23, 1988.[103] Within a year, however, he abandoned the novel in favor of his memoir, letting the one stand in for the other.

A YEAR AFTER THE publication of *After the Last Sky*, and now at work on the novel, Said received news that his dear friend Gold had fallen seriously ill. Dropping everything, he flew to Boston to see him on his deathbed only weeks before his demise on December 31, 1988, at the age of fifty-three.[104] Once again, the two spoke passionately about Asia, Africa, and the differences between East and

West, as well as their shared love of poetry.[105] Gold had just finished his beautiful series "Poems Written During a Period of Sickness," two of which appeared in *The Paris Review* and *The New Republic*. He could not have known it then, but in a few years Said would find himself reflecting on his own illness in his own literary terms before the memories were lost forever.[106]

Several months earlier, Said had been at the epicenter of a breakthrough in Palestinian negotiations. Spurred to action by the intifada, Secretary of State George Shultz invited Said and his longtime collaborator Abu-Lughod to Washington for a meeting on March 26, 1988. His enticing proposal of a three-year transitional period leading to Israel's ceding of the occupied territories recycled elements of the Camp David Accords of 1978 while selling them as a Reagan administration initiative.[107] The invitation, although welcome, was also a provocation. Even though the PLO was the only legitimate representative of the Palestinian people—a position to which Said and Abu-Lughod very loudly adhered—the two were chosen as emissaries because they were American citizens as well as prominent Palestinians who were not members of the PLO. It was Shultz's ploy to dodge Israeli wrath.[108] In the end, the initiative came to nothing. Said later quipped that Shultz "talked about nearly everything but the PLO and self-determination," the chief digression being Said's *Beginnings*, which Shultz declared he had read and was keen to discuss.[109]

Here as elsewhere, Said's political work found its basis in literary criticism. The concerns of *The World, the Text, and the Critic*, for instance, hovered over a request by Arafat in 1988 that Said help translate (as in 1974) a PLO draft statement first rendered by Darwish. As he worked on the declaration, Said felt that it exhibited Arafat's cluelessness about what such a statement should contain. The chairman deleted all the appeals to the international community that Said had carefully worked in while inserting his own lame posturing. Remarkably, although Said was the literary theorist and the PLO leaders the hard-nosed pragmatists, he found the whole experience exasperating evidence of the organization's "postmodern rhetorical anxieties."[110] At the "intifada" meeting of the PNC in Algiers in 1988, Said wryly observed that it was like being at "a convention of grammarians," so minutely did the delegates worry over the wording of their resolutions.

The World, the Text, and the Critic, then, was against the current not only within but outside the university. On the other hand, as a book written by a teacher for teachers, it seemed in some ways to return to the securities of an earlier time. The paradoxical gesture of returning to traditional figures from the eighteenth century and the interwar period in order to create a new intellectual counterforce was subversive at a time when the radicals of supply-side economics were busy tearing down established customs and the self-styled revolutionaries of literary theory were declaring a complete break from the past. For their part, skeptics within theory circles tried to brush off his criticisms as little more than veiled belletrism and even English club conservatism. Of course, Said did not try to hide that he wrote in the manner of—one might say the confines of—the modern British subspecialist of the 1950s and 1960s English department. Well past the time when he cared about impressing the old guard, he illustrated his points on everything from Bach, American diplomacy, and the Boer War with quotations from Samuel Butler, Hopkins, Virginia Woolf, W. B. Yeats, and Henry James. He seemed to be reassuring his audience that everything politically or theoretically difficult in his writing had been humanely expressed before him by the authors they already knew and loved.

This precarious balance between tradition and iconoclasm was evident too in his everyday duties as an educator. Said was surprisingly involved in college service at all levels, and it deeply marked his thinking about practical matters. Even while launching new fields of knowledge, he was engaged in the administration of Columbia College. He weighed in formally, for example, on the balance of English to comparative literature, judged undergraduate poetry contests, chaired a long-standing committee to assess the college's mandate, crossed swords with Trilling in a public exchange over the role of secondary education in preparing students for college-level work, and harangued the provost to support, of all things, library science.[111] He offered a critical response to the report of the World Commission on Culture and Development (UNESCO) titled "Our Creative Diversity," in which he complained that for all its fine points it had not a word to say about encouraging students to think for themselves. He also faulted it for sidestepping the fundamental oddity of university education, which—flying in the face of modernism as well as theory's supposed Copernican break with all that went before—was the need to submit to the authority of a tradition, a discipline, and scholarship.

In the classroom, this emphasis on discipline made him a daunting figure who, according to one *Columbia Daily Spectator* reporter, "command[ed] the telekinetic powers necessary to eject unwanted students from his seminar rooms by sheer force of irate facial expression."[112] Weak or ill-prepared in-class reports would be interrupted, at times with his head facedown on the desk, hands in his pockets loudly playing with pocket change. Or just the opposite, when he would rescue a student giving an inept report with an avuncular nod, by eliciting in the form of a question what the student had failed to say. Every word of Proust's *À la recherche du temps perdu* (*In Search of Lost Time*) must be read in French, he demanded. A student would complain that a philosopher made no sense. He would chide, "This is not scholarship . . . not critical thinking to say something like that." By turns joking and imperious, he consistently held that the labor of interpretation was serious business: "Our brief time in the classroom cannot be squandered."[113] One young colleague wrung her hands, looking for commiseration when she wondered whether she was good enough for a fellowship. He responded, "Get good."[114]

Although many of his students became professors, he had no ambition of making them so. He hated the idea that he might be creating acolytes. Because he had no interest in climbing the university hierarchy or getting tangled in department rivalries, his mission was writing and public speaking. The classroom, to that degree, was a reprieve from all of that, a way to try out ideas, and either beckon or scare his students into taking a stand of their own. Like other Columbia professors who cut their teeth in the low-tech gentlemanly "college," he was telling students, "We want to know what you think, and we're going to be very hard on you."[115] So the focus was on wrestling with primary texts—just the student and the text in dialogue—rather than guild apprenticeships or scholarly apparatuses. He was always completely "there," as Louise Yelin remembered it—no jargon, "no bullshit."[116] And yet "funny . . . very serious, very close to the text," not there to entertain "even when telling a joke," Leon Wieseltier recalled.[117]

He had a unique way of stalking a text. His classes tended to begin very slowly, and he often displayed nerves until he warmed up: "You could almost see the sweat, until he broke through and hit an emotional second wind, now totally absorbed, his art a combination of rigor and improvisation," said a former student, the filmmaker Ric Burns.[118] He himself attested to the "uncomfortable, stomach-churning, palm-sweating anxiety I still feel before (and even during) a class."[119] Arriving home late at night from a four-day speaking tour, he would be up at 4:00 a.m. rereading books he had read dozens of times before, making sure that he entered class prepared.

His children, Wadie and Najla, half expected him to leave his teaching at the door, but on the contrary he read every one of their school assignments, even those that dealt with writers who did not especially speak to him (Dostoevsky, Beckett). Throughout their schooling, about which he pestered them for every detail, he read *all* of their school essays, scribbling comments in the margins that were usually supportive, brief, and a bit uncritical ("You're brilliant"). But he made them feel somehow that he was not just letting them off lightly because he was their dad but was impressed (and a little surprised) by what they could do.[120] When Mariam was being tutored in Hebrew while preparing to apply for a Middle East studies librarian post at Columbia, Said would emerge from nowhere at the end of each lesson to amiably grill her instructor, David Yerushalmi, an Iranian Jew then studying in the Middle East languages and cultures department. "Well, how is Mariam doing, Daud?" he would ask, using the regional version of "David" to show he knew the difference. "She is very good," Yerushalmi would answer, and then Said in his typically childlike, impulsive way blurted out, "I would finish this whole book in two weeks."[121]

For his own graduate students, Said taught a way of doing things, above all, unhurried, expansive, and yet dead serious when it came to the stakes of ideas. He taught by doing rather than laying out a program, opening himself up to knowledge. As for some, like the anthropologist and former assistant Deborah Poole, he taught "the place of rage in scholarship, the role of angry determination, and the importance of that."[122] In regard to the contents of knowledge, he introduced students to philology—its meaning for the present and its long history—about which they knew nothing. But as his Columbia colleague Michael Wood pointed out, he had the talent of learning from them as well, as he admitted to a crowd at the "Third World Literary and Cultural Criticism" conference at Duke University in 1987, when he declared that it was really graduate students at the time, not he, who were responsible for ushering third-world literature into the curriculum.

Only in the mid-1980s did Said begin to venture outside Western literature at his students' urging. Chinua Achebe, Ayi Kwei Armah, Assia Djebar, and others from the global South were all read at his students' behest. His son, Wadie, was important too, introducing his father to younger scholars he did not know, which later led to alliances, and turning him on to the contemporary novelists that his attention to Palestinian issues prevented him from reading.[123] The exception was Philip Roth, with whom Said corresponded and whose *American Pastoral* (1997), about a father's relationship with his politically active and militant daughter, he thought the best novel he had read in a decade. He had, of course, worked for some time to promote Arabic fiction and poetry (he knew the work of the Sudanese novelist Tayeb Salih by at least 1976) and had casually remarked to Engel in November 1972 that he had come across "a really fine novelist called Mahfouz," but the gaps in his reading from South Asia, Africa, and Latin America were obvious by the early 1980s and no longer tolerable to him.[124]

Many of these works, he lamented in 1990 at the University of Kent, were taken up and taught in a frenzy of democratic inclusion that paid little attention to what was intellectually and aesthetically interesting in them. Few works of third-world literature that were not Arab were close to his heart, although the novels of Gabriel García Márquez and the poetry of Constantine Cavafy were exceptions. *Culture and Imperialism* was already in the planning stages by 1987, and it required working through a broad list of third-world writing, which he did with the help of his students.

Many had by then gone on to other things, but with all of them he showed a combination of toughness, irritability, loyalty, and indulgent propping up.[125] In letters to students, he left a record of his brutal frankness when correcting their writing. To one young advisee, he wrote, "Wordy beyond patience." Hyperbole. "Senseless concepts like 'paradigmatic' and 'mental space.'" Your writing is too "self-indulgent, private, and too unsituated to be very good."[126] It wasn't all dressing down. He left his students with the impression that they were as good as the authors they read in class. His early reputation among the profession's elite, and certainly his numerous offers from other schools, were based on the widely shared feeling that he was the best teacher they had ever seen.[127] "Being with him was like being with a playful, alternately super-engaged, super self-absorbed, suddenly very funny, suddenly very angry, or testy friend—a difficult friend who was also your best friend," Ric Burns added. "He could sort of push you around and then be at the same time solicitous."[128] One minute you were in his protected zone and seemed to be all that mattered; the next, when his attention waned, you experienced what one colleague liked to call "the fade" when his mind moved quickly elsewhere.[129]

CHAPTER 9

A FEW SIMPLE IDEAS

Thought is saying no . . . [and] it is to itself that thought says no.

—ALAIN[1]

The fate of public intellectuals in the United States, with its techno-logical panaceas and perfected newspeak, was always shakier than in Europe. The vision of America packaged in Washington think tanks or by culture warriors like Allan Bloom and Roger Kimball occupied the most coveted media real estate. And although the country certainly had public intellectuals—usually news anchors or op-ed columnists—they were rarely philosophers, experimental art-ists, or dissidents. The modern Hazlitts and Wollstonecrafts of the New World, then, did not have to be jailed; they were simply given no airtime on the grounds that "democracy" required regressing to the lowest common denominator. As the closest thing America had to Sartre, Said from the start did his best to find general readers outside the university. But by the 1980s, that quest had become a matter of survival. If he could not find a way to continue thriving, against renewed opposition, in the New York media world, he would be just another footnote in an academic journal.

Said had some of these difficulties in mind when he contrasted his own intellectual style to that of the great German social philosopher Jürgen Habermas—like him, a man of the Left, but unlike him, a third-generation member of the Frankfurt School. The German thinker's solemn disquisitions on topics like "the public sphere" and "the discourses of modernity," Said complained, although obviously learned and urgent, had no moral center, no heart. As far he was concerned, they were "all just hot air."[2] His own career, he ventured, was spun out of only "a few very simple ideas" and a "more unbuttoned . . . mode of proceeding."[3]

The "unbuttoned" shape of those ideas fit his manner of working. Restless and indefatigable, he lurched back and forth without a precise routine to his days. Up at 5:00 or 5:30 in the morning, he worked for an hour or so. Then he would move from his study to the kitchen, make two double espressos, one for him and the other for Mariam, and lay the table for breakfast: an English muffin with orange marmalade often scooped out of the samples he hoarded from hotels and airplanes. Or *labneh* and *zaatar* on pita bread with freshly squeezed orange juice made with a special juicer he had picked out at a high-end appliance shop.[4] He would watch TV in the morning—the news shows—and make an elaborate breakfast that he served Mariam (which his daughter, Najla, thought "cute") and then read the newspaper from cover to cover. He spent another hour or two writing, later shifting to exercise—usually swimming laps at the campus pool or playing a game of squash or tennis. A little more writing followed until he broke to clear his mind with a walk along the edge of Riverside Park. Many of his early encounters with colleagues and students came from such wanderings around Morningside Heights. He was never one to work a fourteen-hour day chained to his desk.

Despite the apparent placidity of the routine, the daily log of his correspondence gives only a small indication of the frenzy of Said's working life. On a single day there were interview requests from the Japanese business newspaper *Nikkei* and KPSB radio, San Diego.

Katrina vanden Heuvel, the editor of *The Nation*, wrote to reassure him that the magazine's coverage of the Iraq war was not as bad as it seemed, asking for suggestions of authors they might commission on the topic. The Hope Foundation invited him to join its telethon; TV5 Paris sent him his itinerary for the *dejeunatoire* following the screening of an Al Jazeera documentary on his life; organizers in Seoul pleaded with him to address the eleventh annual anticorruption conference there; several authors, expressing admiration, sent him their work, seeking endorsements; and, finally, there was a list of a dozen pieces of routine editorial and banking business. Every day the pattern was repeated, only the names of those clamoring for attention changed: UNESCO, the Kahlil Gibran Spirit of Humanity Awards, the Damascus music conservatory, *The Wall Street Journal*, *Le Monde Diplomatique*, Bosnian radio, Irish television, the South African news corporation, a Brazilian magazine—all of them wanting a contribution, an interview, or simply a word or two in response.

No surprise that his abiding interest in piano, when it could be practiced at all, was sporadic—confined to twenty-minute spurts. Phone calls morning and night further broke the office calm, many of them about business and requiring little time, others pure schmoozing or setting up a quick lunch at the Cafe Luxembourg.[5] He called close friends in the early morning hours and pretended to be surprised they were not already up, scolding them for their laziness. One of his idols, the stylistician Leo Spitzer, hated the academic busywork that interrupted thought, once aphoristically remarking, "The telephone of the organizer is the deadly enemy of the desk of the scholar."[6] Said, by contrast, thought the one the other's weapon. "He used the telephone as a virtuoso instrument," according to Don Guttenplan, *The Nation*'s London correspondent and a former student.[7]

The rhythms of work shaped the ideas. Those who knew him well spoke of his taste for Mont Blanc pens and blue bonded stationery, and he would chide his students as they left class on their way to the computer labs that "this is all I need," pulling a fountain pen out of his breast pocket. JoAnn Wypijewski, then an editor at *The Nation*, once made a house call to work with him on an article. After she proposed edits, "he would unscrew the cap on his pen, shake it a little, roll back the sleeves of his French-cuffed shirt, and go to it." And she thought to herself, "Maybe he really was like Balzac, writing everything in longhand."[8] One of his assistants, Zaineb Istrabadi, typed many of his letters and articles from scrawls on finely colored paper sheets.

His collected papers, though, tell a different story. The manuscripts are remarkable not only for the relative absence of revisions but for the intriguing mix of longhand writing—some of it, indeed, in fountain pen on expensive blue paper, but quite a lot of it in pencil on ordinary lined yellow stock or white computer paper. Often mid-page, sometimes even mid-sentence, the text shifts to typed paragraphs and then is interrupted once more by a typed passage from elsewhere cut out and pasted into the space between the lines. A lot of the manuscripts are typed, and his assistants all agree he was a rather good typist.[9] Many pages display all three—handwriting, blocks of pasted text, typed passages—as though he tired of the one before switching to another. Or perhaps it was only that he was on the road, away from his battery of writing machines, high and low tech, or that he had relocated to a chair or a lectern, or had moved from home to his campus office. Or, altogether differently, because writing was for him a sensual experience, it might have been that the different tactilities jostled him out of an impasse.

By the mid-1970s, his apartment was filled from the early hours with the clack of a blue manual Smith Corona typewriter, later the ping of an IBM electric with eraser strip. Whatever the writing implement, he worked from little note cards and fragments of prose on torn pieces of paper from his various trips abroad.[10] By the 1990s and early years of the twenty-first century, all of the topical pieces for *Al-Hayat* and *Al-Ahram* were composed on a laptop. He would later note that "the wonders of the Internet and the speed of electronic exchange have replaced the pen, the typewriter, the hand-carried letter, and to some extent even the library that were the staples of my education."[11] He decided to hedge his bets, using new technologies while cherishing the state of mind encouraged by the more pastoral act of writing with pen and ink.

Of course, he also had his little household tasks. Only he was allowed to operate the expensive espresso machine, and the water had to be Evian or Volvic. Within the family, he was the one in charge of electronic devices: if one needed a new stereo, he would organize the trip to the Wiz and do all of the talking to salespeople.[12] Many of his intimates found it irresistible to dwell on his love of shopping, his knowing his way around the best haberdashers, tailors, and tobacconists, and his taste for pipes, high-end stereos, and cigars. But his preference for nice things was combined with a carefree way with them. As an invited guest of diplomats, he might have been expected to develop a weakness for fine wines and Michelin stars, but the truth is that he preferred run-of-the-mill blended whiskies to single malts and always hated fancy restaurants.

Of all his modes of working, writing was the least fragmented. His essays typically took from two to three days to write and went through three drafts of minor corrections. With some exceptions, he does not seem to have toiled over phrasing or diction. His prose was never sculpted, driven more by ideas than by form, although alert to a mixture of high diction and informality, foreign phrases and colloquialisms. In any case, it flowed out of him in more or less the form it appeared in print, a valuable talent as he faced new challenges in the New York media of the 1980s.

Ever since his breakup with Maire, the difficulty he had sleeping as a schoolboy had developed into an aversion to sleep that endured in later life and was redoubled as a useless tribute to his mother's troubled sleeping, he later speculated, during the final stages of her illness.[13] Whether stemming from Protestant guilt for unproductive time or clinical depression (as his daughter, Najla, surmised), insomnia helped enshrine for him the activity of speech.[14] As time moved on, he typically found his relaxation by taking sudden breaks to which he was as dedicated as work, rushing to a concert on the spur of the moment or planning trips as he did to Spain in 1979, to Tunisia for a month in 1982, and to Morocco with his family in 1988 in the midst of a grueling work schedule.[15] His reading for that reason was more or less on the fly, in airplanes or at home after classes, and the greatest part of his workday remained, essentially, conversations with visitors or on the phone. Although a scholar, he lacked the seclusion usually needed for the job, living rather the distracted life of a journalist.

Such a life involved, naturally, the constant search for new contacts. As Dupee had in the 1960s, the Chicago-born, New York-based entertainment heiress Jean Stein played the role of unofficial agent and all-round promoter in the 1980s and 1990s. The relationship was symbiotic. He revealed to her a world she knew nothing about, advising her editorially on *Grand Street* and introducing her to Middle East poets and intellectuals. In return, she did what she could to open the doors he had not already opened himself, her devotion helped along by a limitless personal affection. They were close enough to be playful, as in this phone message in the summer of 1994:

> Hi, Jean. No need at all to ever call me. I just work for you. I'm just checking in, you know, like those guys who go around punching cards. So I'm just punching a card here to say that I called you at about four something, fifteen. My name is Edward Said . . . and well there you are. I of course would be anxious to, eager, and indeed flattered to get your call. So here I am waiting by the phone anxiously.[16]

Stein had taken over *Grand Street* in 1990 when its founder, Said's dear friend Ben Sonnenberg, was forced to retire after nine years as its editor, his energy gradually sapped by multiple sclerosis. Founded in 1981 in the tradition of the pioneering "little magazines" of the

1920s, *Grand Street* was designed to look "severe" but be fun, a "mix of insolence and information," as Sonnenberg put it.[17] For a time it was the most sought-after venue for frontline artists and journalists, including W. G. Sebald, José Saramago, Jeanette Winterson, Quentin Tarantino, Don DeLillo, and Alice Munro. Said would write seven essays for it over the years.

Both from wealthy families and living in New York, Stein had known Sonnenberg since they were teenagers, although it was Said and Mariam who at a dinner at their flat organized for the purpose reintroduced them to each other after years of being out of touch. She seemed the logical successor at *Grand Street*, having made her reputation with an interview of William Faulkner for *The Paris Review* and securing it with her bestseller (co-edited with George Plimpton) *Edie: An American Biography* (1982), an oral history of one of Andy Warhol's inner circle. Along with her wealthy connections, it helped make her a force in literary Manhattan.

Maneuvering in the media was especially important for Said in the wake of *Orientalism*'s problematic fame. *Time* magazine's flattering profile of him in 1978 was now long gone, and he had become a pariah among the pro-Israel wing of New York publishing after the impact of *The Question of Palestine* had sunk in.[18] Never part of the *New York Review of Books* writers' stable, he had only limited access to the magazine throughout the 1980s and 1990s, until he was finally able to place "The Cruelty of Memory," his long, comprehensive review of the novels of Mahfouz, in 2000.[19] Said's icy relationship with the review's co-editor Robert Silvers was the product of long grievances and came to a head when Silvers published what Said called an "incoherent and scurrilous" review of *The World, the Text, and the Critic* in 1983 by Irvin Ehrenpreis, a Swift scholar. He promptly wrote to Silvers to say that he ought to have been "embarrassed by so laughable and indecent a performance," although he realized this was unlikely seeing that both he and Silvers knew the real purpose behind these "annual attacks on me."[20] Even at *The Nation*, a more welcoming and progressive venue, wealthy pro-Israel donors objected that he was given too much space in its pages. As for the television news shows, stacked more and more with administration parrots, he soon saw that he was being turned into the token Arab, invited only to be shouted down. So he looked for new platforms.

In that pursuit, the contacts he made at Stein's legendary salons were invaluable, although he had already come to know many of the writers and personalities who frequented them. The epicenter of New York literary life, they attracted the likes of Norman Mailer, Warren Beatty, Renata Adler, Jules Feiffer, Joan Didion, and Saul Steinberg. Despite the illustrious company, Stein bestowed on him the unique honor of naming one of the rooms in her apartment the Edward Said Room because of its low tables, Eastern furniture, and exotic decor—especially the piece of calligraphic art that bordered the walls just beneath the ceiling.[21]

Even though he navigated New York society with Mariam in support, he felt an outsider at such events, plagued once again by self-doubt. Well-wishers found his insecurity odd, knowing him well enough to figure out that as he moved about the room, he was quietly torturing himself with the question "What would these people want with little me?"[22] In the next instant, propped up by nervous energy, he mobilized his charm, seizing upon an idea and turning his insecurity into eloquence. Salman Rushdie actually mistook him for a person at ease at a gala for the Sandinistas at the Metropolitan Museum of Art, where he described Said standing "friendly, handsome . . . an expansive talker, a laugher and gesturer, a polymath, [and a] flirt."[23]

Whatever the inner turmoil, this allure obviously helped the networking along. In the more comforting milieu of the university conference circuit, his ability to be at every moment totally "on" in conversation—"socially amazing, none better"—brought followers aplenty and carried over to his sallies into New York society.[24] It was hard not to suspect him of being a little vain, but as the author Marina Warner explained, he "had every right to be . . . burning, intense, graceful. Not just a man with nice features."[25] As a result, she added, there were "lots of friends, many of them women—usually of a definite type—stylish, not too young, intellectual." She herself was not among them, but "there were waves of them," connected to him mainly through politics, for "politics occupied Edward's mind more than literature."[26]

The circuit of these media parties, at any rate, allowed Said to find something even more important: a new circle of friends who not only politically but existentially shared his take on the terrible 1980s. Through the journalist Alexander Cockburn, he met the columnist Andrew Kopkind, and through Sonnenberg he met Elizabeth Pochoda, whose husband was at Pantheon Books and who worked as an editor at *The Nation* when Stein's daughter, Katrina vanden Heuvel, took over the editorship of the magazine from Victor Navasky in 1995. It was through the *New York Review of Books* co-editor Barbara Epstein that he made the acquaintance of Shelley Wanger, who first worked at Condé Nast and later at *Interview* magazine. Wanger in particular gave him the opportunity to try out different, more confessional modes of writing, helping him place his essay on his Cairo childhood in *House & Garden* and put together a volume of his Palestinian essays when few mainstream American presses wanted them. She also paved the way for his "Breakfast with Arafat" at *Interview* magazine and guided his memoir, *Out of Place*, into print.

His triumph at the *London Review of Books* was to have single-handedly turned its reporting on the Middle East in a pro-Palestinian direction. Mary-Kay Wilmers, now the editor, remembers meeting him for the first time in the early 1980s in the *LRB* office dressed in a bright yellow V-necked sweater from which she drew "all sorts of conclusions about sportiness and social life which turned out not to be inappropriate." The U.S. literary critic Richard Poirier, one of his dearest friends with whom he frequently hung out in New York, knew the *LRB*'s then editor in chief, Karl Miller. Wilmers, who took over the paper in 1992, recalls that as a "non-believing, non-practicing, fairly detached" Jew, she was on Israel's side to the extent that she thought about the matter at all. "Meeting Edward changed all that, and for good."[27] His first essay for the paper, appropriately, was on Walter Lippmann, and so about the "journalist's relationship to power—whatever the regime—and the journalist's own power."

Part of his media strategy, but it also reflected his personality, was to mix it up. He did not want all of the writing to be in the same key, given the occasional impatience and anger of his political writing. And the essays on literature and philosophy were not exactly relief, because for many they were a theoretical slog. He looked to show people other sides of his character. When the *LRB* published an essay dedicated to explaining why it took so long to mend an escalator, Said remonstrated with Wilmers. "Why," he asked, "do you never ask me to write pieces like that?"[28] His colleague Michael Rosenthal remembered the same playfulness and willingness to experiment. One day Said decided he wanted to learn to play basketball. He put on his shorts; they went to a nearby court and ran around. "He was terrible, but we had fun."[29]

Having come out of the theory wars, Said had to adjust to the *LRB*'s urbane, conversational style. When the paper edited his articles, he would ring up to tell them they had "massacred" his text, although it usually turned out to be something "quite slight, and easily fixed." Within an hour, he would ring up again to say he had been wrong, and everything was fine, and in the end they edited very little of what he had written. Basically, the *LRB* was happy to have his writing on the Middle East when the New York outlets refused it. His *LRB* pieces on the PLO departure from Lebanon, on his childhood in Beirut, and on exchanges over Zionism influenced the editorial board. By the first intifada of 1987, Wilmers recalls, "we felt the Palestinians had a more or less unanswerable case, and we haven't changed our mind."[30]

The picture was different in his hometown. He had broken into *The Nation* in the late 1960s and as a result had gotten to know

Navasky a little, who in addition to editing the magazine was its publisher, although the relationship was tense. But it was on the fabulous terrace of his early publisher, André Schiffrin, at the beginning of the 1980s that Said first came to know the editors of the magazine well. As an outlet of the liberal Left, *The Nation* had a modest but faithful circulation and a pedigree reaching back to the nineteenth century. Along with *Harper's Magazine*, *The Progressive*, and *The Village Voice*, it became increasingly his sanctuary and mouthpiece in the turbulent decade of Reagan-Bush, even though he was still steadily placing short articles and reviews in *The New York Times*.

But his fit with *The Nation* was not always comfortable. The magazine was rife with class hierarchies and petty insults, and he never felt completely wanted there. Most if not all of his writing was consigned to "the back of the book" in *Nation* jargon—that is, to the arts pages. Apart from his opera column, much of what he wrote for the magazine were book reviews. Even with this shunting of his talents away from political commentary, pro-Israel liberals pressured Navasky to deny him even this level of access after Said and Cockburn expressed in print their support for the presidential candidacy of Jesse Jackson. Jackson had shown particular interest in the Palestine question, meeting informally with Said and others in 1984 in a hotel suite, sitting in his underwear.[31]

Interestingly, Said's outsider status was also his passport, with news outlets consulting him, almost by default, for anything having to do with the Middle East. His counterparts holding up the government's positions included the Iraqi British professor of Middle East studies at Brandeis, Kanan Makiya, who dependably rehearsed Pentagon wisdom, but notwithstanding his establishment patronage neither he nor other native informants supporting the U.S. government line were ever as prominent as Said.[32]

The Nation's columnists, however, helped him stave off alienation. Among them was Christopher Hitchens, for a time a collaborator, co-editor, and speaker on the same platforms in defense of Palestine. With Alexander Cockburn, there was a deeper affinity than with Hitchens, suggested by the title of his review of one of Cockburn's books: "Alex the Magnificent." They had already met in the 1970s through *New Left Review* and deepened their alliance during Cockburn's time at the *Voice* in the early 1980s. Like Said, Cockburn was a "fancy" man, as Wypijewski put it, and the two embraced their contradictions, flaunting their elite educations (Harvard and Oxford), their gorgeous apartments on Central Park West and Riverside Drive, and their derring-do in tipping the scales of public discussion to the left.[33]

One night in a cab on the way to a restaurant, the two impulsively broke out into French, showing off their skills like two "peacocks with their feathers plumed." With Ben Sonnenberg, the three for a time became a "gang" of sorts. Sonnenberg struck almost everyone around him as a beautiful soul, "the most wonderful man on the face of the earth," as Wypijewski put it.[34] Each in his own way slyly witty, the trio formed a mutual admiration society, having dinners together at Sonnenberg's flat whenever Cockburn was in town. Said, who spoke to Sonnenberg every day by phone, would often bring sandwiches over to his house for lunch in order to share the literary gossip both loved, while Said, a bright light in Sonnenberg's life, put him in touch with many of the writers he published in *Grand Street*.[35] Cockburn, for his part, called Said the "lion, because sometimes when he spoke it was as if he were pawing the air, lashing a tail," and then teased him, tugging at his vanity.[36] When Mariam and Wadie were stranded in Washington, D.C., by a snowstorm, Said found himself at a loss for how to entertain his three-year-old daughter, Najla. His solution was to drag her off to Cockburn's flat and then, deep in political conversation, instruct her to amuse herself by looking out the window at the park. Her father, she later recalled, was amazingly empathetic, tender, loving, attentive, but in small doses. He "did his bit, and then it was on to work."[37]

Even as a writer for magazines and newspapers, Said crafted a lucid prose brimming with personality that was, however, more challenging than Hitchens's breezy wit and Cockburn's bold, if inch-deep, reflections. His editors at the trade presses—Elisabeth Sifton and Shelley Wanger—mostly shared Wypijewski's judgment that Said was a fluid and inviting writer for any audience.[38] Their editing of his manuscripts was mostly cosmetic. By contrast, his music columns for *The Nation* struck the editors as too dense, thoughtful but "not what a general reader of a general interest political magazine would expect to find there."[39] He greeted the edits with patience and irony, enduring those at the magazine who found his writing too academic. And he tactfully kept to himself the raves sent to him by serious music critics and musicians, who told him that they only read *The Nation* because of his music columns.

WHEN IT CAME TO Said's "few very simple ideas," neither literary theorists nor journalists were fully aware of the ensemble, or how it fit together. Too colloquial and stalwart for the one, he was too intellectually demanding for the other. Caught between the two, Said set about inventing a lexicon. The vocabulary he devised was not made up of neologisms exactly, just words taken out of their "dynastic" usage (as he put it)—that is, freed from the tyranny of their inherited definitions. He gave everyday words new meanings in part by mastering the art of vague coinages like "affiliation," "inventory," and "eccentricity." "I draw on certain literary texts, literary techniques, matters of interpretation," he once explained, "which . . . taught me a lot about the way ideas are transmitted, formed, and institutionalized."[40] Among these techniques was a rhetoric of sincerity. By liberating words like "equality," "justice," and "pleasure" from their quotation marks, he could repudiate both the cynicism of New York artistes and the political "realism" of Washington think tanks.

Auerbach and Spitzer had taught him that certain words, if properly chosen, define entire peoples. One of Auerbach's most famous and influential essays was dedicated to unpacking the word *figura* (beauty, form, trope, style), while Spitzer assigned the entire second section of a very long monograph to the word *Stimmung* (mood). Throughout the 1980s, Said often talked about these two essays, marveling at their ingenuity in building such large edifices on so small a foundation. If properly mobilized, he proposed, a term could stand in for the writer him- or herself. In the same way that the term "technics" brings to mind Lewis Mumford, or "conspicuous consumption" Thorstein Veblen, we cannot think of the terms "worldliness" and "affiliation" without thinking of Said.

His audience had always been an odd ensemble of New York socialites, crossover journalists, Middle East revolutionaries, and academic phenomenologists. Consequently, his lexicon had to handle difficulty as poems do, suggestively and without limiting words to a single connotation. Said's own *figura* relied on the illusion of physical presence. His key words brought immediacy into his theoretical writing, the kind his editors at *The Nation* and Pantheon thought too convoluted on the first go-round. The pejorative "academic" pointed to a dimension of his writing he wanted very much to retain as well as to coax general audiences to learn from.

We have already seen some of these terms: "autodidact," "amateurism," and the "beginnings/origins" pairing. But one of the most central was his distinction between "filiation" and "affiliation." It might be helpful to trace how he turned words already familiar in one field into a different meaning in another. Roland Barthes, for instance, in "From Work to Text" (1971) wrote of the "myth of filiation" to propose that a text's "paternity" required no authorship, it being rather a direct passage from one word to another without requiring any intervention from the conscious writer. A year earlier, Said's colleague in Columbia's French department Michael Riffaterre (with whom he quarreled in *The World, the Text, and the Critic*) made a similar case using the pairing "Filiation and Affiliation" in order to play with the truism that texts are not actually made up of ideas or things but a recycling of verbal clusters passing from text to text.[41] Said turned the pairing on its head, using "affiliation" for a community of belief as against "filiation," which referred to familial inheritance. His point was that both kinds of belonging can be dangerous when they "reproduce the skeleton of family authority." It is not enough to be against racism or national chauvinism if one repeats their mindless solidarities. Even progressive causes have a dynastic logic when governed by "guild consciousness, consensus . . . class."[42]

Often accused of being too polemical, Said was mostly interested in breaking up the unwritten rules of the professional game where no one is supposed to criticize their colleagues or allies. On the contrary, he seemed to be describing himself in his foreword to Israel Shahak's *Jewish History, Jewish Religion* (1994), where he admired Shahak's commitment "to repeat, to shock, to bestir the lazy or indifferent into galvanized awareness of the human pain that they might be responsible for."[43] In fact, though—and his critics seemed to miss this—he was much more frequently appeasing and at times even evasive. For instance, in reacting to the unseemly alliance between academic criticism and the conservative turn of the 1980s, he expressed himself cagily: its "currents of thought and practice . . . play a role within the Reagan era."[44]

The syntax was typical. Careful to avoid direct accusations or causal links ("play a role within" falls a little short of "is complicit with," for instance), he left himself an escape route. On the other hand, he tore the heart out of adversaries when he wanted to: after the pseudonymous Samir Al-Khalil had insinuated that Said was a closet sympathizer of Saddam Hussein (even though Said had frequently denounced Hussein in print), Said called out the "thuggish tirade" by this "skulking jackal" whose cowardice was made obvious by "his clammy embrace of a nom de plume."[45] It was hardly surprising, then, that in an AIPAC training seminar, pro-Israel cadres were advised that when disrupting public events, "don't cut down a speaker—it's too risky, e.g. Edw. Said and Noam Chomsky . . . Edward Said was fantastic—challenging him will only make you look bad."[46]

After Said was elected president of the Modern Language Association in 1998, Jon Whitman, one of his former students who had moved to Israel to teach at the Hebrew University, loudly resigned from the organization, ostensibly because Said had not shown proper decorum when answering his critics.[47] In his public reply, Said reminded members that his ripostes had been to venomous attacks and that many of these foes he was said to have dehumanized were still close friends.[48] His excoriation of enemies—one thinks of his public responses to Michael Walzer and Robert Griffin, for example—are immensely entertaining, even a little frightening for their verbal aggression. He could certainly rise to invective, as in a letter to *Ha'aretz* when Meron Benvenisti blamed Palestinians for their own dispossession while accusing Said of inventing his own past even as he, Benvenisti, covered up his "shabby role in the ethnic cleansing of Jerusalem" after 1967: "Crude, blustering demagogue that he is, Benvenisti enjoins us to use 'the mangled language of the market-square,' which to judge by the sheer awfulness of his writing is hardly the best medium either for clear thought or for logical exchange."[49] Such examples notwithstanding, mollifying indirection was his more typical mode.

With challenges to his more polemical sides in mind, he remarked in 1983 that some thought him little more than an "undeclared Marxist" and so it was time, he added, to clarify his position.[50] He never really did, though, and others tried with only mixed success.[51] Simple or not, his ideas fall more readily into place when seen against the backdrop of three worldviews he continually learned from, at times exalted, but always held back from uncritically joining: Marxism, psychoanalysis, and feminism.

IT IS REASONABLE TO agree with the Irish poet Seamus Deane that Said was not a Marxist, but only if we recognize the wildly different degrees to which one can be "not a Marxist."[52] Like other opponents of U.S. foreign policy, Said was at times libeled as a sympathizer with "Soviet totalitarianism."[53] The charge was absurd, yet it should not go unnoted that many of the intellectuals to whom he was drawn supported the Soviet Union for much of their lives. These included E. P. Thompson, Emile Habibi, J. D. Bernal, Sadik Al-Azm, and, of course, Gramsci and Lukács. Even more apt, given his professional interests, was the generation of third-world authors who got their start as writing fellows in Poland, East Germany, Czechoslovakia, and other parts of the Soviet bloc. These included his ally and correspondent Ranajit Guha, a historian of South Asia, the Kenyan author and critic Ngugi wa Thiong'o, and the Palestinian poet laureate and close friend Mahmoud Darwish.

Said had always been clear about rejecting membership in communist organizations for both practical and political reasons. But Soviet realpolitik in the Middle East, although a mixed blessing, inspired communist groups within Arab nationalism generally. It was so interwoven with the politics of everyday life that from a Palestinian perspective it was simply part of the landscape and not at all an alien intrusion. At other times, he pretended incomprehension, implausibly turning down a request from his friend and admirer the actress Vanessa Redgrave to be on the board of a left political organization with which she was affiliated on the grounds that "I am most unknowledgeable about Soviet history, and more particularly, the history of Marxism; I would therefore feel like a complete idiot."[54]

From as early as 1969, Said's self-positioning vis-à-vis Marxism and his conditional praise for Soviet foreign policy in the Middle East was openly stated.[55] He repeatedly questioned, though, whether a Marxism devised in the West could ever be relevant outside it: "I have yet to see—to my mind—a satisfactory translation of European Marxism into Arab or Third World terms."[56] For all of Arab nationalism's heroism and rectitude, he once described it as borrowed and inauthentic and for that reason too "inexpensive."[57] Arriving already completed elsewhere, it could never feel the impress of a genuinely Arab stamp. So too communism. In the United States, the organizational Left was so bogged down in debates about whether racism or class struggle was more important that it had little to offer the Palestinian struggle, which is one of the chief reasons he never considered formally joining its ranks.

Apart from a brief visit to Poland on his Guggenheim Fellowship in Beirut, he never set foot in a Soviet bloc country, even at the height of his fame, although invitations were extended.[58] On the other hand, he provoked Hitchens in a revealing moment of anger: "Do you know something I have never done in my political career? I have never publicly criticized the Soviet Union . . . [T]he Soviets have never done anything to harm me, or us."[59] For all the media outcry against "tenured radicals" and Marxist indoctrination in the university, most of the academic Left distanced itself from Marxism or turned it into docile lifestyle transgression. Said was scrupulous about never doing either.[60]

Marxism for Said, at any rate, was always something larger and older than its twentieth-century Soviet or Middle Eastern forms. At its most honorable, it was part of a venerable tradition of the Left that reached back to a time before Marx. His investment in Vico, one could say, was precisely to resurrect an earlier countertradition based on giving dignity back to human labor, to the agency of ordinary people making history, to the class struggles that created the first republics, and to the spirit of humanist breadth rejecting narrow specialization and, like Marx, boldly weighing in on political theory and economics in a poetic spirit. In that light, he delightfully invoked the medieval reformer Cola di Rienzo as one of the founders of humanist thought.[61] Rienzo, the son of a washerwoman and a tavern keeper, an avenger of the abuses of noblemen, and a denouncer of aristocrats, was a brilliant rabble-rouser, having steeped himself in the work of Latin poets and orators in order to use their rhetorical techniques to unify Italy.

Said alluded to other moments of the historical Left by way of Rabelais's Abbaye de Thélème, an anti-authoritarian idyll described in *Gargantua and Pantagruel* (1532), a place where one was able to achieve intellectual and physical fulfillment, free from drudgery and submission to authority.[62] Apart from showing the prehistory of Marx's criticism from below, Said was looking to take humanism out of the hands of self-righteous culture warriors. He had in mind, among others, Hilton Kramer's neoconservative journal *The New Criterion*, for example, whose contributors were busy pontificating about these same classics of "Western civilization" as he was, but for the very different purpose of calling those who exposed the crimes of imperial culture barbarians.

His appraisal of the Left was careful to avoid the balancing act of George Orwell and other self-styled "socialists" whose art was to elude middlebrow censure by denouncing leftist gods—a formula Said knew well from the late journalism of Hitchens and the writing of Leszek Kolakowski, Conor Cruise O'Brien, and others with whom he fought bitterly over the years. In piece after piece, we see him running interference for the Left, humanizing communists and Marxist intellectuals by getting others to see them as full members of a collective intellectual endeavor.[63] Doling out strategic praise for authors he wanted others to read, he promoted a list of broadly social democratic exposés of U.S. foreign policy and the domestic surveillance state. He particularly loved on-the-ground studies of institutional complicity, citing on more than one occasion Frances Stonor Saunders on the cultural Cold War, Nadia Abu el-Haj on the fictions of Israeli archaeology, or Carol Gruber's *Mars and Minerva*, a study of the ways that universities turned themselves into instruments of the War Department during World War I.[64]

"Traveling Theory," one of his most quoted essays, was all about the sapping of intellectual vigor as Marxist concepts like "totality" and "reification" moved away from revolutionary commitments in the actual struggle of parties and movements toward a decontextualized theoretical serenity.[65] There are, of course, many instances when Said articulates an explicitly liberal rather than Marxist political perspective, not only casting suspicion on abusive governments but finding in the very logic of institutions the threat of a new tyranny. The classically liberal model of the fragile individual pitted against organizations can be seen in "Secular Criticism" when he singles out the unlikely trio of T. S. Eliot's Anglican mandarinate, Lukács's vanguard party, and Freud's psychoanalytic community for sharing "vestiges of the kind of authority associated in the past with filiative order"—that is, for losing all reason and fairness when dealing with those outside its ideological "family."[66] As in liberal thought generally, the private individual is portrayed as inevitably threatened by the hierarchy of groups, parties, and parliaments.

Hints of this same centrism can be found in his enthusiasm for Gramsci's contemporary Piero Gobetti, who even inspires a slogan in *Culture and Imperialism*: "the Gobetti factor."[67] As a passionate, young literary intellectual, Gobetti represented for Said a detached philosophical erudition placed in the service of mass mobilization. Gobetti, like Gramsci, was a student at the University of Turin whose outlook changed forever after he witnessed the young Gramsci's skillful role in the Turin labor movement. More than anyone of his generation, Gobetti grasped Gramsci's lesson that it was vital to connect the South, "whose poverty and vast labor pool," Said wrote, "are inertly vulnerable to northern economic policies and power, with the North that is dependent on it."[68] But, again like Said, he was less radical than Gramsci, in solidarity with the Italian Communist Party but never a member of it. During the fascist period Gobetti found that the only consistent and effective defenders of liberal ideals were the organized Left. In that regard, Said implied, aligning himself with the Left only reluctantly and pragmatically, he was the Gobetti of his time.

Yet this too appeared to be another Conradian mask, for there were many counterexamples. In a sardonic aside he once commented that "we liberals" call a situation complex as "a rhetorical signal . . . before a lie is to be pronounced or when a grave and immoral complicity with injustice is about to be covered up."[69] Although he conceded the influence of the Will Rogers–like boldness and clarity of the pragmatist philosopher Richard Rorty, for instance, he was not impressed by his "peremptory liberalism" and hated his America-first politics.[70] Because of his distaste for liberal hypocrisy, close colleagues judged Said "basically Marxist," although of course not communist.[71]

On the other hand, while acknowledging Said's regard for twentieth-century Marxist philosophers, Al-Azm thought "the fundamental structures of his analysis . . . never Marxist," and his Marxism "cosmetic."[72] Chomsky shared this assessment, challenging anyone to show him where, at any point in Said's work, Marxism enters as a serious analytic principle.[73] Deirdre Bergson, a close friend who earlier in life had been active in the Trotskyist movements of South Africa, delighted in Said's confession in his Haverford College commencement speech that he should have studied economics more seriously, but she complained (very inaccurately, it turns out) that he never said a word in any of his work about class.[74]

The attack on Marx in *Orientalism* seemed for many to settle the issue of Said's real sympathies. There, in a move that scholars rightly censured, he corralled Marx into the camp of John Stuart Mill as a man convinced of the inferiority of Indians.[75] And yet one had only to look at Said's alert and prolonged close readings of Marx's *Eighteenth Brumaire of Louis Bonaparte* in "On Repetition" to get the opposite impression. And in the very months that he was writing *Orientalism*, his support for the German communist was stalwart, and even a little defensive:

> It's been said about Marx that he saw this struggle as something exclusively economic; that's a serious falsification . . . He was perfectly aware that the struggle was materially *expressed* and economically characterizable, but he was, I think, enormously sensitive to the shaping dialectic, to the intangible but very real figurations, to the internal unisons and dissonances the struggle produced. That is the difference between him and Hobbes, who saw life as nasty, brutish, and short.[76]

Here, at any rate, Said was clearly accusing bourgeois thought (in the person of Hobbes) of a crude materialism and saying that Marx himself was, among other things, a very early and invaluable cultural critic.[77] What reservations he had seemed designed to encourage third-world intellectuals to free themselves from European icons, no matter how liberatory. And he was eager to show he wanted nothing to do with "solidarity before criticism," a phrase he often used to express how dangerous it was when allies keep silent about each other's mistakes in the name of a common cause. Even Marx, he was implying, a giant of liberation and ethical integrity, could not entirely escape Eurocentrism.

His critique of Marxists, interestingly, was frequently from the left. He complained that professors had diminished the revolutionary force of Marxism by turning it into "principally a reading technique."[78] He was also protective, even agitated, when the core of Marx's writings were treated ineptly or gutted by the politically enfranchised. In a reader's report on Geoffrey Hartman's *Criticism in the Wilderness* in 1976, for example, he found it unforgivable that the author had "swept the whole matter of Marxism and its relationship to Hegelian philosophy out of the room."[79] Samuel Huntington's tribalist screed *The Clash of Civilizations* (1996) conducted its argument without any attention to "the globalization of capital." He quoted Oscar Wilde's *Soul of Man Under Socialism*—"no class is ever really conscious of its own suffering"—adding that for that reason agitators are needed to bring it to consciousness.[80]

Especially in Said's writings on Palestine do the calculations of political economy and the dilemmas of class tensions associated with Marxism play a prominent role. In "The Future of Palestine: A Palestinian View," he laid out what he flatly called "the class role of the intellectual."[81] Again and again, he zeroes in on the weakness of the Arab "national bourgeoisie," which had been unable to create a civil society, and so yielded to its intolerable alternative, the "national security state," while assaulting the Arab free marketeers in his late writing for Middle East newspapers.[82]

Cairo, 1954 (From *Egyptian Streets*)

Mount Hermon application photo
(Courtesy of the Said Family Collection)

As a young man in Cairo
(Courtesy of the Said Family Collection)

Dhour el Shweir looking northeast toward Mount Sannine
(Photograph by the author)

Listening to his father (Courtesy of the Said Family Collection)

Aunt Melia
(Courtesy of the Said Family Collection)

Tiegerman in Kitzbühel (Courtesy of Allan Evans
and the Arbiter of Cultural Traditions)

Arthur Gold, class of 1957
(From the *Nassau Herald*, Princeton yearbook, Princeton University)

Charles Malik
(Courtesy of Getty Images and Corbis Historical)

R. P. Blackmur (Photograph by Charles R. Schulze)

Harry Levin
(Courtesy of Getty Images: The LIFE Picture Collection)

Editors of *Partisan Review*. Standing
(from left): George Morris, Philip Rahv,
Dwight Macdonald. Sitting (from left): Fred
Dupee, William Phillips (Photograph by Maurey
Garber, courtesy of the Garber family)

Sadik Al-Azm
(Courtesy of the Erasmus Prize Foundation)

On the porch in Dhour el Shweir. Back row (from left): Grace, Joyce, Rosy, Samir Makdisi. Front row (from left): Edward, Hilda, Wadie, Saree Makdisi, Ussama Makdisi, Jean Makdisi (Courtesy of the Said Family Collection)

Shafiq Al-Hout
(Courtesy of the Said Family Collection)

Fact-finding tour in Lebanon. (From left) Fredric Jameson, Eqbal
Ahmad, Yasser Arafat, David Dellinger, Don Luce, and Ramsey Clark
(Courtesy of SAADA, the South Asian American Digital Archive)

With John Berger in the Haute-Savoie, France
(Photograph by Jean Mohr)

With Ibrahim Abu-Lughod (Photograph by Jean Mohr)

With Ben Sonnenberg (Photograph by Alexander Cockburn)

Playing piano, November 1983 (Photograph by Jean Mohr)

Jean Stein (Photograph by Brigitte Lacombe)

In Quincy, France (Photograph by Jean Mohr)

With Wadie (Photograph by Brigitte Lacombe)

With Noam Chomsky at Columbia, 1999
(Courtesy of the Said Family Collection)

With Diana Takieddine before the Columbia concert, 1993.
(Photograph by Joe Pineiro, courtesy of the University Archives, Rare
Book & Manuscript Library, Columbia University Libraries)

With Najla (Photograph by Yto Barrada)

At a rally for Palestine in 2000, Union Square, New York
(Courtesy of the Said Family Collection)

With Mariam (Photograph by Karl Sabbagh)

One of many paintings, drawings, and caricatures
(By Robert Shetterly, courtesy of AWTT, Americans Who Tell the Truth)

At his desk late in life
(Still from the film *Selves and Others: A Portrait of Edward Said*,
courtesy of Wamip Films, Paris)

It is reasonable to say, then, that Al-Azm and Chomsky were incorrect to think that the economic and sociological tenets of Marxism were never integral to Said's analyses. They are, on the contrary, particularly evident in his study on the ground of the Arab private sector in *The End of the Peace Process*, but not only there.[83] Aghast at the low level of organization and theoretical awareness among the militants in Beirut in 1972, he gave a structural, rather than personal or partisan, explanation of the morass:

> [We find] the mode of production and the mode of dis-
> tribution to be respectively, immediate consumption and
> dispersion. I mean something like this: since the society is
> essentially a surface, an exterior, it has no memory, no sense
> of dimension . . . Thus production, paradoxically, is con-
> sumption . . . You produce an idea, a product, a movement,
> only to have it *happen*—it lasts only for the consumption . . .
> There is no history.[84]

While engaging its modes of thought and conceptual apparatus, he did, it is true, resist Marxism as well, but for one reason alone: its partisans had not creatively adapted it.

Psychoanalysis stands as another neglected facet of Said's intellectual makeup. His childhood friend Andre Sharon went so far as to say that "[psycho]analysis is the key to Said."[85] Here, too, the record of Said's engagements with the assumptions and procedures of "the talking cure" is tantalizingly inconclusive. Readers tend to forget, or at least discount, his long discussion of Freud in *Beginnings*. Said retrospectively underlined the Viennese doctor's imposing role in the book in the new preface he wrote for *Beginnings*'s reissue in 1985. We can take its placement there as proof of the importance of Freud's theories to his work, for added to his psychological reading of Conrad, and placed alongside his last published work, *Freud and the Non-European* (2003), psychoanalysis bookends his career. The attention he pays to the field, though, would not necessarily please most Freudians.

Close readers of *Beginnings* had only a small taste of his devotion to the psychoanalytic implications of language. Despite treating Freud's writing on dreams, the role of the father, and the Oedipus complex, Said clearly considers the Freudian system predominantly linguistic and textual. Psychoanalysis so obviously relies on revealing the secrets of the unconscious (the "mystic writing pad" in Freud's terms) by dwelling on the etymologies of words uttered involuntarily by the patient in therapy. By the same token, the writer's powers of imagination are for Freud none other than the result of sublimating libidinal drives. In *Beginnings*, Freud is mobilized above all to break out of literary conventions by revealing the motives underlying narrative's temporal and spatial movement and by reconciling ideas with desires.[86] None of the gestures one associates with a psychoanalytic reading (the probing of suppressed symptoms, cathexis, psychosomatic neuroses) seemed of much interest to Said.

His investments, all the same, were personal, not only intellectual. Said began intense analysis as an undergraduate at Princeton and remained in therapy until the end of his life.[87] The turmoil over a father he perceived as distant and unsympathetic, the steep sexual learning curve as he escaped his mother's smothering embrace, a profound insecurity about his own identity, the violent oscillation between boastfulness and self-doubt—all played a part. But he also felt an irreconcilable tension between the movement politics of which he berated himself for not doing enough and the life of the mind he could not live without. His habits of writing were similarly tortured. Instead of letting his ideas unfold in a progression of steady drafts, he bottled them up, letting fragments out in conversation until he could no longer bear it, setting them down in a torrent of writing. Although he let few see it, he lived in agony.[88]

He threw himself into the psychoanalytic literature in the early 1970s, keeping close at hand a comprehensive bibliography prepared at the University of Buffalo's Center for the Psychological Study of the Arts.[89] In part, as he revealed in "Swift's Tory Anarchy," this was because he intended in his Swift study, if not a full-dress psychological interpretation, at least to lay out the conditions that made the range of Swift's psychology possible, from a concern with "fair liberty to an excremental fixation."[90] He was, we know, busy at work in October 1968 preparing a piece (never published) on the connection between linguistics, psychology, and psychiatry for *The Hudson Review* that placed Lacan's 1953 Rome lectures on, among other things, speech and language in psychoanalysis and Chomsky's theories face-to-face.[91] All made perfectly natural his close friendship with the very different intellectual companions, generationally, politically, and in overall sensibility, of Allen Bergson and Jacqueline Rose, one a practicing analyst, the other a psychoanalytic critic of literature.

What even the most attentive readers of *Beginnings* might miss, on the other hand, is the Arab substrate of almost all of his flirtations with the Freudian system. From as early as 1972, Said had written to Sami with a cri de coeur: "The Arabs since Avicenna and Ibn Khaldun (who borrowed from Aristotle) have never produced a theory of mind."[92] It would be a theme he returned to constantly, with ever more desperation and with a determination to set it right. Despite its advanced mental hospitals and brilliant psychological novels, Arab culture was characterized by "an almost total absence of 'psychological science'" in its social theory.[93] On the other hand, Said praised Mahfouz for the psychological depth of his representations of character and for capturing the "special mode of Arabic psychological experience":

> One of the most powerful things about Western culture in all its aspects is that anchoring the whole structure is a working theory of the human mind . . . Since without ego identity and ego stability relations are transitory. What is said is true only for the moment, and dies (metaphorically) thereafter. The connection between language and reality is never investigated.[94]

These larger civic possibilities of psychoanalysis were what Said particularly stressed. He had been taken, for example, with Erik Erikson's essay "The First Psychoanalyst" (1956), particularly his theory of the identity conflicts within the ego and resulting confusion about the subject's productive role in society. For Freud, the visceral appetites of the unconscious are the main players of mental life. In Erikson, by contrast, the ego's psychic needs are for a fulfillment that is plainly social.

In his notes for *Beginnings*, Said described these civic dimensions of psychoanalysis even more baldly. Freud, he noted, wanted to become a lawyer, a politician, a lawmaker—*Gesetzgeber*—before he chose to study medicine. Indeed, when Freud was exiled from Austria in 1938, he carried under his arm a manuscript on Moses, the supreme lawgiver. It is from that angle that Said detected comparisons between psychoanalysis and Vico's *New Science*. For Vico had tied a psychology of humans in prehistory to a study of their economic life, deifying labor in the myths of Hercules and Vulcan, for instance, showing that a fear of thunder originally drove early humans to domesticate nature in agriculture. What Said loved about Vico was reviled by Hannah Arendt, who contemptuously (but accurately) called him an "ideologist of the classless society."[95]

His interest, as he described it, was less psychoanalysis than "political psychology." He found one model in Nadim Rouhana's "The Psychological Bases for Political Behavior: The Case of Denial in Israeli Thought and Policy," which set out to explain the country's displacement of its responsibility for others' suffering by summoning the memory of their people's own.[96] Fittingly, then, in Said's *Freud and the Non-European*, Freud is depicted less as the bold explorer of the unconscious than as someone who cast doubt on the uniqueness of Jewish belonging by observing that Moses was Egyptian. The Jews might trace their bloodline to Abraham, but the rituals and faith that bind them came "from the outside, from a great stranger."[97] Just as iconoclastically, Freud challenged the foreignness of Jews to European culture; they were, in his handling, deeply enmeshed in it, and therefore not really outsiders in the usual sense. And Freud flatly disapproved of Zionism—his *Moses and Monotheism* standing as a historical obliteration of the tidiness of tribal identity as such, and thus opening the door for others to appreciate the common features of Palestinian and Jewish experience.[98]

If psychoanalysis was "textual" for Said in the sense of following Freud's reliance on writing and word choice when decoding the unconscious, in the East it was valuable in a more social and political way than Freud's fixation on the individual psyche might warrant. When one of his academic correspondents, Carl Brown, proposed a conference on psychoanalysis in 1972, Said was enthusiastic but wanted special attention paid to "the Arabic part of the field."[99] Originally, Said encouraged Brown's aim of exposing the many psychoanalytic abuses in the Middle East, among them the psychological torture used by occupying forces in Algeria and the Palestinian territories as well as the Freudian clichés that governed so much Western media coverage. Nasser's motives in the Suez crisis, for example, were once lamely traced to his hatred of his father. But he warned of problems of translation, "since most psychoanalysts don't know the language and most people who know the language know nothing about psychoanalysts."

For all his attractions to psychoanalysis, Said also bent the field to his will. He read André Green, the French psychoanalyst, born in Cairo to secular Jewish parents, and met Christopher Bollas, the author of the important modern psychoanalytic concept of the "unthought known."[100] He was conversant, then, with even out-of-the-way therapeutic and interpretive procedures but also militated against them. Freud the author and stylist rather than the theorist of childhood fantasies or the creativity of dreams is what mattered most. In a typical feint in his letter to Brown, he wrote that "the first psychologists were poets." Rather cagily in the preface to his dissertation (in passages that did not find their way into the book), he fleshed out this statement. The "polemic against the psychoanalytic prejudice of Conrad criticism," he observed, "is no more than an indictment of the sorcerer's apprentice."[101] Whatever magic, in short, that emerges from Freudian literary criticism is already found full-blown in the master (Conrad in this case), which is why Said reserved his admiration for the "power of the sorcerer *in his own hands.*"

Despite everything psychoanalysis offered, he did not believe the mind was "easily recovered by psychological digging."[102] The New York psychoanalytic scene in which he had deep personal roots reaching back to the beginning of his career put him off. On January 9, 1966, only a few years after he joined the Columbia faculty, he described a party at the house of a colleague:

> Watching, the other night at [Quentin] Anderson's; the propriety, confident, and even smug use, appropriation, and arming of themselves with Freud by [Steven] Marcus, [Richard] Hofstadter, convinces me by now that Freud has replaced—or rather (like the founding of Israel) fulfilled the Old Testament for the Jews. The promised land, and the Messiah. Simplicity, wish-fulfillment, the realization of a monumental, sustained fantasy. That all one's urges and instincts originate confidently in one place (Freud), that they go to another where they become fulfilled, themselves—Israel. How perfect and simple. It is an irresistible system, and one that is not only attractive but insidious. *To be avoided at all costs.*[103]

Later, in his Freud book, Said would embrace the rather different account of Jewish belonging of Isaac Deutscher, who in *The Non-Jewish Jew, and Other Essays* (1968) argued that their insecure status in Europe gave Jews like Spinoza, Marx, Trotsky, and Freud at once a privileged perspective and a reason to fight back.[104] Their intellectual triumph could be better explained by social marginality than by either libidinal drives or divine dispensations, and their dissidence drove them not to the safety of a protective fortress but to finding in their own marginality a common cause with the disoriented and dispossessed.[105]

Like psychoanalysis, feminism hovered over Said's career as a troubling question mark. To a degree, it overlapped with psychoanalysis as an exploration of desire, sexuality, and the invention of self. His commitments to "the woman question," at any rate, were of longer duration and more explicit than many have supposed. Deirdre David, a longtime correspondent and former student, put it plainly: "Said *was* a feminist" not just because he was surrounded by bright women, worked with them as equals, and acknowledged their leads but because women were a subordinated group.[106] By American academic feminism, though, he was never persuaded. The progressive political engagements of people like Michèle Barrett in Britain, he remarked, were not for the most part taken up in France and the United States, where "the question of gender has become metaphysical and psychologized."[107] Nor had he overlooked that the first-wave women's movement worked "hand in glove" with imperialism.[108] On the other hand, under different conditions their cause was integral to his own. He worked for years to found the Women's Resource Center in the West Bank and was quick to acknowledge the central role played by women in the intifada.[109]

Only the audacity of feminism, he suggested, would risk angering allies, as he had as a Palestinian, by insisting that left and right were not the only poles of politics. Palestinians shared with struggling women the same "absence, [and] silence" of social groups "banished to the attic, by an act of deliberate, programmatic exclusion."[110] Throughout the 1980s, just as he began to lose interest in literary theory, he saw in feminism a site of "interesting, daring, novel attempts to do something from an historical point of view, across discursive lines in often transgressive ways."[111] He frequently referred to Sandra Gilbert and Susan Gubar's *Madwoman in the Attic* (1979) along with his Columbia ally Jean Franco's *Plotting Women* (1989), Joan Scott's "invigorating and amazing" contestations,

Helen Callaway's *Gender, Culture, and Empire* (1987), and Hélène Cixous's and others' work, which made it "impossible to avoid . . . gender issues in the production and interpretation of art."[112]

No woman in his pantheon had the stature of Vico, of course, but the role of women, especially in his music criticism, was emphatic. Inspired by Catherine Clément's *Opera, or the Undoing of Women* (1988), he railed against the unsettling patterns in Western classicism where women were either the "inspirational muse, and later helpmeet, adjunct, adoring but lesser partner, to some prominent male composer" or a "destructive seductress"—as in Alban Berg's *Lulu* or Richard Strauss's *Salome*.[113] Moving beyond themes to institutions, he commented on the scarcity of serious work on women's role in the production and performance of music. Feminist theory, he complained, had not shown the same sophistication in music criticism as it had in other areas, which was not surprising, because the institution of Western classical music was such a "massively organized . . . masculine domain."[114] Does Beethoven's *Fidelio* flatter or demean women? He was not sure and looked to feminist criticism to find an answer.[115] He regularly corresponded with Rose Subotnik, one of the vanguard proponents of the so-called new music criticism, seeking her advice and in turn using his influence to help her professionally.

Likewise, he felt "twinned," as he put it, to the sociologist Gillian Rose, whose command of philosophy impressed him deeply just as her uncompromising intellectual style—influenced, like him, by Adorno as well as by a great dislike of poststructuralism—was one he felt entirely his own.[116] On the personal side, even before his mother died, women were his closest confidantes, a fact that established his deeply felt personal and professional indebtedness to the insights that only women brought to his life and the special ease he felt around them.[117] When he sought counsel, it was to women, not men, that he turned. Although he complained of his "not very satisfactory" relationships with his sisters, he spoke freely with them about even the most secret sides of his personal life, partly to confess, at times to brag, but always looking for advice.[118] His need for love and affirmation—in Tariq Ali's words, he "was really awful" about needing "to be praised"—led to intimacies that were as intense personally as politically.[119]

Too critical of American feminism to give it center stage, he held up women's scholarship ignored by others, and worked to open doors for women professionally. A colleague in the philosophy department, Akeel Bilgrami, co-taught courses with Said in the last years of his life. Once strolling down College Walk with him, and perhaps recognizing this side of Said's thinking about which so few knew, Bilgrami suggested they do a seminar together on feminism.[120] Said stopped in his tracks—a theatrical gesture he often used, letting his jaw drop as if to say "Don't tell me." The arrested motion was in this case ambiguous, but even though Bilgrami was only ribbing him, Said did not laugh and did not say no. Maybe they would have taught the course, it's hard to say, but he died before they had the chance.

CHAPTER 10

THE THIRD WORLD SPEAKS

A true symphony of discordance.

—SAID, "The Castle"[1]

Apart from the Carter years, the PLO's high-water mark was the nineteenth session of the Palestine National Council in Algiers in 1988, the so-called Intifada Meeting. No longer waiting hat in hand for the great powers to recognize them, the delegates issued a declaration of independence, unilaterally establishing a Palestinian state. In turn, they officially recognized the Jewish state already there, embracing UN Resolutions 242 and 338 acknowledging Israel's right to live "in peace within secure and recognized boundaries" in exchange for Israel's withdrawal from the territories occupied after 1967. All parties would agree to end "all military activity."

It was Said whom the PLO chose to deliver the good news. As the Palestinian representative on the prominent ABC news program *Nightline* on November 15, 1988, he reported ebulliently from Algiers only moments after the declaration was passed, never more visibly at one with the PLO leadership. The program's opening video segment, in fact, portrayed him at Arafat's right hand. There he sat, a trusted counselor discussing drafts of documents that he held in his outstretched hands as an animated Arafat looked on approvingly. During the program, the cameras now focused on him with the skyline of Algiers in the background as he laid out clearly the position he had always held and that was now engraved in the PLO platform: "two states, one Arab, one Jewish . . . that would partition Palestine between them and co-exist peacefully."

The PNC's unanimity was short-lived. In an explosive October 1989 interview for the Kuwaiti newspaper *Al-Qabas* in Paris, Said predicted that the PLO's top-down leadership was pushing the movement over a cliff.[2] He and Abu-Lughod were "disgusted by the negligence, corruption, and incapacity" of a leadership that went about acting the supplicant, treating the U.S. government like a "big white father" when the United States was really acting as an attorney for Israeli interests. He had been "filling [Arafat's] eyes and ears" with news about what was lacking for the last fifteen years to no avail. Writing to the Palestinian diplomat Leila Shahid in 1991, he struck a similar note: "He hasn't so much as called any of us for advice . . . What kind of leadership is that?"[3]

The 1988 meeting had itself sown the seeds of discord. Everyone agreed that unilaterally declaring Palestinian independence and installing the PLO as its provisional government ingeniously narrowed Israel's options. For now its violence would be rightly seen as breaching a nation's sovereignty rather than quelling uprisings within its territories. The position already had high-profile support from, among others, Jerome M. Segal, a research scholar at the Institute for Philosophy and Public Policy at the University of Maryland, who had just published a barrage of op-eds in *The New York Times*, the *Los Angeles Times*, *The Washington Post*, and several other prominent papers proposing an almost identical plan to the one the PNC adopted.[4] The disagreement lay with how the new government would orient itself to the intifada. Given the radicalization of the base, where Palestinian youth faced tanks armed only with stones and slingshots, it was really Israel that needed Arafat, not the other way around. And yet now, gratified by the new attention, Arafat played the moderate, willing to trade land for peace and working hard to "get the Palestinian teenagers to cool it."[5] Said wanted instead not to dampen but to encourage the revolutionary ferment, striking the accusatory note in speeches at the time that the intifada (which was hardly seen this way even by allies) was "surely the most impressive and disciplined anti-colonial insurrection in this century."[6]

Awkward political tensions complicated matters. As Bush *père* prepared to redraw the map of the Middle East with the buildup to war in August 1990, and the first invasion of Iraq in January 1991, Said met the fall of the Berlin Wall in 1989 with mixed emotions. At first he welcomed the event, seeing similarities between the upheavals in Eastern Europe and the intifada.[7] In time he thought better of aligning himself with the likes of French theorists like Jean-François Lyotard, who in the wake of the fall extolled the triumph of U.S. capitalism in a series of "postmodern fables."[8] Said later took relish in ridiculing Lyotard for popularizing the idea that it was better to live without convictions, that noble causes were dangerous, and that consumer culture was liberating. These views, inspired by the fall of communism, Lyotard called the "postmodern condition," and it was Said's frequent target throughout the 1990s.

In June 1990, Said's mother, Hilda, died in Washington, D.C., after a seven-year battle with cancer. His sister Grace, then living in the capital, had been caring for her selflessly, with Said coming down from New York on frequent visits. By then in hospice care and living in Grace's flat, Hilda talked with her son every day for hours on the phone. "What the hell are you talking about for so long?" Grace would ask.[9] His answers were vague: about this or that. His sister could not understand how they filled the time, for it was mostly gossip, but Hilda needed the distractions. For, like her son, she had trouble sleeping. He would "pick her brains about people he knew," although Grace suspected it had less to do with trading news than the need for each other's company. In the last six weeks of her life, metastasis attacked her brain, and she mostly lay unconscious. No matter, he kept vigil by her bed with Grace, both waiting hopelessly for her to awake. Years later, he would admire her courage in refusing chemotherapy despite her doctor's constant entreaties. "I don't want the torture of it," she had explained.

Her dying was more poignant for its symbolism. Hilda had spent the last six years of her life as a nomad shuttling between Beirut, Washington, and New York, with little side trips to visit specialists in London. Like many Palestinians, she had been granted Lebanese citizenship in the 1950s, and so was not technically stateless, but her U.S. visa required regularly leaving and reentering the country.[10] With her children already U.S. citizens, she could easily have become one herself, but this required obligatory stays in the United States for up to a year at a time, which she found unappealing. The terminal illness, at any rate, made travel back and forth impossible, and as a result she overstayed her visa. Deportation proceedings were begun by the Immigration and Naturalization Service, even as she lay on her deathbed. Only her death rendered the order moot, and the judge at the hearing berated the U.S. immigration authorities for their heartlessness.

BETWEEN 1987 AND 1992, Said worked haltingly on a novel about betrayal.[11] By the mid-1990s, as he frequently told Mariam, the betrayal theme had morphed into another one highlighting the impotence of Arab men (a fitting post-Oslo refrain), but by then he had abandoned the project. Set in Beirut on the eve of the political crisis of 1958, it was a story of intrigue—a Middle East John le Carré or Graham Greene novel, although its large international cast of characters made it impossible not to see Conrad's *Nostromo* lurking behind its scenes and situations. Espionage, police repression, politically driven humiliation were the major plot elements. Only forty-five pages were completed in the end, but among them were detailed notes and outlines for the pages he never finished. The backstory actually took place: In 1958, Lebanese Muslims and Druze, inspired by ascendant Nasserism, agitated for Lebanon to join the United Arab Republic. Lebanon's president, Camille Chamoun, a Maronite Christian, responded by calling for a U.S. military intervention, which took place on July 15 and continued until the fighting subsided and the pro-Western Chamoun government was stabilized.

Against this backdrop, the novel revolves around the abduction of a medical student who had taken part in a campus protest against Eisenhower and Dulles and who is betrayed by an informant, later hauled off to a secret prison. One by one, the characters of Said's life reappear in slightly altered form. The medical student recalled Said's martyred Cairene doctor, Farid Haddad, just as Emily, Farid's mother, stood in for Hilda.[12] A powerful but estranged relative, the pompous Michel Saba, who is first seen in his office reading the homilies of Saint John Chrysostom and lecturing everyone on the evils of communism, is a barely disguised Charles Malik. Saba is intent on converting the wayward Farid to Christianity and then, after forcing this submission, handing him over to the Americans.

Said himself is an ambiguous and distorting combination of two different characters: Asaad Francob (the "opposite" of Farid, according to Said's notes), a "chameleon-like" character who talks too much and is having an affair with a journalist with ties to a shady U.S. secret agent; and Sidgi, a distinguished fifty-year-old Harvard PhD in philosophy, whose many published books and international reputation provoke his Beirut peers to humiliate him by demanding that he get a local high school degree before teaching at the university.

Apart from a glimpse into his occasional self-mockery, the novel's fragments provide an invaluable insight into his aesthetic intentions. According to his notes, he thought the best Palestinian writing had managed to balance the "classical/universal and novel/situational"—that is, a middle space between brutal realism and ritual.[13] Beirut cannot but stand for itself in the novel, the literal place

of cosmopolitan delight and degraded civil strife, but it also signi-
fies as a "nascent Arab stage." Francob is not a person so much as a
polemical type, the "completely free man" who can "get away with
anything and accumulate no history." And Sidgi is almost allegori-
cal, a Western intellectual who is "cut off from Arabs and the West,
aware of Jews . . . powerless to change, too honest to affiliate." If
Sidgi is a little less repellent than Francob (who we later learn is the
one who betrayed Farid), Said is just as merciless in portraying him
(with an added touch of Al-Azm) as a polemicist who descended
from aristocratic stock, a man who "never learned how to be cryptic
or allusive . . . like an elephant walking through grass." In one particularly mordant aside, he dwells on his own inauthenticity by describing his alter ego's "disproportionately tall, authentically
Levis-clad body, safari jacket, and Bruno Magli moccasins setting
him apart from the enormous crowd of drab gray-shirted, gray or
khaki trousered and mostly slippered young men and women."

He left the final form of the novel unclear, but not his direc-
tive to explode the "long narrative line" associated with the realist
novel, which he thought guilty of the illusions of continuity. This
he felt untrue to Palestinian experience. "Stay with the fragment,"
he counsels. "I trust its distracted shortness, its always refreshingly
re-begun opening." Only that way would he be able to get over "the
insidious restraint . . . of letting my 'subjectivity' flow forth," as he
put it. With "subjectivity" safely in quotation marks, he wanted to
avoid at all costs the confessional mode of so much bad third-world
lyric poetry and testimonial fiction.

In the end, his own authorial personality overwhelmed him, and
that had a great deal to do with his abandoning the novel. Later,
he would explain his reasons in a remarkable essay inspired by his
friend the South African novelist and Nobel Prize winner Nadine
Gordimer, in which he spoke of the role of authors as social comedi-
ans whose job is done when they have captured existence fearlessly
or beautifully in words.[14] This threat of observing folly and injustice

from outside and above, and then accepting them, gave him pause. The novelist could be completed only by criticism, and that meant saying no to what is, not reproducing it faithfully.

IN SEPTEMBER 1991, just before casting the novel aside, Said organized a conference in London, hoping to firm up and clarify weak PLO bargaining positions in preparation for the Madrid Conference planned for late October. Co-sponsored by the United States and the Soviet Union, the Madrid initiative was meant to revive the peace process by involving Jordan, Lebanon, and Syria in the negotiations. Along with four others from the American Council for Palestinian Affairs, he set out to "break the political logjam."[15] Unfortunately, beset by factional quarrels and the same tired arguments, the effort was a dispiriting failure.[16] Said perceived again the troubling trend in the PLO leadership to hunt for back channels, seeking favors from potentates. Because two superpowers had approached the PLO, its leaders no longer felt obliged to solicit goodwill from the public. If Said had barely been heeded earlier, after the Madrid gathering he was now sidelined more or less completely. The formula for the Oslo disaster was already taking shape.

Meanwhile, with his usual preoccupation with health issues, he called home during a break to get the results of a recent blood test taken to monitor his cholesterol levels. Two years earlier, the family doctor, Charles Hazzi, had noticed suspiciously high white blood cell counts, which were steadily rising—the first signs of a possible cancer. Already alerted to the possibility, Said had begun to worry, and so was more than usually eager to get the latest results. To his surprise, Mariam did not reassure him, telling him instead to contact Hazzi immediately. Alarmed, he pressed her until she broke the bad news to him.

The tests showed he had chronic lymphocytic leukemia.[17] Hazzi played it down, insisting that the condition was not life threatening and that a good hematologist could handle it. Najla and Wadie were dutifully informed but told there was nothing to worry about because their father's life was not in immediate danger. Said responded initially with relief, for despite his hypochondria a real illness, especially a life-threatening one, he wanted no part of, and eagerly sought reassurance.

Only when he was back in New York at Memorial Sloan Kettering did the diagnosis turn brutal. With what he considered tasteless insensitivity, Memorial doctors told him he would soon be dead. Unwilling to accept this verdict, he searched for other opinions and in six months discovered Kanti Rai, an innovative hematologist and oncologist at Long Island Jewish Medical Center who would treat him over the next decade. In time, Rai would become a friend. Said introduced him to the work of Nietzsche, invited him to his seminars, and coaxed Gordimer to show him around South Africa. In return Rai, a native of Jodhpur, India, introduced him to Rajasthani *langas* at his daughter's wedding in 1996. Their mutual affection was strengthened by sharing stories about the misdeeds of the British empire. Said would visit India for the first time a year later, giving lectures in Delhi and Calcutta.

Said was used to keeping feelings to himself. He had a talent for making others believe they were his confidants when, in reality, he withheld his most revealing vulnerabilities and doubts until he felt it time to let them out. And when he did, he told everyone. With the diagnosis now plain, he was resolved to stay mum as Mariam and the children wrestled with its implications. Suddenly, a week afterward, he woke up in the middle of the night and informed Mariam that he wanted to tell the world he had cancer.[18] She wanted him to wait until more tests were out, but he was adamant, and the next day he began telling friends "confidentially" one after the other, as though they were privy to a secret, that he was sick and that the prognosis was dire.

Rai began treating him with immune therapy using monoclonal antibodies in June 1992 but had to resort to the more traditional methods of chemotherapy (Fludarabine and Rituximab) after March 1994.[19] He reserved the summers for the strongest doses of treatment so that Said could recover in time to continue teaching during the academic year. Being both vain and bloody-minded enough to will himself into relative normalcy for the first half decade of the onslaught, Said managed to maintain the illusion of health by keeping a robust physical appearance, managing even a head of hair despite some thinning. But by the end of the 1990s, the chemo had visibly ravaged him; his handsome face was pale and his cheeks sunken. A tumor in his belly gave him the strange appearance of a man both wasting away and putting on weight.

In direct response to the terminal diagnosis, Said began *Out of Place* in May 1992, one of many milestones provoked by his changing prospects.[20] In August of that year, he was fast at work correcting not one but two manuscripts for publication: "my political writings over 25 years," as he described *The Politics of Dispossession* (1994) and *Representations of the Intellectual* (1994). Still referring to his memoir by the original title "Not Quite Right," he reflected on the project in its infancy, saying that he was "beginning to be very engrossed in the joys and, alas, the problems of autobiography."

Four months before his diagnosis but already in a political funk, new energy arrived from an unexpected source. In May 1991, he was invited to South Africa to give the T. B. Davie Academic Freedom Lecture, where he met Walter Sisulu and Nelson Mandela, who had been released from a twenty-seven-year prison stay in February of the previous year.[21] Hosted by the University of the Witwatersrand in Johannesburg before proceeding to the main event in Cape Town, he was the official guest of the African National Congress (ANC), then still the central flame of anti-apartheid resistance. After meeting privately with Mandela briefly, he spent a much longer time with Sisulu (himself a leader who spent many years in prison) discussing the history of ANC struggle. The demise of the ANC, thwarted by a betrayal of its own principles and a corrupt leadership, was not at the time as publicly clear as it later became, although some of Said's close South African friends on the left had none of his uncritical reverence for the organization.[22] He looked past their warnings in the name of importing tactical lessons for the Palestinian movement.

His conversations with Sisulu reanimated his efforts to organize the London gathering four months later, filled as it was with invaluable lessons about the ANC's focus on winning the ethical high ground rather than focusing on doomed military campaigns. This identification with an anticolonial liberation struggle was the best rejoinder he knew to the reactionary spirit of the 1980s. In an era that saw the crushing of the New Jewel Movement of Maurice Bishop in Grenada, the exhaustion of the Sandinistas, a stand-off in El Salvador, and the invasion of Panama, Said saw Palestine's future in a third-world revolutionary movement of a similar type—one that had learned the power of symbols to inspire a vast international following. Of course, this ameliorating gesture was predictably attacked. The PFLP, with which he had once flirted, denounced him for being too "bourgeois," and he broke with its leader, George Habash, who took the hard line in not recognizing Israel at the very 1988 meeting of the PNC in which Said sided with the majority.

His post-ANC media strategies were detectable in *Pontecorvo: The Dictatorship of Truth*, a film he produced and narrated for BBC Television's Channel 4 on May 6, 1992. This fascinating documentary was ostensibly about an Italian neorealist director. But it pursued an anticolonial theme, focusing on Gillo Pontecorvo's deliberately rough black-and-white classic, *The Battle of Algiers* (1966). Said used the film to explore the aesthetics of third-world resistance, though he was disenchanted with Pontecorvo's later work, in which the beauty of ideas gave way to an emphasis on artistic autonomy.

A few years earlier, in 1988, he had called on Pontecorvo in Rome, arriving at his doorstep "with only the slenderest of introductions." A middle-class Jew who grew up under Mussolini, the director had met Picasso, Stravinsky, and Sartre in Paris, where he then lived as a tennis player, later becoming a twenty-four-year-old head of the communist youth movement and leader of antifascist resistance throughout northern Italy. How could a man of such political passions, Said asked, "sublimate them completely in images and music" in his more recent work? Aestheticism, Said suggested, had crippled him.[23] He lamented that the same man who inspired Oliver Stone, Costa-Gavras, and Bertolucci had "all but vanished from the stage of European cinema" at the height of his fame and influence because he did not want producers meddling with his artistic vision. Tragically, Pontecorvo had planned a film on the intifada as well, but this too was a casualty of his perfectionism.

Beleaguered by the times, Said found himself more and more under siege within the Palestinian movement itself. After meeting former president Carter in Virginia on August 24 of that year, he wrote to him in September to get his support for the Welfare Association, a private fund-raising organization for helping Palestinians in the West Bank, Gaza, Israel, and Lebanon. He had been trying to arrange a meeting between Carter and the association's director, George Abed, author of *The Economic Viability of a Palestinian State* (1990).[24]

Despite these and similar initiatives over the previous decade, and partly because of them, in 1989 the PLO leadership unleashed the slanderous rumor that Said was an American collaborator. At the time of the *Al-Qabas* interview following the 1988 Algiers meeting—his first public voicing of doubts about the PLO leadership—he was attacked by Nabil Shaath, then chairman of the PNC Foreign Affairs Committee, along with Marwan Kanafani, former Arab League officer and brother of the well-known Palestinian writer Ghassan Kanafani. Among other things, they insinuated that as a member of the Council on Foreign Relations from 1983 on, Said was in league with Israeli Labor Party politicians.[25] Ironically, Said had agitated for years to have others recognize that pinning the PLO's hopes on "liberal" Israeli labor was a fatal miscalculation. The accusers nevertheless found Said's old-school ties to figures in the State Department and *Foreign Affairs* suspect. His earlier invitation from

David Rockefeller to address the Trilateral Commission (which Said declined) seemed just another stroke in the damning portrait.[26]

The atmosphere was murky enough for an Arab newspaper in Paris, *Al-Youm al-Saba*, to weigh in, defending him against the charge that he had gone over to the other side. Said pointed out that Arafat and Yasser Abed Rabbo, a member of the PLO Executive Committee, had also been invited to the Council on Foreign Relations and were eager to accept. It would be foolish, he said, to refuse the opportunity. In any event, the council was not simply a pernicious pro-U.S. advisory body. It was, as he pointed out in the interview, a "private organization whose members are outstanding personalities interested in U.S. foreign affairs."[27] Its influence on American foreign policy, much of it disastrous from Said's point of view, made it an almost exact counterpart of Chatham House in the U.K. and therefore a place to be heard if one could. His position and intentions were misperceived, it turned out, not only by the PLO but also by its enemies. His Israeli comrade in arms, Israel Shahak, dug up a report prepared by the American Enterprise Institute, whose apparent aim was to stymie Palestinian aspirations by having Said and Walid Khalidi "help Israel to cause a split in the PLO and engage in discussion about Camp David with the Israelis."[28]

Within a year, his political life would enter a second phase, the two halves neatly divided by the Oslo peace agreement of September 1993. In the humiliating aftermath of those accords, signed with great fanfare by Yasser Arafat and Yitzhak Rabin on the White House lawn during the Clinton years, Said broke bitterly with the very PLO chairman he had so relentlessly defended throughout the 1970s and 1980s when Arafat's name could barely be mentioned in public without inviting rebuke. Once again, he was fighting a two-front war.

Pushing back against the age did not mean going unrewarded by it. In June 1991, he became a fellow of the prestigious American Academy of Arts and Sciences (he would be elected a member of the academy only in 2002 after the art critic and board member

Michael Fried, his old grad school friend, intervened to point out that the honor was long overdue).[29] In 1994, UNESCO awarded him the Picasso Medal for lifetime achievement, and in April, along with a teaching award given by the Columbia College Student Council in honor of his skill at paying "tribute to the Core Curriculum," he became the first faculty member to win the Lionel Trilling Award twice, this time for *Culture and Imperialism* (1993), judged a "masterpiece" by the selections committee.[30]

Still, his biggest coups came in the form not of prizes but of platforms. The Reith radio lectures, the BBC's flagship annual series, had been founded by Bertrand Russell and featured over the years the likes of Robert Oppenheimer, Ali Mazrui, and John Kenneth Galbraith. Over the objections of British conservatives writing in the tabloids, Said gave his 1993 lectures on the unique historical role of intellectuals, later commenting to a friend that "it was crazy for me to accept." He had to write six lectures to be published immediately and broadcast with only "about a month to do it."[31] The lectures compensated for the major study on intellectuals he had always planned but never written. Somehow, he managed to get the lectures done, and they appeared as *Representations of the Intellectual*, in much the form he delivered them on air.

With this busy speaking schedule, it was a struggle to keep his family close, although he felt the need sharply now when his health was so uncertain. In 1993, then a freshman in college, Najla accompanied Said on a trip to France for a UNESCO roundtable. One of the participants was the Nobel Prize–winning Colombian novelist Gabriel García Márquez, an author Said hugely admired (he would marvel with friends over the author's novella *No One Writes to the Colonel*).[32] At the reception, García Márquez walked right up to Najla and asked (in French), "Which of my books have you read?" which apparently was the question he asked everyone he met. And not being able to lie in this or in anything else, she quickly answered *rien* (nothing).[33] He found this charming, and Najla pretty, and, grabbing her by the arm, walked her around the room like his date for the rest of the event.

Delightful distractions like these, though, were hard to come by. Although it obviously alarmed him, the leukemia diagnosis did not alter Said's way of life for some years. Only around 1993, when the trajectory of the illness was clearer, did he contemplate serious changes.[34] One of them was to risk performing piano in public. Although he had freely played for students and friends in his apartment (including at his sixtieth birthday party), his only performance after college took the form of playing short passages for illustration purposes during the Wellek music lectures at Irvine. It was time to overcome the performance anxiety that his old roommate John Solum had recognized in him at Princeton. He decided to give a joint performance at the Miller Theatre at Columbia University on April 27, 1993, with Diana Takieddine, a professional pianist and comrade from the 1970s in Beirut, playing a challenging program of works for two pianos by Brahms, Mozart, Chopin, Britten, and Schubert (the performance was repeated at Georgetown). In his opening remarks onstage, he referred to her self-effacingly as the "real pianist."

Performing in public had an unforeseen benefit: it made it impossible for enemies to write him off as a brittle polemicist.[35] The audience found the performance dazzling, with subtle dynamic shifts and lightness of articulation. After the performance, he was at first giddy as after a successful lecture, overjoyed that he had gotten through it. Later he wrote to a colleague to say, with unnecessary modesty, that he was sorry the fellow had missed the concert, "not because it was such wonderful playing (it was ok I guess), but because it was a great Columbia event, from my point of view at least. Afterwards it took me three days to be able to get out of bed."[36] In the weeks leading up to the concert, he had exhausted Takieddine with demands to practice, so eager was he to make the event a success. Some professional musicians in the audience naturally noticed mistakes, a few of them grumbling about them at intermission. Aware that he was not, after all, a professional, he later beat himself up, pouring out his heart on the phone to his friend Allen Bergson that he had been dreadful and had made a fool of himself.[37] The audience reaction suggested nothing of the kind.

Meanwhile, Harvard's courtship again picked up, and this time he decided to accept their overtures.[38] Said's skillful negotiating over salary and perks was legend among his friends, but in this instance there was no gamesmanship.[39] Cambridge was quieter than New York and inseparable in his mind from the monastic intensity he had enjoyed in his grad student years. It would be a nice city to die in, he thought.[40] If it seemed unlikely that he would leave the media and publishing capital of the world, where the best opera in America was staged, he still had many connections in Cambridge, and Najla had after all been born there in 1974.

During a bid almost a decade earlier, he had written to Harry Levin on December 26, 1985, to put his feelings plainly: despite the frenetic pace of New York, he felt a "deepening solitude . . . So one gets lonelier all the time, and the alienating effect of this most rootless and exilic of cities has amplified the loneliness."[41] This was all the truer when contemplating death. But when Said realized that his motives for leaving New York were mostly about what his hometown lacked rather than the attractions of Cambridge itself, he pulled back. On April 22, 1993, he declined the offer from Harvard for good, putting an end to a courtship of two decades.[42] Only four months later, he was asked to assist in the defense of Nidal Ayyad, accused in the World Trade Center bombings, by helping the lawyers assess the "grammatical styles of two notes/letters that the United States plans to introduce as evidence in its case in chief." Said curtly declined three weeks later.[43]

With the help of the French sociologist Pierre Bourdieu, Said found a second major platform. He was invited to give a series of lectures at the Collège de France in 1996, forming the core observations that would, with many changes, lead to his last book, *On Late Style*

(2006).[44] Writing in August to "Cher Pierre Bourdieu," he explained his plans for the lectures with a characteristic lack of confidence: "In the end, I decided—despite everything—to give the lectures in French; it will at the very least be an adventure."[45] Said's self-doubt was again misplaced. Marina Warner, a British historian and novelist, made the trip to Paris to hear the last of Said's lectures on Adorno and was taken with his idiomatic fluency and his ability to engage with participants in French after the talk. The audience apparently felt the same, for his lecture on Wagner was packed, and a formal dinner followed at the home of Leila Shahid, the first woman ambassador of Palestine, then stationed in Paris.[46]

WITH SAID LARGELY SIDELINED by the PLO, music took on an even greater prominence in his life. For one thing, it offered a way of knowing and feeling that many of his colleagues could not find in their critical arsenal; for another, it carried none of the unpleasant baggage of rival critical schools or political strife. As a result, it began to find its way even into books that seemed not to be about music at all—*Culture and Imperialism*, for instance, his promised sequel to *Orientalism*, and *On Late Style*.

For all its erudition and elegance, *Culture and Imperialism* was strangely turned in on itself. The long shadow of Operation Desert Storm (1991) darkened its pages and its mood. There were dangers, as he had learned from earlier abandoned projects, in writing a work of such scope, and indeed the scholarly apparatus of *Culture and Imperialism* seemed a little ad hoc. Hundreds of titles were mentioned, usually in passing, but without reference to the vast corpus of work on imperialism as an economic process or as a system that assumed so many distinct historical forms. How to write about imperialism without speaking about the intricate international machinery of modern capitalism? As though to compensate, he put his trust in literary critics whose work was embroiled in economic theory.

As a critic of "reification"—society's tendency to turn all personal relationships into things for sale—Lukács was just such a
critic.[47] Digging through the formal and thematic features of novels in order to find traces of historical trends, Said was never more
Lukácsian than in *Culture and Imperialism*. Of course, his admiration went much further back. Still, it was the precise borrowings from Lukács that mattered here, for they were not the ones he
had highlighted in his earlier essays. Writing to Jean Starobinski
in 1967, he extolled Lukács for many of the same reasons that his
American colleagues faulted him, praising the Hungarian Marxist's
interpretive model, which traced the continuities between works of
literature and "world-views . . . socio-cultural conditions" with an
astounding "theoretical subtlety."[48] Prior to the book's appearance,
he worried that these political readings of fiction might be misread.
Writing to his former co-adviser Monroe Engel in 1989, he fretted: "I
don't want you to think of me as treating literature only as a vehicle
for my convictions, but of seeing it as part of (dare one say it) global
processes which have been sanitized out of it."[49]

There were good tactical reasons, Said thought, for treating only
part of what authors intended. *Not* getting to the bottom of what
they might fully mean allowed him to mobilize agreed-upon understandings for specific purposes. It was a classic post-*Beginnings*
gesture of sacrificing mandarin finesse for principled clarity and a
habit that recalled Gramsci's riposte to the influential intellectual
Benedetto Croce, who had chastised the communist movement
for its crude treatment of certain concepts. Gramsci agreed, but
added that watering down difficult ideas is a feature of all mass
movements and necessary for their dissemination. Said's comment
in a letter to *The Times Literary Supplement* in 1992 assessing recent
books by two younger theorists was typical: they "sometimes allow
the subtlety of their nice theoretical webs to obscure the underlying
disparities of power . . . Why not instead study the work of writers
like Edward Thompson who opposed imperialism openly? Or of Indian and African nationalists of the same period?"[50]

It is obvious, at any rate, how little questions of aesthetic form troubled Said when interpreting literature in *Culture and Imperialism*. He unabashedly defended the reading of novels for what they revealed about a historical period, saying it did not diminish the value of the work of art but supplied "complex affiliations with their real setting."[51] Levin's remarks in *The Gates of Horn* more or less captured his former student's view: "The major tendency of the novel, in the modern West, has been that deliberate resolve on the part of writers to confront, to reflect, and to criticize life."[52] Setting his sights on this resolve, Said followed in the steps of that book, published the year Said graduated from Harvard, by dwelling on this contest between "separable content" and "belletristic philandering," as Levin put it.[53] At least as a tactical matter in these projects, the former won out for both of them.

The labor of this massive study was spectacular, stretching Said's narrative powers to the limit. In letters, he referred anxiously to its "slightly too large framework."[54] Perhaps its best-known parts—the controversial chapters on Jane Austen's *Mansfield Park* and Verdi's *Aida*, which prompted a number of indignant published replies defending Austen's feminist integrity and Verdi's anticolonial politics—suggested a study primarily designed to show how works of art quietly encode and disavow a violent imperial relationship.[55] The underlying premise was that true artistry absorbs its environment so sensitively that it bears witness to values it lacks the power to diagnose.

This at-times-ridiculed aspect of the study—Al-Azm sneered, "It's hardly news to say that the culture of an imperial country reflects imperial attitudes"—barely touched the book's ambitions, though.[56] Warmly received in many quarters (Chomsky considered it, along with *The Question of Palestine*, his most important book), and already in its fifth printing by June 1993, *Culture and Imperialism* bore little resemblance to the popular summaries of it found, for example, in *Time* magazine.[57] This "plum pudding of a book," wrote Robert Hughes, is about "how the three big realities of empire—imperialism, 'native' resistance, decolonization—helped shape, in particular, the English and French novel."[58]

Culture and Imperialism, though, had far greater ambitions. Unwilling to see imperialism as a "mental attitude" alone, Said tightly moored the book's argument to the hard facts of land acquisition, which is only another way he brought economics into an argument that seemed to neglect it: "By 1914, the annual rate [of land appropriation] had risen to an astonishing 240,000 square miles, and Europe held a grand total of roughly 85 percent of the earth as colonies."[59] At every turn, Said reminded readers that everything from trade imbalances to ore extraction and colonial education systems was traceable to battles over square footage. Like *Orientalism*, whose final chapter moved from Napoleon's Egypt to the U.S. State Department, the book's coda turned its eye on the here and now of empire, laying out a case for how transnational corporations are involved in what amounts to a war on "public space."[60]

The brute physicality of land and the fact that the globe had only so much of it gave the book a groundedness it would not otherwise have had, and so helped him fend off the charge (leveled by his friend and political ally Sami Al-Banna among others) that he was too much the idealist, giving center stage to images and ideas over the real determinations of weapons, money, and natural resources. Said was, in fact, stressing the intractable permanence of land, the boundaries of place, and the imperious centrality of the English language. His fixations on geography were obvious to visitors to his apartment, where he at times pulled out one of those large-format maps that generals and war strategists use in the Situation Room to study the balance of forces for the coming battle. There he proceeded to show them exactly what Palestinians were up against, the various Bantustans that confined them, the roads that cut through their territories choking off transportation and preventing access, much like the township system in South Africa under apartheid.[61]

Without mentioning the Israeli occupation of Palestine directly in *Culture and Imperialism*, he clearly had it in mind in detailing earlier acts of conquest in India, Africa, and Southeast Asia. But he did so while considerably stretching his earlier concept of imaginative geography in a move that Al-Banna and others thought far too idealist. He was never more forceful than in *Culture and Imperialism* in making the claim that the right to settle or work on a plot of land is "reflected, contested, and even for a time decided in narrative."[62] The legal authority over land is usually bestowed on those with a claim to inheritance or previous settlement. Both are propped up by what are essentially stories about one rather than another version of the past. Ultimately, law conforms to the story that wins over the largest audience.

This apparent collision in his argument between the formative power of ideas and the hard materiality of land was another sign of a project at war with itself. The tension could be discerned in his use of the term "imperialism" itself. In the book's opening movement, Said boldly, and somewhat dubiously, reversed the commonly understood temporal order of imperialism and colonialism. Conventionally, the latter is thought to have come first, a pragmatic and unsystematic process of private ventures and holding companies from the fifteenth to the nineteenth century, in which resources are stolen, labor enforced, and settler communities established abroad, eventually with the help of the crown. The East India Company would be a paradigm of this kind of operation.

In the more commonly accepted account, imperialism is understood as the late nineteenth-century financialization of this earlier process. Unlike colonialism, imperialism exerts control from afar through punitive trade agreements, International Monetary Fund interest rate manipulations, government sanctions, and World Bank austerity plans. Instead of by occupying other countries, setting up bureaucracies, or training a native elite, power is asserted by the threat of military intervention and the institution of sanctions, as well as by more temporary military occupations. Said reverses this chronology. In *Culture and Imperialism* he considers imperialism not the extension of a system based on the theft of resources and the coercion of labor but a primal urge, even a lust, for conquest and racial subjugation that predates colonialism: "a protracted, almost metaphysical obligation to rule subordinate, inferior, or less advanced peoples." He further argued, and just as iconoclastically, that colonialism "has now largely ended," a position that contradicted many of his earlier statements on the subject.[63]

Here too one found a conflict with another ambition of the book left untouched in the *Time* magazine review and other mainstream sources. Neither his general nor his academic audience picked up on his clear agenda in the book, which was to extol the golden age of the anticolonial liberation movements of Frantz Fanon, Patrice Lumumba, Amílcar Cabral, and others. He was insisting not only that their experiences were still relevant but that they provided better models for understanding the contemporary imperial system than those currently popular in the academy. This theoretical indecision about whether colonialism does or does not still exist was reflected in the book's contrasting emotional registers in which close readings mixed with honorific accounts of unsung heroes and the grandeur of scholarly assessment gave way to stories of the harshness of imprisonment, hunger, and torture suffered by the empire's rebels and gadflies. These latter elements gave the book a rabble-rousing feel that sat awkwardly alongside its weighty bibliography and occasional uncertainty.

Despite this clash of ideas, Said held the project together with one consistent desire. Whatever else he did, he wanted here at last to begin to locate an original, completely indigenous, third-world theory, which for years he had complained was lacking. At one point, he seemed to have found one version of "purely native" forms of dissent in the Bengali historian Ranajit Guha's "dharmic protest," but he hunted for more examples.[64] To that end, key words were summoned in the book's chapter titles and headings that suggested its uneasy attempts at unity: "discrepant experiences," "resistance and opposition," "consolidated vision." But here too he worked against himself, settling into an overall organization that stressed "two sides" and "two visions."

The musical image of counterpoint was one expression of this binary: two melodies superimposed, blending sounds but keeping the two melodic lines independent of each other as though harmony were an accident along the horizontal journey rather than the chord's collective union in vertical sound. As in *Orientalism*, he was looking for common ground, insisting on mutual respect for the differences among peoples, but with no interest at all in the sort of mythical and absolute fissure between East and West found in the poetry of Kipling. With that in mind, he set out to destroy the West's "rightward-tending damnation" that sees anything nonwhite, non-Western, non-Judeo-Christian as being outside its ethos, and ridiculed with equal fervor the likes of the Iranian sociologists Ali Shariati and Jalal Al-e-Ahmad, who considered the West "an enemy, a disease, an evil." Yet his image of "two sides" and "two visions" left him with the unsatisfactory dyad of East versus West all the same.[65]

In some ways his least radical book, *Culture and Imperialism* brought *Orientalism*'s divided sympathies to an even higher pitch. At times, he seemed to subscribe to the "two superpowers" language of the American news cycle that in essay after essay he had spoken against.[66] Some passages gave the impression that the primary conflict in the world was between white and dark races, two fatally segregated outlooks that clashed with the assuaging notes of his opening chapter, "Overlapping Territories, Intertwined Histories."[67] Thinkers in the West, Marxist, feminist, structuralist, and psychoanalytic, were, with few and grudging exceptions, guilty of blindness toward imperialism, he charged.[68] Even Raymond Williams, whom he had rightly praised for just the opposite, was suddenly in the dock as a thinker for whom "the imperial experience is quite irrelevant."[69] Strangely forgotten in such a comment were the explicitly anticolonialist writings of poets, novelists, and essayists of former times like Denis Diderot, Blake, W. E. B. Du Bois, H. G. Wells, and Nancy Cunard.

All of Europe was characterized until 1904 by "an uncontested imperialist enthusiasm," he declared, although (again of two minds) he later softened the accusation or withdrew it altogether. In that latter mood, he spoke instead about the "almost Copernican change in the relationship between Western culture and the empire" in the early years of the century when a renaissance of fresh thinking and the revolutionary energies unleashed by Russia allowed many intellectuals to recognize that World War I was basically a squabble among the European powers over control of colonial territories.[70]

Then, after the apparent concession, he returned assertively to his initial claim: Western missionaries, anthropologists, Marxist historians, even the liberation movements themselves, all expressed a paternalism toward Africa, denying it sovereignty: "The general cultural situation . . . conformed to this kind of pattern."[71] He carefully chronicled the "great Enlightenment insights" into racism and the tracts that revealed the immorality of the colonial project by Bartolomé de Las Casas, the Abbé Raynal, Kant, and Herder. But one got only the vaguest sense of just how frank and sustained had been their attack on the whole imperial enterprise. Nor was mention made of the sympathetic reaction in Europe to the uprisings in Algeria and Egypt in the late nineteenth century, or the briefly successful Zulu wars against the British in the 1870s—all historical turning points that showed that his own critique and that of postcolonial studies were descended from a long lineage of anticolonial thinking that neither adequately acknowledged.[72] Although he wove them skillfully together in a broad pedagogical pattern, the argumentative threads became at times hopelessly tangled.

Two essays from this period, his boldest statements on the culture wars, gave an insight into the reasons for this balancing act. The most impressive of the two was "The Politics of Knowledge" (1991). Opening with an anecdote about delivering a draft of the introduction to *Culture and Imperialism* at a "major research university" (Rutgers), he described being attacked during the Q&A by a woman, a black historian "of some eminence" on the faculty.[73] Apparently, he was roughly handled, the charge being that he mentioned no living non-European women in his paper. An old nemesis in the audience, an Arab Orientalist, later joined her, assailing him along similar lines.[74] Months afterward, clearly injured, he was still grumbling about the encounter to friends.

In the essay, he pointed out that affirming the existence of a nonwhite "other" is not itself an argument and certainly not a progressive one. A race, a gender—neither is the beginning or end of a person. Were one to assume that it was, as the Rutgers professor had done, the absurd corollary would be that a "fifth-rate pamphlet and a great novel have more or less the same significance." What matters in the end, Said argued, is *"how* a work is written and *how* it is read." It is perfectly imaginable, in other words, that anticolonial sentiments can be expressed by reading Yeats or Shelley critically. Within months, he came out with another essay along similar lines for the Africanist journal *Transition,* this time tackling the canon debates.[75] Old-guard conservative critics like E. D. Hirsch, he charged, were exaggerating the changes that had actually been made to college reading lists, which were still mostly filled with the likes of Shakespeare and T. S. Eliot. At the same time, he objected to the "silliness" of younger professors and grad students who publicly attacked senior scholars as racists or pilloried their peers for being politically incorrect.

Much of the ambivalence of *Culture and Imperialism* came from Said's attempt to fit the square peg of the militant liberation movements into the round hole of the new postcolonial consensus. Postcolonialism's new wave of scholars, many of them from former colonial territories or related by birth or family name to those who were, broke into Western academic life for the first time. By the same token, they were from a generation formed under Reagan, on the one hand, and postmodernism, on the other. From South Asia, Latin America, and the Middle East, often from well-to-do families with political connections, many migrated to the metropolitan university in part because of the openings Said had created. But once there, and feeling their newfound power, they subscribed to a "big bang" theory that no resistance to colonialism had existed before them. The idea seemed to be that one had to be a member of an oppressed racial, ethnic, or national group in order to resist imperial injustices, and an equation was drawn (one Said had always opposed) between what one knows and what one is. In a setting marked by the end of the postwar economic boom (1972) and the fall of the Berlin Wall (1989), the thematic emphases of postcolonial studies hardly corresponded to Said's, which had to do with the creation of new states, the petitioning of governments, and media battles in the public sphere. The motives of postcolonial studies, by contrast, might be described as a general loathing for a Western entity vaguely dubbed "modernity."

Although postcolonial studies had been invented in English departments, it was far from only literary. Drawing on French and German social and aesthetic theories, it produced mixed kinds of writing, works of philosophy that combined ethnography and history in a language riddled with Marxist and anarchist terms and attitudes. It spread rapidly from the humanities to every wing of the social sciences, and it was just as likely to find postcolonial scholars in anthropology, history, and geography as in comparative literature. "Postcolonial theory," then, was the name that came to represent a somewhat contradictory bid to "other" Europe using the concepts of a select school of European philosophers in a politically ambiguous rejection of "Western man." Said was in this way caught between stodgy traditionalists upset by anything new and a vanguard that to him had thrown out some of the most critical thinking of the past on the grounds that it was white and male. He had become the nominal father of a field that he was reluctant to disown but that no longer resonated with his vision.

The intensity of his dismay was, as usual, much clearer off the record. His revealing correspondence with Camille Paglia, an exuberant stylist teaching at a small arts college in Philadelphia, was a case in point. Paglia had scandalized academia with an uproarious essay, "Junk Bonds and Corporate Raiders" (1991), as Said was finishing *Culture and Imperialism*. This unshackled assault on academic back-scratching was also an attack on theory, which from her point of view had taken all the fun out of art.[76] A feminist who for the most part wrote about sexuality and pop culture, she fenced in this essay for the classics, contending that the 1960s counterculture (from which she drew her inspiration) had happily killed off the clichés of modernism and had rescued New Criticism. She made it clear to everyone that poststructuralists like Lacan, Derrida, and Foucault were the "real fossilized reactionaries of our time." Said gently reprimanded her for going a little too far on occasion but said he couldn't agree more with her thesis that theory was "dangerous" to students.[77]

His frustrations had their impact on the classroom as well and threw him off his game. At odds with the drift of academic fashions, he taught less as the decade wore on, complaining that students had lost their critical sense and were unable to take a position: "I insult them, coax them, and cajole them . . . but they don't debate anymore. They take everything I say as some kind of professional counsel."[78] His earlier balancing of harsh criticism with warmth and encouragement was less and less in evidence. Although he remained a powerful presence in the classroom, he was not always kind to the students, pouncing on mistakes and showing impatience.[79]

As a result of his inner turmoil, his intentions in *Culture and Imperialism* lay hidden in forests of misdirection. In one of the book's turbulent middle chapters, for example, he mulled over authors like Thomas Mann and André Gide who had managed to take imperialism as their theme while casting a pall on it but who could not go so far as to give natives their own voice or get beyond a pessimistic exoticism. The very point of *Culture and Imperialism* as a sequel to *Orientalism* was to move from the negative to the positive. The idea was not to show what Europe had done wrong but to give third-world intellectuals the floor, which for all its revolutionary fervor *Orientalism* had not done. Hence, the book rests on a hierarchy, exalting heroes of third-world emergence like Tayeb Salih, Jean Genet, and George Antonius who unlike Mann and Gide conveyed the three-dimensionality of their own cultures on their own terms, laying out alternative systems of value with new points of departure found in the periphery itself.

These somewhat didactic contrasts were hard to miss, and the book was full of them, communicating clearly the gradations of good, better, and best in matters of culture and imperialism. As a consequence, even though these promotional gestures were necessary for the political line in the sand he wished to draw, many of the more subtle strands of his argument were missed. One of the most defining lay in the remarkable section titled "A Note on Modernism."

He wrote in full awareness of the fact that the modernist writings of Gertrude Stein, Joyce, Kafka, and Mallarmé were not just another literary school taught in college. For decades, professors had placed modernism at the very center of literary education, making it the standard against which all great writing should be measured. But they did so, he thought, tendentiously. Modernism's familiar repertoire of the ineluctable, the impenetrable, and the self-referential had become the credo of an urbane hopelessness. The well-wrought themes of modernist anguish, emptiness, and silence, he argued, are not all that can be found in the novels of Virginia Woolf and the poetry of Ezra Pound. In fact, they reflect "the critic's impasse, not the literature's difficulty."[80] He had once complained to Trilling that the almost universal critical applause for modernism in the academy had a habit of stressing the "dark, confused side of its nihilism," forgetting that side of it represented by Nietzsche, who possessed a "revitalized sense of rational learning and a radically *constitutive* sense of the human sciences," that is, a strong sense of how the different approaches to studying society and culture, from economics to sociology and music, express themselves without priority in humanist inquiry alone.[81] The university may offer a sane redoubt against the stridency of politics, but politics enters the university in a deflected way through modernism, which takes the form of a mental space to moot despair in the low-stakes environment of aesthetic taste.

This aspect of his argument brought him closer to Lukács. He always wondered why so many American critics had kept the great Marxist at arm's length when he had so much to say about how literary movements or aesthetic strategies (supposed to be tooth-less in this regard) help shape a society's political outlooks.[82] He could personally relate to the Hungarian philosopher's ability to acrobatically dodge official censure, being dissident while surviving constant pressure from above and on all sides, in his case, as an independent thinker in the Soviet sphere. It is not clear, surpris-ingly, that Said knew much of Lukács's writings on culture and imperialism from the 1930s and 1940s, which explored the effects of imperial attitudes on the philosophy and arts of Germany post-Bismarck until the collapse of World War I.[83]

At any rate, he never mentions Lukács's works from this period, although he clearly sensed the links Lukács had established between modernism and the "imperialist period" (in the philosopher's words), for his arguments in the book closely resemble them. A decade earlier, Said had even argued that Lukács's social theories were deeply rele-vant to the Middle East and that they "resemble the wide-ranging discussions that have been taking place in the Islamic world."[84] It is not surprising, then, that he also shared Lukács's reservations with modernism, although it certainly was unexpected to many of his readers, because as a modern British specialist modernist artists were the very subject of his teaching and he seemed to use their writings as his point of departure in his essays.[85]

And yet focusing on the imperial attitudes that lurk beneath the surface of culture, and perhaps reflecting also on his own counter-experiments with a ritualized Arab realism, he found a reason fi-nally to put into words his dissatisfaction. Not as an art form but as a worldview or (in Lukács's words) an "ideology," modernism tended to raise the senses over ideas and viewed humans as solitary, asocial, unable to enter relationships. Said shared this complaint and added his own. He deplored modernism's "extremes of self-consciousness, discontinuity, self-referentiality, and corrosive irony."[86] There would never be an indigenous third-world theory unless this modernist consensus was seen as a metropolitan point of view rather than a generally human fate. The European intellectual in this way acknowledges imperialism's harm but accepts no responsibility for it and assures us there are no alternatives. Despite modernism's cultural riches and global scope, its bold restructuring of historical time, and its irreverence toward convention, it created an irony of form that "substitutes art . . . for the once-possible synthesis of the world empires."[87] By disabling the critical sense and forestalling initiative, it was, in Conrad as much as anyone, a crucial part of that imperial system itself.

THROUGHOUT THE 1990S, eager to keep at least one side of his life free from controversy, Said came to see music as a bulwark against despair in an American political culture that increasingly saddened him. Even then, the strategy was not always effective. Responding to a warm letter from the bestselling novelist Patricia Highsmith in 1988, he recounted that his piece on pianists had been accepted by The New York Times but killed at the last minute by the executive editor, Abe Rosenthal, "simply because it was by me."[88]

The Western classical repertoire lay just beneath the surface of even his most political and literary prose and played a significant role in Culture and Imperialism. Looking back on Beginnings in 1987, for example, he attributed the book's structure to its ventriloquism of diverse voices, which he likened to the harmonic choruses of polyphony.[89] Palestinian history had been witness over twenty years to a "droning ground bass of land alienation," a true "continuo."[90] And so too Vico's use of repetition resembled the cantus firmus or chaconne, devices in which a "ground motif anchors the ornamental variations taking place above it."[91] The tension between harmony and melody in Wagner's *Das Rheingold*, he observed, was very much like the tension between system and species in history as a succession of events.[92]

Even teaching literature took on a musical cast. He invited students to his apartment, playing piano to illustrate how musical pieces tell stories and how the thematic departure and return of the hero in the novel echoes the structure of the fugue, just as the interplay of characters resembles the passing of the melody among soloists in a concerto grosso.[93] His own attempts at literature were saturated with musical terms and sensibilities, as in this grandiloquent fragment from a grad school poem:

> The world does not tell its time from the east
> Where crashing noises mix with silly bleats
> And the sun's rays imprison as in modal rounds . . .
> Hanging was a simple dream from which to awake
> And sing the destined rounds, refreshed, louder.
> Ours was not a sage view for we clamored for new
> harmonies.[94]

Some of the themes of *Orientalism* were expressed here very early. In the poem above, a culture out of key, his people's struggles turned into a bad musical, and the East destined to follow the West unless it can devise "new harmonies." In "Hans von Bülow in Cairo," a poem written in the same period, we find a related but different theme, Europe's romance with Oriental escape. The baron Hans Guido von Bülow, one of the most famous conductors of the nineteenth century, actually did move to Cairo's drier climate late in life to recover from illness.[95] Said uses this historical incident to draw a bitter portrait of the "old tonesmith" shaking dust from his slippers, tortured by the heat, recalling the glorious days with Franz Liszt's daughter Cosima before she left him for Wagner, looking out over an indifferent Nile from his veranda with "wordless, gleaming fury" as death approaches.

The term "contrapuntal" in *Culture and Imperialism* was an obvious part of this effort to expand music's metaphorical reach. An offspring of his earlier interest in polyphony, it pointed to a furtive dissonance within the dominant trends of his time. Polyphony, after all, is a genre of harmony that holds independent voices together in unison without merging them, keeping a number of contradictory positions in play, but also on occasion meeting at a point where they momentarily blend. The rising and falling of two or more melodic lines charts spatial progress as in a line graph. *Culture and Imperialism* was, among other things, an experiment in summoning this spatial dimension of musical notation and vocabulary in order to develop ideas about the geographic imagination.

Many of the book's readers took the term "contrapuntal" loosely to mean a more supple, nonconfrontational kind of reading—one aware of different plotlines but without a preference for any one of them.[96] Ultimately, the term was more polemical than that. In an essay titled "The Music Itself: Glenn Gould's Contrapuntal Vision," for example, he blamed mechanical reproduction and the celebrity system for forcing the Canadian pianist to be at home in the "opposing hosts of counterpoint." In this case, the image is not one of harmony but one of confrontation.[97] There was something troubling for Said, in other words, about Gould's mastery of counterpoint, which was "to play God," for it involved "the complete management of time, the minute subdivision of musical space, and absolute absorption of the intellect."[98] He elsewhere referred to counterpoint as "academic" and "rule-bound in a very vigorous way," hardly the image of openness that it implied for its 1990s audience.[99] The "contrapuntal" is above all an image about space, as the Gould essay showed with its long discussion of the relevance to counterpoint of Pythagorean geometry and the role of "adjacency" in musical composition.

The spatial dimensions of music had been an implicit motif in Ferruccio Busoni's *Sketch of a New Esthetic of Music* (1907), which for Said was one of the great unread books of the humanist tradition, a revolt staged against the boring "lawgivers" of the music world. The book anticipated a familiar Saidian theme by looking to performers to renovate the now stale or incomprehensible works of composers, treating the repertoire less as a collection of museum pieces and more like the launching pad for a philosophical quest. But like much else in Said's canon the affinity was conflicted. In his bid to get to the higher unfettered meanings of music, Busoni had promoted its nonrepresentational and immaterial dimensions, which did not mesh well with the territorial emphases of *Culture and Imperialism*. Even more, Busoni associated himself with the controversial theories of his turn-of-the-century contemporary Heinrich Schenker, whom Said disliked intensely.

There is little doubt, though, that Said's spatial view of music was negatively influenced by the Schenkerian method. For its devotees, the surface elements of tonal music are subordinated to an elemental structure. Some musicologists had even compared Schenkerian analysis to aspects of nineteenth-century philology.[100] Just as the latter hunted for a primordial language, subordinating all other languages to it, the former operated on the principle of "tonal space" where the tonic triad was the autonomous core and the neighboring notes its ornaments.[101] Said's antipathy to this approach was probably amplified by the fact that in his neighborhood on Manhattan's Upper West Side, the Mannes School of Music was a hotbed of the Schenkerian method. This might have darkened his review of a performance by one of the school's celebrated graduates, Murray Perahia, once a "very fine pianist," according to Said, whose recitals were now "boring and safe . . . like the votary of an unknown cult coming to an altar decorated like a nineteenth-century ballroom."[102]

This focus on a centralized ur-structure contrasted sharply with Said's fascination with Busoni, whom he loved for being a dashing risk taker and unruly poet. He called him "an intellectual and a visionary," both inside the system and a critic of it.[103] Nowhere did Busoni live up to Said's impressions more than when he wrote that "we admire technical achievements . . . yet they are outstripped, or cloy the taste, and are discarded."[104] For these were exactly Said's feelings in grad school when he scribbled to himself a note describing the disastrous effects of the music world's obsession with technical perfection: "Almost any intelligent listener of music, or reader of music criticism, will tell you that music criticism as it is practiced today, is shabby, boring . . . and witless."[105] The reason, he would go on to say, was that music criticism, like performance, had been turned into "a specialized rarity." How could professional pianists stir our emotions or make us grow when they hide themselves away from the world, constantly practicing in order to compete on the music circuit?[106]

In response, Said looked for models for his own criticism in those practicing musicians who strove to demystify music: Charles Rosen in *The Classical Style* (1971), Glenn Gould's essays, Pierre Boulez's *Orientations* (1985), and Adorno (himself a minor composer), whose *Philosophy of New Music* (1949) Said championed in a series of popular seminars delivered at Columbia in 1982 and 1983.[107] Having only recently discovered him, he wrestled with Adorno's writing, often antagonistically, until the end, particularly in the last five years of his life. It was only after Glenn Gould died in 1982 that Said considered writing a book-length study on music, although he contented himself for the next decade with occasional articles in *Vanity Fair*, *The Nation*, and *Le Monde Diplomatique*. Not until 1989 did anyone see the point of urging him to integrate these scattered musical ideas with his established work on empire, language, and intellectuals.

The Critical Theory Institute at Irvine invited him that year to give the Wellek lectures, requesting that he speak about music. He accepted warily, knowing he was entering new territory with immense demands on technical fluency. The odd essay on music could be written off as a sideline, but a sustained theoretical reflection opened him up to a different kind of scrutiny. He produced three lectures, one on extreme performance, another on musical transgression, and the last on the solitude and affirmation of melody that would appear as *Musical Elaborations* (1991). Like *Orientalism*, it delighted some and infuriated others, especially a few musicological guardians of the fold.[108] Its argument was built on the claim that music requires silence. "The most silent of the arts," he noted, music "is also the most . . . esoteric and difficult to discuss."[109] A decade later, he came back to the idea in a proposal for a long-form study of Bach and Beethoven—one he intended to be, of all things, a major statement on globalization to rival the work of Francis Fukuyama, Paul Kennedy, and Benjamin Barber on the subject.

Just as Orientalists called Said a pretender, a few musicologists thought him a "fish out of water."[110] It was clear that he was stepping on toes. Above all, *Musical Elaborations* was meant to shatter music's autonomy and its mystical isolation from rational meaning and social experience. A number of musicologists were taken aback, some because they were offended, others because they felt that in certain wings of their enterprise—the New Musicology, for instance—they had already set this program into motion.[111] In fact, though, he was as much a pioneer as they. Said's dozen and a half music essays of the 1980s on the social conditions of music were published at about the same time as the books that defined their movement, and Said in turn, far from pretending to be the sole innovator, introduced his grad students to the work of the New Musicology in seminars in the early 1990s.[112]

One of the leading figures of the movement, Rose Subotnik, in any case had no trouble accepting him as part of a common cause, not least because of their warm personal correspondence: "I know few scholars who have listened so attentively to what I had to say, or conversed so generously without personal acquaintance."[113] His reception, then, wildly enthusiastic among nonspecialists, also won adherents among professionals, even if some met his criticisms with indignation. As at so many other times in his career (in the Swift project and in *Orientalism*, for example) they objected that he should refrain from lobbing missiles when he lacked an insider's expertise. The most ill-tempered and dismissive response, perhaps, came from the scholar Kofi Agawu in a review of *Musical Elaborations* titled "Wrong Notes."[114]

Many music scholars, on the other hand, praised his insights precisely because they were not pedantically fixated on guild jargons. After his recital in 1993 at Columbia's Miller Theatre, for example, he was implored by Walter Frisch, the head of the music department at Columbia, to teach a course for them. Frisch had been won over by Said's major point about music's doubtful autonomy: "We are trying to be more of an intellectual integrated department in which the previously separate programs in historical musicology, music theory, and ethnomusicology have been effectively merged."[115] A few years later, he was invited to give a keynote at the European Arts Forum in Salzburg sponsored by the European Union and the Salzburger Festspiele—"the first Arab to be invited," he proudly told a friend.[116] Clearly there were specialists who valued his opinion.

Probably his richest encounter with the music establishment took place posthumously when the revered musicologist Ralph Locke took up Said's reading of Verdi's *Aida* in *Culture and Imperialism*. Apart from showing that he considered Said a force to be contended with, his response displayed all the mixed feelings Said's intervention had unleashed in official music circles. Locke's intricate, luxuriantly argued chapter in his book *Musical Exoticism* (2009) drew on learned references to Verdi correspondence and on an intimate command of Verdi's score and libretto with the idea, first, of praising Said for opening up new understandings of the opera. He pointed out certain musicological mistakes, but interestingly, his most telling charge was political, and not musical at all. Said, he argued, overlooks Verdi's own anti-imperialist sentiments as well as the possibility that the representation of ancient Egypt in the opera may be playing the role not of the khedive Ismail's patriotic gestures to the nation's illustrious past but of a stand-in for imperial Britain. Said, he suggests, paints Verdi as an Orientalist, whereas he supported radical elements of the Risorgimento in Italy and was plainly anticolonial in his sentiments.

Locke shrewdly noticed what many readers missed: that Said's argument is geographic. However, in this case he neglected to specify how. Said is talking not so much about the bloated exoticism of a famous Italian's fantasy about the Orient (as most assume) as about a major artistic opening night at a newly built opera house on Egyptian soil imposed on the busiest part of downtown Cairo—one that effectively divided the East and the West portions of the city. As Said puts it, *Aida* "is not so much *about* empire as *of* it." On the one side, hotels, trains, broad tree-lined boulevards, electricity, modern life, and on the other, unpaved streets and hand-drawn carts.

Said was trying to demonstrate that a cultural event intended to have one kind of national significance in fact had another. The khedive hoped that because Verdi represented the best of the West, the modernizing of Cairo by virtue of this staged premiere would amount to an argument against Ottoman domination. In the end, though, the event signified submission to an art form that could only be understood as a symbol of European empire and its grandiose attitudes to the world. Most readers would not have known about Said's personal relationship to *Aida* in that setting, his coming-of-age in music as a concertgoer and starry-eyed amateur during his formative years in Cairo, where he attended performances in the very khedival opera house in which *Aida* had premiered in 1871.

He still recalled these experiences in his unfinished novel *Elegy*, where he lingered over the parade of characters, sounds, and smells of a concert of the Cairo Symphony Orchestra. There, white-shirted Western performers, Armenian impresarios, a "wizened Sudanese doorman," a "mixed" girl (Italian, Greek, American) married by a "young Palestinian, and a noble Yugoslav conductor" fill out the scene. The logic of his case against imperial geography in the *Aida* passages of *Culture and Imperialism* had to do, then, not with bad representations of the "other" but with the sovereign art form of the European bourgeoisie plopped down in the middle of cosmopolitan Cairo in order to occupy its vital center. Even worse, Verdi, the creative artist as an imperial "I," commercializes opera, an art form that ought to rely much more on collaboration.[117]

The exchange with Locke revealed the dangers for critics moving too easily between Said's political and his musical outlooks. He certainly expressed sides of his character in music that are found nowhere else. The startling range of his selected essays over three decades in *Music at the Limits* (2008) reveals a boisterous virtuosity as well as often hair-raising judgments as a reviewer. Quite unlike his conduct in his own field, he spoke in the heat of the moment like a man with nothing to lose (Rosen's "sloppy garrulousness," Strauss's "bombast and neo-Wagnerian extravagance," Pollini's "almost frightening boredom" and "appalling display of bad-tempered virtuosity").[118] The privilege of being an amateur offered him the freedom to indulge in ideas for which there were no direct political or professional stakes. In the spell of its emotional effects, he at times spoke of music as an almost mystical, pre- or nonlogical realm, as though enjoying the ineluctable spaces he denied himself when writing about literary modernism.

If mixed overall, the impression Said left on Daniel Barenboim, one of the most revered conductors and pianists of his generation, was ecstatic. Barenboim flatly declared that "Edward knew everything" when it came to music, from the basic to the obscure—performance histories, the repertoires (by year) of major festivals, the keys and tempos of obscure works, and the great works of obscure composers. The two men shared a view of how Western classical music took shape. "Edward," Barenboim recalled, "was one of the few people who really believed and understood that the development of music was one organic process that started with the Gregorian chant, the pre-Baroque, the Baroque, the classical chords, the Romantic movement, chromaticism, which led evolutionarily and naturally to atonal music."[119]

This meant that the break of Arnold Schoenberg with tonality, the creation of the twelve-tone system, was not a revolutionary step at all but an "absolutely unavoidable and logical continuation of the stretching of the harmonic world through chromaticism taken to its utmost limit." If Said delighted in displaying this mastery of minutiae, especially when debating experts, Barenboim went even further.[120] Said, he claimed, had a "refined knowledge of the art of composition and orchestration" that surpassed that of most performers with whom he had collaborated in a long career.[121]

If meeting Barenboim by chance in a London hotel in 1993 changed Said's life (they spoke every day by phone, and Barenboim confessed that he "loved" Said), the conductor was not the only musical star in his orbit. Thrilled by the musician's life, Said watched from the sidelines, at times the starstruck fan, at others the upstart. His relationship with the experimental opera director Peter Sellars represented some of both.[122] On the one hand, he corresponded with him like an ally, inviting him to give seminars at Columbia; on the other, he walked a line, considering Sellars's modern-dress productions of Mozart's *Don Giovanni* and *Così fan tutte* by turns "cleverly constructed" and gimmicky—anti-establishment but shorn of the class conflict found in Mozart's original.[123] Sharing a stage with the legendary violinist Yehudi Menuhin at the Institute of Contemporary Arts in London in July 1991, he began a correspondence with him that lasted for two years. Menuhin had been swept away by Said's essay in *Grand Street* on *Aida*, "The Imperial Spectacle," and Said, repaying the compliment, applauded the "brave words" of Menuhin's "wonderful Knesset speech," which accused the Israeli government of "governing by fear" in the West Bank with "contempt for the basic dignities of life."[124]

Said (like Menuhin) found in music a way of relating to those who spoke a different language. Paying his respects to an ailing C. L. R. James on Railton Road in Brixton in 1987—then a slightly dystopian landscape of run-down buildings and harassing policemen—he found it hard at first to find common ground. James, a native of Trinidad and the author of *The Black Jacobins*, a groundbreaking early study of the Haitian slave rebellion, and a highly original study of cricket as a working-class art form, certainly shared Said's anti-imperial convictions. Said had made the pilgrimage, in fact, to honor James's contributions to art and to black liberation. But even though, like Said, James had lived for a long time in the United States and praised autodidacts (and was himself one), his political experiences were starkly different.

James had spent much of his life in Trotskyist parties organizing labor or battling with Caribbean nationalist leaders in a bid to create a West Indian federation. His tastes as a critic went much more in the direction of popular culture (especially Hollywood film) than Said's. More than anything, though, by the time of his visit, James's familiarity with Said's stature was limited. Only a few weeks earlier, the great civil rights activist and former Black Panther Stokely Carmichael had visited, and it was not clear James (who was not one to stand on ceremony) knew exactly who he was.[125] Only when Said mentioned that he played piano did the two men settle in. In the hour and a half they spent together, they talked almost exclusively about Beethoven's sonatas and their dislike of Verdi and Puccini. Later, Said sent James a cassette of Gould's performance of The Goldberg Variations, to which James warmly replied in a short handwritten letter, thanking him "a million times" and encouraging him to keep sending anything that, like the Bach, brought one back to the "days when . . . tempo and tone were primary."[126]

Although on this occasion, the two agreed, overall Said had more adventurous tastes than James. Said frequently complained, in fact, of the tedious solemnity of the concert circuit—the "alienating social ritual of the concert itself" and its passive audiences together made for an almost "sadomasochistic experience."[127] A few hypocritical sprinklings of more daring work by Olivier Messiaen or Dmitri Shostakovich hardly made up for the sugary Italian operas, the same conservative Austro-Germanic symphonies wheeled out each season at the Met. If as a performer he stuck to classics like Schubert, Beethoven, and Bach, as a listener he was drawn to experimental composers like Boulez, Hans Werner Henze, the second Viennese school, Leoš Janáček, György Ligeti, and Cage.

The albums he listened to at home were, if not always avant-garde, more adventurous than usual symphony hall fare: John Adams's *Death of Klinghoffer*, Erich Wolfgang Korngold's *Die tote Stadt*, Harrison Birtwistle's *Triumph of Time*. It was certainly remarkable, though, that in his massive collection of CDs, LPs, and cassettes at home his classical interests were almost entirely Western European. There was a large sampling of Eastern European composers to be sure, among them Janáček and Bartók, but almost no Russians apart from a single Tchaikovsky, one Mussorgsky, the inevitable *Rite of Spring*, and a bare sampling of Shostakovich's symphonies. In popular music, though, there were many more Arab pieces than his writings suggest, including the popular composer and folksinger Marcel Khalife.

He reveled in the life of musicians and fantasized about being one, for his original hopes at Mount Hermon and Princeton never really left him. In the end, though, his critical powers found their energy in words and ideas, not sound and silence. In his rendezvous with Tiegerman at his cottage in Kitzbühel on summer vacations, he would perplex the man with a dazzling knowledge of theories of the musical avant-garde. But this left the pianist cold, for all Tiegerman cared about was playing.[128] It was only with Barenboim that Said could indulge a mutual love for theorizing music, but even so, the two at times exchanged roles.

On the one hand, he was the confidant and equal, on the other, a fan gushing about performing a four-handed piece with Barenboim backstage before a concert (Schubert's Fantasy in F Minor), likening his friend's playing to that of an orchestra because of its sweep and musicianship. In turn, Barenboim admired Said's talent for bringing social critique into music and benefiting from its special ways of knowing. Doing so in other spheres would demand all of Said's improvisational skills in the years ahead as the political walls closed in and he was forced to abandon a Palestinian state in favor of a Palestinian ideal.

CHAPTER 11

TWO PEOPLES IN ONE LAND

Change the battlefield from the street to the mind.[1]

After 1993, Said's political life revolved almost completely around his goal of a one-state solution in Israel/Palestine. He had to agree with Chomsky that a flat demand for an immediate single state based on one person, one vote would be a "gift to the Israeli right wing."[2] Consequently, both men were eager to distinguish between initial and subsequent steps. The former would proceed by stages, first a two-state settlement, then closer accommodation, then the easing of borders, and finally some federal arrangement leading to a binational system.

Ahead of the curve, he was once again bitterly attacked by both the Palestinian and the Israeli sides. The essays he wrote and interviews he gave in the wake of the signing of the Declaration of Principles, as the Oslo accord of 1993 was officially known, would eventually fill five volumes (a separate accord was signed in 1995). Initially, the agreement was warmly, even jubilantly, greeted by key players in the Palestinian and Israeli camps as well as the better part of public opinion (both Jewish and Arab), especially in the United States.

As the Palestinian leadership saw it, the Oslo accord's chief achievement was the creation of the Palestinian Authority with limited self-governance in the West Bank and Gaza. But there was no agreement on the status of Jerusalem, the illegal settlements, the right of Palestinian return, or recognition of Palestine as a sovereign state. Although the treaty promised peace between Israel and Palestinians and had been universally heralded in the media, Said took on the lonely task of showing it to be a betrayal—not the less-than-perfect attainment of a deal, as the press characterized it, but "the end of the peace process." He lived this last decade of his life, according to his son, Wadie, in a permanent state of rage and hurt.[3]

His allies pleaded with him not to draw this line in the sand. Whatever the shortcomings of the agreement, intransigent opposition would risk isolating him. Tactically, the better plan surely was to bide one's time.[4] His broadsides against the deal were nevertheless relentless, and all the more abrasive when measured against his generally conciliatory approach until then, as Oded Balaban observed in "The Other Edward Said," an essay that appeared originally in Hebrew in the Haifa journal *Masharef*.[5] Balaban documented that despite the bad press he had received to the contrary, Said's position had been heretical for much of his career, recognizing the state of Israel before others in his own camp, stressing the sufferings of the Jewish people, not only those of his own, and insisting on mutual recognition.

To those who took the trouble to notice, it was obvious that his collaborators had always included Israeli and Jewish men and women of science and the arts, and he was willing to engage with spokespeople he disagreed with or disliked, like Rabbi Michael Lerner, even if he drew the line with others, like the American political theorist Michael Walzer, who mobilized the exodus myth as though only Jews had experienced exile. Even more, he had for some time been reaching out to dissident journalists and the New or Revisionist historians within Israel itself such as Tom Segev, Amira Hass, and Ilan Pappe, not all of them anti-Zionist. He felt particularly indebted to the research on Gaza by Sara Roy, a child of Holocaust survivors from the Lodz ghetto who chose to live in multicultural America rather than Israel and who wrote compellingly about the deliberate "de-development" of the Gazan economy. In turn, many of them acknowledged that their own research relied on the openings he had earlier provided.

One of the least known of Said's quiet allies was Rabbi Elmer Berger, the founder and president of American Jewish Alternatives to Zionism, whose "humanistic universalism" exemplified Judaism as a religion of universal values, not the exceptionalism for which the Israeli state clearly stood.[6] Paradoxically, these exchanges were helped along by the legalizing of Israeli-Palestinian dialogue within Israel following "the Rabin-Arafat handshake," for it made their arguments less taboo and allowed them more freely to circulate.[7] At the same time, the minor concessions wrung from the Israeli side by Oslo made Said's own access to Palestine easier. "This is the first time in my life since I left Palestine at the end of 1947," he mused, "that I've been to the West Bank and Gaza and Israel on a regular basis."[8]

The accords themselves were finalized as undemocratically as the government they credentialed. Hanan Ashrawi, one of the principal PLO negotiators, recounted in *This Side of Peace* (1995) that the agreement was reached in complete secrecy in Oslo, Norway, without any public discussion and without anyone even informing the PLO negotiating team about the agreement until it was a fait accompli. On her way from Tunis to Washington for the eleventh round of negotiations, she was simply handed the agreement and told nothing could be changed. She knew something dramatic had happened in early September 1993, when she received a cryptic call from a colleague who reassured her that "the back channels have delivered." Abu Ala and Hassan Asfour, two academic figures out of touch with Palestinian realities, initialed the separate peace under the instructions of Arafat's second-in-command, Abu Mazen, in the presence of the Norwegian foreign minister. The two, who were quite marginal to the process, had read none of the negotiating team's reports, painstaking factual studies, or strategic list of fall-back positions.⁹

Ashrawi bluntly told Abu Mazen, "This will backfire." Indeed, none of the key objectives were achieved. What Israel recognized was not the right of Palestinian self-determination and statehood but the right of the PLO to be the representative of the Palestinian people and to be allowed to return to Gaza and the town of Jericho in the West Bank. This was the banner under which Arafat argued that the Palestinian movement had been saved. As Ashrawi observed, a fatal process had been set in motion. Because the PLO and Israel were officially at peace, the entire Arab world could now begin to normalize relations with Israel.

Said was not alone in judging the treaty a surrender. But he was the only one who denounced it with a venomous sarcasm designed to burn bridges. He branded Arafat Israel's Buthelezi, the administrator of a Bantustan, and compared the new Palestinian Authority to the government of Vichy.¹⁰ For the next decade, in three extraordinary collections of essays, he staked out alternatives with seemingly limitless invention, experimenting with autobiography, anecdote, diatribe, and philosophical musings from every possible angle. From a literary and artistic point of view, this work was much more than an assortment of op-eds or occasional pieces for the Arab press. The essays represented some of his most elegant and nuanced writing and thinking. The point was even more dramatic in that despite the collections' considerable length—amounting to more than one thousand printed pages—they were only part of what he wrote, the rest scattered over small, mostly Arab publications.

In *Peace and Its Discontents* (1993)—"the first of my books to have been written start to finish with an Arab audience in mind"—he described "the vulgarities" of the White House ceremony, "the degrading spectacle" of Yasser Arafat thanking everyone for what amounted to a suspension of his people's rights, and "the fatuous solemnity of Bill Clinton's performance, like a twentieth-century Roman emperor shepherding two vassal kings through rituals of reconciliation and obeisance."[11] In time, Arafat would hit back by banning Said's books in the West Bank and Gaza.[12] Meanwhile, Said's manifestos threw many of his closest allies off balance, including his good friend Sami, who feared that climbing out on this limb might make him politically irrelevant. Said responded angrily that his friend's position was similar to those who kept silent during the Vietnam War, not a tactical move, only opportunism.[13]

Said's central slogan in *Peace and Its Discontents*—"Two Peoples in One Land"—would from this moment on signal a militant new direction.[14] Behind it lay decisive structural shifts. First, the Palestinian and Jewish populations had over time become demographically intertwined. Many of the younger generation of Palestinians were Israeli citizens, and they identified with their country, wanting to fight for equality within it. Ironically, the labor force that Israel used to build and expand the illegal settlements was largely made up of Palestinians, giving them a financial stake in their own displacement. Palestinian youth could now access Arab television and CNN and, while comparing their own condition with that of their peers abroad, aspired to consumer comforts and a bit of normalcy instead of a permanent state of siege. Under the previous polarization, Arab activists in solidarity with Palestine refused to visit the territories. They despised the idea of legitimizing Israel in any way. But this had the unfortunate effect of depriving the region of material support and intellectual expertise, a problem the one-state solution promised to alleviate.[15] Gradually refined over half a decade, Said's post-Oslo position received its clearest public expression in a feature he wrote for *The New York Times Magazine* on January 10, 1999, titled "The One-State Solution."

The grim geographic facts seemed to offer no other option. Oslo had given its blessing to "seven discontinuous Palestinian islands amounting to 3 percent of the land surrounded and punctuated by Israel-controlled territory."[16] Said realized that the idea that Israelis and Palestinians could live together as equal citizens in a single democratic state might seem utopian. On the other hand, what could be bleaker than the illusion that Palestinians could have a state of their own, so disarticulated, militarily terrorized, and embargoed had the territories become. The two-state solution that he had long fought for was simply no longer possible. If that notion limped on in the United States' ever more cynical promises of future sovereignty, it was gradually obliterated by the slicing up of Palestinian land into atomized territorial pockets divided by Israeli settlements and a permanent army presence. Said reasoned that because the whole purpose of Israeli strategy had been to make a future Palestinian state impossible, it had succeeded too well for the older deceptions to be credible. He was not so much calling for the creation of a single state. It already existed, although only in the form of an apartheid state with two different and unequal sets of laws, rights, and privileges.

Although unpopular in the post-Oslo euphoria, the demand for a single democratic and secular state in Palestine was not new. It had been mooted from as early as 1948, and there were good historical reasons for lending the idea support. As a Christian in the Middle East who, like others, had to navigate inherited colonial arrangements, Said was only too aware of the pitfalls awaiting multiethnic political arrangements based on identitarian allocations of power. In Bilad al-Sham, the French had devised a system where representation was affixed to religious identities, dividing parliament into percentage allotments. By custom, if not by the terms of the constitution, for example, the presidency of Lebanon was reserved for a Maronite, the prime minister for a Sunni, the Speaker of Parliament a Shiite, and the foreign minister a Greek Orthodox. Intended to keep confessionalism at bay by giving each religion its own constituent power, the arrangement also wrote these differences indelibly into formal political structures.[17] To appreciate Said's antipathy to a Jewish or Muslim state, it was important to understand his familiarity with this earlier failed system.

By far the most prominent international spokesman for the cause, he was at the same time persona non grata with the new Palestinian Authority, just as he was at last addressing an Arab audience on more than an occasional basis. From the mid-1990s onward, he wrote by his own account twenty-four journalistic articles a year, syndicated twice monthly. It was a challenge, he conceded, to remain fresh throughout the bleak task of going over old ground for a public that either quickly forgot or refused to hear.[18] The principal venues were *Al-Hayat* (The Life), a pan-Arab newspaper with a circulation of two hundred thousand based in London, founded in Lebanon, with a multinational editorial staff; and *Al-Ahram* (The Pyramids), an English-language newspaper of Arab affairs based in Cairo. At first, he wrote his articles in Arabic, quite clearly and expressively according to his assistants, although the editors wanted them in English so they could be translated by their staff. Those translations, however, were often awkward, even at times unintelligible unless one had read the English first, and often needed to be corrected by his Iraqi assistant Zaineb Istrabadi or by Mariam.[19]

Writing regularly for Arab newspapers changed his style. In a letter to Abdulrahman Al-Rashid of *Al-Majalla* (The Magazine) in 1990, he confessed, "I've never had an Arab audience before, and the discipline of trying to address people on a monthly basis has been very good for clarity of thought and soundness of expression." The downside was having to be constantly on guard: "I can write more freely about Arab concerns in an English or American or French journal than in an Arab one."[20] Several Palestinian strategists came over to his earlier, once unpopular positions on Oslo, including Ashrawi, who, consenting uncomfortably to be in attendance on the White House lawn for its signing, conceded in retrospect that a clearer break would have been the better choice.[21]

As he addressed an Arab audience, Said discovered a more populist tone. Officially, he had always been more or less at war with American popular culture, protesting (inaccurately) that it meant nothing to him. "Naj," as he called Najla, fought back, turning him on to the Irish singer and songwriter Sinead O'Connor and delivering the comforting news that her music was a takedown of Thatcher's Britain and that she supported the Irish Republican Army. She forced him to listen, and eventually he claimed that her music excited him, and he found in O'Connor's lyrics affinities with Yeats.[22] To his surprise and delight, Najla pointed out that the alt-rock singer Ani DiFranco wrote for *The Nation*. Meanwhile Wadie, who disliked classical music intensely, chided his father for not having enough blue-collar tastes and did his best to make a case for the political revolt in heavy metal music.

One could find passing allusions to the likes of Joan Collins, Mary Tyler Moore, Diane Keaton, and John le Carré scattered throughout his writing, but his forays into popular culture had mostly to do with the colonial and Arab worlds. He wrote, among others, about the doyenne of traditional Arab vocal music, Umm Kulthum, Arabic cinema, the celebrated Egyptian belly dancer and film actress Tahia Carioca, Joe Sacco, the Maltese author of graphic novels about life in the occupied territories, and the Tarzan movies he saw as a boy in Egypt.[23] The spirit of these sources made him feel more of the place while in his American exile, and pervading the Palestinian political essays, they captured a different tenor of his writing. The new mood had much to do with his visit to Israel and the occupied territories in June 1992, just after his diagnosis. For the first time in forty-five years he returned with Mariam, Wadie, and Najla "to show my family where I was born, the house I grew up in, the school I was sent to."[24] The news that he had leukemia and the increasing political isolation were pushing him back to his beginnings.

IN SETTING OUT IN 1992 to write his memoir, *Out of Place*, Said did not so much fail as refuse to finish the novel he had worked on fitfully for five or so years after 1987. In a dramatic turnaround given his lifetime of teaching, toward the end of his life he even rejected the novel as a literary form, saying it no longer had meaning. Although he set to work in earnest only in the early 1990s, the memoir really had its origins earlier in the "Cairo Recalled" essay in *House & Garden* in 1987, and even more in 1988, when he successfully pitched a story about his childhood to James Atlas of *The New York Times Magazine*.

"Not to be boastful," he wrote in his letter to Atlas, but "no one to my knowledge of my background—American, Palestinian, academic, etc.—has done what I propose to do . . . a chronicle of encounters . . . a somewhat fraught and perhaps even dangerous experience."[25] In fact, with the exception of Mohammed Shukri's *For Bread Alone* (1972), a visceral autobiography about stealing to live in a time of famine and about a sexual and literary coming-of-age in Morocco of the 1940s and 1950s, no one in the Arab world had written a book at once so confessional and psychologically fraught.[26] As it turned out, *Out of Place* would be Said's most widely read book in the region.

Shortly after beginning the memoir, he admitted to a friend that "the central problem is how much to reveal, and how much to hide, and how the two are related to each other." He confided anxiously to those around him that Rosy, Jean, Joyce, and Grace were not going to be happy with the way he treated their parents and that they would likely resent his decision to leave the sisters largely out of his "game of disguises and revelations." In fact, they found it galling because, as Grace put it, "we all felt as sisters that he got the best part of the deal . . . He made it seem like he was the persecuted one, but he was not."[27] He escaped to Cairo for three weeks in 1994 to get away from family distractions and to have the peace of mind to work on the memoir, whose urgency seemed greater two years later. The leukemia treatments over 1994–95 had been unsuccessful, however savage their effects on his body, and he was hit with two bouts of pneumonia in February and August 1996, the second of which very nearly killed him.[28]

He had always meant to call the book "Not Quite Right" and

held on to the title until just before the book went to press. He probably reasoned in the end that the theme of exile lodged in the word "place" would be cleaner and less ambiguous than the discarded title, which suggested, nevertheless, the inner spirit of the book, which is not about exile, after all, but about being odd, awkward, and at home nowhere. The problem was how to reveal the psychological complexities of a representative Arab of a certain type—touching on that "theory of mind" that he had earlier complained Arab culture lacked—but to do so without parading his own symptoms for others to ogle at. "To know oneself," he wrote in an unpublished 1977 essay, "is no invitation to morbid self-consciousness."[29]

About a painfully observant boy in a world whose grandeur was primarily aesthetic, the book inevitably evoked Proust for many reviewers. As it did for Said, who referred to the book as "a Proustian meditation" in part because, like Proust, he dwelled on his younger self as though it were not really him, only an alien creature that resisted all explaining.[30] Said regularly taught a popular seminar in the 1970s devoted entirely to the great novelist, requiring students to read the multivolume novel whole and in French. The story was probably too well known to him not to have forced its way into his own—the unhealthy longing of a son for his mother, the loneliness of privilege, and the frustrations of an adventurous mind having vicariously to witness others' adventures. For all that, Said's chronicle of the exotic world of the upper classes was entirely un-Proustian in its sensibilities. In place of Proust's period sentences, Said gives us acerbic asides. Nothing like Proust's languor can be found in *Out of Place*'s typical sentences about the world of wealth and seclusion: "a WASP from the Northeast, very much a creature of that world's fully paid up citizens—morally righteous, confident, generally patronizing."[31]

With its publication, Said's seven years of toil on the book came to an end, a project written sporadically on odd days in the hours before dawn. Coy about its novelistic aspects, and aware of what it was taking the place of, he set about dodgily referring to it as a

work of "documentary fiction."[32] Whatever its genre, it was a culmination and, more than any other book, the one that brought all his
talents into one place. Although Said praised her for guiding him
through hundreds of pages of "overwritten and inchoate prose,"
Shelley Wanger, his editor at Pantheon, claimed that the pages he
gave them, in fact, needed little revision: "He knew exactly how to
do it."[33] For years the structure had been fully formed in his head,
the manuscript finally written in longhand on blue, yellow, and
white paper in a continuous flow with almost no crossing out.[34]

All of his books had made a mark, and at least three of them
were considered major events, but the public acclaim for *Out of Place*
was universal. Along with enthusiastic reviews and the *New Yorker*
prize for nonfiction, the memoir prompted fan letters from Nobel
laureates (Nadine Gordimer and Kenzaburo Oe) and movie stars,
among them Emma Thompson, Jodie Foster, and Vanessa Redgrave.[35] Their admiring notes joined those of childhood friends and
distant relatives who after being out of touch for years thanked him
for the forgotten world he had managed to revive. His childhood
romance with Hollywood was as strong as ever and not softened
by his own celebrity. He had, after all, testified that year before the
European Parliament, attended the Herbert von Karajan Centrum
in Vienna, and given the first Spinozalens at the Nieuwe Kerk (New
Church) at The Hague in November. No matter, the notes from his
screen idols made him feel like a starstruck child and moved him
to recall the time he met Danny Glover, Warren Beatty, and Annette
Bening at a party and was too flustered to know what to say.[36]

"Dear Edward," wrote Gordimer in September 2000, "you spoke
of wanting to write a novel. I wonder—this too—whether in these
last months you might have begun."[37] Surrounded by novelists—he
was good friends with Salman Rushdie and friendly with Philip
Roth and Paul Theroux—he dodged the question even while inviting it.[38] In an interview in *Time* magazine as he embarked on the
writing of that book, he toyed with his interlocutors, announcing
that his planned memoir of the vanished world would address an

era with so few traces that "I can let memory play all the tricks it wants. I want that, actually. Then maybe I'll write some fiction."[39] In time, that comment seemed a feint. In the view of his childhood friends and his sisters, it was the photographic realism of the book that stood out. He remembered everything with prodigious accuracy, faithful even to the smallest details of facial gestures and tone of voice.

If he confided to friends a vague intention of someday withdrawing from the world to write a novel, he rarely let on to those around him that he already had. After Said gave Tariq Ali the courage to finish his own cycle of novels about Pakistan, Ali asked him, "Have you ever thought of writing a novel or a play script?"[40] "No," he answered, "I don't think I could. What would I write about?" Maybe the response was just part of the old self-doubt—that strange combination, as Barenboim noted, of being at once "so sure and so insecure." His sentences often ended with the phrase "don't you think?" which was not just clearing his throat but testing his views against another's. But Said also just liked to fib. At age eleven he had an appendix operation that left a huge scar. When Najla asked him about it, he said he had been gored by a bull while studying bullfighting in Spain. He liked playing the game of fiction when the truth was neither here nor there. To impress Mariam in the early days of their courtship, he told her he had dated Candice Bergen. At dinner with another couple years later, one of them bragged of meeting a famous film star. "Edward beats you," Mariam replied. "He once went out with Candice Bergen." Realizing that everyone would start bombarding him with questions about his intimacies, he calmly laughed and said, "Did you really believe me? I was joking."

He had a novelist's knack for noticing details, remembering what a person was wearing, how he cocked his head, the limpness of his hand when greeting. Such moments leap out of the best passages of *Out of Place*, as when he describes the "cretinous cackle" of the mother of Abie, his cousin in Queens, or in some of the more merciless sketches in his short story "An Ark for the Listener":[41]

Marguerite was, it seemed, the result of hours of arranging and restless pushing, kneading, pulling and jerking. She was a sequence of corners that at each moment threatened an explosion into swimming fat; not the pleasant dumply fat of her older sister Ne'mé, but a powerful, hairy, even muscular fat that might have swept you aside saying *"that* is where you belong—stay there!"[42]

Not owning up to his fiction had partly to do with feeling his strength in traits that militated against it. Patricia Highsmith, the celebrated author of *Strangers on a Train* (1950), *The Talented Mr. Ripley* (1955), and other novels, was moved by the political vigor and no-nonsense directness of his essays and wrote to him diffidently as a fan for just that reason.[43] Kenzaburo Oe, similarly, in a series of long and deferential letters, went way beyond praise for Said's "strong, intensive, and moving style"; he found Said's political essays an "enduring" corrective to his own fiction:[44]

I have somehow failed to tell you, my dear Said, that your book gave the incentive for me to resuscitate myself as a novelist . . . The materials of my novels had become too much involved with my own life, on the one hand and, on the other, with esoteric mysticism. If I had kept on writing that way, my novels would have lapsed into perverted confessions of faith. In such a state of mind I received the Nobel Prize in Stockholm, feeling it to be a kind of burden.[45]

In a stream of tender, closely typed faxes of some length, Gordimer expressed a very similar view. Here, another world-class novelist put herself at the feet of the New York critic: "You are the raven that feeds me today—although the raven is too Poe-ish a bird for you, and the dove too mild and complaisant for your great spirit."[46] The exchange was part of an intimacy "beyond respect, more like a loving friendship that cannot easily be described," as Said's oncologist,

Kanti Rai, who witnessed the camaraderie firsthand, put it.[47] She sent Said her Nobel acceptance speech, saying that his political essays inspired its central theme on writers as witnesses. Looking for advice and reassurance, she filled her letters with the irreverence of a co-conspirator. When V. S. Naipaul won the Nobel in 2001, for example, she gleefully gave Said a running account of the awards ceremony in Stockholm, calling Naipaul "the Greta Garbo of laureates" for ditching the official ceremonies and snubbing his fellow prizewinners when they gathered at the Grand Hôtel bar.[48] All the other laureates despised him, she added.

In the absence of a novel of his own, there were some who floated the idea that the real fictional creation was Said's own life. The fact was that several novelists made him a central character in their books. One of these romans à clef was Ahdaf Soueif's *Map of Love*, where he appears as Omar al-Ghamrawi, an internationally famous Egyptian American conductor and political writer, tall, with black hair "greying at the temples . . . and dark, dark eyes"; and Dominique Eddé's *Cerf-volant* (*Kite*), where he appears as Farid Malek, a Syrian transplant to Alexandria, a brilliant activist who wants to change the world.[49] Both authors zero in on his gestures and idiosyncrasies: in Soueif, "the way he walks into the room, the energy crackling off him, the heads turning to look . . . Isabel is in love with him . . . She can't help it. Lots of women couldn't. And as far as I can see, it never did them any harm."[50] And in Eddé, "his hands were elegant and nervous. He had long mobile fingers that jabbed the air, punctuating everything, even when at rest . . . Curious about everything, he wanted it all: adventure and comfort, anchorage and open sea."[51]

In R. F. Georgy's *Absolution: A Palestinian Israeli Love Story*, he appears as himself, the moral compass behind Avi, an Israeli prime minister who, when studying at Columbia, learned under his tutelage to acknowledge Palestinian suffering. In "Goodbye Instructions" (1973), a poem cycle by a former student from the early 1970s, David Lehman, an imaginary Edward, as teacher, holds forth: "There's no point flexing / your muscular good intentions. / I never promised to answer / your delightfullest questions."[52] Said appeared, named and unnamed, as a character in a number of other books and films, including *The Other* (1999), a French-Egyptian feature film directed by Youssef Chahine in which Said again appears as himself.

Although *Out of Place* helped his reputation with audiences he had not reached before, he had always hit a wall when it came to France. Despite his lectures at the Collège de France, *Orientalism*'s well-received French translation in 1980, and his lifelong orientation to everything French, he had always slightly frightened the literary establishment. Major cultural outlets on television and the big publishing houses (Gallimard, for example) resisted him. The intellectuals of the Parisian Parnassus, many of them left renegades now on the political right, considered him competition. His public presence, they could see, was very much like the *nouveaux philosophes* Bernard-Henri Lévy, Alain Finkielkraut, and André Glucksmann, and yet he was on the left, spoke their language, could play piano, lecture on Beethoven and Wagner, and had found a seat at the table of the political establishment. *Out of Place* helped him break through this invisible wall. By 2003, he was awarded an honorary degree at the Sorbonne, and just after his death a special tribute was held in his honor at the Bibliothèque Nationale.

A lover of novels, he quite logically concluded that writing them himself was neither necessary nor particularly inviting. Over the last decade of his life, his views on the matter were very close to those of his friend Israel Shahak, whose fascinating letter to him about *After the Last Sky* came with some unexpected reservations: "I will not hide from you the fact that some aspects of the book are such as provoke my disagreement. I don't mean politics at all. I mean that the book is too poetical (and vague) for my taste; too much influenced by the Palestinian poetry, which I confess to you that I greatly dislike—contrary to the Palestinian prose."[53] Why were the Palestinians so easy to expel in 1948? he asked. "One of the reasons may be too much poetry and specially of poetry which is not self-critical."

It is evident from "The Limits of the Artistic Imagination," a little-known but seminal lecture he delivered in 1995 at Macalester College, that his own view mirrored Shahak's. This lecture was written not long after he abandoned his novel of betrayal and with *Out of Place* well under way.[54] He took the lecture as an occasion to explain what one can and cannot do in fiction and, although gingerly and with respect, took up Gordimer's "fine book" *Writing and Being* (1995), which grew out of her Nobel acceptance speech. He judged too romantic her view that fiction is more durable than life. And he reproached the usual conceits of awards ceremonies where the uncomfortable facts of the real-world literary marketplace go unmentioned.

What we are seeing in the third world, he went on to say, is a new aesthetic, one that hardly registers in the metropolis because it is raw, didactic, and unashamedly political. In fact, Said had earlier defended Hanan Ashrawi's dissertation (which he had helped supervise) when her advisers objected that she held up third-world literature (and Palestinian narrative in particular) as "an instrument of revolution and change" in which the literary imagination appeared as a confrontation and a chronicling of historical events.[55] As the New York media chattered on about globalization, he continued, the third-world author's locale was ignored. Moreover, art itself, at least one that is not inauthentic, is threatened by the curse of technocratic specialization. It is not the auteurs who bring these matters to our attention, he concluded, much less show a way out. It is the intellectuals as diagnosticians, political analysts, catalysts, and interpreters. Cockburn and Wypijewski, then a couple, riffed on this talent of his for combining the indefinite and open-ended with the emphatic, giving him cuff links fashioned as typewriter keys for his sixtieth birthday, one of them a semicolon, the other an exclamation mark.[56]

· · ·

AT MIDNIGHT ON MONDAY, May 10, 1999, Said wrote to a friend to say that Eqbal Ahmad, his comrade in arms, had died only hours before in Islamabad of complications from a surgery for colon cancer. The note was hastily scribbled after returning from Ahmad's Upper West Side flat, where he had gone to console his wife, Julie. In those familiar rooms it was somehow easier to visualize the many times Eqbal sat barefoot and cross-legged on the floor, a drink in hand, sizing up a political crisis or reciting poetry in four languages into the early morning. Said's melancholy was tinged with regret for their recent quarrel over an Indian science award he wanted Ahmad's help in securing for Kanti Rai—an impossible task that Said thought his friend could miraculously bring about and was angry when he didn't. Losing him now when he himself was so frail was crushing. And Ahmad died needlessly, it turned out. The Pakistani hospital where he had been sent was ill-equipped to handle one of chemotherapy's routine side effects, the heart attack that carried him away.[57]

In the early years of the twenty-first century, he confided to Rai, his oncologist, that he had wanted to write a book about Ahmad, putting into words what his activism and modesty had prevented him from writing himself. Ahmad left behind no major writing, only a scattering of political essays later collected in a volume of selected writings with a foreword by Chomsky.[58] He bequeathed instead a series of sympathetic encounters, witty observations, and organizational wisdom attractively passed along by word of mouth mostly, although happily (if only partially) archived in a collection of interviews by the Armenian American alternative radio broadcaster David Barsamian.[59] Said found Ahmad's lack of bookkeeping and his disregard for acclaim as alluring as his shared political commitments and wanted to capture the intellectual and spiritual lightning that the man had failed to record himself. It was, after all, Ahmad who was responsible for pushing Said early in his career to focus on moral agitation rather than military action to achieve his aims. As early as 1970, Ahmad had addressed the Organization of Arab Students with the then-unpopular argument that public relations were more important than guerrilla actions, and his comments influenced Said's thinking profoundly.[60]

By the time of the second, or Al-Aqsa, intifada of 2000, this advice would become especially valuable. The media, in Said's view, were by then determining the course of the conflict. Said believed ever more strongly that the name of the game was the "war of images and ideas," a battle to make the Palestinian story as sophisticated and persuasive as Israeli *hasbara* (literally, information intended for the outside world, but more colloquially, propaganda).[61] The way forward for liberation struggles lay in "flexible, mobile political forces who relied more on initiative, creativity, and surprise than they did on holding fixed positions."[62]

The End of the Peace Process, a collection of essays written between 1995 and 1999, tried to show how it was done. The book represented his most creative political thinking of the post-Oslo period. Isaac Newton, Theodor Herzl, Nelson Mandela, and Elizabeth Taylor—all were summoned in the polychromatic essays of the book, which gave the one-state solution a higher calling and deeper philosophical register. Covering subjects as varied as the German cultural critic Walter Benjamin, the French historian Jules Michelet, and the Martinican poet and parliamentarian Aimé Césaire, he also experimented with leaving the grand discourses of state politics behind and instead, as in *After the Last Sky*, throwing himself into the lives of ordinary Palestinians. His achievement in this respect was particularly marked in three of the book's most moving and personal works of political journalism, "On Visiting Wadie," "Scenes from Palestine," and "West Bank Diary."[63]

The one dedicated to his son particularly stood out. With no special prodding from his father, the New York–schooled, very Americanized Wadie learned Arabic on his own and then, in 1994, after graduating from college, went to study at the American University in Cairo. As soon as the AUC experience was over, he announced he would spend a year in Palestine. His father did not believe him.

When it was clear that Wadie was serious, Said tried to fathom the significance of the act, because he himself had been unwilling to do the same, even though there had been some unstated pressure to make such a gesture. His old friend and collaborator Abu-Lughod, for example, had left his job at Northwestern to spend the last decade of his life teaching at Birzeit in Ramallah. In general, the Oslo debacle, along with his declining health, pushed Said to look for a more personal connection with Palestine than had been available from the usual choreographed trips to the Middle East to make a film or give a lecture, the most recent example being a trip to the West Bank in February and March 1997 to make the film *In Search of Palestine* for the BBC.

Wadie's initiative made him think again. Said's former student Ashrawi, then working for the Palestinian Authority in Ramallah, knew very well that he wanted desperately to be welcomed as one of their own by Palestinians living in the territories. That he was not hurt him deeply.[64] Wadie not only showed the way but opened doors, acting as his planner and guide, driving him from town to town, arranging the logistics, introducing him to the day-to-day workings of the territories, and above all bringing him into contact with young people to whom Said otherwise had no access.[65] Given the patriarchal culture, his being there with his son suggested a greater commitment to the place.

Depending on one's point of view, Oslo had either made the Palestinian national struggle no longer possible or brought it to a perverse realization. Either way, it was now gone from his agenda. The move freed him up to criticize more caustically the U.S. government and to hammer away at his idea of Palestinianism as a universal ethos of inclusiveness that included the need to move beyond any definite or localized belonging. Unfortunately, unlike when he was writing *Orientalism*, Said could no longer count on a left-leaning common sense.

It was with a spirit of defiance, then, that his last political essays from 1995 to 2003—which he gathered together shortly before his death in *From Oslo to Iraq and the Road Map* (2004)—took up the broad assault on civic freedoms after 9/11, the launching of permanent war by the U.S. military in the Middle East and North Africa, and the frightening authoritarianism at home. There he complained of "the levels of lobotomized cheerleading in the intellectual sector" and found the "'experts' (the worst was that pig [Fouad] Ajami)" a disgrace.[66] He railed against the Patriot Act, passed in October 2001, which represented what he called "an Israelization of U.S. policy."[67] The United States seemed more and more ruled by fundamentalist Christian sects, which "are, in my opinion, a menace to the world."[68]

This was not to say that his focus had shifted entirely to domestic issues. Despite a dedicated global following, Said confronted a certain degree of skepticism in the Middle East itself. In Israel and the territories, his influence was already considerable. In Israeli academia, especially among the younger generation, *Orientalism* had become more or less required reading. His work also resonated nicely with the revolt within Israel itself against the Ashkenazi establishment as well as the protests against its various white papers falsely portraying Israel as a multicultural society of tolerant inclusiveness.

Countering that portrait, a movement among Mizrahi Jews sought to bring that multiculturalism to realization and, in doing so, adduced Said, who had always welcomed diversity in the region by persistently writing about Arabs, Palestinians, and Oriental Jews as having a similar sensibility and destiny. Despite impediments, his work was circulating in the region. *The Question of Palestine* appeared in Hebrew as early as 1981. A year before that, his comrade and friend Shahak wrote to him from Israel to say "your name is known here to a considerable extent."[69] Because of the florid Arabic translation of *Orientalism* and *Culture and Imperialism*'s sheer length and erudition, the two books made less of an impact in the Arab world than the political essays, particular those of *The Politics of Dispossession*, which were very influential. Although by the 1980s

Said was very widely known in the region, it was not as a cultural or literary critic, even though *The World, the Text, and the Critic* had been translated into Arabic by the Syrian Ministry of Culture in a pirated edition that remained unavailable outside Syria. Najah al-Attar, the first woman to head the ministry, invited Said four times to the country, and he vehemently rejected the offer each time because of domestic repression and Syria's betrayal of the Palestinians during the Israeli invasion of Lebanon.[70] She, however, recognized, as others have since, that Said's greatness—and it is perhaps his singular achievement in the Arab world—was to have impressed upon everyone the vital importance of the intellectual as society's social conscience, diagnostician, and setter of agendas.

In Palestine, intellectuals resented his care in mentioning the suffering of the Jews in the Holocaust and thought it outrageously provincial to argue that "the U.S. must be the primary focus of our work," in the sense of influencing the opinions of the U.S. public upon which Israel's life support ultimately relied.[71] His frequent agitation for more "creativity" in advancing the Palestinian cause, or his quoting of Césaire's line that "there is a place for all at the Rendezvous of Victory," for instance, although high-minded, seemed to many too far from the field of battle and out of contact with the enormity, say, of the Gazan crisis, where people's homes were routinely reduced to rubble by Israel's bulldozers. Even those who had embraced Oslo never considered it anything more than another step toward an independent, sovereign Palestine. Was it not betrayal then, some wondered, when he wrote that "exile seems to me a more liberated state," or when he concluded that Palestine was "precisely irrecoverable . . . We are moving away from it. It is not to create the beautiful place with orchards and so on. I don't believe in a final coming-home"?[72] He was, in the view of many activists, not only out of touch with these statements but letting his Americanism show.[73]

Although he might have appeared this way to impatient partisans, Said was never an interloper safely housed in a Manhattan high-rise. Even after Oslo, he was recruited by Ashrawi to sit on the board of the Palestinian Human Rights Commission and worked for other organizations under the new governmental authority.[74] And he continued to raise money, make films, and agitate. His ongoing personal involvement was illustrated by an encounter with Ibrahim Ammar, an enterprising Palestinian student who arrived in London at twenty-one with a pair of blue jeans, two sweatshirts, and a small suitcase. After attending Said's lecture at the Houses of Parliament, he waited in line to talk to him. Finally standing before him, he casually mentioned that he would appreciate any ideas for financial assistance so that he might continue his schooling. Said replied that he would see what he could do. Ammar left gratified but sure that this "legend among us Palestinians," as he put it, would forget his promise the moment he left the hall. Within a month a check for fifteen hundred pounds arrived in the mail.[75]

The new directions in Said's writing and speaking sprang not from fatigue or defeatism but from an unpleasant collective reality. A lack of sovereignty had forced Palestinians to reimagine nationalism as a general plight rather than a form of belonging based on blood and soil. By contrast, Israel's national ideal was borrowed from nineteenth-century Europe, as Uri Eisenzweig, a scholar trained in Israel and France, had persuasively argued while endorsing Said's case for the "imaginary spatial structures" of Zionist territory.[76] These convictions were at the center of "The Landscape of Palestine: Equivocal Poetry," a conference he helped organize with Abu-Lughod, Khaled Nashef, and others much later at Birzeit University in the West Bank, which sought to expose the fictions of Israeli archaeology.[77] In his view Zionism, to put it plainly, had created a European colonial enclave in Palestine, and it was important for Palestinians not to repeat the offense.

This clash of appearances between America and the Middle East lay behind the strange events of late June and early July 2000, when, after a family visit to Lebanon to give two public lectures, he returned to a media frenzy. Some public officials and journalists were calling him a terrorist. As part of a packed schedule, Said had taken time from his talks in the country to tour southern Lebanon, a "security zone" recently vacated by the Israeli military, which had been forced out of the country by the Lebanese resistance after a twenty-two-year occupation.

Following a visit to the notorious Khiam prison, Said chatted with journalists, some of whom followed the entourage, which included his family and a close friend, Fawwaz Traboulsi, who had organized the tour. They proceeded to the Fatima Gate on the border with Israel, where they found a heap of stones on the Lebanese side of the fence as well as three Hezbollah party officials, who looked on. As with all visitors to the area, the men invited the group to throw a symbolic stone in the direction of a fence on the other side of which, and at some distance, stood a guard tower that as far as the group could see was unoccupied. Someone speaking Arabic in the entourage encouraged Said to throw a stone, and Traboulsi agreed to join in. Said's stone barely made it to the fence, falling limply to the ground.[78] A photographer from the newspaper *Assafir* and a crew from Al-Manar TV were the ones who had followed them to the gate. Later that evening, the photographer from *Assafir* brought the photograph to Said's hotel for him to have a look. Meanwhile, the sister-in-law of a good friend—the novelist Elias Khoury—asked if she could distribute the photograph through Agence France-Presse, where she happened to work. Said saw no harm and readily agreed.

That night Hezbollah aired a clip of the event on local television.[79] Because to everyone who was there the action seemed little more than harmless theater, the outcry that followed struck them as bizarre. Said, who had always argued for peaceful coexistence between the Palestinians and the Jews, was portrayed as a violent anti-Semitic fanatic. The New York tabloid *Daily News* featured a photograph of his stone throwing on its second page under the provocative title "Columbia Prof Admits to Stoning."[80] In the ferocious media attack, Paula Zahn on CNN was particularly uncivil when interviewing him, so much so that Said decided not to waste time with mainstream news outlets thereafter. In the uproar, pro-Israel faculty members, students, and donors worked relentlessly for months to have him dismissed from the university, or at least to force the university to embarrass him by issuing a public denunciation. Some professors from the medical, business, and engineering schools were particularly aggressive, drowning the provost's office with up to fifty emails and calls and winning over one of the trustees.[81]

A number of colleagues rallied in support, as did large sectors of the public. In the heat of the affair, Columbia's provost, Jonathan Cole, after a delay of two months, issued an official statement at the request of student government leaders. In a five-page letter quoting John Stuart Mill and the Columbia Faculty Handbook, Cole pointed out that no laws had been broken and no indictments filed, and that it was only Said's political views that made this an issue at all. Citing academic freedom, his announcement effectively quashed the campaign, although it limped on for several weeks and never completely died. The criticisms did not all come from the pro-Israel side. Some of his allies thought he trivialized the act in interviews, stressing that he threw a "pebble" aimed at no one in a "symbolic gesture of joy."[82] In the face of Israeli state violence, they asked, why not turn the tables by proudly owning the gesture?[83] The act was, in fact, trivial but in the minds of some had left a question mark about his life's work, and that sent him into a prolonged depression.[84]

BEING DONE WITH FICTION, at least as an author, mirrored other contradictions. As Barenboim wryly observed, Said invested more and more time in classical music just as the Western public had begun to lose interest in it. Meanwhile, Said had not abandoned his quest to make classical music less forbidding to the public, although the effort was soon merged with a plan to give Palestine itself a profile in the classical world. By chance in 1989, he saw with

Mariam a "CBS This Morning" segment featuring Saleem Abboud Ashkar, a twelve-year-old Palestinian who had just performed with the Israeli Philharmonic Orchestra. Said immediately recognized that "the boy is very talented, but he will never be allowed to succeed in Israel."[85] He contacted George Abed, then the head of the Palestine Welfare Organization, asking him to track down the young pianist. Later that year, a meeting was arranged, and on several successive days in Paris, the two met for several hours. After the audition, which involved long conversations about life in general, Said confirmed the boy's skills, persuading the Al-Qattan Foundation to support his education.

A few years later, in 1993, the Palestinian National Conservatory of Music was established. Said was consulted by the founders and played a constructive role in making the institution a reality, contributing the ten thousand dollars he received for the *New Yorker* prize for *Out of Place*. He reasoned that if Palestinian youth could learn to focus through music—the anxieties of the occupation were more than distracting—they might concentrate on their other studies as well. The conservatory, though, would need the highly trained musician-instructors that Palestine did not have at that time, and recruiting them from Europe required Israeli visas that were practically impossible to obtain. In response, Said asked Barenboim for help. The conductor quickly and efficiently organized a procedure for German musicians to come to teach. Swept up in the experience, and at the request of the director of the conservatory, Suhail Khoury, Barenboim promised to build a Palestinian orchestra. His involvement grew on all fronts. In March 1998, Barenboim was performing in Jerusalem as Said was finishing a film for the BBC on the West Bank. Taking advantage of their proximity, he arranged for Barenboim to play at Birzeit, where the conductor performed a four-handed Schubert piano piece with Abboud Ashkar himself.

As it happened, that very year Barenboim had been invited by the German cultural minister to help organize forthcoming celebrations in Weimar, which had been named the European Capital of Culture of 1999.[86] Wanting to avoid the tired themes associated with that famous city—on the one hand, Goethe and Schiller, on the other, the nearby concentration camp of Buchenwald—he called on his recent experience to propose instead a workshop with young Israeli and Arab musicians, a maximum of fifteen or so. Barenboim presented Said with the happy opportunity, pointing out that "we can do something that is not just music." "Absolutely," Said responded.[87] Eventually, to their surprise, more than two hundred Arab musicians applied. In August, Barenboim along with Said and the cellist Yo-Yo Ma selected a group of "seventy-eight Arab and Israeli musicians aged eighteen to twenty-five" to attend a musical workshop in Weimar.[88] The West-Eastern Divan Orchestra was born. Within a few years, annual workshops for the musicians were set up in Spain until in 2005 they performed in Ramallah itself in a memorial concert for Said and in solidarity with Palestine.

No one supposed this symbol of Israeli-Arab cooperation would bring about peace. Apart from embodying understanding at a time when Said was promoting a one-state solution in Israel/Palestine, what it actually could do, they thought, was offer an education through music as "a spiritual exercise." Said and Barenboim had long militated against *Musikwissenschaft* (musical science), the drills and procedures involving acoustics, bodily exercises, and reading disciplines designed to produce performing marvels who knew little else.[89] Barenboim had long observed that Said did not go about problems scientifically, rather artistically, and this became another reason to invest in musicians who were fully realized individuals. They used the same pedagogical principles later instituted at the Barenboim-Said Akademie in Berlin and that remain in place today: all-around training combining the study of performance with the study of history, politics, and aesthetics. Educating through music, not music education—that was the idea.

Applauded throughout the world, the orchestra nevertheless led to frictions in Said's family. Although the West-Eastern Divan concept had always meant to operate on a level above the Israel/

Palestine conflict, the Boycott, Divestment, and Sanctions (BDS) movement led by Omar Barghouti began to boycott the orchestra, believing that the collaboration hurt the Palestinian cause by normalizing relations with a pariah state rightly condemned for its violations of international law. Grace, the grassroots activist of the family, in particular was critical. Her perspective, like Said's, was colored by her extensive time in the United States. A graduate of Teachers College, which sat just north of Columbia's campus, she had escaped the civil war in Beirut in 1983, first living with her brother and Mariam in their New York apartment but, finding the city too overwhelming, later moving to Washington.[90] For much of the 1990s and after Said's death, she worked for divestment from Israel. "We Palestinians," she joked, decided to "use our Christianity by getting a foot in the door of the churches on this issue but without excluding our Muslim friends." Later a stalwart in the BDS movement, she remained convinced that although Said disliked the "rigidity" of the BDS movement at times, he would have taken his stand with it critically. In the last years of his life, he had already supported targeted divestment and boycotting the settlements and was furious with his colleague the progressive historian Eric Foner for refusing to support defunding the settlements.

For most of the Said family, then, the orchestra's existence was galling, especially as conditions in Palestine deteriorated over the first decade of the twenty-first century. They were swayed, apparently, by the vigorous, and from Mariam's point of view quite unfair, BDS publicity campaign against it. Mariam dug in, staying on as the orchestra's main organizer and promoter side by side with Barenboim after Said was gone. She felt that her husband's legacy in the organization that he considered one of his proudest accomplishments had to be preserved, and that it was ill-advised for the National Conservatory of Music to sever its ties with Barenboim in 2005. For one thing, keeping it alive led to an important organizational spin-off, the Barenboim-Said for Music center in Ramallah, which was always more than a school or youth orchestra, more an all-encompassing cultural experience for Palestinians from the West Bank, inside Israel and the diaspora. The pilot program that began with Barenboim and the National Conservatory of Music in the mid-1990s is still thriving and is funded by the Regional Government of Andalusia, Spain, and the Foreign Ministry Office of Germany, as well as through individual donations.

Although his friendship with Barenboim added to his musical credibility and enriched his personal and artistic life, the bond between them was intellectually complementary if not always congruent. When publishing their dialogues on music before live audiences in New York, they hinted at their union of unlike minds by calling it *Parallels and Paradoxes: Explorations in Music and Society* (2002). On one occasion, debating whether music and literature shared fundamental traits, Said took the view that musical notation was a "text" more or less like that of a novel in the sense that both required interpretation. Barenboim couldn't agree, saying that whatever words can describe makes music unnecessary.[91] It is true that an actor can deliver the simple word "no" in a thousand ways, emphatically, aggressively, understandingly. But as a word, "no" has a meaning that a text of music—basically "black spots on white paper"—does not. "How can you read that?"[92]

They parted ways also on the matter of "silence." Said speculated that silence undercuts music as a waste and a loss whereas in literature (silence as the unsaid) is preserved in the word and part of its meaning.[93] Authors may at times read their work aloud, but essentially they compose in silence and their audience consumes the work in silence. As a conductor, Barenboim could not think silence an absence. "Sound needs the silence that precedes it . . . You hang on to that first note as a listener, but in every phrase there are silences in order to breathe, in order to get more intensity . . . Music is expressive only because there is silence that interrupts it . . . And the silence after is louder than the original chord."[94]

On the big issues, they affected each other's thinking. Barenboim looked up to Said's talent for tracing musical patterns in the political world and at times emulated it. At a dinner party in London toward the end of Said's life, with all the guests listening intently—Tariq Ali, Jacqueline Rose, Stuart and Catherine Hall, Mariam, and a withdrawn Said, who held his tongue, ceding the floor to his friend—Barenboim spoke at length, about ten minutes or so, slowly developing the idea that the Oslo Accords were like the failed tempo of a concert, the pace unable to catch up to the score, until it fell into the abyss.[95]

CHAPTER 12

THE RACE AGAINST TIME

He who is not malign does not live serenely.

—THEODOR ADORNO[1]

"My watch," Said once wrote about his childhood, "guarded my life like a sentinel." Now a grown man, he had to live with the consequences: "Nine p.m. still represents 'lateness.'" As the beer with peanuts he shared with Mariam while watching the news gave way to scotch, and it being too late by then to call anyone, the workday was over. He would need at least a little sleep to prepare for the next day's assault.[2] The lesson might have been slow in coming, but he had learned that wasting time was also a way of spending it and that amusements were retaliation against his self-imposed regimes.[3] As Mariam confessed, "he wasted time aplenty," and Christopher Hitchens ribbed him that he dropped the names of too many TV shows not to have watched them when no one was looking.[4] The completed task, at any rate, was less important than the constant activity.

In *The Last Interview* (2004), the documentary film made just before his death, his friend the journalist Charles Glass listened as

Said offered a litany of the facts of his life over the last few years. He could no longer read. Under the cloud of chemo, it was beyond him even to listen to music. Wadie was startled to see his father falling asleep in a living room chair at 7:00 p.m., a book falling out of his hand, and Najla had to remind him of the names of simple household things.[5] With sadness, Glass begged him to be happy with what he had managed to get done. Playing down the drama, Said stuck to the story he told whenever anyone told him to take it easy—that the idea of rest made him sick and that sleep was already a kind of death. He was planning a second volume of *Out of Place*, bringing the story up to the present, and there were other projects too.[6]

He did not always handle crises so sensibly. Years before, in 1983, he sat with Mariam beside the hospital bed of Wadie, who was gravely ill with osteomyelitis. After posting vigil for several hours, he suddenly jumped from his chair to remind Mariam that they had concert tickets and needed to be on their way. Mariam looked up at him uncomprehendingly and thought, "How can you think of such a thing?" "I am not going," she flatly said. Undeterred, he tried to coax her: "It will be good for you." She was adamant. Not only did he leave, but he returned home only very late, well after the concert had finished, going on the offensive as soon as he walked through the door: "Why are you still up?" And then it struck her that he couldn't cope. The situation overwhelmed him, and all he could do to dodge collapse was fall back on routine.[7] He often dealt with his own illness in the same way.

The last four years of his life were spent pulling together three short books, but only one appeared before his death: *Freud and the Non-European*, which, despite its title, had almost nothing to do with the mysteries of the unconscious and everything to do with his own childhood home, Egypt, about which Freud had been obsessed for most of his life. Based on a lecture he delivered at the Freud Museum in London, it was a kind of revenge against the lecture's intended venue, the Sigmund Freud Museum in Vienna, which withdrew its invitation because of the scandal caused by the rock-throwing incident.

Like the posthumous *Humanism and Democratic Criticism* (2004) and *On Late Style* (2006), *Freud and the Non-European*, although suggestive, was written in a single key. With little time, he settled for primer-like books, not worrying too much about style, taking a stand on what mattered most in any way he could. To make up for a certain flatness of expression, he returned to ethical basics defiantly announced. The defining tone of his last years came through clearly at a debate in New York in 2001 about America's role in the world between (among others) Christopher Hitchens, on one side, and the Egyptian novelist Ahdaf Soueif, on the other. After much venomous back-and-forth onstage, Said jumped to his feet from the audience during the Q&A to ask, "Why does no one talk of truth and justice anymore?"[8]

Fatigue made progress slow as he worked on the three books, forcing him to put off others (on Eqbal Ahmad and the book on Beethoven and Bach) to some point in the future. Of the leukemia treatments that plagued him, the worst was Campath, a particularly nasty drug whose side effects included itching, constant headaches, and shortness of breath. In thick black pen strokes on the inside flap of a manila folder containing the manuscript of a talk on humanism, he jotted down a diary entry sometime in 2000: "This lecture was given . . . on three successive nights during chemotherapy. How I managed I cannot easily say, but I did with . . . my hair falling out."[9] At this point in his life, he lost interest in novelty. He preferred muscular reaffirmations from new vantage points. His reassertion of old articles of faith (the urgent political force of humanism, the threat to thought posed by an uncritical scientism) had a different ring now, as though their mood during the early years of the twenty-first century's "war on terrorism," although still undaunted, was also slightly doomed.

· · ·

SAID SENSED THAT WHEN he was gone, his critics would pounce, for he would not be there to hold them in check with an angry reply. The indignities of disrespect joined those of physical decline. In August 2003, he was traveling back from southern Portugal, where he and Mariam had been vacationing with Jean Stein. On the last night of their stay, the weather was exceptionally beautiful, the soft breeze off the ocean comforting him as he read a book by Talal Asad in preparation for a lecture on religion he was to give in 2005 in Scotland. It was to be a high-profile event—Henry James had delivered the first of its kind there—and Said was determined to begin his preparations early. But he was already feeling wretched and feverish. For the first time in all their travels after 9/11, they were asked by the airline to call in advance to confirm their flight and supply their passport numbers. "I don't like these questions," he confided to Mariam, sensing the problems to come. In bed that night, he became delirious from the fever and had to be put in a wheelchair as they headed for the Faro airport.

Sitting forlornly in the terminal with a military bag of books on his lap (it doubled as his medicine bag), he watched everyone else get on the plane. But the TAP officials refused to board him. His name had tripped a warning, apparently, and they demanded he first be cleared by the U.S. embassy in Portugal, which in turn sought approval from Washington, where it was then midnight. Airport security opened his bag strewing medicines and books about. Humiliated, a sickly man in a wheelchair, he spoke weakly but angrily: "I was born an American citizen. I've lived in the States for forty-five to fifty years." When they finally relented, the point had been made. Cockburn used to mock him gently for his hyperbole when complaining of the latest "filthy diatribe" against him in *The New Republic*, adding, "I know you don't care about the feelings of a mere black man such as myself."[10] Now the charge seemed strangely literal. Whether the airline held him at the gate out of run-of-the-mill ethnic profiling or targeted him for his political activities on orders from U.S.

immigration, the result was the same. He was considered exotic as a boy in Cairo for being an American; now the officials of his own country did not seem to think him genuinely theirs.

The year before had been very different. In October 2002, he flew to neighboring Spain to receive with Barenboim the Premio Príncipe de Asturias de la Concordia (the Prince of Asturias Concord Prize) for founding the West-Eastern Divan Orchestra. A low-key Nobel Peace Prize, it came with a handsome award of twenty thousand euros each and a Miró sculpture. But even the recognition came with some embarrassment. In the last few years, he found cold comfort in the fact that the monstrous swelling that usually attacks the lymph nodes of the neck with his kind of cancer largely passed him by, although after 1995 he began to develop protuberances in the jowls and below the jaws requiring medical intervention.[11] For the most part, the swelling targeted his abdomen instead, nestling dangerously and inoperably between the heart, spinal column, and liver. This meant he could continue lecturing without distracting his audience with an obvious deformity. Usually his bulging stomach, although noticeable, could be partly concealed by loose-fitting suits.

He did not want his compromised body to make him seem pathetic ("I don't do victimhood," he insisted in an interview with *New York* magazine just after the appearance of *Out of Place*), and so was happy that Rai never told him to cut back on his plans or to curb his lifestyle.[12] Rai had devised ways of managing the disease without his undergoing chemo until later in the treatment, and he was able to delay the even more invasive experimental drug regimen Rituxan for several years. He made the best of his life of labs and hospitals by bringing his work to the doctors themselves, delivering "Timeliness and Lateness: Health and Style" at the College of Physicians and Surgeons of Columbia University in 2000 with Rai in attendance.[13] In the endless routine of visits to chemo, he made friends, not just acquaintances, with the staff, speaking to them with genuine warmth, remembering not just their names or those of their significant others but details of their doings, even years afterward.[14]

But not every indignity could be dodged. By April 2003, after he received an honorary degree at the Sorbonne, a lymphoma caused by the leukemia made his abdomen swell beyond its usual size so that his ceremonial sash would not fit. He sat passively as attendants hovered around him tying two sashes together to complete his uniform. Even worse, when the stone-throwing incident hit the papers a few years earlier, a student wrote a tasteless letter to the *Columbia Daily Spectator* mocking him for being fat, not realizing that the midriff bulge was a tumor.[15] *The Washington Post* piled on with a malicious ad hominem remark: "The silver-haired man in the smock, cap, and stylish sunglasses seems a little too old, a little too portly . . . to be hurling stones in the direction of Israeli soldiers."[16]

His political enemies found ways to snub him. King's College Cambridge, where his old ally Tony Tanner had been a fellow, turned him down for an honorary degree when others half his stature were given the honor without a second thought. Said had spent much of October and November 2002 in Cambridge giving four keynote lectures that filled the seven-hundred-person theater to capacity, with many turned away. But the influence of his old nemesis Ernest Gellner, who had trashed *Culture and Imperialism* in *The Times Literary Supplement* in 1993 on the grounds that culture did not matter and that the Western empires did more good than harm, followed Said to Cambridge. At the rancorous council meeting of King's fellows, a handful of supporters of Israel did what they could to block the degree, and in order to keep the peace, the majority acquiesced.[17] Ian Donaldson and a few other scholars fought back, forcing a reconsideration, but the decision arrived too late. Donaldson delivered the announcement that the honorary degree was his on the day Said fell into his final coma.[18]

Since at least *The Question of Palestine* two decades earlier, he had been under attack, but just before and after his death his political foes seemed especially eager for revenge. If not as extreme as the assassins of reputations hired by magazines like *Commentary* (Edward Alexander's "Professor of Terror" in 1989 was probably the most notorious example), former students emerged to disown him or write books warning of the dangers of his dubious charisma.[19] Given Said's own strong sense of loyalty, the most dispiriting betrayal came from his former ally and collaborator Christopher Hitchens, who had lately turned to the political right after being exposed for funneling information to Ken Starr's lieutenants during the Clinton impeachment investigation. Railing against abortion and denouncing "Islamo-fascism," he had become a reliably pro–U.S. foreign policy guest on television roundtables and a member of a select group of Washington insiders.

The days of hanging out with Said and the "gang" in New York were gone (in fact, Hitchens dropped Ben Sonnenberg cold after the latter stopped editing *Grand Street* and was no longer useful). Aware that Said was dying, Hitchens went ahead anyway with the publication of "Where the Twain Should Have Met" for *The Atlantic Monthly*, which appeared only a few weeks before the end. Ostensibly commemorating *Orientalism*'s twenty-fifth anniversary, Hitchens used the occasion to condescend, pretending to correct Said's "errors" in the book, recycling all the old canards against it, and posing as an erudite fluent in German and conversant in Goethe when he was nothing of the kind. Ignoring the whole point of *Orientalism*'s campaign against the artificial severing of neighboring cultures, he accused Said of being a man ideally poised to bridge the cultures of East and West who instead drove a wedge between them.

Even some who seemed to praise him—the London-based Australian journalist and memoirist Clive James, for instance—resorted to left-handed compliments, whittling away at his stature while laying a few verbal land mines along the way. Instead of acknowledging Said's nimble maneuvering between warring civilizations, James cast a shadow on his enviable connections. "There are some bright people in the East," wrote James, "who thought of Said as just another international operator doing well out of patronizing them, and with less excuse," as though Said were not from "the East" and not an Arab as well as an American intellectual. Like others, James looked at the doubleness of the immigrant experience and saw only self-contradiction.

Although it was not meant as such, the term "lateness" fit many of the academic counteroffensives surprisingly well. The timing of the backlashes (Robert Irwin's *For Lust of Knowing*, for example) suggested cowardice, Irwin waiting thirty years to publish his remarks until Said could no longer respond to them. Said's verbal bruisings of Bernard Lewis, Robert Griffin, and Michael Walzer among others might have made him think twice about facing his target, but in any case they were not easy to forget. Said reviled the tactic in a review of V. S. Naipaul in the *New Statesman* in 1981 alluding to the novelist's habit of sniping at third-world peoples from the pages of *The Atlantic Monthly*: "Does he . . . risk their direct retaliation . . . like Socrates liv[ing] through the consequences of his criticism? Not at all."[20] A related strategy was simply to erase his name. When *The New York Times* in its memorial for Sonnenberg listed all the famous people who had written for *Grand Street*, it excluded Said, one of the journal's most frequent contributors.[21] So too the online list of celebrity recipients of the Bowdoin Prize at Harvard, which conspicuously omits Said's name.

A different kind of damage was inflicted by former intimates struggling for closure. A decade and a half after his death, Dominique Eddé published *Edward Said: Le roman de sa pensée* (2017; *Edward Said: His Thought as a Novel*), a largely autobiographical tell-all in which she casts herself as his neglected muse.[22] A few of Said's friends recoiled from its staginess—her playing on the *W* of his middle initial as the "double you" of his identity, for example, or the comparison of his divided self to the right- and left-hand parts of a piano score.[23] Carefully embedded slights made Said appear, at just the times others found him charming, an unsavory figure, as though she wanted to hurt the man she claimed to admire.

Billing itself as both, the book was more novel than study, building itself around Said's fascination with Conrad (as though this were news) and proposing that Albert Camus and George Orwell were major touchstones, when, in fact, he loathed them.[24] Because Eddé mistook *Beginnings* for his first work and found his memoir "cold," she fell back on the line that his life was the novel. But she went even further. Unfamiliar with his fiction and poetry, she argued that he'd never had the courage to throw himself at the mercy of the imagination as novelists and poets must. For to do so would mean entering dangerous emotional territory that resists the control of the critic's strong sense of what ought to be. The charge revealed how little she knew him. It ignored his emphatic defense throughout his life of the neglected rights of critics when set against the usual pieties about artists in the general culture.

IN THE FINAL YEARS, Said put aside his cautions about displeasing the profession or appearing out of step with its fashions. With little to lose and time running out, he thought it was a good season to put his principles on the line in as plain a way as possible. And yet, on the phone with his childhood friend Charlie Blythe, he was feeling emotional under the influence of the cancer drugs. Close to tears, he became irate with himself for caring too much about status and getting the right invitations.[25] He wrung his hands, confessing to another friend that he felt wretched buying expensive clothes when so many in the world were struggling.[26]

In two major lecture series, a flurry of essays, and a short book (*Humanism and Democratic Criticism*), his writings in the early twenty-first century on the vitality of humanism so closely paralleled those of the early 1980s that undated manuscripts in the archive from the one period are easy to confuse with the other. Age, if anything, had made him more combative, even if the effects of chemo had softened the edges of his prose and made its earlier three-dimensionality plainer and more declarative. The temporizing of *Culture and Imperialism*, at any rate, was behind him as he pursued projects that directly confronted the critical mainstream. For many of his colleagues, humanism had long conjured images of slave owners lecturing colored people on the benefits of reason. If the term had been unpopular in the early days of his career, by the beginning of the twenty-first century it had become for almost everyone around him a slogan that evoked every crime of Western civilization. University administrators still solemnly invoked it, but that discredited it even more.

He acknowledged that humanism had been used at times to "drape current praxis in a cloak of decency" and that "effusions about *humanitas*"—the former secretary of education William Bennett's sanctimonious *Book of Virtues* (1993) was one example—provided moral cover for atrocities (Said's example was the carpet bombing of Cambodia). We all know the ironies well, he added, when Israeli soldiers broadcast Simon and Garfunkel songs while standing watch over the massacres in the Sabra and Shatila refugee camps outside Beirut in 1982. But such examples, he countered, were only half the story. Not only in Europe but in China and the Arab world, humanism had always been bound up with training in the liberal arts. It represented no less than a revolution in learning based on the study of books, especially the forgotten wisdom of the past, and the passion to make knowledge generally accessible. Within Taoism, Confucianism, Sufism, and the Brahmo Samaj in India, among others, one found traces of the same agnosticism, skepticism toward the supernatural, and emphasis on human choice found in the most admirable strains of Western humanism.

There was every reason to deny that it represented, in any fundamental sense, the spirit of European racists like David Hume and Cecil Rhodes. For to dispense with humanism was to jettison also the maverick secularity of Thales and Anaxagoras, the philological study of Roman law in Varro, the preservation of Oriental learning in the Islamic golden age (Averroës, Avicenna), the great rediscovery of Egypt in Neoplatonism, the creation by scholasticism of the first European universities, the madrassas of the Maghreb and the Levant, and the triumph of reading in the Italian Renaissance of Poggio Bracciolini and Erasmus.

Against the early twenty-first-century world of niche markets, wars of extermination, and unrestrained biotechnology, Said argued, only humanism's strong sense of preserving the past stood as an impediment. The social role of the intellectual only became clear in the way humanism had historically entered the political sphere. In a review of a book on the influential journalist and presidential adviser Walter Lippmann, he found everything an intellectual ought not to be: accommodating, cowardly, supercilious toward the weak, defiantly middlebrow.[27] Among intellectuals, Lippmann's alter ego for him was Chomsky. At an event at Columbia, Said introduced his friend before a lecture by recounting a recurring fantasy in which he liked to indulge. He imagined Chomsky, he explained, sitting on one side of a boardroom table across from Zbigniew Brzezinski, Robert McNamara, Alexander Haig, and Tom Brokaw. Despite being outnumbered, he "[made] them squirm," destroying the arguments of these apologists and warmongers until "all . . . [were] carted off to the Hague for trial."[28] By lifting "a corner of the wall-to-wall carpet on which liberal Americans have pranced for three decades," Chomsky exemplified humanism's intellectual combat mode.[29] Lippmann, by contrast, never risked a thing.

While embracing the intellectual's social role, Said with characteristic unpredictability latched on to Julien Benda's seminal study, *La trahison des clercs* (1928; *The Treason of the Intellectuals*). The gesture was puzzling, because by "treason" Benda meant polluting the intellectual vocation by getting involved in politics.[30] Here was a man who thought democracy vile and believed that intellectuals formed a holy order whose members ought to live a reclusive, even ascetic life (his models were Socrates and Jesus). On the other hand, Said extolled Benda's secular Christian ideals. The humanities did, in fact, have a spiritual dimension, if by "spirit" one meant force of mind and ethical resolve. After September 11, 2001, such a model was attractive when many opinion makers seemed to want to do away not just with this or that dissident view but (as Said put it) with "thought itself."[31]

As death approached, he found it impossible not to reckon with his own field of study, facing what role, if any, it played in the intellectual's vocation. For that reason, he returned to the concerns of essays he had written in the 1970s and early 1980s on comparative literature and translation.[32] The very arcaneness and unfashionability of comparative literature, he observed, could not hide the fact that it contributed a great deal to questions of war, human rights, and foreign policy.[33] Concretely, in the youth rebellions of the 1960s, he found evidence of the "interanimation of traditions" made possible by the first translations of transformative works of radical thought that appeared in English for the first time between 1963 and 1972 (Fanon, Gramsci, Cabral, and others).[34] Above all, Said found in the field's willingness to swim against the stream a safeguard against the pretensions of techno-scientific exactness. Broad comparisons made specialization impossible. And unlike so many of the natural sciences, his discipline had continually reinvented itself, questioning its own pro-Western biases, and (just as important) pushing its object of study beyond literature into philosophy, music, history, political science, and sociology.[35]

Whatever powers were gleaned from their data, social scientists were relatively ill-equipped to make sense of society as a single interconnected body of material goods, cultural processes, and imaginative projections. In his early notes for a course on the Frankfurt School, he jotted down what he considered Adorno's major themes. One of them—"science, fact: a threat to liquidate all philosophy"—stood out. For it suggested that humanists understood better than the sciences that "facts" are themselves framed by, and find their meaning in, a comprehensive social theory in which language, values, and ideas all play a part.

One of the most profound social changes of the twenty-first

century—the conquest of writing by digital communications—was also one about which literary humanists and comparatists had a great deal to say.[36] The movement from paper and ink to a backlit screen meant abandoning the physicality of the text, the tedious and exacting labors of producing it, and the imaginative effort required by readers holding a book in their hands without the aid of hypertext. It was not simply nostalgia to want to hold on to the intellectual world that the older technology of writing allowed when not doing so had such disastrous consequences on the critical faculties. From essay to essay, he made the same sort of case: progressive thinking meant preserving traditions, not destroying them.

ALTHOUGH UNPOLISHED, HIS POSTHUMOUS study *On Late Style* was also unguarded. To that degree, it might have revealed more about his thinking late in life than he intended. More than any other of his books, it represented an almost equal balance between his musical and his literary sensibilities. Taking its leads from a famous essay by Adorno on Beethoven's late musical works (which included *Missa solemnis*, *Fidelio*, and the late sonatas), the book rather roughly, given his admiration for Adorno, set out to reverse its terms. Adorno's point had been that in late style composers feel free to rely on conventions rather than continue proving their originality. Said, dwelling on the heroic bitterness of certain exceptional novelists and composers, reveled in their Promethean desire to disrupt conventions.

All the same, lurking everywhere in the book were hints about how physical demise turns great minds into helpless witnesses. Falling short of implying that at death's door his rebellious spirit had collapsed, he was still forced to mull over the abyss where the possible and the inevitable meet: "I became quite fed up with politics."[37] Some uncertainty lingered within him about whether he had lost the drive to change the world, or whether he was intrepid enough to be, as he wrote of Genet, *contre-moi-même* (against myself). Like the artists he confronts in *On Late Style* itself, he wanted none of the amiability and official ingratiation of a venerable age. On the other hand, the traditions to which he clung were not about reactionary calm but, as in music, material for variation within no prescribed form. He loved to point out that the term *inventio* in music does not mean invention as normally understood—the creation of something from nothing—but the endless development of a received motif.

Because late style as a theme dated back to the years surrounding his diagnosis (it comes up in seminars in the early 1990s and takes full shape in three lectures in 1993), it might appear to be patterned suspiciously on the figure of his own cross.[38] It would be inviting to guess that heightening an already dramatic gesture, he was casting himself as some sort of Oedipus at Colonus, who, taboo in the eyes of the villagers (Oedipus had killed his father and married his mother), enters Colonus blind, wronged, and punishingly truthful, most of all about himself.

As it turns out, no real symmetry existed between lateness as an idea and his approaching death. Rather, his move to the problem of lateness was in some ways inevitable given the progression of the philosophical problems of beginnings, middles, and endings that he considered at each stage of life. Earlier in his career, he had held up the apparently conservative idea of continuity (Vico's idea that the past could be repeated in an original way), discovering within it a radical alternative to modernism's supposed ruptures with everything past. In a similar way, he meant to deprive lateness of its complacency, but not only late in life. He had considered the problem of lateness already in *Beginnings*, where he zeroed in on the writer who "begins to view himself as nearing the end of his career, tempted with the idea of going on" even after his writing had "reached its conclusion."[39]

At sixty-seven, Said was hardly an old man when he was composing the books and lectures of his final year. In his own mind, then, the figure of Oedipus in *On Late Style*, or alongside it of Richard Strauss (who died at eighty-five), was not very close to his own. If his later thinking lacked some of the grace and precision of his earliest essays, he was more than capable of stroking his audience while battering down its defenses. As he put it in an essay for *Al-Ahram*, "The essential thing about works of genius is that they hide or eliminate all the traces of the labor that went into them."[40] Deceptive simplicity had for a long time been a major rhetorical tool. But was style enough? He worried about still having something to say, nodding toward Yeats, who greeted old age by looking back on a career "reduced to a foul rag-and-bone shop."[41] He had not forgotten seeing Sartre in 1979, frail and unimpressive, his protégés leading him around by the nose. He sadly observed, "Great old men are liable to succumb either to the wiles of younger ones, or to the grip of an unmodifiable belief."[42] If vulnerable to flattery, and he always had been, he was at least not going to fall victim to dogma.

Not the idea, then, so much as the phrase "late style" is what he took from Adorno's short essay "Late Style in Beethoven" (1937). Said was eager to point out, in fact, that he was departing from Adorno's thesis. The book eventually published as *On Late Style*—assembled skillfully by Michael Wood from Said's partial drafts for the book and other lectures and writings never intended for inclusion—should be thought of more as the culmination of two decades of thinking about Adorno than as a commentary on the Beethoven essay per se. He had begun his serious exploration of Adorno's work only in the late 1970s. Until 1984, he had written or spoken very little about the great German thinker.[43] In the fall of 1983, he offered a seminar mostly dedicated to Adorno along with the work of Walter Benjamin, Herbert Marcuse, and Lukács, whom he called the "enabler and precursor" of them all.[44]

As one of the two or three most influential philosophers of the twentieth century, Adorno represented a nimble synthesis of aesthetics, psychoanalysis, epistemology, and empirical sociology. Affiliated from the age of twenty-four with the Frankfurt School, he, along with other Marxist intellectuals, developed a unique methodological amalgam. After 1932 and the rise of Nazism, the institute moved to Columbia University and then later to California to continue its research before returning to Germany after the war. In a barrage of seminal studies, written in a philosophically unyielding but also clear, angry, and at times despairing prose, they exposed capitalism as a threat to freedom, taste, morality, and thought. Gullible American policy makers disastrously embraced a narrow scientism, they argued, even as the country's corporate mass culture carried on and perfected the Nazis' World War II–era mind control by entertaining its citizens to the point of mental and emotional death.

Adorno was the unusual critic in a field dominated by aesthetes and musicologists who drew parallels between Bach's arithmetical compositions and the mechanization of bourgeois reason.[45] Said spoke from Adorno's vantage point when he called the Metropolitan Opera the "citadel of unresolved corporate and aesthetic interest."[46] As harsh as Said could be on Strauss in *On Late Style*, Adorno was even more unyielding, accusing Strauss's late work of being like a "Bazaar of the World" right next to the Grand Hotel: "everything offered for display and sale, everything accommodated."[47] Said, though, found Adorno too sweeping in his condemnations of Strauss and Arturo Toscanini, whom Adorno dismissed as "a disorder of late capitalism, his *Meisterschaft*, or mastery," a tyrannical parody of the assembly line. Said quite differently praised Toscanini for relieving concert performances of their traditionalism and sentimentality.[48] But he followed Adorno closely when railing against the seedier sides of the big celebrity pianist parade (Said often fumed about New York's mafia of piano performers, among them Vladimir Ashkenazy) and the warping powers of the classical music market. Adorno put the study of the composition, production, reproduction, and consumption of music on a serious footing for the first time, and this more than anything Said applauded and closely studied.

Yet Said did not worship Adorno any more than his other intellectual heroes. Adorno's pessimism bothered him: he "injects

Marxism with a vaccine that renders it immobile."[49] Eloquent when probing the bad dream of a society where all human relations have become financial transactions, Adorno in his descriptions of the market's evil genius gave no space to popular struggles or resources of hope. Saying no to everything, Said added, makes lateness uninteresting; there must be a constructive element. Said pushed a large swath of Adorno's best work to the side for that reason, and the Adorno who appealed to him was primarily the music theorist and the author of the agonized collection of postwar autobiographical fragments *Minima Moralia* (1951).

It was to be expected, then, that his earlier praise for Adorno (in *Musical Elaborations*, for example) was grudging. Only Adorno's work right before and after World War II, Said claimed, was truly good—namely, his famous study on the "culture industry" with his Frankfurt colleague Max Horkheimer along with *Philosophy of New Music* and *Minima Moralia*. Said almost certainly did not read, or read closely, the books that many consider the pinnacle of Adorno's thinking: *Aesthetic Theory* (1970) and *Negative Dialectics* (1966). In effect, he seriously foreshortened Adorno's range of interests, declaring that he was a philosopher whose "main subject was music," ignoring his work on Kierkegaard, television, Heidegger, German literature, and a host of other subjects.[50] A harsh critic of jazz and Tin Pan Alley, the bane of folkloristic composers like Stravinsky, Bartók, and Smetana, Adorno had himself written musical compositions in the New Viennese style exemplified by Arnold Schoenberg's twelve-tone school. Said took care to internalize the principal message, as he saw it, of Adorno's music theory: "The commodity form dominates all musical life"; that is, capitalism, by turning everything into a utility for which one willingly pays, has not spared music, destroying both its autonomy and its transcendence.[51] At the same time, anything that in Adorno smacked of the Hegelian tradition, Said shunned, but that, to most of his readers, was Adorno through and through, if critically.

Said, then, was really revising, and even contesting, Adorno's reflections on late style. How does one explain the remarkable shifts in style of major artists at the end of their careers? For Adorno this cannot be done with a cheap recourse to psychology, reducing the musical piece to the person, though the appeal of doing so is easy to understand. The disembodied, "almost idyllic" tone of Beethoven's final piano sonatas—so unlike the fireworks of the *Eroica*, for instance—can then easily be seen to signal the tranquility and resignation of old age.[52] But the operation divests art of its independence, making it a mere appendage of biography.

In a psychological approach, it would go without saying that a mature composer, if he were a genius, would double down on his earlier rebelliousness and throw out all convention in quest of a new language. But Beethoven did just the opposite, filling his late pieces with gratuitous "formulas and phrases of convention," aimless trills and appoggiaturas.[53] Having invented willfully throughout his life, the artist finally reins in desire in favor of the laws of form. The artwork is in this way given back its status as a revolt against reality rather than its servant. Late style is not about age at all for Adorno except insofar as it takes a long time for the artist to understand aesthetic form's indifference to reality.

Said's stress on the earthly and the worldly could not be more alien to Adorno's view here, just as his understanding of late style was relentlessly psychological. Reviewing Maynard Solomon's *Late Beethoven* (2003), he applauded the very habits of the biographer that Adorno reviled. Everything was geared to exploring the late works' "private striving and instability" as well as charting Beethoven's disturbing transformation from extrovert to introvert. The late work of the master was not, as we would expect (and as Adorno maintains), a lesson finally learned but an abdication and a flight from the necessary tasks that the declining powers of age dissuaded him from taking. The late pieces of Beethoven are contorted, knotty, and eccentric because of profound disappointment and withdrawal: his refusal—as Said puts it, quoting the Greek Alexandrian poet Constantine Cavafy—of "direct engagement with [his] own time."[54]

Late in life, Cavafy had begun to rival Hopkins as the poet on whom Said relied to express his hidden emotions. For hours after dinner he would read him aloud to Mariam, and if not Cavafy, then Wordsworth. Cavafy's "nonmetaphorical, almost prosaic un-rhymed verse" (as Said put it) captivated him for its capacity to chart the larger, mostly urban Hellenic world (above all Alexan-dria), often set in classical times and ignoring the modern Arab world around it. Significantly, Said called this art an "aesthetic of non-production"—an anti-voluptuous facing down of the temp-tations of the elegiac in order to look reality in the face. In Cavafy, it was clear that Said allowed himself feelings he usually fled in actual life—this "lapidary calm" in the face of a world turned out badly, a melancholic disenchantment without reconciliation or remedy in which having survived was the only victory. When it came time for Said's memorial, his sister Jean thought they should read a poem of Hopkins. But knowing what no one else seems to have known as well—this late-life immersion in the Alexandrian poet—Mariam stepped in to insist that Cavafy was the only choice. In the end, Najla delivered his "Waiting for the Barbarians," a mordant portrait of a citizenry's flight from the public square, "bored by rhetoric and public speaking," ceding its right to confront the rulers because of the threat of an external enemy that never arrives.

A sense of abjuring resolution governed his take on Adorno. On this question, the two agreed. But again and again, Said returned to the idea, absent in Adorno, that late works are not merely bris-tly, unsweet, or deliberately unpleasing (Adorno implies that these qualities are like lashes of the master in full command, keeping the audience on edge) but "episodic, fragmentary, unfinished," filled with "difficult and often mystifyingly unsatisfactory conclusions"— the exact definition Said gave late style in his book on Freud in 2003.[55] The focus moves, in short, from the intentionally off-putting to the unresolved.

Said was clearly wrestling with his own biography (and psy-chology), although not in the way we might expect. In the 2003 interview "Traveling with Conrad," for instance, he provides us with a rather unflattering portrait of the novelist. Although identifying with Conrad's self-doubt, he noted that the author's late style was sadly "full of reminiscences . . . self-quotation." Although revered late in life, Conrad was haunted by the fear that his fiction was now ordinary and that he had descended into a kind of mannerism.[56] Said understood this as a warning, the result perhaps of having earlier explored the problem head-on in the neglected essay "Too Much Work" (1999)—its title a pun alluding to the risks of adding too many writings to an already bulging oeuvre. The great geniuses who tend to inspire biographies are known for their "scarcely imaginable gifts of invention" and for qualities more divine than human. If, though, their lives are examined in everyday detail—"the marital problems, the bad teeth and rascally dentists, the difficulties with money, etc."—a "disappointingly humdrum portrait emerges." Mozart was, among other things, a fawning courtier, Einstein a mediocre violinist and uninspiring teacher, Goethe a boring administrator in the tiny duchy of Weimar. Alongside talents "unending in their richness," banality shadowed their genius at every turn.

The entire book meant to place despair, fatigue, and misanthropy under scrutiny. He wished to behold intellectual giants who succumbed late in life to the temptations he now felt himself and that he was determined to work through.[57] Something of that grim determination, along with the central place of Adorno in his study, was evident in a *Ha'aretz* interview with the Israeli journalist Ari Shavit in 2000 in which he exclaimed, "I'm the last Jewish intellectual. You don't know anyone else. All your other Jewish intellectuals are now suburban squires . . . I'm the last one. The only true follower of Adorno."[58] This was not the first time he had used the image. On a panel at a conference of Jewish progressives organized by the journal *Tikkun* in December 1988, his co-panelist Michael Walzer, ostensibly to keep peace, urged the audience to forget history and move on. A woman named Hilda Silverman then spoke from the floor saying she was confused: "Our entire raison d'être as Jews is history. The phrase 'never again' is our watchword, and now you're telling the Palestinians to forget history?!" At that point, Said responded to her call and, taking the mic, said, "Allow me to be the last Jewish intellectual."[59]

In a letter to Said in 1978, the radical journalist I. F. Stone put his finger on at least one of Said's motives for the provocation. There he brought to the foreground what Said already knew well, that the brunt of anti-Semitism had shifted from Jews to Arabs in the modern West. Praising a recent article by Said in the *New Statesman*, Stone admired his ability to "affirm the great gifts and worth of your oppressed and rejected people" and then concluded, "Yours have become the sensitive 'Jews' and mine the 'goyim.'"[60]

Wadie interpreted his father's gesture a little differently. It was significant that the Shavit interview took place just before the second intifada and the "war on terrorism" that followed 9/11, a period when all bets were off and Israel would ramp up its occupation without fearing reprisals. In a defensive posture, Shavit felt himself beaten in the interview, losing ground, and so resorted to ruses of insinuation and evasion. Annoyed, Said took stock of his interlocutor and thought to himself: "Look at you. You claim to be representing a people and a civilization, and you don't get it at all. You're not understanding what it means to be a Jewish intellectual, one committed to worldliness and universal justice. You may have the weapons and the resources, but intellectually and morally you've already lost, and it's just a question of when others figure it out."[61]

A lot of the book, then, took its leads from the chapter on Jean Genet, where he identifies Genet's genius for love, passion, and revolution as *rigueur dans le désespoir* (toughness in the face of despair). In the chapter on Mozart, for example, Said laments the composer's dismal view of human nature revealed in the title of his opera *Così fan tutte*—"everyone acts this way," that is, deceives their lovers and betrays their friends.[62] Mozart's lightheartedness hid an abiding darkness, its "closed system" of melody and parody dressing up a plot that revealed its characters' emptiness and unsatisfied longing.

Mozart's was a cynical unchanging order that Said indirectly condemned as morally and politically unacceptable, as was that of Richard Strauss (given his own chapter in *On Late Style*), who in his late work of the mid-twentieth century actively sought to go back to the eighteenth century by composing reactionary confections that showcased tonal harmonies and showed off his own talents for artifice as a way of retreating from the world of human affairs.

The trials of confidence Said endured as he worked on the book were probably clearest in the "Lingering Old Order" chapter on Luchino Visconti's 1963 film adaptation of Giuseppe Tomasi di Lampedusa's novel *The Leopard*. Like the main character of his novel, Lampedusa was a Sicilian aristocrat and very much a part of that Italian materialist tradition Said had embraced in Gramsci, Vico, and Gobetti. Even more, Lampedusa captured beautifully that combination of old-world decay, the stubborn arrogance of a colonized people, and the tragedy of being an anachronism, which recalled the Arab agony in twenty-first-century America. The Sicilians confused oldness with greatness: "For more than twenty-five centuries we've been bearing the weight of a superb and heterogeneous civilization, all from outside, none made by ourselves, none that we could call our own . . . For two thousand and five hundred years we've been a colony . . . we're worn out and exhausted."[63]

In one scene, Don Fabrizio, the proud but bored patriarch of a decaying rural estate, receives an emissary from the Turin government looking for the heads of old families to enter parliament in order to give the new regime legitimacy. The prince declines the offer of a seat in the senate with words that must have made Said think of his time on the PNC: "I belong to an unfortunate generation, straddling two worlds, and ill at ease in both . . . What would the government do with an inexperienced legislator who lacks the faculty of self-deception, an essential requisite for those who wish to guide others? No, I cannot lift a finger in politics. It would get bitten off . . . The Sicilians never want to improve. They think themselves perfect. Their vanity is greater than their misery."[64] Glimmers of the outlook were genuinely his own, familiar as he was from the ordeal of Oslo with the comforting truth that dirty politics are better left to smaller minds. He could not really deny, as much as he wanted to, the accuracy of Don Fabrizio's portrait of futility, and he confided to those who had yet to read it, "You have something very special waiting for you."[65] But just as with Cavafy, Lampedusa savored a pessimism that was not Said's, just a feeling whose danger lay in being attractive at moments of weakness.

In an intimate correspondence with Kenzaburo Oe a year before his death, Said gave voice to doubts he had never expressed before. "What most readers of Vico have missed," he ventured, "is his pessimistic outlook . . . No matter how hard we try, we are limited in a sense not just by our minds, but by our own standpoints, our own time . . . My favorite writer Joseph Conrad put it well: we live, as we dream, alone."[66] Pushing aside this surrender to melancholy, Oe, like Gordimer before him, reminded Said that they looked to him for bucking up, recalling that he had once compared Said to Simone Weil as she meditated on death in London in 1943 and, like Weil, he had not been seduced by the gloom of it.[67] A selection of Said's political essays had just been translated in Japan, appearing as *Propaganda and War*—a more candid title than its American counterparts and a glimpse into how he was perceived abroad. In their turbulent exchange, the two writers spoke of plans to push back against what Oe called the "united cultural imperialisms of America and Japan." As each sought the other's solace, Said reassured Oe with the observation that however weak were the weapons of literary language and imagery in the face of military aggression, they at least were "central to the whole enterprise of democratic citizenship."[68]

The rallying tone seemed a reproach to Adorno, whom Said began to see as a late nineteenth-century mind banished by accident to the twentieth century. Although Said shared much with Adorno's disillusioned romanticism, it was time to check his devotion to a thinker whose only real revenge on the zeitgeist was to insult it. He knew he was not going to win, not only because of the geopolitical forces arrayed against him, but also because of the audiences for whom evidence was never enough. He would be defeated, he reasoned, by the superior power of incessantly repeated lies. But he was also haunted by the modernist truths just over the shoulder of his consciousness, of infertility and dashed dreams. The script was already written, and the story would probably end badly.

Those who took their lessons straight from the bleak visions of Hardy's *Jude the Obscure* or Conrad's *Nostromo* he could not accept. In a letter to a well-wisher, he refused to hedge: "I'm afraid I cannot agree that the situation is 'hopeless.' Where cruelty and injustice are concerned hopelessness is submission, which I believe is immoral."[69] Just before his death, John Berger lamented that this "subversive cosmopolitan" who had thrown his life at the cause of Palestinian statehood had not moved the needle very much.[70] For all his personal charm, and the almost scary array of intellectual and moral weapons, the central political objective of his life seemed as far away as ever.

His old friend Andre Sharon saw just the reverse, reflecting on how changed the world had become at his hands. Rather than conforming to America, he brought America over to him, or a significant swath of its intellectuals anyway, creating a high-minded dissidence for the professional classes in which anti-imperialism was the new common sense, multicultural authority much less rare, and the force of culture in political struggle an acceptable version of the facts. A friend joked with him, saying, "I don't know what you're fighting about . . . You've won."[71] He probably would have found a way to win again in the age of Trump. He certainly had predicted its unthinkable bid to let Israel simply annex all Palestinian lands even as his version of the one-state solution has lately emerged as a viable option among those seeking a just end to the Palestinian agony. Still, Blackmur's words, which he doubtless recalled, were troubling: "The next age may not be literate in any sense we understand."[72]

. . .

LOOKING BACK, THE SQUABBLE over his travel documents at the Faro airport in August 2003 had been a bad omen. By the end of September, Said was dead. The proximity of the two events sent friends looking for answers. A myth circulated—Sonnenberg was one of those convinced—that Said had been too cavalier, risking an evening swim in the Atlantic with a compromised immune system.[73] If he had not been so rash, they thought, he might have lived for years. The reality was otherwise. Although chronic lymphocytic leukemia is usually a treatable disease, he unluckily fell into a group with a complication known as Richter's syndrome. In such cases the leukemia quickly multiplies and spreads into a fast-growing large B-cell lymphoma. Rai suspected that he had the condition when treating him in the hospital after his return from Portugal. Eventually, the autopsy confirmed Rai's diagnosis.

In the weeks after his return from Portugal, Said set about calling friends and former students, urging them to write responses to Hitchens's slanders in the *Atlantic Monthly* piece on *Orientalism*. The new semester had just begun, and with a major lecture abroad to prepare for, there was much to be done. Having returned with a fever, on Sunday, September 21, he told Mariam he felt a little better and was going to spend the day writing the introduction to *From Oslo to Iraq and the Road Map*. On Monday, though, Najla sensed something was terribly wrong. Observing him around the apartment, she found him no longer coherent. Wadie and his wife, Jennifer, who then lived only a block away, noticed the same thing, immediately contacting Mariam at work and then calling Kanti Rai urgently as Mariam rushed home. The doctor urged them not to panic, to take their time, so Wadie and Mariam slowly dressed him—he was no longer able to stand or walk—helping him onto the sofa before taking him downstairs to the car for the drive to the Long Island Jewish Medical Center by 7:30 that evening. On the way, Mariam anxiously caressed his hand, while he, still aware of his surroundings, gently squeezed hers to calm her nerves.

At the emergency room, they could see at once his condition was dire. Rai's face was grave. Taken immediately to intensive care, he was allowed visitors in the evenings but by Tuesday and Wednesday was already in a coma. On Wednesday afternoon Rai met with the family to say there was no hope. A massive viral and bacterial infection now filled his lungs, and he would be gone by morning. Do not stay to the bitter end, he advised them. The ICU's whirring machines set off a piercing alarm when the patient's heart stops, and given the likely trauma, patients' families are not even allowed into the room. Said's sister Grace had come up from Washington, joining the others around the bed to say their goodbyes. By 7:00 p.m., the sadness was too much for Najla—this watching over his labored breathing while staring at the monitor to see if his heartbeats would get stronger. She and Mariam kissed him goodbye and left together. Grace, Wadie, and Jennifer stayed another hour until Kanti persuaded them to leave. On Thursday morning, September 25, at 6:40 a.m., Mariam got the call that fifteen minutes before he had passed away.

He chose not to be buried in Palestine. The political symbolism of his life made the desecration of his grave an unfortunate possibility. Instead, drawing on Mariam's family connections, he selected a small Quaker cemetery perched on a grassy, tree-lined shelf of a steep hill in Brummana, Lebanon. There his simple black marble slab rests, his name appearing in English above and in Arabic below. Like the cemetery itself, the plot is tucked away from the world, almost secreted, in a way entirely unfitting a life like his own, except for the encroaching signs of modernity marring the general splendor of the valley. Modern high-rises vie with cypress trees to border the verdant triangle of the graveyard, which, although small, is too large for the number of Quakers buried there. And although it faces south toward Palestine overlooking a mountain range towering above Beirut, even the final resting place was not quite right.

NOTES

ABBREVIATIONS USED IN THE NOTES

Frequently Cited Works by Said

ALS: *After the Last Sky*
B: *Beginnings*
C&I: *Culture and Imperialism*
CI: *Covering Islam*
CR: *Culture and Resistance*
EPP: *The End of the Peace Process*
ESR: *The Edward Said Reader*
FNE: *Freud and the Non-European*
HDC: *Humanism and Democratic Criticism*
IES: *Interviews with Edward Said*
JC: *Joseph Conrad and the Fiction of Autobiography*
LS: *On Late Style*
ME: *Musical Elaborations*
ML: *Music at the Limits*
O: *Orientalism*
OI: *From Oslo to Iraq and the Road Map*
OP: *Out of Place*
PD: *The Politics of Dispossession*
PeD: *Peace and Its Discontents*
PP: *Parallels and Paradoxes*
PPC: *Power, Politics, and Culture*

PS: *The Pen and the Sword*
QP: *The Question of Palestine*
RE: *Reflections on Exile*
WTC: *The World, the Text, and the Critic*

Archives

CZ: Constantine Zurayk Papers, American University of Beirut.

EWSP: Edward W. Said Papers (1940s–2006), MS 1524, Rare Book and Manuscript Library, Columbia University Library. All references to this archive in the notes will follow the format box:folder:series.subseries. For example, 48:1:II.1 refers to box 48, folder 1, series II, subseries 1.

FBI: Edward William Said, FBI Vault.

HL: Harry Levin Papers, Levin-Said Correspondence, MS Am 2461 (859), Houghton Library, Harvard University.

HT: Edward W. Said, Harvard University Graduate Student Transcripts.

IW: Ian P. Watt Papers (SC0401). Department of Special Collections and University Archives, Stanford University Libraries, Stanford, California.

MH: Northfield Mount Hermon School Transcripts; Said 18790MH.01, 02, 03.

PT: Undergraduate Academic Files, box 169, Said, Edward (1957), AC198, Princeton University Library.

ST: Edward Said Papers of the Center for Advanced Study in the Behavioral Sciences Records (SC1055), Department of Special Collections and University Archives, Stanford University Libraries, Stanford, Calif.

Interviews

Abu-Deep: Kamal Abu-Deep, 1/18/16, Oxford, U.K.
Abu-Lughod: Lila Abu-Lughod, 4/15/18, New York
Al-Azm: Sadik Al-Azm, 12/19/15, Berlin
Al-Banna: Sami Al-Banna, 3/30/16, 4/6/16, 4/8/16, Bethesda, Md.
Al-Hout: Bayan Hout, 2/26/17, Beirut
Ali: Tariq Ali, 6/2/16, London
Alpers: Svetlana Alpers, 12/5/17, New York (correspondence)
Ammar: Ibrahim Ammar, 5/5/17, Woodbury, N.J.
Ashrawi: Hanan Ashrawi, 6/7/18, Ramallah
Atassi: Mohammad Ali Atassi, 11/28/16, Beirut
Barenboim: Daniel Barenboim, 1/22/17, New York
Barsamian: David Barsamian, 5/7/18, Boulder, Colo.
Bender: John Bender, 4/1/17, Minneapolis
Berger: John Berger, 12/2/15, Antony, France
Bergson, A.: Allen Bergson, 9/23/15, New York
Bergson, D.: Deirdre Bergson, 9/23/15, New York
Bilgrami: Akeel Bilgrami, 3/25/17, New York
Blythe: Charles Blythe, 11/30/15, Cambridge, Mass.
Brieger: Gottfried Brieger, 12/1/15, Detroit
Burns: Ric Burns, 6/6/16, New York
Carnicelli: Tom Carnicelli, 8/3/16, Maine
Carroll: Clare Carroll, 12/4/15, New York
Chomsky: Noam Chomsky, 2/12/16, Cambridge, Mass.
Cole: Jonathan Cole, 1/11/16, New York
Cortas: Nadim Cortas, 11/26/16, Beirut

David: Deirdre David, 12/11/15, New York
Davis: Lennard Davis, 11/16/18, New York
Delaney: Sheila Delaney, 6/23/17, Vancouver
Dickstein: Morris Dickstein, 4/9/18, New York
Eddé: Dominique Eddé, 7/8/16, Beirut
Fahy: Sandra Fahy, 4/1/16, New York
Farer: Tom Farer, 7/15/17, Denver
Fried: Michael Fried, 12/2/15, Baltimore
Friedman: Robert Friedman, 12/18/15, New York
Gallagher: Dorothy Gallagher, 7/19/16, New York
Ghazoul: Ferial Ghazoul, 4/6/16, Cairo
Gindy: Nadia Gindy, 5/4/17, Cairo
Glass: Charles Glass, 2/24/16, New York
Greene: Gayle Green, 8/8/17, Berkeley, Calif.
Grimshaw: Anna Grimshaw, 2/7/18, Atlanta
Guttenplan: Don Guttenplan, 1/5/16, 1/6/16, London
Habachy: Nazeeh Habachy, 1/23/16, New York
Hadidi: Subhi Hadidi, 12/9/15, Paris
Hakim: Carol Hakim, 4/10/17, Minneapolis
Hovsepian: Nubar Hovsepian, 2/10/16, California
Idriss: Samah Idriss, 4/28/17, Beirut
Istrabadi: Zaineb Istrabadi, 1/6/16, Bloomington, Ind.
Kardouche: George Kardouche, 5/10/16, Egypt (Red Sea)
Khairallah: Assaad Khairallah, 11/25/16, Beirut
Khalidi, M.: Muhammad Ali Khalidi, 4/11/18, Toronto
Khalidi, R.: Rashid Khalidi, 4/13/18, New York
Khalidi, T.: Tarif Khalidi, 12/15/15, Beirut
Lehman: David Lehman (correspondence)
Lentin: Ronit Lentin, 1/18/16, Dublin
Locke: Ralph Locke (correspondence)
Malik: Nabil "Bill" Malik, 8/17/18, Portsmouth, R.I.
Margaronis: Maria Margaronis, 3/12/16, London
McLeod: Alexander McLeod, 12/3/15, Nashville
Miller, J.: Hillis Miller, 1/7/16, Connecticut
Mintz: Alan Mintz, 1/5/16, New York
Mitchell: W. J. T. Mitchell, 12/14/15, Chicago
Mohr: Jean Mohr, 4/28/17, 5/5/17, Geneva
Musallam: Basim Musallam, 12/17/15, Cambridge, U.K.
O'Connell: Dan O'Connell, 8/13/18, New York
Painter: Karen Painter, 12/16/15, Minneapolis
Parry: Benita Parry, 11/23/18, Mynydd Llandegai, Wales
Piterberg: Gabriel Piterberg, 12/3/15, Los Angeles
Poole: Deborah Poole, 4/4/16, Baltimore
Rai: Kanti Rai, 12/21/15, Great Neck, N.Y.
Richetti: John Richetti, 4/1/17, Minneapolis
Rose: Jacqueline Rose, 2/10/16, London
Rosenthal: Michael Rosenthal, 12/22/15, New York
Sabbagh: Karl Sabbagh, 2/23/16, London
Said, G.: Grace Said, 11/25/16, Beirut
Said, M.: Mariam Said, 9/29/15, 8/14/16, 7/11/17, New York
Said, N.: Najla Said, 5/30/16, 8/16/16, New York

Said, W.: Wadie Said, 2/16/16, 3/10/19, Columbia, S.C.
Said Makdisi: Jean Said Makdisi, 11/25/16, Beirut
Seidel: Frederick Seidel, 8/15/16, New York
Shaheen: Mohammad Shaheen, 2/15/16, 11/25/16, Beirut and Amman
Sharon: Andre Sharon, 2/19/16, New York
Sifton: Elisabeth Sifton, 1/20/17, New York
Solum: John Solum, 12/11/15, Westport, Conn.
Soueif: Ahdaf Soueif, 4/2/17, London
Stein: Jean Stein, 3/24/17, New York
Stern, D.: David Stern, 4/14/16, Cambridge, Mass.
Stern, M.: Michael Stern, 12/22/15, San Francisco
Traboulsi: Fawwaz Traboulsi, 1/24/16, Beirut
Wanger: Shelley Wanger, 4/27/16, New York
Warner: Marina Warner, 12/16/15, London
Wieseltier: Leon Wieseltier, 12/9/15, Washington, D.C.
Wilmers: Mary Kay Wilmers, 2/22/16, London
Wood: Michael Wood, 5/27/16, Princeton, N.J.
Wypijewski: JoAnn Wypijewski, 2/26/16, New York
Yelin: Louise Yelin, 12/7/15, New York
Yerushalmi: David Yerushalmi, 7/26/16, Jerusalem

PREFACE

1. Soueif.
2. Hamid Dabashi, "The Moment of Myth," *CounterPunch*, Oct. 2, 2003.
3. *RE*, xi.
4. Blythe.
5. Conversation with EWS and Elias Khoury, New York, ca. May 2001; Sontag to EWS, May 5, 2001, and Gordimer to Sontag, April 9, 2001, EWSP, 28:15:I.1.
6. Khalidi, T.
7. FBI, 54, Aug. 20, 1979.
8. FBI, 11, July 12, 1982; FBI, 4, Aug. 28, 1991.
9. Said read these lines aloud at Ahmad's memorial at Hampshire College, Sept. 18, 1999; https://www.youtube.com/watch?v=zfqor65wguk. See also Stuart Schaar, *Eqbal Ahmad: Critical Outsider in a Turbulent Age* (New York: Columbia UP, 2015), 72.
10. Alexander Cockburn, "Edward Said: A Mighty and Passionate Heart," *CounterPunch*, Sept. 25, 2003.
11. Mohammad Shaheen, ed., *Edward Said: Riwayah lilajyal* [Edward Said: A story for the future] (Beirut: Arab Institute for Research and Publication, 2004).
12. Ibid.
13. Rosenthal; Mitchell.

1. THE COCOON

1. Jean Said Makdisi, *Teta, Mother, and Me: An Arab Woman's Memoir* (London: Saqi, 2005), 329. Hereafter cited as *Teta*.
2. Emanuel Hamon, dir., *Selves and Others: A Portrait of Edward Said* (2004).
3. Nadia Gindy, "On the Margins of a Memoir: A Personal Reading of Said's *Out of Place*," *Alif: A Journal of Comparative Poetics* 20 (2000): 285.
4. Said, G.

5. Gindy, "On the Margins of a Memoir," 286.
6. Annalise Devries, "Utopia in the Suburbs: Cosmopolitan Society, Class Privilege, and the Making of Ma'adi Garden City in Twentieth-Century Cairo," *Journal of Social History* 49, no. 2 (2015): 351–73.
7. Hoda Guindi, "Of the Place," *Alif: A Journal of Comparative Poetics* 25 (2005): 10.
8. Said, G.; *Teta*, 49.
9. Said, G.
10. Said Makdisi.
11. *Selves and Others.*
12. Gindy, "On the Margins of a Memoir," 287.
13. *Teta*, 37–38.
14. *OP*, 93.
15. Said, G.
16. Gindy, "On the Margins of a Memoir," 290.
17. *OP*, 135.
18. Sharon.
19. Kardouche.
20. Laura Robson, *Colonialism and Christianity in Mandate Palestine* (Austin: University of Texas Press, 2011), 127.
21. *RE*, 270.
22. Sharon.
23. Habachy.
24. Guindi, "Of the Place," 10.
25. *Teta*, 318.
26. *RE*, 273.
27. Aida Fahoum to EWS, 1999, EWSP, 48:16:II.1.
28. EWS, "Palestine, Then and Now: An Exile's Journey Through Israel and the Occupied Territories," *Harper's Magazine*, Dec. 1992, 48.
29. Charles Malik, "The Near East: The Search for Truth," *Foreign Affairs* 30 (1952): 233.
30. Max Rodenbeck, *Cairo: The City Victorious* (New York: Alfred A. Knopf, 1999).
31. Nabil Matar, *The United States Through Arab Eyes* (Edinburgh: Edinburgh University Press, 2018).
32. EWS, "Leaving Palestine," *New York Review of Books*, Sept. 23, 1999.
33. *OP*, 205.
34. Ibid., 165–67.
35. Guindi, "Of the Place," 10.
36. *OP*, 96–97.
37. *Teta*, 77.
38. Ibid., 295.
39. Ibid.
40. Allan Evans in *Ignace Tiegerman: The Lost Legend of Cairo*, arbiterrecords.org/catalog/ignace-tiegerman-the-lost-legend-of-cairo/.
41. Henri Barda in Allen Evans, *Ignaz Friedman: Romantic Master Pianist* (Bloomington: Indiana University Press, 2009), 221.
42. Ibid., 229.
43. Samir Raafat, "Ignace Tiegerman: Could He Have Dethroned Horowitz?," *Egyptian Mail*, Sept. 20, 1997, www.egy.com/judaica/97-09-20.php.
44. *Ignace Tiegerman: The Lost Legend of Cairo.*

45. *RE*, 274.
46. EWS, "Cairo Recalled: Growing Up in the Cultural Cross Currents of 1940s Egypt," *House & Garden*, April 1987, 32.
47. Allan Evans to EWS, Oct. 22, 1987: "It was a revelation to get a dose of Tiegerman's observations and an understanding of his aesthetic."
48. Barda, in Evans, *Ignaz Friedman*, 223.
49. *OP*, 198.
50. Said, G.
51. Hilda Said to EWS, Nov. 21, 1966, EWSP, 28:16:II.2.
52. Said Makdisi.
53. Justus Reid Weiner, "'My Beautiful Old House' and Other Fabrications by Edward Said," *Commentary*, Sept. 1, 1999. Said's response can be found in his "Defamation, Zionist Style," *Al-Ahram*, Aug. 26–Sept. 1, 1999; and in Munir K. Nasser, "They Attack Me to Discredit Palestinians' Right of Return," *Bir Zeit Newsletter* (Fall 1999): 14.
54. Keith Schilling to EWS, Jan. 18, 2000, EWSP, 30:18:I.1.
55. EWS, "Palestine, Then and Now," 51.
56. Sent to the author on Feb. 20, 2016.
57. Said Makdisi.
58. *OP*, 144.
59. The Right Reverend Sir Paul Reeves to EWS, May 29, 1991, EWSP, 15:12:I.1.
60. Malik, "The Near East: The Search for Truth," 231.
61. EWS, "A Palestinian Voice," *Columbia Forum* 12, no. 4 (Winter 1969): 29.
62. Habachy.
63. Undated handwritten notes, EWSP, 77:32:II.4.
64. Mohammad Shaheen, "Remembering Edward Said: A Glimpse of His Life and Thought," sent to author on Jan. 4, 2016.
65. Shaheen.
66. O'Connell.
67. EWS to Jacoby, Feb. 21, 1984, EWSP, 7:8:I.1.
68. Shaheen.
69. Said, M.
70. *Teta*, 19, 42.
71. *OP*, 230.
72. Said Makdisi.
73. *OP*, 12.
74. EWS to Wadie Said, 1967, EWSP, 28:16:II.2.
75. *OP*, 54, 57.
76. Gindy, "On the Margins of a Memoir," 288.
77. Said, G.
78. Said Makdisi.
79. *Teta*, 14.
80. Ibid., 16, 18.
81. EWS, "My Guru," *London Review of Books*, Dec. 13, 2001, 19.
82. Cortas; Said, G.
83. Wadad Makdisi Cortas, *A World I Loved: The Story of an Arab Woman* (New York: Nation Books, 2009).
84. Ibid.
85. Habachy.
86. Gindy, "On the Margins of a Memoir," 285.
87. Jean Said Makdisi to the author, Sept. 12, 2017.

88. EWSP, 77:32:II.4.
89. *OP*, 114.
90. Ibid., 124.
91. Ibid., 123.
92. Éric Rouleau, "Cairo: A Memoir," *Cairo Review of Global Affairs* (Fall 2010).
93. *QP*, xiv.
94. *OP*, 122.
95. "Orientalism and After: An Interview with Edward Said," *Radical Philosophy* 63 (Spring 1993), EWSP, 80:31:II.5.
96. To take one of many examples, M. Cherif Bassiouni, "The AAUG: Reflections on a Lost Opportunity," *Arab Studies Quarterly* 29, no. 3–4 (Summer/Fall 2007): 29: "Until 1967, Edward Said was basically an Anglophile professor of comparative literature . . . [with] no commitment to Arab nationalism."
97. EWSP, 77:32:II.4.
98. EWS, "Leaving Palestine."
99. Gindy, "On the Margins of a Memoir," 286.
100. *RE*, 274.
101. Ahdaf Soueif, *Mezzaterra: Fragments from the Common Ground* (New York: Anchor, 2010), 253.

2. UNSETTLING

1. *FNE*, 54.
2. CV for Harvard Application, 1957, HT.
3. *PPC*, 412.
4. Ibid., 47.
5. Ibid., 69.
6. Harry Levin, *The Power of Blackness: Hawthorne, Poe, Melville* (1958; New York: Alfred A. Knopf, 1970), 4.
7. EWS, "Commencement Speech," Northfield Mount Hermon School, June 2002; sent to the author on Dec. 11, 2015.
8. *OP*, 84.
9. *PP*, 4; *RE*, xii.
10. *OP*, 233.
11. Ibid., 134, 141.
12. Ibid., 263–64.
13. EWS, interview by Jean Stein, Aug. 19, 1993; sent to the author by Stein on Feb. 23, 2017.
14. Howell-Griffith to Gordon F. Pyper, Feb. 17, 1951, MH.01, 20.
15. Price to Director of Admissions, Jan. 8, 1951, MH.01, 22.
16. Badeau to Dr. Howard Rubendall, Nov. 8, 1950, MH.01, 26.
17. EWS to Director of Admissions, Mount Hermon School, Feb. 4, 1951, MH.01, 2.
18. Ibid., 3.
19. Brieger.
20. Davis.
21. Poem sent to author by Peter Weis, Mount Hermon archivist, on Dec. 12, 2015.
22. *OP*, 43–44.
23. Ibid., 248.
24. Brieger.

25. Weis to author, Dec. 11, 2015.
26. *OP*, 17.
27. Ibid., 19.
28. Hilda Said to Rubendall, Sept. 21, 1951, MH.02, 20.
29. Hilda Said to Rubendall, Feb. 18, 1952, MH.02, 26-29.
30. Jean Said Makdisi, *Teta, Mother, and Me: An Arab Woman's Memoir* (London: Saqi, 2005), 84. Hereafter cited as *Teta*.
31. Letters sent to the author by Marina Warner on Jan. 16, 2015.
32. EWS, "Defamation, Zionist Style," *Al-Ahram*, Aug. 26-Sept. 1, 1999.
33. Hilda Said to Rubendall, Oct. 13, 1952, MH.02, 36-38.
34. Hilda to Rubendall, Jan. 9, 1953, MH.02, 43.
35. Ethel R. Maddern to Princeton, June 22, 1953, PT, 21.
36. Fischer to EWS, June 22, 2000, EWSP, 48:20:II.1.
37. *OP*, 278.
38. *Teta*, 85.
39. Hilda to Rubendall, Jan. 9, 1953, 43.
40. *Exiles: Edward Said*, directed by Christopher Sykes (BBC2, 1986).
41. *OP*, 330.
42. Ibid., 279.
43. HT, 64.
44. EWS to Rubendall, March 13, 1958, MH.03, 26.
45. Yerushalmi.
46. *OP*, 233.
47. Said, N.
48. Said Makdisi.
49. *OP*, 222.
50. Because of illness, his speech was delivered by his son, Wadie.
51. *OP*, 145.
52. *PPC*, 206; *OP*, 205-206.
53. EWS, interview by Stein.
54. Ibid.
55. Ibid.
56. Ibid.
57. Bergson, A.
58. Said, N.
59. EWS to Michael Rosenthal, March 10, 1973, EWSP, 5:5:I.1.
60. Rubendall to Professor Ludwig, Nov. 26, 1957, MH.03, 14.

3. AN IVIED APPRENTICESHIP

1. Hopkins to Robert Bridges, May 21, 1878, quoted in *WTC*, 41.
2. EWS, "Commencement Speech," Northfield Mount Hermon School, June 2002.
3. Elaine Hagopian, "Ibrahim and Said," *Arab Studies Quarterly* 26, no. 4 (Fall 2004): 6; Habachy. Erich Segal was still writing to Said in Oct. 1976 to send him his piece "Slouching Towards America" in *The New Republic*, in which, among other things, he praises Levin for exposing the myth of the American golden age (EWSP, 29:27:I.1).
4. J. Merrill Knapp, Rhodes Scholarship Recommendation, Nov. 19, 1956, PT, 29. The sentiment is repeated by G. E. Bentley in his recommendation for Said to Harvard, Feb. 24, 1957, which adds that his talents and conviviality come "in spite of his somewhat exotic background" (HT, 34).

5. Abigail Klionsky Oral History Project—Dr. Gerald Sandler ('57), Seeley G. Mudd Manuscript Library, Princeton.
6. McLeod.
7. PT, 13.
8. HT, 36.
9. Carnicelli.
10. Bergson, A.; Bergson, D.
11. PT, 25; Carnicelli; Solum.
12. Fried.
13. Farer.
14. Solum.
15. Said, G.
16. Solum.
17. Habachy.
18. McLeod.
19. Solum.
20. *OP*, 291.
21. Habachy; McLeod.
22. Solum.
23. EWS, Statement of Purpose, HT.
24. Warner.
25. Marie-Hélène Gold to EWS, Jan. 18, 1989, EWSP, 78:5:II.4.
26. Marie-Hélène Gold to EWS, Sept. 19, 1999, EWSP, 48:11:II.1.
27. Ibid.
28. *ESR*, 421.
29. *WTC*, v; *OP*, 285, 277.
30. Carnicelli; Fried; EWS Memorial Tribute to Arthur Gold, Feb. 26, 1989, EWSP, 78:5:II.4.
31. Fried.
32. Edward W. Said ('57), "Nasser and His Canal," *Daily Princetonian*, Oct. 11, 1956, 2.
33. Wadad Makdisi Cortas, *A World I Loved: The Story of an Arab Woman* (New York: Nation Books, 2009), 136–37.
34. Interestingly, his son, Wadie, would write his senior honors thesis at Princeton on Nasser's participation in Bandung and Egypt's role in fostering Afro-Asian solidarity.
35. Farer.
36. *OP*, 250, 274.
37. EWS to Dire, May 1, 1959, EWSP, 30:3:I.1.
38. EWS, "My Guru," *London Review of Books*, Dec. 13, 2001, 19–20. "It was Ibrahim who introduced Arabs in America to the world of national liberation struggles and post-colonial politics" (ibid., 20).
39. PT, 13.
40. EWS to Rubendall, Oct. 29, 1957, MH.03, 9.
41. "Orientalism and After: An Interview with Edward Said," *Radical Philosophy* 63 (Spring 1993): 1, EWSP, 80:31:II.5.
42. EWS to Princeton University, Oct. 14, 1957, PT, 3.
43. HT, 32 (Jan. 2, 1958).
44. *OP*, 287.
45. EWS to Harvard, 1957, HT.
46. *OP*, 264.

47. EWS to Albert Sonnenfeld, Oct. 27, 1978, EWSP, 5:9:I.1.
48. HT, 59.
49. Ibid., 53.
50. WTC, v.
51. R. P. Blackmur, *A Primer of Ignorance*, ed. Joseph Frank (1940; New York: Harcourt, Brace & World, 1967), 71.
52. EWSP, 77:32:II.4; he uses the phrase in "Sense and Sensibility," *Partisan Review* 34, no. 4 (Fall 1967): 632.
53. RE, 247.
54. Ibid., 253; Fried. See EWS, "Sense and Sensibility": "Blackmur's unique classroom mode, as described by Arthur Gold . . . was to describe how one becomes intimate with literature" (629).
55. RE, 249.
56. R. P. Blackmur, *Language as Gesture: Essays in Poetry* (New York: Harcourt, Brace, 1952), 403.
57. ESR, 424; B, 256-57.
58. Blackmur, *Language as Gesture*, 3, 12.
59. EWSP, 97:20:III.1.
60. Blackmur, *Primer of Ignorance*, 100.
61. Ibid., 13-14.
62. R. P. Blackmur, *The Lion and the Honeycomb: Essays in Solicitude and Critique* (1935; New York: Harcourt, Brace, 1955), 293.
63. ALS, 173-74.
64. OP, 265.
65. But which Heidegger? In Malik's curious preface to O. Frederick Nolde's *Free and Equal: Human Rights in Ecumenical Perspective* (Geneva: World Council of Churches, 1968), 7, he adopts, on behalf of humanism, the language of Heidegger's notorious rejection of humanism.
66. Said, M.
67. Ibid.
68. Charles Malik, "The Near East: The Search for Truth," *Foreign Affairs* 30 (1952): 236.
69. Ibid., 238.
70. Ibid., 243.
71. Ibid., 256-60.
72. Charles Habib Malik, *The Problem of Coexistence* (Evanston, Ill.: Northwestern University Press, 1955), 8.
73. Charles Habib Malik, *A Christian Critique of the University* (Downers Grove, Ill.: Intervarsity Press, 1982), 23.
74. See Said's respectful but testy correspondence with William Spanos in which he reviles Heidegger as a reactionary and a mystic (Aug. 4, 1972), EWSP, 5:2:I.1; (Jan. 5, 1979), EWSP, 5:10:I.2; (May 22, 1980), EWSP, 5:19:I.1, and his early critical review of Ihab Hassan's *Dismemberment of Orpheus*, "Eclecticism and Orthodoxy in Criticism," *Diacritics* 2, no. 1 (Spring 1972): 2-8. He does, however, cite Heidegger more forgivingly in the unpublished "The Second and a Half World," EWSP, 77:32:II.4.
75. PPC, 158; EWS to Richard Kuhns, Jan. 25, 1973, EWSP, 5:4:I.1.
76. OP, 292.
77. "Orientalism and After: An Interview with Edward Said."
78. Rosenthal.

79. EWS to Alfred Dunhill Limited, Nov. 26, 1991, EWSP, 16:2:I.1.
80. Blackmur, "In the Country of the Blue," in *Primer of Ignorance*, 180. See also EWS note on Blackmur, EWSP, 97:14.III.
81. EWSP, 97:2:III.1.
82. EWSP, 81:1:III.1.
83. Ibid.
84. Ibid.
85. Ibid.
86. David Stern, Said's student at Columbia who went on to Harvard for graduate study, remembers Levin as "a horrible Harvard type, stodgy, very Brahmin, who would pontificate a lot" (Stern, D.).
87. *OP*, 289.
88. Harry Levin, *Refractions: Essays in Comparative Literature* (Oxford, U.K.: Oxford University Press, 1966), 323, 339.
89. *OP*, 288.
90. Fried.
91. EWS to "Dash," Nov. 29, 1972, EWSP, 5:3:I.1: "I became quite sentimental . . . I started to think back over his work, his effect on his students, his effect on me, and I found that he was still more of a teacher than most people realize."
92. Harry Levin, *The Gates of Horn: A Study of Five French Realists* (Oxford, U.K.: Oxford University Press, 1963), 4.
93. EWS to Levin, June 12, 1965, HL.
94. Harry Levin, *Grounds for Comparison* (Cambridge, Mass.: Harvard University Press, 1972), 19.
95. Ibid., 6; and Levin, *Gates of Horn*, ix.
96. EWS, "Phenomenology, Structural Thought, and Literature," American Council of Learned Societies application, Oct. 14, 1965, ST, 17-19.
97. Levin, *Refractions*, 65.
98. Levin, *Gates of Horn*, 16.
99. Levin, *Refractions*, 240-41.
100. Levin, "Two *Romanisten* in America: Spitzer and Auerbach," in *Grounds for Comparison*, 111.
101. EWS to Harry Levin, Oct. 9, 1972, HL. As late as 1970, already a well-known professor, Said is still signing his letters to Levin "your admiring student Edward Said."
102. Levin, *Grounds for Comparison*, 41, 46, 123.
103. Ibid., 127.

4. THE SECRET AGENT

1. Undated, but ca. 1957-62, EWSP, 77:32:II.4.
2. EWSP, 77:32:II.4.
3. A colleague from Harvard [signature unclear] to EWS, Dec. 16, 1967, EWSP, 28:22:I.1.
4. Delaney; Said Makdisi.
5. Bergson, A.
6. EWSP, 81:1:III.1 and 77:32:II.4.
7. Said Makdisi.
8. Ibid.
9. EWS to Wadie Said, June 2, 1965, EWSP, 28:16:II.2.
10. Hilda Said to EWS, Nov. 21, 1965, EWSP, 28:16:II.2.

11. Henry Caraway Hatfield, a member of her doctoral committee, wrote to Maire from Berlin on March 18, 1968, cc'ing Levin calling her work "at times brilliant" while griping that a writer "who uses words like 'chthonic' or 'appolonisch' *must* get them right or makes the reader extremely skeptical . . . At times it sounds as though *The Magic Mountain* had been written by an existentialist in collaboration with Susan Sontag," HL.

12. Farer; also Said, G.; Bergson, A.; Blythe.

13. EWSP, 97:3:III.1.

14. *EPP*, 69.

15. EWSP, 77:32:II.4, 21.

16. Christopher Hitchens, *Hitch-22: A Memoir* (New York: Twelve, 2010), 385.

17. EWS, "An Ark for the Listener," EWSP, 77:2:II.3.

18. Mariam Said to author, Sept. 25, 2018.

19. Mary McCarthy, "On F. W. Dupee (1904-1979)," *New York Review of Books*, Oct. 27, 1983.

20. Leon Trotsky, *The Russian Revolution*, ed. F. W. Dupee, trans. Max Eastman (New York: Anchor, 1959), vii–viii.

21. James Wolcott, "Enemies for Ever," *London Review of Books*, May 18, 2017, 14.

22. Ibid., 16; McCarthy, "On F. W. Dupee (1904-1979)."

23. Rosenthal.

24. EWSP, 110:11:III.3. Said, however, defended Trilling publicly against Alfred Kazin's portrait of him in *The New York Review of Books* as a snob and self-promoter. With eighteen others, Said wrote a letter of protest that appeared in the *Times* on June 25, 1978.

25. EWS to Engel, Nov. 29, 1972, EWSP, 5:3:I.1.

26. Bergson, A.

27. Rosenthal; Wood.

28. Davis.

29. Rosenthal.

30. EWSP, 110:11:III.3.

31. EWS to Engel, Nov. 29, 1972.

32. Guttenplan.

33. *RE*, xxii. In "Sense and Sensibility," *Partisan Review* 34, no. 4 (Fall 1967), he takes a page from the New Critical handbook by admiring Georges Poulet and Blackmur for evading "the game of research" and preferring "the rich irregularity of things."

34. EWS, "At Miss Whitehead's," review of *The Sixties: The Last Journal, 1960–1972*, by Edmund Wilson, *London Review of Books*, July 7, 1994, 2.

35. Seidel.

36. EWS to Starobinski, Nov. 22, 1967, EWSP, 30:3:I.1.

37. Barthes to EWS, Aug. 25, 1972 [incorrectly dated 1975], EWSP, 5:1:I.1 (trans. author and Emilie Pons).

38. Allen Bergson to author, Sept. 24, 2015.

39. Said, M.

40. *RE*, 235.

41. Khalidi, T.

42. EWS, "A Configuration of Themes," *Nation*, May 30, 1966, 659-60.

43. Levin to EWS, May 31, 1966, HL.

44. HL.

45. *RE*, 555.
46. EWS, "Conrad and Nietzsche," in *Joseph Conrad: A Commemoration*, ed. Norman Sherry (London: Macmillan, 1976), 65.
47. Said, N.
48. Conor Cruise O'Brien, Edward Said, and John Lukacs, "The Intellectual in the Post-colonial World: Response and Discussion," *Salmagundi*, no. 70/71 (Spring–Summer 1986): 70–71. In a review in *TLS* on Oct. 12, 1984, Said lauded Benita Parry for being the first critic to engage with "the most important aspect of Conrad's writing"—its latent imperialism.
49. "Traveling with Conrad," interview with EWS and Peter Mallios, Feb. 28, 2003, EWSP, 80:41:II.5.
50. O'Brien, Said, and Lukacs, "Intellectual in the Post-colonial World," 74, 72, 73. See EWS to Robert Boyers of *Salmagundi*, Oct. 29, 1985 (EWSP, 8:17:I.1), where he describes this testy exchange.
51. Mitchell.
52. "I am the Cunninghame Graham figure in the duo with Conrad—the opposite" ("Traveling with Conrad").
53. *JC*, 80–81.
54. *RE*, xxii; EWS, "Conrad and Nietzsche," 72.
55. EWSP, 97:3:III.1.
56. EWS, "Conrad and Nietzsche," 71.
57. *RE*, 267; EWS, "Sense and Sensibility," 629.
58. EWSP, 97:31:III.1.
59. Bergson, A.
60. *JC*, 57.
61. Raymond Williams and Edward W. Said, "Media, Margins, and Modernity," in Raymond Williams, *The Politics of Modernism: Against the New Conformists* (London: Verso, 1989), 187.
62. *ESR*, 423.
63. Ibid., 39.
64. *JC*, vii; cf. *RE*, 563.
65. *JC*, 60, 58, 38, 17.
66. EWS to Geoffrey Hartman, Dec. 4, 1967, EWSP, 30:3:I.1.
67. Quoted in Richard Macksey and Eugenio Donato, "The Space Between—1971," in *The Structuralist Controversy: The Languages of Criticism and the Sciences of Man* (Baltimore: Johns Hopkins University Press, 1972), x.
68. EWS to Richard Kuhns, Jan. 25, 1973, EWSP, 5:4:I.1. "Read a lot of Deleuze but think, although he's very brilliant, he needs a good editor" (EWS to Richard Macksey, Feb. 7, 1973, EWSP, 5:5:I.1). Said thought Deleuze politically conservative but his theory of knowledge "revolutionary" (EWSP, 97:1:III.1; *B*, 377).
69. An idea found also in "An Unpublished Text," quoted in Claude Lefort's editor's preface to Maurice Merleau-Ponty, *The Prose of the World*, trans. John O'Neill (1969; Evanston, Ill.: Northwestern University Press, 1973), xiii.
70. *JC*, 38, 119.
71. Ibid., 49.
72. EWS, "Labyrinth of Incarnations," *RE*, 11; EWSP, 97:27:III.1.
73. EWS to Chomsky, March 13, 1972, EWSP, 28:12:I.1.
74. Lucien Goldmann, *The Hidden God: A Study of Tragic Vision in the "Pensées" of Pascal and the Tragedies of Racine*, trans. Philip Tody (1955; London: Verso, 2016), 235.

75. *OP*, 256.
76. See, for example, *PPC*, 6; *RE*, 16.
77. EWS, "Sense and Sensibility," 628, where he writes that E. D. Hirsch's idea that understanding is really the understanding of necessity is taken without acknowledgment from "Heidegger's writing about Hölderlin." Gerald Graff et al. to EWS, Feb. 20, 1969, EWSP, 5:1:I,1.
78. *JC*, 195–96.
79. *B*, 323.
80. *LS*, 78.
81. EWS, review of *Joseph Conrad: A Psychoanalytic Biography*, by Bernard C. Meyer, *Journal of English and Germanic Philology* 67, no. 1 (Jan. 1968): 176–78; *JC*, 102.
82. EWS, "Phenomenology, Structural Thought, and Literature," American Council of Learned Societies application, Nov. 15, 1965, ST, 17–19.
83. EWSP, 97:1:III.1.
84. *PPC*, 225.
85. Joseph Farag, *Palestinian Literature in Exile: Gender, Aesthetics, and Resistance in the Short Story* (London: I. B. Tauris, 2016), 118 (of his typescript).
86. EWS, "Diary: My Encounter with Sartre," *London Review of Books*, June 1, 2000, 42–43.
87. Ali.
88. EWS, "The Arab Portrayed," in *The Arab-Israeli Confrontation of June 1967: An Arab Perspective*, ed. Ibrahim Abu-Lughod (Evanston, Ill.: Northwestern University Press, 1970), 6.
89. EWS, "Diary."
90. Maurice Merleau-Ponty, *The Phenomenology of Perception*, trans. Donald Landes (1945; London: Routledge, 2012), 466.
91. EWS, "The Totalitarianism of Mind," review of *The Savage Mind*, by Claude Lévi-Strauss, *Kenyon Review* 29, no. 2 (March 1967): 256.
92. Ibid., 258.
93. Ibid., 249.
94. Ashrawi; Bergson, A.; Khalidi, T. See, for example, his miscellaneous notes on structuralism, as well as his forty-nine-page general account of the movement in EWSP, 97:27:III.1.
95. Chomsky.
96. EWS to de Man, Jan. 7, 1968, EWSP, 30:3:I.1.
97. *PD*, xv.
98. Ibid., xvi.
99. EWS, "A Palestinian Voice," *Columbia Forum* 12, no. 4 (Winter 1969): 27.
100. Lehman to EWS, Feb. 28, 1973, EWSP, 5:6:I.1.
101. Stern, D.
102. EWSP, 76:18:II.3.
103. EWS to Robert Alter, Nov. 2, 1967, EWSP, 28:9:I.1.
104. EWSP, 76:18:II.3.
105. Ibid.; EWS to Quentin Anderson, Nov. 28, 1967, EWSP, 28:9:I.1.
106. EWS to Ronit and Jerome Lowenthal, Dec. 15, 1967, EWSP, 28:22:I.1.
107. Including many of the original notes for *Beginnings*. See EWSP, 97:2:III.1.
108. EWS to Ronit and Jerome Lowenthal, Dec. 15, 1967.
109. Chomsky.
110. EWS, "Himself Observed," review of *George Steiner: A Reader*, *Nation*, March 2, 1985.

111. Jerome Lowenthal to EWS, Jan. 7, 1968, EWSP, 28:22:I.1.
112. EWS to Levin, June 28, 1965, HL.
113. EWS to Robert Alter, April 2, 1968, EWSP, 28:22:I.1.
114. See Barbara Epstein, "The Rise, Decline, and Possible Revival of Socialist Humanism," in *For Humanism*, ed. David Alderson and Robert Spencer (London: Pluto, 2017). Goldmann, she observes, "was also active in Hashomer Hatzair, a socialist Zionist organization critical of capitalism for its propensity to isolate humans from one another."
115. Harry Levin, *Grounds for Comparison* (Cambridge, Mass.: Harvard University Press, 1972), 37.
116. EWS to Robert Alter, Nov. 2, 1967, EWSP, 28:9:I.1.
117. Bell to EWS, Nov. 1, 1966, EWSP, 110:18:III.3.
118. EWS, "Swift as Intellectual," in *WTC*, 72. "That realm has come to resemble the ambiance of a club" (73).
119. EWS to Trilling, Jan. 1973, EWSP, 5:4:I.1.
120. EWS to Maud Wilcox, Dec. 11, 1980, EWSP, 5:22:I.1.
121. EWS, "Swift's Tory Anarchy," *Eighteenth Century Studies* 3, no. 1 (Fall 1969): 48.
122. R. P. Blackmur, *A Primer of Ignorance*, ed. Joseph Frank (1940; New York: Harcourt, Brace & World, 1967), 13.
123. EWS, "Notes on the Characterization of a Literary Text," *MLN* 85, no. 6 (Dec. 1970): 768.
124. EWS, "Swift as Intellectual," 74.
125. Ibid., 54.
126. EWS to George Mayhew, Feb. 3, 1968, EWSP, 30:3:I.1.
127. EWS, "Swift's Tory Anarchy," in *WTC*, 57.
128. EWS, "Swift in History," EWSP, 110:16:III.3.
129. EWS to Angus Fletcher, Nov. 28, 1968, EWSP, 28:9:I.1.
130. EWSP, 76:18:II.3.
131. EWS to Israel Shahak, Dec. 14, 1977, EWSP, 30:13:I.1.
132. EWS to "Robert," April 2, 1968, EWSP, 28:22:I.1.
133. Blythe.

5. BEFORE OSLO

1. EWSP, 77:32:II.4. Undated, but ca. 1957–62. In the early 1960s, he submitted this and other poems to *The Sewanee Review, Evergreen Review,* and other literary magazines.
2. Lorette to EWS, Oct. 20, 1972, EWSP, 5:2:I.1.
3. Guttenplan.
4. Rosenthal.
5. Mintz.
6. Levin to Hatfield, April 30, 1968; HL.
7. Leibowitz to EWS, May 5, 1968, EWSP, 28:22:I.1.
8. Stern, M.
9. *PPC*, 209.
10. Michael Stern, "Professors Show Little Enthusiasm for Election Strike," *Columbia Daily Spectator*, Nov. 4, 1968.
11. Friedman.
12. Eqbal Ahmad to BBC Television, Dec. 7, 1992, EWSP, 29:14:I.1.
13. Yelin.
14. Michael Stern, "Radicals Interrupt Nearly 40 Classes in NROTC Drive," *Columbia Daily Spectator*, Feb. 27, 1969.

15. Friedman.
16. Stern, M.
17. Trilling to EWS, March 3, 1973, EWSP, 5:4:I.1.
18. EWS to Trilling, Jan. 25, 1973, EWSP, 5:4:I.1.
19. Michael Widlanski, "350 Hear Debate on Mideast War at Campus Forum," *Columbia Daily Spectator*, Oct. 25, 1973.
20. Ahmad Besharah, "Re-focusing on the Middle East," *Columbia Daily Spectator*, April 16, 1970.
21. Mintz.
22. Delaney. A clarification of his stand on violence can be found in "Chomsky and the Question of Palestine" (1975), in *PD*, 333, and "Identity, Negation, and Violence" (1988), in *PD*, 346, written during the first intifada.
23. EWS, "Traveling with Conrad," interview with Peter Mallios, Feb. 28, 2003, EWSP, 80:41:II.5.
24. Bergson, A.; Farer; Delaney.
25. Najla Said, *Looking for Palestine* (New York: Riverhead Books, 2013), 10.
26. EWS, "Palestine, Then and Now: An Exile's Journey Through Israel and the Occupied Territories," *Harper's Magazine*, Dec. 1992, 47.
27. EWS to "Dash," Nov. 29, 1972, EWSP, 5:3:I.1; EWS to Tom Farer, April 6, 1973, EWSP, 5:6:I.1.
28. EWS to Farer, April 6, 1973.
29. EWS to Dickstein, Jan. 27, 1973, EWSP, 5:4:I.1.
30. EWS to Monroe Engel, Nov. 29, 1972, EWSP, 5:3:I.1.
31. *PD*, 5.
32. Mariam Said, introduction to *A World I Loved: The Story of an Arab Woman*, by Wadad Makdisi Cortas (New York: Nation Books, 2009), xxx.
33. *PD*, 271.
34. Said Makdisi.
35. Beirut was "the expatriate capital of the Arab world." After the Israeli invasion of 1982, however, that role "was over." *Exiles: Edward Said*, directed by Christopher Sykes (BBC2, 1986).
36. EWS to Chomsky, Nov. 7, 1973, EWSP, 5:3:I.1.
37. EWS to Sami Al-Banna, Feb. 7, 1973; EWSP, 5:5:I.1.
38. EWS, "Michel Foucault as an Intellectual Imagination," *boundary 2* 1, no. 1 (Fall 1972): 1-36.
39. EWS, "My Guru," *London Review of Books*, Dec. 13, 2001, 20.
40. *PPC*, 208; EWS, "Palestine, Then and Now," 54.
41. Shafiq Al-Hout, *My Life in the PLO* (London: Pluto Press, 2011), 107.
42. EWS to Sami Al-Banna, Feb. 7, 1973.
43. *B*, 34.
44. EWS, "Molestation and Authority in Narrative Fiction," in *Aspects of Narrative: Selected Papers from the English Institute*, ed. J. Hillis Miller (New York: Columbia University Press, 1971), 47-68.
45. Miller; see also the correspondence between Said and Ian Watt for evidence of his rise to prominence in Conrad circles (IW).
46. EWS to Carol Malmi, March 6, 1978, EWSP, 30:6:I.i.
47. EWS to Michael Rosenthal, March 10, 1973, EWSP, 5:5:I.1.
48. EWS to "Erwin," March 20, 1973, EWSP, 5:5:I.1.
49. EWS to Engel, Nov. 29, 1972, EWSP, 5:3:I.1.
50. EWS to "Dash," Nov. 29, 1972, EWSP, 5:3:I.1.

51. Said, N.
52. EWS to Monroe Engel, June 28, 1973, EWSP, 5:6:I.1.
53. Davis.
54. EWS to Ferial Ghazoul, Jan. 6, 1973, EWSP, 5:4:I.1.
55. Said, M.
56. Abdallah Laroui, *The Crisis of the Arab Intellectual* (1974; Berkeley: University of California Press, 1976), 3.
57. Ibid., 5.
58. Ibid., 6.
59. EWS to Farer, April 6, 1973.
60. EWS, "Living in Arabic," *Al-Ahram*, Feb. 12–18, 2004.
61. EWS to Richard Macksey, Jan. 2, 1973, EWSP, 5:5:I.1.
62. Ibid.
63. EWS, "Living in Arabic."
64. EWS to Rosenthal, March 10, 1973.
65. EWS to Richard Macksey, Feb. 7, 1973, EWSP, 5:5:I.1.
66. EWS to Farer, April 6, 1973.
67. Jean Bodin (1576) and Jean-Baptiste Chardin (1680) made use of Khaldun's historiography and popularized him in France. Vico addresses the work of Bodin in *The New Science*.
68. *RE*, 564; *EPP*, 244; EWSP, 71:8:II.2.
69. *WTC*, 36.
70. Ibn Khaldun, *Muqaddimah: An Introduction to History*, trans. Franz Rosenthal (1377; Princeton, N.J.: Princeton University Press, 1967), 756.
71. *The Qur'an*, trans. Tarif Khalidi (New York: Penguin Classics, 2009), sura 55: "The All Merciful . . . He created Man / He taught him eloquence."
72. EWSP, 77:19:II.4.
73. Al-Hout.
74. EWS, "Speaking and Language," *New York Times Book Review*, Feb. 20, 1972, 21.
75. EWSP, 97:23:III.1 and 104:8:III.
76. EWS, "Linguistics and the Archeology of Mind," *International Philosophical Quarterly* 11, no. 1 (March 1971): 104–34. He had been at work on this essay since at least 1968, having written to publishers to obtain copies of Chomsky's *Theory of Syntax* and Lacan's *Discours de Rome: Réponses aux Interventions* (1953) in preparation.
77. Chomsky to the author, Feb. 13, 2016.
78. For a sense of the care with which Said studied technical aspects of Chomsky's linguistics, see his notes on *Cartesian Linguistics*, EWSP, 97:3:III.1.
79. EWS to Chomsky, March 13 and April 15, 1972, EWSP, 28:12:I.1.
80. EWS to Chomsky, April 15, 1972.
81. EWS to Chomsky, March 13, 1972.
82. EWS to Chomsky, March 4, 1972, EWSP, 28:12:I.1.
83. Ibid. Said criticized Chomsky for using mostly Israeli rather than Arab sources.
84. EWS, *"Al-tamanu' wa al-tajanub wa al-ta'aruf,"* *Mawaqif* (March 1972). Said wrote the piece originally in English under the title "Witholding, Avoidance, and Recognition," EWSP, 72:14:II.2.
85. EWS to Sami Al-Banna, July 31, 1972, EWSP, 30:4:I.1.
86. Najm to EWS, Dec. 13, 1971, EWSP, 72:14:II.2.

87. EWS, "Notes on the Arab Intellectuals at Home and Abroad," undated lecture to the Association of Arab-American University Graduates (AAUG), ca. 1977, EWSP, 77:2:II.3.
88. Adonis to EWS, Oct. 25, 1971, EWSP, 72:14:II.2.
89. Sadik Al-Azm, *Self-Criticism After the Defeat*, trans. George Stergios (1968; Beirut: Saqi, 2011), 165.
90. EWS, "Witholding, Avoidance, and Recognition," 2.
91. EWS to Sami Al-Banna, July 31, 1972.
92. EWS, "Witholding, Avoidance, and Recognition," 23-24.
93. Ibid., 2.
94. Ibid., 7-9.
95. EWS, "Arabs and Jews," *Journal of Palestine Studies* 3, no. 2 (Winter 1974).
96. EWS to Amr Armenazi, May 30, 1973, EWSP, 5:6:I.1.
97. EWS to George Kardouche, July 5, 1973, EWSP, 5:6:I.1.
98. EWS to Armenazi, May 30, 1973.
99. Ibrahim Abu-Lughod, *Resistance, Exile, and Return: Conversations with Hisham Ahmed-Fararjeh* (Birzeit: Ibrahim Abu-Lughod Institute of International Studies at Birzeit University, 2003), 72. Bayan Nuwayhed Al-Hout, herself a notable activist, wrote a prehistory of the PLO in a dissertation titled "The Palestinian Leaderships and Institutions (1917–1948)," published in Arabic in 1981.
100. Al-Hout, *My Life in the PLO*, 121.
101. Mariam Said to the author, Oct. 31, 2017.
102. Chomsky.
103. Hovsepian.
104. Al-Hout, *My Life in the PLO*, 58.
105. Al-Hout.
106. Said, G.
107. Alexander Cockburn, "The Failure of the P.L.O. Leadership," *Nation*, March 12, 1988, 330.
108. *PD*, 101.
109. EWS, "Solidly Behind Arafat," *New York Times*, Nov. 15, 1983.
110. EWS, "Meeting with the Old Man," *Interview*, Dec. 12, 1988, 112–15, 194.
111. *IES*, 42.
112. EWS, "Rhetorical Questions," *New Statesman*, May 8, 1978.
113. *RE*, 231.
114. EWSP 111:32:II.2; cf. *WTC*, 40.
115. *ESR*, 423. For a case in point, see "Interpreting the Algiers PNC" (EWSP, 70:2:II.2), published as "Palestine Agenda," *Nation*, Dec. 12, 1988.
116. EWS to *Middle East*, April 22, 1979, EWSP, 30:4:I.1.
117. EWS to Halliday, June 8, 1979, EWSP, 5:11:I.1.
118. *PD*, 226.
119. Najla Said, *Looking for Palestine*, 32.
120. Al-Azm.
121. EWS to Robert Alter, Aug. 13, 1979, EWSP, 30:4:I.1.

6. THE GENTILE INTELLECT

1. Keats to Benjamin Robert Haydon, May 10-11, 1817, in *Letters of John Keats to His Family and Friends*, ed. Sidney Colvin (London: Macmillan, 1925), 14–17.
2. FBI, Feb. 28, 1983.

3. For example, EWS, "Intellectuals and the Crisis," in *EPP*, 119.
4. EWS, "Identity, Negation, and Violence," in *PD*, 341–59.
5. Wypijewski.
6. See, for example, EWS to "Emile," Feb. 7, 1975 (EWSP 30:8:I.1), about setting up an Arab foundation and Arab studies institute with Suliman S. Olayan. Or his letter to the Honorable James Carter, Sept. 16, 1992, for help in getting human rights recognition for Palestine (EWSP, 17:6:I.1).
7. Christopher Hitchens, *Hitch-22: A Memoir* (New York: Twelve, 2010), 386.
8. EWS to Salim Tamari, Feb. 21, 1972, EWSP, 5:1:I.1. Birzeit, located on the outskirts of Ramallah, became a university in 1975.
9. Foxworthy to EWS, March 18, 1976, EWSP, 29:24:I.1.
10. Elaine Hagopian, "Ibrahim and Edward," *Arab Studies Quarterly* 26, no. 4 (Fall 2004): 3–22; EWS to Kuwaiti ambassador, Nov. 19, 1973 (EWSP, 30:10:I.1), for the purpose of establishing a chair of Arabic at Columbia.
11. Fouad Moughrabi, "Remembering the AAUG," *Arab Studies Quarterly* 29, no. 3–4 (Summer/Fall 2007): 97–103.
12. EWS to Abourezk, Feb. 12, 1980, EWSP, 5:16:I.1.
13. EWS, interview by W. J. T. Mitchell, in *Edward Said and the Work of the Critic: Speaking Truth to Power*, ed. Paul A. Bové (Durham, N.C.: Duke University Press, 2000), 43.
14. "Prepared Statement of Edward W. Said," with Abu-Lughod, "Questions and Discussion," U.S. Congress, House, Special Subcommittee on Investigations of the Committee on International Relations, The Palestinian Issue in Middle East Peace Efforts, Hearings, 94th Cong., 1st sess., Sept. 30, 1975 (Washington, D.C.: U.S. Government Printing Office, 1976), 28–31, 31–36, 36–62.
15. EWS, "Contemporary American Society and the Palestine Question," July 19, 1979, EWSP, 83:III.1.
16. EWS to Patricia M. Derian (assistant secretary for human rights and humanitarian affairs at the U.S. State Department), Sept. 12, 1980, EWSP, 5:20:I.1.
17. Elaine Hagopian, "Reversing Injustice: On Utopian Activism," *Arab Studies Quarterly* 29, no. 3–4 (Summer/Fall 2007): 57–73.
18. Al-Banna.
19. Hagopian, "Ibrahim and Edward."
20. Hovsepian.
21. Farer.
22. FBI; David Price, "How the FBI Spied on Edward Said," *CounterPunch*, Jan. 13, 2006.
23. FBI.
24. Price, "How the FBI Spied on Edward Said."
25. *PPC*, 171; *PD*, 30.
26. Shafiq Al-Hout, *My Life in the PLO* (London: Pluto Press, 2011), 9, 78.
27. Al-Banna.
28. Jim Schachter, "Said Says He Would Not Take Offer to Be Palestinian Rep," *Columbia Daily Spectator*, Nov. 15, 1977.
29. David Margules and Megan Gallagher, "Press Service Calls Said Sadat's Pick," *Columbia Daily Spectator*, Nov. 16, 1977.
30. *PD*, xxii.
31. EWS to "Erwin," March 20, 1973, EWSP, 5:5:I.1; *PPC*, 271.
32. *B*, 373.

33. EWS to Monroe Engel, Nov. 29, 1972, EWSP, 5:3:I.1.
34. EWS, "Between Worlds," in *RE*, 563.
35. *RE*, 319.
36. Barbara Harlow, conversation with author, ca. 1998.
37. *RE*, 322.
38. Ibid., 48–49.
39. Ibid., 56–57.
40. EWS to David Grossvogel (*Diacritics* editor), July 10, 1973, EWSP, 5:6:I.1.
41. Klein to EWS, March 11, 1977, EWSP, 109:1:II.1.
42. Engel to EWS, n.d., EWSP, 28:22:I.1.
43. Wieseltier.
44. Tanner to EWS, July 7, 1976, EWSP, 29:25:I.1.
45. EWS, "Interview," *Diacritics* 6, no. 3 (Fall 1976): 30–47.
46. EWSP, 40:23:II.1.
47. See Mohammad Shaheen, ed., *Edward Said: Riwayah lilajyal* [Edward Said: A story for the future] (Beirut: Arab Institute for Research and Publication, 2004).
48. See EWS to Ellen Graham, June 2, 1976, EWSP, 29:25:I.1. His evolving views on poststructuralism were plainly revealed in this generally positive readers report on Geoffrey Hartman's *Criticism in the Wilderness*, where he complained that Hartman exhibits at times "the side of Derrida I find most unconvincing, the residual Husserlian tendentiousness and pomposity."
49. *HDC*, 11–12, 51.
50. EWSP, 97:1:III.1.
51. EWS, "The Return to Philology" (talk delivered at the American University of Cairo, Dec. 1994), EWSP, 75:1:II.3.
52. *ESR*, 436.
53. *B*, 378.
54. Ibid., 316.
55. EWS, "Witholding, Avoidance, and Recognition," 22, EWSP, 72:14:II.2.
56. EWSP, 77:32:II.4. This observation, a fragment, is buried among drafts of his fiction and poetry and undated (ca. early 1960s).
57. EWS, "Witholding, Avoidance, and Recognition," 23.
58. Max Harold Fisch, introduction to *The Autobiography of Giambattista Vico*, trans. Max Harold Fisch and Thomas Goddard Bergin (Ithaca, N.Y.: Cornell University Press, 1944), xxi.
59. One of its organizers, Giorgio Tagliacozzo, was in Said's New York milieu, working as a lecturer on the history of ideas at the New School between 1946 and 1961. He joined Donald Phillip Verene to found the Vico Institute in 1974. Both regularly corresponded with Said (EWSP, 29:21:I.1, 29:22:I.1, 29:24:I.1).
60. John Simon to EWS, July 30, 1980, EWSP, 5:16:I.1.
61. EWS, "Michel Foucault (1927–1984)," *Raritan* 4, no. 2 (1984): 188.
62. EWS, "An Ethics of Language: The Archaeology of Knowledge and the Discourse of Language by Michel Foucault," *Diacritics* 4, no. 2 (Summer 1974): 31.
63. Ibid., 28.
64. Yelin.
65. EWS, "Ethics of Language," 28.

66. EWS, "Michel Foucault as an Intellectual Imagination," *boundary 2* 1, no. 1 (Fall 1972): 2.
67. EWS to Cixous, Jan. 15, 1973, EWSP, 5:4:I.1.
68. Foucault to EWS, n.d. (ca. Dec. 1972), EWSP, 5:3:I.1 (trans. Emilie Pons and the author).
69. EWS to Foucault (in French), Jan. 15, 1973, EWSP, 5:4:I.1 (my translation).
70. By 1979, Said understood Foucault to be a supporter of Israel. EWS, "Diary: My Encounter with Sartre," *London Review of Books*, June 1, 2000.
71. EWS, "Foucault as an Intellectual Imagination," 5.
72. Ibid., 25.
73. Ibid., 2.
74. EWS, "Michel Foucault (1927–1984)," 192.
75. Ibid., 194. In "An Ethics of Language," Said identifies Foucault's suppressed sources as Michael Polanyi, Thomas Kuhn, and Georges Canguilhem.
76. *B*, 334, 337.
77. EWS to Louise Adler, Sept. 16, 1981, EWSP, 5:5:I.1.
78. EWS, recommendation for James Merod, Oct. 23, 1981, EWSP, 5:6:I.1.
79. Gabriel Kolko, *Main Currents in Modern American History* (New York: Harper & Row, 1976), vii–viii.
80. EWSP, 31:3:I.2; EWS to Raskin, March 25, 1983, EWSP, 6:21:I.1.
81. Jonah Raskin, *The Mythology of Imperialism: A Revolutionary Critique of British Literature and Society in the Modern Age* (New York: Monthly Review Press, 1972), 3–4, 11–12.
82. *Columbia Daily Spectator*, Nov. 22, 1977.
83. Levin to EWS, July 29 [incorrectly marked June 29], 1976, HL.
84. EWS to Levin, Aug. 2, 1976, HL.

7. FROM SAIGON TO PALESTINE

1. From a U.S. Air Force songbook, sent by Keith and Anne Buchanan to EWS on Sept. 12, 1987, EWSP, 10:9:I.1.
2. Khalidi, T.
3. *O*, 5.
4. *WTC*, 282, 250.
5. *O*, 22.
6. Ibid., 20.
7. Daniel Martin Varisco, *Reading Orientalism: Said and the Unsaid* (Seattle: University of Washington Press, 2007); Ibn Warraq, *Defending the West: A Critique of Edward Said's "Orientalism"* (Amherst, N.Y.: Prometheus Books, 2007); Robert Irwin, *For Lust of Knowing: The Orientalists and Their Enemies* (London: Penguin, 2006).
8. EWS to Ms. Toby Gordan, March 22, 1978, EWSP, 111:2:II.1.
9. EWS to Levin, Jan. 26 and Feb. 7, 1978, HL.
10. Said, M. Chomsky thought the arrangement plausible: "We talked about all of these things."
11. Chomsky to EWS, Aug. 7, 1976, EWSP, 29:25:I.1.
12. For drafts of *Orientalism*, see EWSP, 47:19:II.1 and 47:20:II.1.
13. Not just Vietnam. The book appeared only a year before socialist revolutions in Nicaragua, El Salvador, Grenada, and the Philippines.

14. EWS to Shahak, Jan. 7, 1978, EWSP, 116:33:II.4.
15. EWS to Ferial Hopkins, April 19, 1976, EWSP, 29:24:I.1; Research Statement to the Center for Advanced Study in the Behavioral Sciences (1975–76); *PPC*, 168.
16. EWS to Ferial Hopkins, April 19, 1976, EWSP, 29:24:I.1.
17. EWS to Roger Owen, July 19, 1976, EWSP, 29:25:I.1.
18. EWS to Roger Owen, July 19, 1976.
19. Al-Banna.
20. Ibid.
21. Tom Farer to EWS, June 14, 1976, EWSP, 29:25:I.1.
22. Cole.
23. Alpers.
24. Cole.
25. Alpers.
26. Chomsky to EWS, July 28, 1976, EWSP, 29:25:I.1.
27. *O*, 307.
28. Seymour M. Hersh, "The Gray Zone: How a Secret Pentagon Program Came to Abu Ghraib," *New Yorker*, May 24, 2004.
29. M. Cherif Bassiouni, "The AAUG: Reflections on a Lost Opportunity," *Arab Studies Quarterly* 29, no. 3–4 (Summer/Fall 2007): 29–30.
30. EWS, "Diary: My Encounter with Sartre," *London Review of Books*, June 1, 2000, 42.
31. Naseer Aruri, ed., *Middle East Crucible: Studies on the Arab-Israeli War of October 1973* (AAUG Monograph Series, 1975); Abdel-Malek to EWS, June 14, 1976, EWSP, 29:25:I.1.
32. Abdel-Malek replied, reasonably, that Said's relevant work barely existed until after 1970–71. Abdel-Malek to EWS, July 9, 1976, EWSP, 29:25:I.1.
33. EWS to Abdel-Malek, July 14, 1976, EWSP, 29:25:I.1.
34. A charge made, among others, by James Clifford, "On Orientalism," in *The Predicament of Culture: Twentieth-Century Ethnography, Literature, and Art* (Cambridge, Mass.: Harvard University Press, 1988); see EWS, "A Palestinian Voice," *Columbia Forum* 12, no. 4 (Winter 1969): 24–31.
35. *PD*, 15; EWS to Mr. Locke of *The New York Times Book Review*, Nov. 22, 1972, EWSP, 5:4:I.1.
36. Burns.
37. EWSP, 71:8:II.2; EWS, foreword to J*ewish History, Jewish Religion: The Weight of Three Thousand Years*, by Israel Shahak (1994; London: Pluto Press, 1997); EWSP, 70:16:II.2.
38. *PD*, 391.
39. Nancy Elizabeth Gallagher, "Interview with Albert Hourani," in *Approaches to the History of the Middle East: Interviews with Leading Middle East Historians* (Berkshire, U.K.: Ithaca Press, 1996); *PD*, 391. Heikal was the editor in chief of the Cairo daily newspaper *Al-Ahram* (1957–74). Abdullah Laroui, *La crise des intellectuels arabes: Traditionalisme ou historicisme?* (Paris: Maspero, 1974), 2, 5.
40. Basim Musallam, "Power and Knowledge," *MERIP Reports* 79 (June 1979): 20.
41. Jessup, interestingly, was E. P. Thompson's grandfather.
42. Gallagher, "Interview with Albert Hourani," 39.
43. EWS, "Unfinished Intellectual Work," EWSP, 71:1:II.2.
44. EWS to Zurayk, Feb. 18, 1974, EWSP 30:5:I.1.

45. EWS, "The Special Relationship Between Thoughts and the Intellectual," trans. from the Arabic by Joseph Farag, *Al-Majallah*, Jan. 30, 1990, 24-25.
46. Hani A. Faris, "Constantine K. Zurayk: Advocate of Rationalism in Modern Arab Thought," in *Arab Civilization: Challenges and Responses*, ed. George N. Atiyeh and Ibrahim M. Oweiss (Albany: State University of New York Press, 1988), 4.
47. "Unfinished Intellectual Work," EWSP, 71:1:II.2.
48. Ibid.
49. Ibid.
50. EWS to Tom Farer, Feb. 13, 1976, EWSP, 30:23:I.1.
51. Emanuel Hamon, dir., *Selves and Others: A Portrait of Edward Said* (2004).
52. *O*, 6.
53. *ESR*, 436; *O*, 14.
54. Roger Scruton, *Thinkers of the New Left* (London: Longman, 1985). Said's photograph appears on the cover of the American edition alongside that of Lacan, Sartre, Foucault, and others.
55. EWS, Obituary for Raymond Williams (draft), EWSP, 67:1:II.2.
56. Yelin.
57. Conversation with the author, fall 1982, New York.
58. EWS, "Raymond Williams," *Nation*, March 5, 1988; *PD*, 93; Raymond Williams and Edward W. Said, "Media, Margins, and Modernity," in Raymond Williams, *The Politics of Modernism: Against the New Conformists* (London: Verso, 1989), 178.
59. EWS, "Raymond Williams."
60. *PD*, 93.
61. Raymond Williams, "Media, Margins, and Modernity, 178.
62. Raymond Williams, *The Country and the City* (Oxford, U.K.: Oxford University Press, 1973), 289.
63. Ibid., 302.
64. Ibid., 279.
65. Ibid., 285-86.
66. *B*, 353-54.
67. In his Gauss lectures, Said assigned Foucault's "Questions on Geography," which appeared in *Herodote* (1976); *WTC*, 220.
68. EWS to Ferial Ghazoul, Feb. 28, 1978, EWSP, 30:7:I.1. The thirty-page lecture in French was untitled: EWSP, 116:33:II.4.
69. EWS, "Arabs, Islam, and the Dogmas of the West," *New York Times Book Review*, Oct. 31, 1976; see EWSP, 90:8:II.2.
70. EWS to Dr. Mary Ellen Lundstein, Nov. 21, 1978, EWSP, 5:9:I.1; West to EWS, n.d. (ca. 1978), EWSP, 5:9:I.1.
71. Said, G.
72. Said Makdisi.
73. Kairallah.
74. Al-Azm.
75. EWS to Al-Azm, Nov. 10, 1980, EWSP 30:15:I.1.
76. There would be two other translations of *Orientalism* into Arabic. Highly regarded translations of Said's other books and essays can be found by, among others, Fawwaz Traboulsi, Mohammad Shaheen, and Subhi Hadidi. Traboulsi's translation of *Out of Place* is the most widely read of Said's books in the Arab world.

77. Al-Azm.
78. Abu-Deeb.
79. Varisco, *Reading Orientalism*, 23.
80. Ibid.; Warraq, *Defending the West*, 19; Irwin, *For Lust of Knowing*, 283.
81. Irwin, *For Lust of Knowing*, 197.
82. Ibid., 296.
83. Mahdi Amel, *Hal al-Qalb li ash-Sharq wa al-'Aql li al-Gharb?* [Intelligence for the West and passion for the East?] (Beirut: Dar al-Farabi, 1985).
84. Mintz.
85. Jacques Berque, "Au dela de 'l'orientalisme,'" *Qantara: Le Magazine de l'Institut du Monde Arabe* 13 (Oct./Dec. 1994).
86. Warner.
87. EWS to Westminster College, May 24, 1982, EWSP, 6:11:II.1.
88. Shahak to EWS, Sept. 5, 1993, EWSP, 29:11:I.1.
89. *PD*, 307.
90. The proceedings were published in *Journal of Palestine Studies* 16, no. 2 (Winter 1987): 85–104.
91. Kairallah.
92. Wieseltier.
93. On Feb. 4, 1982, Said wrote to Dr. P. S. van Koningsveld at the University of Leiden delighted to see his thesis regarding Snouck Hurgronje's career in espionage validated.
94. *O*, 93.
95. EWS, "Interview," *Diacritics* 6, no. 3 (Autumn 1976): 45.
96. EWS, "The Problem of Textuality: Two Exemplary Positions." *Critical Inquiry* 4, no. 4 (Summer 1978): 673–714.
97. *WTC*, 183.
98. Quoted by Wood; Mitchell.
99. EWS, "An Exchange on Deconstruction," *boundary 2* 8, no. 1 (Fall 1979): 71.
100. Burns.
101. *O*, 52.
102. Ibid., 11.
103. Ibid., 204.
104. Wood.
105. *O*, 8.
106. Martin Kramer, "Said's Splash," in *Ivory Towers on Sand: The Failure of Middle Eastern Studies in America* (Washington, D.C.: Washington Institute for Near East Policy, 2001), 27–28.
107. Aijaz Ahmad, *In Theory: Classes, Nations, Literatures* (London: Verso, 1992), 197.
108. David Riesman to EWS, March 19, 1975, EWSP, 29:21:I.1.
109. "Edward Said: Bright Star of English Lit and P.L.O.," *New York Times*, Feb. 22, 1980, A2.
110. *QP*, 56–57.
111. EWS, "Projecting Jerusalem," *Journal of Palestine Studies* (Autumn 1995): 5–14.
112. "Alice" to EWS, Jan. 4, 1974, EWSP, 30:5:I.1.
113. Mary Ann Lash to EWS, March 15, 1978, EWSP, 54:6:II.1.
114. EWS to William Warner, Sept. 27, 1978, EWSP, 5:9:I.1.
115. *QP*, 218.

116. Zurayk to EWS, Feb. 20, 1980, EWSP, 53:7:II.1; EWS to Ronit Lentin, March 17, 1981, EWSP, 5:25:I.1.
117. According to Clare Carroll, these included Diana Trilling, John Romano, and Quentin Anderson.
118. EWSP, 48:16:II.1.
119. See, however, Clovis Maksoud, *The Arab Image* (Delhi: Ramlochan, 1963), 12.
120. Said also promoted *Many Voices, One World* (UNESCO, 1981), an official report chaired by the Nobel Peace Prize laureate Seán MacBride calling for a "new world information order." MacBride not coincidentally oversaw another UNESCO report, *Israel in Lebanon* (1983), which unanimously concluded that Israel was guilty of war crimes in Lebanon. The committee labeled Israel's actions "ethnocide" (*PD*, 247–50).
121. EWS to Shahak, Jan. 7, 1978. Chomsky called Said's media criticism "close to my own"; Chomsky.
122. EWS to Alan G. Thomas, Nov. 4, 1992, EWSP, 17:2:I.1. He was particularly fond of Debray's *Teachers, Writers, and Celebrities: The Intellectuals of Modern France* (1981).
123. EWSP, 75:21:II.3.
124. *PD*, 65.
125. EWS, "Palestinian Voice," 24.
126. EWS, "Notes on the Arab Intellectuals at Home and Abroad" (undated speech to the AAUG), EWSP, 77:2:II.3.

8. AGAINST FALSE GODS

1. *JC*, 28.
2. EWS to "Mr. Mann," July 15, 1978, EWSP, 5:9:I.1.
3. Abdel-Malek to EWS, June 11, 1978, EWSP, 30:6:I.1.
4. EWS to Al-Banna, July 31, 1972, EWSP, 30:6:I.1.
5. Salman Rushdie, *Joseph Anton* (New York: Random House, 2012), 233–34.
6. Najla Said, *Looking for Palestine* (New York: Riverhead Books, 2013), 36; EWS, "The Acre and the Goat," *New Statesman*, May 11, 1979, 685–88.
7. Said, *Looking for Palestine*, 85.
8. EWS to Tony Tanner, Aug. 4, 1979, EWSP, 30:5:I.1.
9. EWS to Ellison Findly, Oct. 1, 1982, EWSP, 6:16:I.1.
10. Unsigned letter to EWS, June 27, 1982, EWSP, 6:13:I.1.
11. Anonymous to EWS, March 19, 1990, EWSP, 13:18:I.1.
12. Deborah Poole to Joy Hayton, Sept. 23, 1985, EWSP, 8:14:I.1.
13. Jim Naughton, "The Emerging Voices of the Palestinians," *Washington Post*, June 7, 1988.
14. Poole.
15. Cole.
16. EWS, "Leaving Palestine," *New York Review of Books*, Sept. 23, 1999.
17. Said Makdisi.
18. *IES*, 19–35; EWS to *Middle East*, April 2, 1979.
19. EWS to To Whom It May Concern, Nov. 20, 1989, EWSP, 13:6:I.1.
20. EWS to Musa Mazzawi, Aug. 9, 1983, EWSP, 7:2:I.1.
21. Ibid.
22. EWS to Kalid el Fahoum and Yasir Arafat, Feb. 16, 1983, EWSP, 75:25:II.3.

23. *RE*, 118; *WTC*, 4, 25; Fred Halliday, *The Making of the Second Cold War* (London: Verso, 1983), a book that Said promoted. See also *WTC*, 25; *C&I*, 27, 284; *PD*, 54.
24. Miller.
25. *C&I*, 37.
26. Conor Cruise O'Brien, Edward Said, and John Lukacs, "The Intellectual in the Post-colonial World: Response and Discussion," *Salmagundi*, no. 70/71 (Spring–Summer 1986): 69; Wood.
27. President and Mrs. Reagan to EWS, Dec. 1987, EWSP, 10:15:I.1.
28. EWS to Gary F. Waller, Dec. 17, 1981, EWSP, 6:7:I.1. *The Shadow of the West*, written and narrated by EWS, directed by Geoff Dunlop (VATV in association with Kufic Films, 1982).
29. Burns.
30. EWS, Commencement Lecture, AUC, June 17, 1999, EWSP, 31:10:I.2.
31. *PS*, 41; David Gerrard, "Said Leads Undergrad Seminar," *Columbia Daily Spectator*, Jan. 21, 2000.
32. Taken from his quotation of Morris Lazerowitz's *Studies in Metaphilosophy* (1964), EWSP, 97:1:III.
33. In Michael Waldman's "Question of Edward Said," *Columbia Daily Spectator*, March 4, 1982, Said reported that he was "working on a large study of the role of the intellectual in the 20th century."
34. EWS to Massimo Bacigalupo, Oct. 5, 1979, EWSP, 5:12:I.1: "two books of criticism coming out next year"—*The World, the Text, and the Critic* and the book on Gramsci and Lukács; EWS to Wilcox, Nov. 19, 1979, EWSP, 5:14:I.1.
35. Said knew Bernal's story from Gary Werskey's *Visible College: Scientists and Socialists in the 1930s* (New York: Viking, 1978), a book he assigned in his seminars in the early 1980s.
36. EWS to Wilcox, Nov. 19, 1979.
37. EWS to National Endowment for the Humanities, Oct. 12, 1979, EWSP, 5:13:I.1.
38. Anderson to EWS, April 24, 1978, EWSP, 30:6:I.1. In 1977, Said read the interwar Marxist cultural debates found in *Aesthetics and Politics*, Paul Feyerabend's *Against Method* (a critique of science by a former scientist), Adorno's *Minima Moralia*, and Lucio Colletti's *Marxism and Hegel*. EWS to New Left Books, Sept. 27, 1977, EWSP, 30:13:I.1.
39. EWS to Wilcox, Nov. 4, 1980, EWSP, 5:21:I.1.
40. EWS to Bacigalupo, Oct. 5, 1979.
41. EWS to Wilcox, Dec. 11, 1980, EWSP, 5:22:I.1.
42. EWS to Albert Sonnenfeld, Aug. 23, 1978, EWSP, 5:9:I.1.
43. Dan O'Hara to EWS, April 12, 1983, EWSP, 83:11:III.1.
44. Michel Chodkiewicz to EWS, Feb. 3, 1983, EWSP, 6:21:I.1.
45. EWS to Wilcox, Dec. 11, 1980.
46. EWS, "The Problem of Textuality: Two Exemplary Positions," *Critical Inquiry* 4, no. 4 (Summer 1978): 673.
47. EWS to Kamal Abu-Deeb, Dec. 8, 1977, EWSP, 29:27:I.1.
48. EWS to Monroe Engel, Nov. 29, 1972, EWSP, 5:3:I.1.
49. Jacqueline Onassis to EWS, Oct. 16, 1989, EWSP, 13:3:I.1.
50. EWS to Jonathan Arac, April 19, 1976, EWSP, 29:24:I.1.
51. *WTC*, 191.
52. Yelin; Dickstein; Ghazoul.

53. Gold to EWS, Aug. 26, 1978, EWSP, 5:7:I.1.
54. *PPC*, 198.
55. EWS to Herb Leibowitz, Dec. 4, 1967, EWSP, 28:22:I.1.
56. *PPC*, 198; *HDC*, 12, 32, 39, 136.
57. *RE*, 144.
58. *HDC*, 39.
59. EWS, "Comparative Literature as Critical Investigation," 14, EWSP, 70:16:II.2.
60. Ibid.
61. *RE*, 125-26.
62. *O*, 141. See also "Renan's Philological Laboratory," in *Art, Politics, and Will: Essays in Honor of Lionel Trilling*, ed. Quentin Anderson, Stephen Donadio, and Steven Marcus (New York: Basic Books, 1977), 59-98.
63. *O*, 140.
64. *HDC*, 71.
65. Noam Chomsky, *Language and Responsibility* (New York: Pantheon, 1979), 175.
66. *WTC*, 249-51; EWS, "An Ethics of Language," *Diacritics* 4, no. 2 (Summer 1974): 32; Donald Phillip Verene, preface to *On the Study Methods of Our Time*, by Giambattista Vico (Ithaca, N.Y.: Cornell University Press, 1990), 7.
67. Rosenthal.
68. EWS, Seminar Notes for "History of Critical Theories" (1971), EWSP, 83:1:III.1.
69. Ibid.
70. EWS, "Beginnings," *Salmagundi* 2, no. 4 (Fall 1968): 45. Here his approach to Hegel was more affirmative: "Paraphrasing Hegel, we can say that formally the problem of beginnings is the beginning of the problem" (41).
71. Ali.
72. EWS to Albert Sonnenfeld, Oct. 27, 1978, EWSP, 5:9:I.1.
73. EWS to Anders Stephanson, Feb. 23, 1976, EWSP, 29:23:I.1.
74. EWSP, 66:6:II.2.
75. EWS, "On Critical Consciousness: Gramsci and Lukács," EWSP, 78:10:II.4; *RE*, 565.
76. *WTC*, 290.
77. Ibid., 291.
78. EWS, "Beginnings," 45. His correspondence with his editors (EWSP, 40:23:II.1) and his notes to *Beginnings* (EWSP, 65:2:II.1) confirm that his book was a direct response to Kermode.
79. EWS, "On Critical Consciousness, 4.
80. Ibid., 11.
81. Massimo Bacigalupo to EWS, Sept. 21, 1979, EWSP, 5:12:I.1.
82. Marginal note to Jean Stein interview of EWS, Aug. 23, 1993, New York.
83. EWS, Obituary for Raymond Williams (draft), EWSP, 67:1:II.2. The obituary appeared in *The Nation* on March 5, 1988.
84. See also his ambivalence about whether Gilles Deleuze was conservative (EWSP, 97:1:III.1).
85. Raymond Williams and Edward W. Said, "Media, Margins, and Modernity," in Raymond Williams, *The Politics of Modernism: Against the New Conformists* (London: Verso, 1989), 182; *WTC*, 5; *PD*, 316; *WTC*, 267.
86. EWS, "Conspiracy of Praise," *MERIP Reports* 15 (Nov.-Dec. 1985).

87. His position on facts is clearest in a letter to the UN Development Programme on March 7, 2003; what matters is how they are related to a hypothesis and how truth is related to interest (EWSP, 28:6:I.1).

88. EWS to "Doris," June 8, 1978, EWSP, 30:6:I.

89. EWS to Jameson, Nov. 9, 1977, EWSP, 30:7:I.1.

90. *PPC*, 56–57.

91. Miller.

92. EWS to Lawrence Lipking, Feb. 5, 1981, EWSP, 5:2:I.1.

93. *PPC*, 192: "In 1988 . . . or thereabouts, there was a tremendous flurry of stuff . . . rereading Fanon but trashing him at the same time. I felt that it was really a misreading, or a betrayal, of Fanon." Bhabha's essay describing Fanon as a figure of psychic ambivalence rather than revolutionary change appeared in *New Formations* (Spring 1987).

94. EWS to William Bernhardt, Oct. 14, 1972, EWSP, 5:2:I.1.

95. Lindsay Waters to EWS, April 2, 1981, EWSP, 5:26:I.1.

96. Not including books he wrote with others and his pamphlet *Yeats and Decolonization* (Cork: Cork University Press and Field Day Pamphlets, 1988).

97. *RE*, 152.

98. There were, however, other models: Sarah Graham-Brown's photo essay *The Palestinians and Their Society* (1980), Susan Meiselas's *Nicaragua* (1981), and Malek Alloula's *Le harem colonial* (1986).

99. Mohr.

100. Ibid.

101. *ALS*, 6.

102. Derrida to EWS, Jan. 10, 1987, EWSP, 8:17:I.1 (my translation).

103. Carol Coulter to EWS, June 24, 1988, EWSP, 11:12:I.1.

104. Monroe Engel to EWS, Jan. 5, 1989, EWSP, 13:14:I.1.

105. EWS, Obituary for Arthur Gold, Feb. 26, 1989, EWSP, 78:5:II.4.

106. Monroe Engel to EWS, Jan. 5, 1990, EWSP, 13:14:I.1; William E. Cain, "Studying America's Aristocrats: An Interview with Arthur R. Gold," *ALH* 2, no. 2 (Summer 1990): 358–73.

107. "The Shultz Meeting with Edward Said and Ibrahim Abu-Lughod," *Journal of Palestine Studies* 17, no. 4 (Summer 1988): 160.

108. George Shultz, *Turmoil and Triumph: My Years as Secretary of State* (New York: Scribner's, 1993), 1029.

109. *PD*, xxviii; Susan Schendel (Shultz's assistant) to the author, Dec. 12, 2015.

110. EWS, "Palestine Agenda," *Nation*, Dec. 12, 1988, 637; *PD*, 147.

111. EWS to Karl Kroeber, March 5, 1974, EWSP, 30:11:I.1; EWS to Jonathan Cole, May 7, 1990, EWSP, 13:24:I.1.

112. Ben Letzler, "Sometimes Wrong, Never in Doubt," *Columbia Daily Spectator*, Jan. 28, 2000.

113. Stern, D.

114. David.

115. Stern, D.

116. Yelin.

117. Wieseltier.

118. Burns.

119. EWS, "An Unresolved Paradox," *MLA Newsletter* (Summer 1999): 3.

120. Said, N.

121. Yerushalmi.
122. Poole.
123. Said, N.
124. EWS to Engel, Nov. 22, 1972, EWSP, 5:3:I.1.
125. Ruth Halikman, "West Advocates," *Columbia Daily Spectator*, Oct. 18, 1993.
126. EWS to "Jimmy," Dec. 16, 1972, EWSP, 5:4:I.1.
127. Miller.
128. Burns.
129. Davis.

9. A FEW SIMPLE IDEAS

1. Alain, a.k.a. Émile Auguste Chartier, "Propos sur la religion" (1924). In *OP*, Said describes reading Alain during his year off in Cairo in 1957 (285).
2. *PPC*, 205.
3. Ibid., 139.
4. Poole; Said, N.
5. Said, W.
6. Harry Levin, *Grounds for Comparison* (Cambridge, Mass.: Harvard University Press, 1972), 129.
7. Guttenplan.
8. Wypijewski.
9. Carroll; Said, W.
10. Said, W.
11. EWS, Mount Hermon Commencement Speech, June 2002.
12. Said, N.
13. Greene.
14. Said, N.
15. Said Makdisi.
16. Phone message from EWS to Jean Stein, Nov. 19, 1994. Sent by Stein to the author on Feb. 24, 2017.
17. Ben Sonnenberg, "My Montparnasse," *Raritan* 10, no. 4 (Spring 1991).
18. His media access was not entirely cut off. James L. Greenfeld invited him to attend a *New York Times Magazine* editorial luncheon on March 14, 1989, with the hope that their exchange would generate an article (EWSP, 12:6:I.1).
19. Except for letters to the editor. See, however, Barbara Epstein to EWS in March 1989 asking him to write on the Albanian novelist Ismail Kadare (EWSP, 12:8:I.1).
20. EWS to Silvers, Jan. 9, 1983, EWSP, 7:21:I.1.
21. Wanger.
22. Ibid.
23. Salman Rushdie, *Joseph Anton* (New York: Random House, 2012), 232–33.
24. Warner.
25. Ibid.
26. Ibid.
27. Wilmers.
28. Ibid.
29. Rosenthal.

30. Wilmers.
31. Hovsepian.
32. EWS, "Who's in Charge?," *Arena Magazine*, April 4, 2003, 40; Glass.
33. Wypijewski.
34. Ibid.
35. Said, M.
36. JoAnn Wypijewski, "Mementos," sent to the author on Feb. 19, 2016.
37. Said, N.
38. Sifton.
39. Margaronis.
40. *PPC*, 76.
41. Michael Riffaterre, "A Stylistic Approach to Literary Theory," *New Literary History* 2, no. 1 (Autumn 1970): 39, 46.
42. *WTC*, 19–20.
43. EWSP, 70:16:II.2.
44. WTC, 118.
45. EWS to *Independent*, Aug. 29, 1990, EWSP, 71:6:II.2.
46. Notes sent to EWS by Chomsky, July 20, 1985, EWSP, 8:17:I.1.
47. Whitman to MLA, Sept. 11, 1998, EWSP, 70:8:II.2.
48. EWS to MLA, Oct. 8, 1998, EWSP, 70:8:II.2.
49. EWS to *Ha'aretz*, Aug. 28, 2000, EWSP, 71:1:II.2.
50. *WTC*, 28.
51. For example, Mahdi Amel, Aijaz Ahmad, Manfred Sing and Miriam Younes, Gilbert Achcar, and others. The best of these was Ahmad's because of its understanding of Said's literary points of departure.
52. Seamus Deane, "A Late Style of Humanism," *Field Day Review* 1 (2005): 198.
53. In, for example, *The New Republic*; *RE*, 141. Appearing in a review of *Orientalism* by Said's former student Leon Wieseltier, the scurrilous charge inspired Said's response to the magazine on April 10, 1979: "This is red-baiting a la McCarthy and Cohn, and only that" (EWSP, 5:15:I.1).
54. EWS to Redgrave, Oct. 9, 1992, EWSP, 17:5:I.1.
55. EWS, "A Palestinian Voice," *Columbia Forum* 12, no. 4 (Winter 1969): 31, where he argued that Soviet support, although vital, was also late and insufficient.
56. EWS, "Palestinian Prospects Now: Edward W. Said Speaks with Mark Bruzonsky," *Worldview* 22, no. 5 (May 1979): 8.
57. EWS, "Palestinian Voice," 27.
58. A speaking tour was arranged for him in Cuba, for example, in 2000 but abandoned for scheduling reasons: Cuban Book Institute to EWS, March 23, 2000, EWSP, 31:2:II.2; EWSP, 32:49:II.2; EWS to Alexander G. Bearn, Feb. 8, 2001, EWSP, 31:2:II.2.
59. Christopher Hitchens, *Hitch-22* (New York: Twelve, 2010), 386.
60. Yelin; Rosenthal; Al-Banna.
61. *HDC*, 21.
62. Ibid.
63. In his enthusiastic recommendation letter for the American socialist economist and *Monthly Review* co-editor Harry Magdoff, whom he compared to Socrates (EWSP, 8:2:I.1).
64. *ESR*, 435.
65. *WTC*, 238–41.

66. Ibid., 19–20.
67. *CI*, 50.
68. *CI*, 49; *PPC*, 335.
69. EWS, "The Limits of the Artistic Imagination," EWSP, 75:21:II.3.
70. Mitchell.
71. Traboulsi; Wood.
72. Al-Azm.
73. Chomsky.
74. In the Q&A session after his Haverford commencement speech, he was asked, "What do you think should be fixed?" Said replied, "Economics, the economics." Bergson, D.
75. Aijaz Ahmad, *In Theory: Classes, Nations, Literatures* (London: Verso, 1992); Mahdi Amel, *Hal al-Qalb li ash-Sharq wa al-'Aql li al-Gharb?* [Intelligence for the West and passion for the East?] (Beirut: Dar al-Farabi, 1985).
76. EWS, "Interview," *Diacritics* 6, no. 3 (Fall 1976): 36.
77. *QP*, 56.
78. *RE*, 143; EWS, "Interview," *Diacritics*, 39.
79. EWSP, 29:25:I.1.
80. *WTC*, 78.
81. EWSP, 77:24:II.4.
82. EWS, "Notes on the Arab Intellectuals at Home and Abroad" (undated speech to the AAUG), EWSP, 77:2:II.3.
83. *EPP*, 30.
84. EWS to Sami Al-Banna, Feb. 7, 1973, EWSP, 5:5:I.1.
85. Sharon.
86. *B*, 158.
87. Macleod.
88. Said, M.; Said, W.
89. EWSP, 112:25:III.2.
90. EWS, "Swift's Tory Anarchy," *Eighteenth-Century Studies* (Fall 1969): 60.
91. EWS to Jack Goellner, Johns Hopkins University Press, Oct. 28, 1968, EWSP, 97:23:III.1.
92. EWS to al-Banna, July 31, 1972, EWSP, 30:6:I.1.
93. EWS, "Witholding, Avoidance, and Recognition," EWSP, 72:14:II.2.
94. EWS to Al-Banna, July 31, 1972.
95. Hannah Arendt, *The Portable Hannah Arendt*, ed. Peter Baehr (New York: Penguin, 2000), 169.
96. A fellowship proposal submitted to Said for his opinion; see EWS to Nadim Rouhana, Aug. 9, 1983, and the proposal itself (EWSP, 7:3:I.1).
97. Said quoting Josef Yarushalmi, in *FNE*, 31.
98. *FNE*, 41; *EPP*, xiv; *PD*, 119.
99. EWS to Brown, Dec. 6, 1972, EWSP, 5:4:I.1.
100. Rose.
101. EWS, "Joseph Conrad and the Fiction of Autobiography," undated draft, EWSP, 46:1:II.1.
102. EWS, "Linguistics and the Archaeology of Mind," *International Philosophical Quarterly* 11, no. 1 (March 1971).
103. EWSP, 110:11:III.3.
104. *FNE*, 53.
105. *FNE*, 52. See in this respect, EWS, "A Jew Without Jewishness," review of *The Counterlife*, by Philip Roth, *Guardian*, March 13, 1987.

106. David.
107. *PPC*, 61.
108. Ibid., 217.
109. EWS to unstated addressee, Oct. 31, 1989, EWSP, 13:3:I.1.
110. *RE*, xx.
111. *PPC*, 147.
112. *ME*, xv.
113. Ibid., 43.
114. Ibid., 44.
115. EWS, "Music," *Nation*, Feb. 7, 1987, 160.
116. Rose; *FNE*, 72–75.
117. Said, M.
118. *OP*, 11; Said, G.
119. Ali; Wypijewski.
120. Bilgrami.

10. THE THIRD WORLD SPEAKS

1. EWS, "The Castle," written in 1952, MH.
2. Interview with EWS in *Al-Qabas*, Oct. 7–8, 1989, reprinted in *Israel & Palestine Political Report* 153 (Oct. 1989): 4.
3. EWS to Shahid, March 28, 1991, EWSP, 15:3:I.1.
4. Jerome M. Segal to EWS, May 16, 1988, EWSP, 11:5:I.1; EWS to *Nation*, July 2, 1990, EWSP, 71:8:II.2.
5. Jerome M. Segal, "Why Israel Needs Arafat," *New York Times*, Feb. 7, 1988.
6. EWS, "Response," *Critical Inquiry* 15, no. 3 (Spring 1989): 634–46.
7. EWS, "Freedom and Resistance," EWSP, 78:5:II.4.
8. Jean-François Lyotard, "The Wall, the Gulf, the System," in *Postmodern Fables*, trans. Georges Van Den Abbeele (Minneapolis: University of Minnesota Press, 1997), 67–82.
9. Said, G.
10. Tariq Ali, *Conversations with Edward Said* (Oxford, U.K.: Seagull Books, 2006), 125, 123.
11. Draft and notes of the novel sent to the author by Michael Wood, Aug. 8, 2016.
12. "Emily" was the name of Farid Haddad's mother and, interestingly, also his Queens cousin Abie's mother, whom he treats so roughly in *OP*.
13. Hanan Ashrawi to EWS, March 3, 1980, EWSP, 5:19:I.1.
14. EWS, "The Limits of the Artistic Imagination," EWSP, 75:21:II.3.
15. EWS et al., July 2, 1991, EWSP, 30:3:I.2.
16. *OP*, 215.
17. *ESR*, xi.
18. Said, M.
19. Rai.
20. *OP*, 216.
21. EWS, "Said's Lost Essay on Jerusalem: 'The Current Status of Jerusalem,'" *Jerusalem Quarterly* 45 (2011): 57–72.
22. Bergson, D.; Parry.
23. *RE*, 291.
24. EWS to Carter, Sept. 16, 1992, EWSP, 17:6:I.1.
25. On March 31, 1998, he presented "A Conversation with Edward Said on the Middle East," *Council on Foreign Relations Annual Report*, July 1,

1997–June 30, 1998, 6, 61. In Sept. 1989, with Cyrus Vance and Richard W. Murphy presiding, he was asked formally to respond to a CIA report on Syria.

26. Rockefeller to EWS, April 31, 1984, EWSP, 7:18:I.1.
27. Interview with EWS in *Al-Qabas International*, 4.
28. Chomsky to EWS, April 6, 1982, Chomsky Papers, MIT.
29. Elena Cabral, "CU Professors Awarded Fellowships at Academy," *Columbia Daily Spectator*, June 12, 1991.
30. Becky Geller, "Ceremony Honors Professors," *Columbia Daily Spectator*, April 12, 1994.
31. EWS to George Rupp, June 10, 1993, EWSP, 29:7:I.1.
32. Phone conversation with the author, Aug. 2003.
33. Said, N.
34. *OP*, 215.
35. Said, W.
36. EWS to George Rupp, June 10, 1993.
37. Bergson, A.
38. For the inside story on his recruitment to Harvard, see the correspondence in IW.
39. Wood.
40. Habachy.
41. EWS to Levin, Dec. 26, 1985, HL.
42. Nathaniel Daw and Saara Bickley, "Said Rejects Offer to Teach at Harvard," *Columbia Daily Spectator*, April 22, 1993.
43. EWSP, 29:12:I.1.
44. His lectures at the Collège de France, which differ in some respects from *On Late Style*, were given under the general title "For a Reinterpretation of Cultural Forms."
45. EWS to Bourdieu, Aug. 1, 1996, EWSP, 31:3:I.2 (my translation).
46. Rose.
47. In a letter to Jean Starobinski, Nov. 22, 1967, Said noted his admiration particularly for Lukács's *Geschichte und Klassenbewusstsein* (1923; *History and Class Consciousness*), where the concept of reification is elaborated (EWSP, 30:3:I.1).
48. EWS to Starobinski, Nov. 22, 1967.
49. EWS to Engel, Feb. 7, 1989, EWSP, 12:2:I.1.
50. EWSP, 71:12:II.2.
51. *C&I*, 13.
52. Harry Levin, *The Gates of Horn: A Study of Five French Realists* (New York: Oxford University Press, 1963), viii.
53. *C&I*, 5.
54. EWS to Monroe Engel, Feb. 7, 1989.
55. Susan Fraiman, "Jane Austen and Edward Said: Gender, Culture, and Imperialism," *Critical Inquiry* 21, no. 4 (Summer 1995); Ralph Locke, "*Aida* and Nine Readings of Empire," *Nineteenth-Century Music Review* 3 (2006).
56. Al-Azm.
57. Chomsky.
58. Robert Hughes, "Envoy to Two Cultures," *Time*, June 21, 1993, 60.
59. *C&I*, 8.
60. Ibid., 292.

61. Cole.
62. C&I, xii–xiii.
63. Ibid., 9; see, for example, Conor Cruise O'Brien, Edward Said, and John Lukacs, "The Intellectual in the Post-colonial World: Response and Discussion," *Salmagundi*, no. 70/71 (Spring–Summer 1986): 69.
64. EWS to Harvard University Press, Jan. 11, 1996, EWSP, 29:6:I.1.
65. C&I, 28, 30.
66. Ibid., 332.
67. Ibid., 24, 65.
68. Ibid., 53, 278.
69. Ibid., 41.
70. Ibid., 194.
71. Ibid.
72. Locke, "*Aida* and Nine Readings of Empire," 59.
73. The historian in question was Nell Painter. See H. L. Gates to EWS, Jan. 3, 1992, EWSP, 16:7:I.1.
74. EWS, "The Politics of Knowledge," in *RE*, 372–74.
75. EWS, "Identity, Authority, and Freedom: The Potentate and the Traveler," in *RE*, 387.
76. Camille Paglia, "Junk Bonds and Corporate Raiders: Academe in the Hour of the Wolf," *Arion: A Journal of Humanities and the Classics* 1, no. 2 (Spring 1991): 176–77.
77. EWS to Paglia, Aug. 15, 1991, EWSP, 15:21:I.1.
78. Conversation with the author, New York, Oct. 1997.
79. Bilgrami.
80. EWS to Lionel Trilling, Jan. 25, 1973, EWSP, 5:5:I.1.
81. Ibid.; *B*, 376.
82. *RE*, 63.
83. For example, *Deutsche Literatur im Zeitalter des Imperialismus* [1947; German literature of the imperialist period], *The Young Hegel* (1938), and *The Destruction of Reason* (1933, 1942, 1954).
84. EWS, "Opponents, Audiences, Constituencies, and Community" in *The Anti-aesthetic: Essays on Postmodern Culture*, ed. Hal Foster (Port Townsend, Wash.: Bay Press, 1982), 141.
85. C&I, 186.
86. Georg Lukács, "The Ideology of Modernism," in *The Lukács Reader*, ed. Arpad Kadarkay (Oxford, U.K.: Blackwell, 1995), 187–88; C&I, 188.
87. C&I, 189.
88. EWS to Highsmith, June 17, 1988, EWSP, 11:6:I.1.
89. *PPC*, 77.
90. "Reflections on Twenty Years of Palestinian History," EWSP, 70:16:II.2.
91. *WTC*, 114.
92. EWS, "The Totalitarianism of Mind," review of *The Savage Mind*, by Claude Lévi-Strauss, *Kenyon Review* 29, no. 2 (March 1967): 262.
93. Stern, M.
94. EWS, from the poem "Retrospect," EWSP, 77:32:II.4.
95. EWS, "Hans von Bülow in Cairo," EWSP, 77:32:II.4.
96. *RE*, 562.
97. EWS, "The Music Itself: Glenn Gould's Contrapuntal Vision," in *Glenn Gould: By Himself and His Friends*, ed. John McGreevy (Toronto: Doubleday, 1983), 54.

98. *ML*, 5.
99. Ibid., 253.
100. Nicholas Cook, review of *ME*, *Music and Letters* 73, no. 4 (Nov. 1992): 617–19.
101. *ME*, xix: "Classical music participates in the differentiation of social space, its elaboration if you will."
102. Ibid., 84.
103. Ibid., 119.
104. Ferruccio Busoni, *Sketch of a New Esthetic of Music* (New York: G. Schirmer, 1911), 2.
105. EWS, graduate student notes, EWSP, 77:32:II.4.
106. Seminar notes, "Music, Cultural Analysis, and Critical Theory," 1987, EWSP, 77:32:II.4.
107. EWS, "The Future of Criticism" (1984), in *RE*, 165–72. The author attended these seminars.
108. Cook, review of *ME*.
109. EWSP, 77:18:II.4.
110. Painter.
111. *ME*, xvii.
112. See *ML*, 3–95, especially "Music and Feminism." He assigned, for example, Alan Durant's *Condition of Music* (1984) and Richard Leppert and Susan McClary's *Music and Society* (1987) in a seminar in 1991.
113. Subotnik to EWS, June 1, 1987, EWSP, 10:4:I.1.
114. Kofi Agawu, "Wrong Notes," *Transition* 55 (1992): 162–66.
115. Frisch to EWS, April 30, 1993, EWSP, 29:7:I.1.
116. Abu-Deeb; Archive of the Salzburger Festspiele.
117. *C&I*, 116–17.
118. *ML*, 200, 161, 152.
119. Barenboim.
120. For example, EWS to *London Review of Books*, Sept. 9, 1997, EWSP, 29:8:I.1.
121. *ML*, ix.
122. *ME*, 66, 122, 137.
123. *ML*, 89.
124. Menuhin to EWS, July 25, 1990, EWSP, 13:29:I.1; EWS to Menuhin, June 17, 1991, EWSP, 15:15:I.1.
125. Grimshaw.
126. James to EWS, Aug. 13, 1987, EWSP, 10:8:I.1.
127. *ML*, 206.
128. Allen Evans, *Ignaz Friedman: Romantic Master Pianist* (Bloomington: Indiana University Press, 2009), 242.

11. TWO PEOPLES IN ONE LAND

1. *EPP*, 56.
2. Eli Sanders, "Chomsky, Said Criticize 'So-Called Peace Process,'" *Columbia Daily Spectator*, April 12, 1999.
3. Said, W.
4. Al-Banna.
5. Oded Balaban, "The Other Edward Said," *Masharef* 23 (Winter 2003).
6. EWS to Roselle Tekiner, March 8, 1989, EWSP, 12:7:I.1; Dr. Naseer Aruri, "A Jewish Thinker in the Tradition of Humanistic Universalism," *Washington Report on Middle East Affairs* (Jan./Feb. 1997): 24, 84.

7. Ella Shohat, "The 'Postcolonial' in Translation: Reading Said in Hebrew," in *Edward Said: A Legacy of Emancipation and Representation*, ed. Adel Iskandar and Hakem Rustom (Berkeley: University of California Press, 2010), 343.

8. *CR*, 5.

9. Ashrawi.

10. *PeD*, 121.

11. Ibid., 7.

12. Alexander Cockburn, "Said's Legacy," *Mother Jones*, Sept. 30, 2003.

13. Ashrawi.

14. *PeD*, 119–25.

15. *CR*, 5, 13, 17.

16. *EPP*, xvi.

17. Musallam.

18. EWSP, 31:1:I.2.

19. Istrabadi.

20. EWS to Al-Rashid, Sept. 25, 1990, EWSP, 14:1:I.1.

21. Ashrawi.

22. Said, N.

23. "My interest now in popular culture, so far as I'm interested in it, [is] in the Arab world" (*PPC*, 156).

24. EWS, preface to *After the Last Sky* (New York: Columbia University Press, 1999), vi.

25. EWS to Atlas, Feb. 1, 1988. Atlas agreed to the piece so long as it was autobiographical and not political: Atlas to EWS, Feb. 24, 1988, EWSP, 10:23:I.1, also 30:23:I.1.

26. Mitchell.

27. Said, G.

28. Said, M.

29. EWS, "On Critical Consciousness: Gramsci and Lukács," EWSP, 78:10:II.4.

30. *ESR*, 420.

31. *OP*, 83.

32. Don Guttenplan to EWS, Dec. 16, 1994, EWSP, 29:10:I.1; *Exiles: Edward Said*, directed by Christopher Sykes (BBC2, 1986).

33. *OP*, viii; Wanger.

34. Said Makdisi. He claimed to have a photographic memory, telling his sisters, "You don't have it."

35. *New York Times*, May 5, 2000, EWSP, 31:3:II.2.

36. Said, N.

37. Gordimer to EWS, Sept. 13, 2000, EWSP, 28:13:I.1.

38. Roth to EWS, Feb. 4, 1985, EWSP, 8:2:I.1; EWS to Theroux, Sept. 12, 1990, EWSP, 14:4:I.1.

39. Robert Hughes, "Envoy to Two Cultures," *Time*, June 21, 1993, 60.

40. Ali.

41. *OP*, 239.

42. EWS, "An Ark for the Listener," EWSP, 77:2:II.3.

43. Highsmith to EWS, May 27, 1988, EWSP, 11:6:I.1.

44. Oe to *Grand Street* about EWS, Sept. 9, 2003, EWSP, 28:13:I.1.

45. Oe to EWS, Jan. 28, 2002, EWSP, 28:13:I.1.

46. Gordimer to EWS, Oct. 7, 2001, EWSP, 28:13:I.1.

47. Rai.
48. Gordimer to EWS, Jan. 8, 2002, EWSP, 28:13:I.1.
49. Ahdaf Soueif, *The Map of Love* (London: Bloomsbury, 1999), 51; Dominique Eddé, *Kite*, trans. Ros Schwartz (London: Seagull, 2012), published originally as *Cerf-volant* (Paris: L'Arpenteur, 2003).
50. Soueif, *Map of Love*, 49.
51. Eddé, *Kite*, 114–15.
52. David Lehman, "Goodbye Instructions," in *Some Nerve* (New York: Columbia Review Press, 1973).
53. Shahak to EWS, Oct. 6, 1986, EWSP, 28:15:I.1.
54. EWS, "The Limits of the Artistic Imagination," EWSP, 75:21:II.3.
55. Ashrawi to EWS, March 3, 1980, EWSP, 5:19:I.1.
56. JoAnn Wypijewski, "Mementos," sent to author, Feb. 19, 2016.
57. Said, M.
58. Eqbal Ahmad, *The Selected Writings of Eqbal Ahmad*, ed. Carollee Bengelsdorf et al. (New York: Columbia University Press, 2006).
59. Eqbal Ahmad, *Confronting Empire*, forewords by Edward W. Said and Pervez Hoodbhoy (Cambridge, Mass.: South End Press, 2000).
60. Ahmad to Tim May and Frank Hanly, BBC Television, Dec. 7, 1992, EWSP, 29:14:I.1.
61. *OI*, 98, 102.
62. *EPP*, 278.
63. Ibid., 11, 74–107, 249–55, 303–11.
64. Ashrawi.
65. Said, W.
66. Tom Farer to EWS, March 12, 1991, EWSP, 15:3:I.1.
67. *OI*, 155.
68. Ibid., 228–29.
69. Shahak to EWS, June 25, 1980, EWSP, 5:16:I.1.
70. Hadidi.
71. EWS to Zahi Khoury, July 20, 1989, EWSP, 12:14:I.1.
72. Ibid.; EWS, "Palestine, Then and Now: An Exile's Journey Through Israel and the Occupied Territories," *Harper's Magazine*, Dec. 1992, 51.
73. Discussion with Carol Hakim, Jens Hanssen, and Joe Farag, April 10, 2017, Minneapolis.
74. Ashrawi.
75. Ammar.
76. Eisenzweig to EWS, Nov. 10, 1979, EWSP, 5:14:I.1.
77. EWS, "Palestine: Memory, Invention, and Place," quoted in Elaine Hagopian, "Palestinian Landscape," a review of *The Landscape of Palestine: Equivocal Poetry*, ed. Ibrahim Abu-Lughod, Roger Heacock, and Khaled Nashef, Trans Arab Research Institute.
78. Said, M.; Said, W.; Traboulsi.
79. Traboulsi to author, March 31, 2018.
80. "Columbia Prof Admits to Stoning," *New York Daily News*, July 8, 2000, 2.
81. Cole.
82. Karen W. Arenson, "Columbia Debates a Professor's 'Gesture,'" *New York Times*, Oct. 19, 2000, B3.
83. Hovsepian.
84. Said, M.
85. Ibid.

86. Barenboim.
87. Ibid.
88. *ML*, 261.
89. Barenboim.
90. Said, G.
91. *PP*, x.
92. Barenboim.
93. *PP*, 29.
94. Barenboim.
95. Rose.

12. THE RACE AGAINST TIME

1. Theodor Adorno, *Minima Moralia: Reflections from Damaged Life* (1951; London: Verso, 1999), 25.
2. *OP*, 105.
3. Wood.
4. Said, M.
5. Said, W.; Said, N.
6. Rai.
7. Said, M.
8. Soueif.
9. EWSP, 78:13:II.4.
10. Alexander Cockburn, "Edward Said: A Mighty and Passionate Heart," *CounterPunch*, Sept. 25, 2003.
11. Rai.
12. Emily Eakin, "Look Homeward, Edward," *New York*, Sept. 27, 1999.
13. EWS, "Timeliness and Lateness: Health and Style," talk delivered at the Faculty of Medicine, College of Physicians and Surgeons of Columbia University, Dec. 12, 2000), EWSP, 75:12:II.3.
14. Rai.
15. Ben Letzler, "Edward Said: Fat," *Columbia Daily Spectator*, Sept. 25, 2000.
16. Quoted in Awi Federgruen and Robert Pollack, "Rock-Throwing by Said Should Not Be Excused," *Columbia Daily Spectator*, Sept. 5, 2000.
17. Shaheen.
18. Mariam Said to author, Feb. 24, 2019.
19. H. Aram Veeser, *Edward Said: The Charisma of Criticism* (New York: Routledge, 2010).
20. *RE*, 116.
21. Alexander Cockburn, "Remembering Ben Sonnenberg," *CounterPunch*, Sept. 16, 2010.
22. Dominique Eddé, *Edward Said: Le roman de sa pensée* (Paris: La Fabrique, 2017).
23. Khalidi, R.
24. Camus's "jejune formulae" and so on (*C&I*, 176, 179); Orwell's "Cold War polemic . . . comfortably protected from history's 'unquiet fuss'" and so on (ibid., 21, 27).
25. Blythe.
26. Abu-Deeb.
27. EWS, review of *Walter Lippmann and the American Century*, by Ronald Steel, *London Review of Books*, March 5–18, 1981, 7.
28. EWS, "Introduction to Noam Chomsky," EWSP, 75:11:II.3.

29. EWS, "Chomsky and the Question of Palestine," in *PD*.
30. Aijaz Ahmad, *In Theory: Classes, Nations, Literatures* (London: Verso, 1992).
31. *HDC*, 71.
32. These included "Intellectuals and Comparative Literature," EWSP, 111:20:II.3; and "Comparative Literature as Critical Investigation" and "Translation and the New Humanism," EWSP, 70:16:II.2.
33. Especially in essays for the Arab press: "Millennial Reflections: Heroism and Humanism," *Al-Hayat*, Jan. 12, 2000; and "Humanism: Backlash and Backtrack," *Al-Ahram Weekly*, Sept. 27–Oct. 3, 2001.
34. Dan Laidman, "Prof. Said Speaks on Humanism," *Columbia Daily Spectator*, Feb. 17, 2000.
35. *PPC*, 70; Harry Levin, *Grounds for Comparison* (Cambridge, Mass.: Harvard University Press, 1972), 92.
36. EWS, "Humanism and Heroism," *Al-Ahram*, Jan. 6–12, 2000.
37. *PPC*, 191.
38. At the Italian Academy for Advanced Studies (Columbia University), at the University of London, and at Wolfson College, Oxford.
39. *B*, 260.
40. "Too Much Work" (1999), EWSP, 71:12:II.2, published in *Al-Ahram*, Feb. 7, 2001.
41. *B*, 261.
42. EWS, "Diary: My Encounter with Sartre," *London Review of Books*, June 1, 2000.
43. David Shapiro to EWS, April 5, 1984, EWSP, 7:11:I.1; Andreas Huyssen to EWS, Jan. 9, 1984, EWSP, 7:7:I.1; the essay in question was "Remembrances of Things Played" (1985). See *ML*, 17–19.
44. EWSP, 97:9:III.1.
45. *ML*, 272–73.
46. Ibid., 153.
47. Ibid., 33.
48. Ibid., 51.
49. *LS*, 14.
50. Ibid., 21.
51. Class notes for the seminar "Culture and Criticism," EWSP, 97:4:III.1.
52. Theodor W. Adorno, "Late Style in Beethoven," trans. Susan H. Gillespie, *Raritan* 13, no. 1 (Summer 1993): 102–107.
53. Ibid.
54. *ML*, 300–301.
55. *FNE*, 28–29.
56. EWSP, 80:41:II.5.
57. EWS, "Adorno as Lateness Itself," in *Apocalypse Theory and the Ends of the World*, ed. Malcolm Bull (Oxford, U.K.: Blackwell, 1995), 264–81.
58. *PPC*, 458.
59. Hovsepian.
60. Stone to EWS, 1978, EWSP, 28:15:I.1.
61. Said, W.
62. EWS, "*Così fan tutte* at the Limits," *Grand Street* 16, no. 2 (Fall 1997): 93–106.
63. Giuseppe di Lampedusa, *The Leopard*, trans. Archibald Colquhoun (1958; New York: Pantheon, 1960), 205.
64. Luchino Visconti, *The Leopard* (film), 1963; cf. the novel, 209.

65. Phone conversation with the author, June 2003.
66. EWS to Oe, March 6, 2002, EWSP, 28:13:I.1.
67. EWS interview with Oe, *Grand Street*, 1995, EWSP, 80:19:II.5.
68. EWS to Oe, n.d. (ca. Jan. 2002), EWSP, 28:13:I.1.
69. EWS to Rachel Feldhay Brenner, Dec. 11, 1991, EWSP, 15:28:I.1.
70. Berger.
71. Sharon.
72. R. P. Blackmur, *A Primer of Ignorance*, ed. Joseph Frank (1940; New York: Harcourt, Brace & World, 1967), 7.
73. Wypijewski, "Mementos," sent to the author on Feb. 19, 2016.

SELECTED BIBLIOGRAPHY

BOOKS BY SAID

After the Last Sky: Palestinian Lives. Photographs by Jean Mohr. New York: Columbia University Press, 1986.

The Arabs Today: Alternatives for Tomorrow. Cleveland: Follet, 1972.

Beginnings: Intention and Method. Baltimore: Johns Hopkins University Press, 1975.

Conversations with Edward Said (interview with Tariq Ali). Oxford, U.K.: Seagull Books, 2006.

Covering Islam: How the Media and the Experts Determine How We See the Rest of the World. New York: Pantheon, 1981.

Culture and Imperialism. New York: Alfred A. Knopf, 1993.

Culture and Resistance: Interviews by David Barsamian. Cambridge, Mass.: South End Press, 2003.

The Edward Said Reader. Edited by Moustafa Bayoumi and Andrew Rubin. New York: Vintage, 2000.

The End of the Peace Process: Oslo and After. New York: Pantheon, 2000.

Entre guerre et paix. Translated by Béatrice Vierne. Preface by Tzvetan Todorov. Paris: Arléa, 1997.

Freud and the Non-European. New York: Verso, 2003.

From Oslo to Iraq and the Road Map. New York: Pantheon Books, 2004.

Humanism and Democratic Criticism. New York: Columbia University Press, 2004.

Interviews with Edward Said. Edited by Amritjit Singh and Bruce G. Johnson. Jackson: University Press of Mississippi, 2004.

Israël, Palestine: L'égalité ou rien. Translated by Dominique Eddé and Eric Hazan. Paris: La Fabrique, 1999.
Joseph Conrad and the Fiction of Autobiography. Cambridge, Mass.: Harvard University Press, 1966.
Musical Elaborations. New York: Columbia University Press, 1991.
Music at the Limits. New York: Columbia University Press, 2008.
On Late Style: Music and Literature Against the Grain. New York: Pantheon, 2006.
Orientalism. New York: Vintage, 1978.
Out of Place: A Memoir. New York: Vintage, 1999.
Peace and Its Discontents: Essays on Palestine in the Middle East Peace Process. New York: Vintage, 1993.
The Pen and the Sword: Conversations with David Barsamian. Chicago: Haymarket Books, 1994.
The Politics of Dispossession: The Struggle for Palestinian Self-Determination, 1969–1994. New York: Pantheon, 1994.
Power, Politics, and Culture: Interviews with Edward Said. Edited by Gauri Viswanathan. New York: Vintage, 2001.
The Question of Palestine. New York: Times Books, 1979.
Reflections on Exile and Other Essays. Cambridge, Mass.: Harvard University Press, 2000.
Representations of the Intellectual. New York: Pantheon, 1994.
The World, the Text, and the Critic. Cambridge, Mass.: Harvard University Press, 1983.
Yeats and Decolonization. Cork: Cork University Press and Field Day Pamphlets, 1988.

BOOKS WITH OTHERS

Acts of Aggression: Policing Rogue States. With Noam Chomsky and Ramsey Clark. New York: Seven Stories, 1999.
Blaming the Victims: Spurious Scholarship and the Palestinian Question. With Christopher Hitchens. New York: Verso, 1988.
The Entire World as a Foreign Land. With Mona Hatoum and Sheena Wagstaff. London: Tate Gallery, 2000.
Intellectuals. With George Steiner, William Pfaff, and John Lukacs. Edited by Robert Boyer. Saratoga Springs, N.Y.: Skidmore College, 1986.
Nationalism, Colonialism, and Literature. With Terry Eagleton and Fredric Jameson. Minneapolis: University of Minnesota Press, 1990.
Parallels and Paradoxes: Explorations in Music and Society. With Daniel Barenboim. Edited by Ara Guzelimian. New York: Vintage, 2002.
A Profile of the Palestinian People. With Ibrahim Abu-Lughod, Janet L. Abu-Lughod, Muhammed Hallaj, and Elia Zureik. Chicago: Palestine Human Rights Campaign, 1983.
Reaction and Counterrevolution in the Contemporary Arab World. With Walter Carroll and Samih Farsoun. N.p.: AAUG, 1978.

EDITED BOOKS

The Arabs Today: Alternatives for Tomorrow. With Fuad Suleiman. Columbus, Ohio: Forum Associates, 1973.
Henry James: Complete Stories, 1884–1891. New York: Library of America, 1999.

Kim. By Rudyard Kipling. London: Penguin, 1987.

Literature and Society: Selected Papers from the English Institute, 1978. Baltimore: Johns Hopkins University Press, 1980.

INTRODUCTIONS, PREFACES, FOREWORDS, AFTERWORDS

"Afterword: The Consequences of 1948." In *The War for Palestine: Rewriting the History of 1948.* Edited by Eugene Rogan and Avi Shlaim. London: Cambridge University Press, 2001.

Foreword to *Beyond the Storm: A Gulf Crisis Reader.* Edited by Phyllis Bennis and Michel Moushabeck. Brooklyn: Olive Branch Press, 1991.

Foreword to *The Fateful Triangle: The United States, Israel, and the Palestinians,* by Noam Chomsky. Chicago: Haymarket, 1983.

Foreword to *I Saw Ramallah,* by Mourid Barghouti. Cairo: American University of Cairo Press, 2000.

Foreword to *Jewish History, Jewish Religion: The Weight of Three Thousand Years,* by Israel Shahak. London: Pluto Press, 1997.

Foreword to *Language and Colonial Power: The Appropriation of Swahili in the Former Belgian Congo, 1880–1938,* by Johannes Fabian. Berkeley: University of California Press, 1986.

Foreword to *The Oriental Renaissance: Europe's Rediscovery of India and the East, 1680–1880,* by Raymond Schwab. Translated by Gene Patterson-Black and Victor Reinking. New York: Columbia University Press, 1984.

Foreword to *Peace Under Fire: Israel, Palestine, and the International Solidarity Movement.* Edited by Ghassan Andoni, Huwaida Arraf, Nicholas Blincoe, Hussein Khalili, Marissa McLaughlin, Radhika Sainath, and Josie Sandercock. New York: Verso, 2004.

Foreword to *The Performing Self: Compositions and Decompositions in the Languages of Contemporary Life,* by Richard Poirier. New Brunswick, N.J.: Rutgers University Press, 1992.

Foreword to *Selected Subaltern Studies.* Edited by Ranajit Guha and Gayatri Chakravorty Spivak. Oxford: Oxford University Press, 1988.

Foreword to *Thoughts on a War.* Edited by Phyllis Bennis et al. Edinburgh: Canongate, 1992.

Foreword to *Unholy Wars: Afghanistan, America, and International Terrorism,* by John Cooley. London: Pluto Press, 1999.

Introduction to *The Cairo Trilogy: Palace Walk, Palace of Desire, Sugar Street,* by Naguib Mahfouz. London: Everyman's Library, 2001.

Introduction to *The Language of Modern Music,* by Donald Mitchell. London: Faber & Faber, 1993.

Introduction to *Mimesis: Representations of Reality in Western Literature,* by Erich Auerbach. Princeton, N.J.: Princeton University Press, 2003.

Introduction to *Moby-Dick,* by Herman Melville. New York: Vintage, 1991.

Introduction to "*Saint François d'Assise*: An Excerpt from an Opera in 3 Acts and 8 Tableaux," by Olivier Messiaen. *Grand Street* 36 (1990).

Introduction to *Three Novels,* by Joseph Conrad. New York: Washington Square Press, 1970.

"Introduction: Homage to Joe Sacco." In *Palestine,* by Joe Sacco, Seattle: Fantagraphics Books, 1997.

"Introduction: The Right of Return at Last." In *Palestinian Refugees: The Right of Return.* Edited by Naseer Aruri. London: Pluto Press, 2001.

Preface to *Beirut Reclaimed*, by Samir Khalaf. Beirut: Al-Nahar Press, 1993.
Preface to *CIA et Jihad, 1950–2001: Contre l'URSS une désastreuse alliance*, by John K. Cooley. Paris: Autrement, 2002.

UNPUBLISHED WORK

Creative
"An Ark for the Listener" (short story, 1957–65)
"Betrayal" (novel draft, 1987–92)
Elegy (novel draft, 1957–62)
Poetry: "The Castle," "A Celebration in Three Movements," "Desert Flowers," "The early morning gently forges . . . ," "Hans von Bülow in Cairo," "Little Transformation," "Old People of the Village," "Requiem," "Retrospect," "Song of an Eastern Humanist," "Vision's Haze," "Windy corners of empty corridors . . . ," "Wistful Music"

Essays and Lectures
"Adonis and Arab Culture" (address to the UN, October 3, 1980)
"The Arab Nation: What Future?"
"The Arabs and the West and the Legacies of the Past"
"Comparative Literature as Critical Investigation"
"Freedom and Resistance"
"Great Issues of Our Time: India and Palestine"
"History, Literature, and Geography" (1994)
"Intellectuals and Comparative Literature"
"Introduction" to B. Rajan (on Milton and the East India Company)
"Jonathan Swift" (Columbia lecture, May 4, 1967)
"Language as Method and Imagination"
"Lecture on Critical Theory"
"Literary Criticism and Politics?"
"Literary Criticism and the Problematic of Language"
"Living with Conrad"
"The Media and Cultural Identity: National Authority or Exilic Wandering?"
"Modernity and Critical Consciousness"
"Note on the Arab Intellectuals at Home and Abroad"
"On Critical Consciousness: Gramsci and Lukacs"
"Response to Richard Kuhns's 'Affect and Reality in Philosophy and Literature'"
"The Second and a Half World"
"T. E. Lawrence Lecture"
"Translation and the New Humanism"
"Unresolved Geographies, Embattled Landscapes"
"Witholding, Avoidance, and Recognition" (published only in Arabic)

FILMS BY SAID

In Search of Palestine, a segment of "Films for the Humanities and Sciences." Directed by Charles Bruce. BBC, 1998.
In the Shadow of the West, a segment of *The Arabs: A Living History*, a ten-part series. Directed by Geoff Dunlop. Landmark Films, 1986.

The Palestinians. With Ibrahim Abu-Lughod. Two-part documentary. Directed by David Edgar. BBC Channel 4, 1988.
Pontecorvo: The Dictatorship of Truth. BBC TV, 1992.

FILMS ABOUT SAID

Exiles: Edward Said. Directed by Christopher Sykes. BBC2, 1986.
The Other (El Akhar, L'autre). French/Egyptian feature film. Directed by Youssef Chahine. 1999.
Out of Place: Memories of Edward Said. Directed by Makoto Sato. 2006.
Selves and Others: A Portrait of Edward Said. Directed by Emmanuel Hamon. Wamip Films, 2004.

VERY SHORT SELECTION OF FILMS OF SAID'S LECTURES
AND INTERVIEWS

"Altered States," *Relative Values.* Directed by Jake Auerbach. BBC, 1991.
"The Arab World: Who They Are, Who They Are Not." With Bill Moyers. April 1, 1991. www.youtube.com/watch?v=eI6mjFL80xE.
"Edward Said: The Last Interview." Directed by Michael Dibb. Icarus Films, 2004. www.youtube.com/watch?v=CxW0uJBWVIY.
"Edward Said on Orientalism." Directed by Sut Jhally. Media Education Foundation, 1998. www.youtube.com/watch?v=fVC8EYd_Z_g.
"End of Millennium Conversation: Sebastiao Salgado, Eduardo Galeano, Edward Said, South African National Assembly Speaker Frene Ginwala, Noam Chomsky, Manning Marable, Film Maker John Pilger." *Democracy Now!,* Dec. 29, 2000. www.democracynow.org/2000/12/29/end_of_millennium _conversation_sebastiao_salgado.
"Global Empire: A Conversation with Edward Said." Tariq Ali, 1994. www .youtube.com/watch?v=YvR3qeroQ2M.
"In Conversation—Daniel Barenboim and Edward Said." BBC, 2005.
"The MESA Debate: The Scholars, the Media, and the Middle East." With Christopher Hitchens, Bernard Lewis, and Leon Wieseltier. Nov. 22, 1986. www.youtube.com/watch?v=hnVHuA6xlOo.
"Professionals and Amateurs." Edward Said: Representations of the Intellectual, *The Reith Lectures* 4. BBC Radio 4, July 14, 1993. www.bbc.co.uk /programmes/p00gxqz0.
Raymond Williams and the Legacy of His Work. British Film Institute, 1989.
"The Reith Lecturer Interview: Edward Said." BBC Radio 4, 1993. www .youtube.com/watch?v=7R-mOAtzEc4&t=449s.

VIDEO PRIMERS ON *ORIENTALISM*

Clip from Aladdin: www.youtube.com/watch?v=fgbuTSxky3A.
"Edward Said: An Introduction to Orientalism." MACAT: Macat Analysis. www.youtube.com/watch?v=1aNwMpV6bVs.
"Orientalism" (Eilwen Jones). www.youtube.com/watch?v=UI-cbPX8hoI.
"Orientalism Explained" with clips from Disney's *Aladdin, Indiana Jones, Pirates of the Caribbean,* and so on (Dania Khan and Sarah Kaddour). www.youtube .com/watch?v=dH4s7ezptv4.

SELECT LIST OF PARTIAL BIBLIOGRAPHIES

Yasmine Ramadan, "A Bibliographical Guide to Edward Said," *Alif: Journal of Comparative Poetics*, no. 25 (2005), 270–87.
Eddie Yeghiayan, "A Bibliography" (prepared for the Wellek Lectures of 1989), https://www.lib.uci.edu/about/publications/wellek/said/index.html.

ARCHIVES

EA: The Eqbal Ahmad Papers, 1956–1999. Archives, Hampshire College, Amherst, MA 01002.
NC: Noam Chomsky Papers, Chomsky-Said Correspondence, MC 600, Box 85, MIT Library.

ACKNOWLEDGMENTS

I should pay tribute first to those whose writing on Said I found especially insightful: Eqbal Ahmad, Sadik Al-Azm, Paul A. Bové, Alexander Cockburn, Ferial Ghazoul, Nadia Gindy, Hoda Guindi, Nubar Hovsepian, Conor McCarthy, W. J. T. Mitchell, Basim Musallam, Jean Said Makdisi, Mariam Said, and Michael Wood. For early scholarship undertaken when Said was still alive, my gratitude goes to the late Michael Sprinker for his groundbreaking anthology, *Edward Said: A Critical Reader* (1992). For insights into Said's personal relationship to music, I would like specially to thank Jean Said Makdisi and Daniel Barenboim, whose comments were particularly thought-provoking. Mohammad Shaheen's poetically precise work on Said's legacy is the most important to be found in Arabic. My thanks to him for his constant and attentive correspondence, intellectual support, and personal warmth.

I relied heavily on the resourceful scholarship of those who read my manuscript in whole or in part. For their invaluable advice and merciless editing, and also for their global understanding of the broad connections and implications, I owe a great deal to Keya Ganguly, the late Benita Parry, Mariam Said, and above all Ileene Smith, my editor at Farrar, Straus and Giroux. My gratitude to all four is immeasurable. Let me mention also those who read portions of this manuscript in an earlier form: Lorna Burns, Katie R. Muth, Marco Gato, the editors of *Kitap Zamani*, Basak Ertur and Rasha Salti, Adel Iskandar and Hakem Rustom, Ghazi-Walid Falah and Colin Flint, Rashid Khalidi, and Jay Williams. In a general sense, I relied on the sensitive close reading and friendship of Michal Kobialka, Tim Heitman, Elise Linehan, Dan Sass, Silvia López, Chris Chiappari, and Lyes Benarbane. For giving me an early platform to discuss Said's work and for his cantankerous insights, I embrace the late A. Sivanandan. Let me also thank Andrew Wylie for kindly approaching me to write this book, and Jacqueline Ko, Tracy Bohan, and Emma Herman for shepherding me through the intricacies of intellectual commerce.

For personal details and the dispelling of myths, I leaned on Said's sisters Jean and Grace as well as his children, Najla and Wadie, and most of all his wife, Mariam. Apart from the willingness of close friends, critics, and classmates to be interviewed, several kindly shared private photographs, correspondence, and previously unpublished writings. For this, I give thanks to Lila Abu-Lughod, the late Sadik Al-Azm, Akeel Bilgrami, Noam Chomsky, Dominique Eddé, Sandra Fahy, Anna Grimshaw, Elaine Hagopian, Bayan Al-Hout, George Kardouche, David Lehman, Alex McLeod, Alan Mintz, Jean Mohr, Gabriel Piterberg, Jacqueline Rose, Karl Sabbagh, Andre Sharon, Ahdaf Soueif, the late Jean Stein, Marina Warner, and Michael Wood. Deirdre and the late Allen Bergson, in addition to sharing with me a beloved photograph, painted Said's early academic life in unforgettable colors.

I relied on a number of specialized archives that provided me with needed materials. I would especially like to express my gratitude to Peter Weis at the Northfield Mount Hermon School for his generous assistance and thoughtful commentary. For explaining the importance of the Constantine Zurayk archive at AUB, as well as Arab political organizations in a Palestine already under siege before 1948, my thanks to Kaoukab Chebaro, who was then the head librarian at AUB. Two colleagues of mine at the University of Minnesota translated letters, essays, and passages of key books available only in Arabic. My regards, then, to Joseph Farag and (given the amount of time he spent with me) especially Nabil Matar, to whom I am indebted not only for his translations but for his encouragement. Thanks also to Bashir Abu-Manneh, who put me in touch with key players in Said's life at an early stage of my research.

My time in Beirut was brief but transformative. The ins and outs of Said's second city after New York were opened up for me (along with Dhour el Shweir and Brummana) through the generosity of Nadim and Asdghik Cortas, who made my time there both rewarding and enjoyable. Thanks too to Sonja Mejcher-Atassi and Mohammad Ali Atassi for inviting me into their home and giving me a much-needed course on the new political terrain of the Middle East in the years after Said's death. For heterodox views on the complexities of the region, and for their critical take on Said's place within it, my thanks to Carol Hakim and Jens Hanssen. As part of my Beirut stay, I must also acknowledge the kindness of Syrine C. Hout, who assisted me with making contacts, and Assaad Khairallah for his irreverent anecdotes about Said in his Arab element.

The book depended throughout on the help of my research assistants—first, Abhay Doshi, whose energy and discernment I counted on; later, and just as expertly, Jacqueline Patz, who picked up where he left off; Jasmine Wu, for her invaluable help with photographs; and Emilie Pons, who in addition to tracking down for me key files from the archive called on her native French to confirm (and at times edit) my translations. Let me acknowledge also the poorly recompensed but expert legal advice of Thomas Johnson.

I want, finally, to acknowledge the support I received from the University of Minnesota's College of Liberal Arts and the university's vice president for research. Two of the more difficult chapters were written in the intellectual camaraderie I enjoyed as a fellow at the Camargo Foundation in Cassis, France, in the fall of 2017. Given Said's identification with French culture and his lifelong attachment to the (eastern) Mediterranean, writing in this environment seemed fitting, and in many ways a return home. Apart from the view of Cap Canaille, Camargo gave me a supportive cohort of artists and scholars whom I would like here to thank collectively, but even more Patricia Hampl for her work behind the scenes to make my stay in Cassis possible. In the name of their love of French culture and our sorties together, I would like to mention Teddy and the late Jim Gesell, whose support for the humanities in an age of technoscience has for me and many others made the difference between being published and silence.

INDEX